The Business of Tourism

T0313753

HAGLEY PERSPECTIVES ON BUSINESS AND CULTURE
Philip Scranton, Susan Strasser, and Roger Horowitz, Series Editors

Beauty and Business: Commerce, Gender, and Culture in Modern America, edited by Philip Scranton

Boys and Their Toys: Masculinity, Technology, and Class in America, edited by Roger Horowitz

Food Nations: Selling Taste in Consumer Societies, edited by Warren Belasco and Philip Scranton

Industrializing Organisms: Introducing Evolutionary History, edited by Philip Scranton and Susan Schrepfer

Commodifying Everything: Business and Culture in Modern America, edited by Susan Strasser

The Technological Fix: How People Use Technology to Create and Solve Problems, edited by Lisa Rosner

The Business of Tourism

Place, Faith, and History

EDITED BY PHILIP SCRANTON
AND JANET F. DAVIDSON

PENN

University of Pennsylvania Press

Philadelphia

10   9   8   7   6   5   4   3   2   1

Published by
University of Pennsylvania Press
Philadelphia, Pennsylvania 19104-4112

Library of Congress Cataloging-in-Publication Data

Scranton, Philip.
   The business of tourism : place, faith, and history / edited by Philip Scranton
and Janet F. Davidson.
      p.   cm. (Hagley perspectives on business and culture)
      Includes bibliographical references.
   ISBN-13: 978-0-8122-3968-3
   ISBN-10: 0-8122-3968-7 (cloth : alk. paper)
   1. Tourism—Economic aspects.   2. Tourism—Social aspects.   I. Scranton, Philip.
II. Davidson, Janet F.
G155.A1 B8865   2006
338.4'791 22

                                                                        2006045666

Contents

Preface

PHILIP SCRANTON

Today, tourism is big business. Cities, regions, and nations, along with businesses at all scales, view tourism as providing massive infusions of consumer spending, and in preparing for that, sizable investments in infrastructures and magnets for tourism—hotels, guide services, festivals, specialized transport networks, Web sites, and so on. Yet how can we understand tourism historically and in context(s)? That question animated the Hagley Center for the History of Business, Technology and Society's Fall 2004 conference, "Consuming Experiences." Those of us on the program committee (the series editorial team: Roger Horowitz, Susan Strasser, and me) learned a good deal about the state of tourism studies from colleagues who submitted proposals for the conference—not least that the historical dimension of thinking about tourism had frequently been more gestured toward than closely researched and that the business dimensions of tourism, with some exceptions, had been broadly eclipsed by cultural and representational studies of tourism, which recently have commanded the center stage for research.

Asking how tourism was created, planned, sold, and delivered, by whom, and in what political, technological, and commercial contexts (more than what it meant and to whom), being concerned more with practice than with the projection of images and ideologies, Hagley's conference (the basis for the present volume) probed the mechanisms and the implications of tourism as business enterprise. To be sure, as coeditor Janet Davidson documents in the Afterword, ours was far from the first effort to examine tourism as history and as commercial activity. Nevertheless, *The Business of Tourism: Place, Faith, and History*, surfaces as an intervention, as a view of work-in-progress, in a field that continues the work of defining its core questions, methods, and terrains.

We identified three intriguing thematic elements within the larger landscape, presented here as Commodifying Place, Engaging Religion, and Marketing Communism. Others may be interested in the history of ClubMed or in revisiting the Grand Tour, but we sought to identify spaces for discourse and debate somewhat distinct from the current mainstream.

Commodification is a core capitalist process, translating that which once was free and outside the cash nexus into something that depends upon and explicitly focuses on a cash exchange. Think about panoramic views or beaches, for access to which one can be charged, or consider the transition of some religious sites as destinations for faithful penitents to being spots that urge or demand donations from visitors. More substantively, as the essays in Part I indicate, commodifying place was a demanding challenge a century or more ago. In this regard, as Waleed Hazbun shows in this volume's opening essay, Thomas Cook (& Son) moved from offering British workers train rides to temperance festivals to planning and delivering elaborate, upper- and middle-class tours of the ancient Middle East. What were these travelers buying? How did their Euro-entry to contested, Egyptian domains generate difficulties and longer term tensions? Hazbun's employment of theoretical perspectives from actor network theory in this work is particularly engaging and rich with implications for future research.

Kenneth Perkins picks up similar themes in reviewing organized French tourism ventures to North Africa commencing in the mid-nineteenth century, the institutions and politics central to their efforts, and the unintended consequences of France's World War II humiliation and resistance, not least France's postwar dilemmas concerning colonial territories. Going to the desert was not just a complex, and at times risky, tourist agenda; it also interacted, however indirectly, with local voices—for opportunity, for independence, and so on—that France had long ignored. Philip Whalen revisits France and its cultural terrain in his remarkable study of the Dijon gourmand fairs in the interwar decades. Festivals of marketing and (over)consumption, the gastronomical fairs also confirmed regional identity, brought many thousands to the district in often-straitened years, and permitted local folks to preen and strut, given that the food they created and delivered was stunning, rich, and distinctive.

Place matters in tourism's commodification process, but so too, and not without irony, does religion. Once upon a time, as Brian Bixby shows in "Consuming Simple Gifts," the Shakers were a carefully ambitious sect, seeking converts to their faith, which stressed celibacy, hard work, and occasional rhythmic dancing as honoring God. More than six generations after roughly 1800, their clear, if somewhat unusual, belief system failed to sustain the Shakers, despite their efforts to evangelize and bring in converts from the World. In time, encountering their religious ideals and their mundane practices became a destination experience for travelers to and within America, as many nineteenth-century "visitors" evidently regarded stopping at a Shaker community as an element in the new, western hemisphere Grand Tour. However, in the twentieth century, "Shaker" lost its sectarian referent and became a term signaling simple design and rocketing prices for original artifacts. Here, religion was decanted from social practice and tourist experience over a century's time.

Aaron Ketchell presents a more directly commercial engagement with religion, exploring the religion-and-entertainment site, Silver Dollar City, at the country-culture magnet of Branson, Missouri. There, a bland version of Protestant evangelism reaches out to the millions who arrive to experience a nostalgic past, a posture that fosters creativity of an intriguing sort. Across the Atlantic, religion is also centrally connected to tourism, but in a sharply different fashion. Molly Hurley Dépret reveals to us a religiously fractured Belfast, Northern Ireland, where touring, in those classic-black Austin cabs, the sites of outrages by Protestants or Catholics proves good business for taxi drivers. How informal is this tourism business, and who are the clients and how do they stay safe? Just a few of the host of questions that Hurley Dépret's research can trigger.

Our third section focuses, quite peculiarly, on "Marketing Communism"—why and with what implications? Well, we found that the boundary between capitalism and communism regarding tourism was quite intriguing, as disjunctures between East and West abounded, regarding almost all elements of a tourism experience. Moreover, the Stalinist/Communist state was, apparently, more actively involved in controlling entry and exit than elsewhere, long before 9/11, which generated practices in this arena resonant with early Bolshevik or early Cold War anxieties. That said, the third portion of this text gives you a chance to see the Stalinist vacation system (?) in operation through Anne Gorsuch's remarkable essay. Following this, we offer a second look at socialism's dilemmas, through Patrick Patterson's study of Soviet-bloc tourists in Yugoslavia after 1960. The "Marketing Communism" segment closes with Evan Ward's vivid review of the Castro system's interest in global tourism and in creating the necessary facilities (hotels, boat trips, etc.). The funds central to such innovations came to Communist Cuba by way of Spain's leading enterprises, in the 1980s and after, despite American hostility and embargoes.

Place, religion, and communism/socialism are not the standard topic set for research in tourism's history, to be sure. However, our Hagley group would argue that research in spaces rarely visited can (but only can) generate insights into social, economic, and political processes that have been tossed aside when nationalist, progress-centered or other, related master narratives have been unfolded. We hope that the essays here included will help enable readers interested in tourism's past to distinguish hype from content, analysis from promotional text, and nationalism from entrepreneurialism. We look forward to your reactions to these essays and would be delighted to hear responses from "users." The coeditors' email addresses are scranton@crab.rutgers.edu and davidsonjan@hotmail.com, respectively.

Acknowledgments

The coeditors are delighted to acknowledge invaluable assistance at Hagley from the remarkable Carol Lockman, the research center's anchor staff administrator, and from the institution's permanent staff, whose expertise in managing public events makes presenting our conferences a smooth and professional process. Roger Horowitz and Susan Strasser, this series' coeditors, proved crucial in helping select the papers for the "Consuming Experiences" conference from the much larger set of proposals offered. We also wish to express our appreciation to the University of Pennsylvania Press, whose senior editors' interest in continuing the essay collection series, based on Hagley conferences, made it possible to deliver this seventh Hagley conference research compendium.

Part I
Commodifying Place

Chapter 1

The East as an Exhibit

Thomas Cook & Son and the Origins of the International
Tourism Industry in Egypt

WALEED HAZBUN

On approaching the Arundel Mills shopping mall, located outside of
Baltimore, Maryland, visitors are greeted by the sight of what appears to
be an ancient Egyptian temple transported from the banks of the Nile
complete with massive hieroglyph-covered columns and monumental-
sized statuary. This structure forms the grand entranceway to one of the
mall's main attractions, Muvico's Egyptian 24 megaplex movie theater.[1]
Walking past the ticket counter across the glass mosaic map of the Nile
or sitting in stadium-style theaters decorated with Egyptian-themed
murals, the moviegoer becomes embedded within an adventure story-
line. Operating in a highly competitive business, the mall designers constructed this "fusion" of the experiences of movie watching, shopping,
and travel in an effort to fashion Arundel Mills as a theme-park-like
"destination" that seeks to "maximize retail sales."[2] While most visitors
(and the designers themselves) tend to associate this kitschy themed
environment with images from Hollywood's imagination,[3] this chapter
traces the roots of the construction of such "cinematic" adventure experiences and their commercial uses back to the transformation of the
experience of travel to Egypt in the late nineteenth century and the
simultaneous birth of the international tourism industry.[4]

During the second half of the nineteenth century, the practice of
travel, long associated with experiences of learning and discovery in the
form of the Grand Tour, was increasingly being eclipsed by the rise of
popular, leisure tourism.[5] In the process, Daniel J. Boorstin explains,
"foreign travel . . . became . . . a commodity."[6] This essay explores how
Egypt became the first major region outside of Europe to witness this
transition through which travel to a distant, exotic territory was made
more convenient and increasingly affordable in the form of Thomas

Cook & Son's package tours. Making Egypt accessible for international tourism required not only navigating the geographic distance across the Mediterranean but also traversing what Edward Said calls "imaginative geographies" about the Orient developed in Western scholarship about the Middle East (Orientalism).[7] These imaginative geographies, as Derek Gregory explains, are "constructions that fold distance into difference through a series of spatializations."[8] These differences—defined in social, cultural, and mental terms—were marked by spatial "partitions and enclosures" which would do much to shape the modalities of tourism development in Egypt.[9]

In *Colonising Egypt*, Timothy Mitchell argues that many European and North American travelers to Egypt in the nineteenth century sought to tour Egypt as if it were an exhibition similar to those they might have visited at the London, Paris, or Chicago world's fairs.[10] There, scenes of "the East" were rendered in elaborate dioramas, featuring native Egyptians brought in to provide visitors with donkey rides through the streets of "Cairo." However, once European and North American visitors arrived in the actual Egypt they were shocked and disoriented by what they encountered. Urban Cairo was "at first . . . indescribable, except as disorder."[11] Mitchell explains: "although they thought of themselves as moving from exhibits of the Orient to the real thing, they went on trying to grasp the real thing as an exhibit."[12] Visitors often struggled to find a vantage point from which to separate themselves from this world "and thus constitute it as a panorama."[13] Mitchell uses this *metaphysical* concept, which he calls "the world-as-exhibition," to portray the ways western power transformed and colonized Egyptian society, economy, and landscape in its attempt to construct a readable social order, a calculable commodity-based economy, and a political society that could be governed as a machine.[14]

In a series of rich essays about the culture of travel to Egypt in the nineteenth century, Derek Gregory explores how a certain experience of "Egypt" was made accessible and intelligible to European and North American visitors.[15] Focusing on scripting and visualization, the micro-practices these travelers developed, he notes that travel writers often "described Egypt as a text or series of texts" through which "travel became an intrinsically hermeneutic project."[16] Gregory emphasizes the "intimate connections between reading and sightseeing" in which travelogues, guidebooks, and photography defined travel itineraries, modes of sightseeing, and objects of gaze.[17] These micro-practices operated within a complex field defined by other agents and practices ranging from the knowledges and skills of local guides and merchants to "the emerging protocols of archaeology" and "the operating strategies of tour companies."[18]

This chapter, which can be read as an extension of Gregory's project, examines the role played by the development of new business enterprises and practices in forging a tourism economy in Egypt. It places the rise of popular tourist travel to Egypt within the larger context of the development of tourism as a heterogeneous global industry. By contrasting the dynamics of tourism development in Europe to those in Egypt—a contrast shaped by differing forms of cultural interaction, spatial arrangements, and business practices—I show how the structure of the tourism economy built in Egypt both constrained the tourist practices of western travelers and precluded the agency of local Egyptians and non-westerner visitors in shaping the political economy of tourism.

Initially, "what transformed mere travelers into tourists was the rise of an industry that defined, organized, and commodified 'tourist' experiences."[19] The early development and expansion of tourism as a business owes much to the efforts of the British firm Thomas Cook & Son, a pioneer in organizing and promoting the practice of popular leisure travel. These efforts helped create a tourist market in the transportation and accommodation sectors, leading first to the development of a European tourism infrastructure in the 1850s and 1860s and eventually to the proliferation of tourism-related businesses, commercializing all aspects of the travel experience. As travel became cheaper and more convenient, the practice of leisure tourism spread throughout the industrializing societies of Europe and North America. In the 1870s and 1880s, as the firm was losing some of its competitive advantages and market share in a growing industry, founder Thomas Cook's son, John Mason Cook, led the expansion of the company's operations into Egypt. There he saw new opportunities that could transform the family firm into a modern corporation. J. M. Cook soon established a vertically integrated tourism business based on the firm's control over Nile transportation, several hotels, and hundreds of agents, guides, porters, and servants across Egypt. Tourism became a major economic enterprise in Egypt, prospering with the rise of Egyptology as a field of knowledge and the expansion of British control over the country. By building an extensive tourism business in Egypt the firm considerably expanded its overall size and profits and, in the process, gave rise to what we now call the international tourism industry.

While exploring how Thomas Cook & Son's successful operations in Egypt were facilitated by technological innovations and reliant on British colonialism, which Cook played a role in advancing, this chapter highlights business practices Cook developed that helped convert the experience of travel to Egypt into commodity consumerism. The firm "industrialized" travel in Egypt allowing more people to visit the country and, once there, to see more sights in less time and at less cost. Cook did so by insulating the tourist from the burdens and risks of local economic transactions and other forms of uncertainty such as trusting local guides. These business practices and the form of travel in Egypt they promoted helped define the nature of the cultural and economic relationship constructed between Western visitors and Egyptian society. These practices physically and culturally isolated the tourist, yet freed him or her from independent interactions with the local economy by using modern "industrial" techniques to organize the movement of people, their arrangement within physical space, and the pace and point of view of their tours.[20] As the experience of travel became less interactive and more guided by predetermined itineraries, designed to maximize visual consumption of Orientalist images of "timeless Egypt," it prefigured the highly staged, "cinematic" experiences of the Egyptian 24 megaplex movie theater.

John Mason Cook and contemporary commentators often argued that the firm's effort to develop a tourism industry along the Nile promoted technical, economic, and social progress leading to the "prosperity of Egypt." These claims, however, remain suspect as they ignore how the structure of tourism blocked Egyptians' agency as entrepreneurs, tourists, and interpreters of their territory's monuments and history. Promoting alternative modes of tourism development is feasible, but requires the development of alternative business practices, and with them, alternative modes and cultures of touring that challenge and dissolve the imaginative geographies of colonial era travel.

In the Wake of Napoleon

While visitors to Muvico's Egyptian 24 might view the images around them as reflecting the impressions of intrepid explorers or adventurous archeologists, such as Indiana Jones, they are less likely to realize that the space they are walking though is largely a product of European colonialism, which generated both the field of Egyptology and the international tourism industry.[21] Beginning in the sixteenth century, commercial and diplomatic ties between European states and the Ottoman Empire facilitated the travel of a trickle of explorers and antiquities collectors to Egypt and up the Nile River.[22] Interest in ancient Egyptian artifacts and culture was growing in Europe when Napoleon invaded Egypt in 1798, transforming the nature of European ties with Egypt and opening the door for the expansion of travel in the early nineteenth century. French military control lasted only a few years as the British teamed up with the declining Ottoman Empire to defeat Napoleon. The invasion's most lasting impact, however, was not the product of Napoleon's soldiers but of the troop of engineers, scientists, historians, artists and map-makers he brought to survey and document Egypt's natural and historical geography. The results of this scientific mission were published as *Description de l'Égypt*—twenty-three monumental tomes released between 1809 and 1828. These volumes and the discovery of the Rosetta Stone, which enabled the decipherment of hieroglyphics, helped advance the field of Egyptology and excite popular interest in travel to Egypt.[23]

The flow of archaeologists, explorers, and adventures grew in the early 1800s as Muhammad Ali, the autonomous Ottoman governor of Egypt, centralized the territory's administration and extended his control into Upper Egypt. The "adventurous travelers" of this era "undertook the troublesome journey in search of new 'knowledge,' romantic encounters, and exotic experience."[24] By the middle of the century a new wave of travelers joined the flow, inspired by the increased circulation of travelogues and images, which soon included photography.[25] This growth was assisted not only by a more settled political climate under increasing British influence, regular steamship travel across the Mediterranean, and the end of health quarantines,[26] but also by the publication of the first manuals produced to assist travelers through the historical sites and practicalities of travel.

In 1843, John Murray released *Modern Egypt and Thebes*, a condensed version of a scholarly survey of ancient Egyptian history and monuments written by John Gardner Wilkinson, one of the founders of modern Egyptology.[27] It included details about Alexandria and greater Cairo, where European-run accommodations were becoming available, as well as practical planning information for travelers. Republished in 1858 under the title *Hand-Book for Travelers in Egypt*, it became a standard reference guide.[28] This and similar volumes helped transform and standardize the experience of travel to Egypt. Commodities in their own right, they recommended what supplies to buy, where to buy them, whom to hire, and which sights to visits. Moreover, they enabled visitors to become increasingly more like European leisure tourists, purchasing a known commodity and visiting *tourist* attractions, in contrast to the explorers and travelers seemingly in search of new knowledge and experiences. "What brings the tourist to the Orient" was not the challenge of exploring the unknown, but "the desire to identify the already defined signs of exoticism as exotic."[29]

The journey, however, remained costly and slow paced; it required much preparation as well as continual negotiation during the trip. Travelers generally had to rely on a hired *dragoman* to assist with the logistics of travel. The multilingual dragoman, a term derived from the Arabic word for translation, generally came from one of several Mediterranean nationalities but also included characters such as "Osman Effendi," a

Scottish convert to Islam.[30] These intermediaries acted as interpreters as well as guides, though most travelers and guidebooks considered their knowledge of ancient Egyptian antiquities limited and untrustworthy. Many travelers even complained about how dependence on their dragoman prevented them from direct experience of the Orient, noting with relief that "while on the banks of the Nile he is kept in his place as a servant."[31] As helpful as he might be (especially when traveling on to Palestine and Syria), the dragoman often generated mixed feelings. Guidebooks routinely noted that many were unscrupulous and that "It often requires considerable moral courage to keep these individuals in their proper places, for the more useful and capable they are the more easy is it for their employers to lose control over them."[32]

The highlight of most trips was the journey up the Nile and back, conducted on a *dahabiyyah*, a large, sailed houseboat. Selecting a boat and crew, then outfitting it from the bazaars and stores in Cairo, even with the help of a dragoman, might take considerable time and effort as travelers found what they needed and bargained for a reasonable price. Travelers setting off for a Nile voyage would not only need to bring from home or buy items such as clothes, a small library of books, and personal items, but also had to secure bulky furniture including a mattress, iron bed stand, wash tub, and drawing table.[33] For many visitors the greatest annoyance was dealing with local Egyptians who often crowded around travelers seeking *bakshiish,* a term used to refer to both tips and handouts. Murray's *Hand-Book* warned, "Strangers justly complain of the torment of the people of the village, who collect around them like a swarm of flies, forcing their troublesome services upon them to their great discomfort and inconvenience. It is the duty of the traveler's dragoman to prevent this."[34] However, as Cook's company history reported: "while the dragomans kept beggars and touts at bay it was clear that they usually did so in order to funnel all available tourist cash into their own pockets. . . . These extractions were the stuff of Victorian tourist tales."[35]

Even as the obstacles travelers faced decreased around mid-century, the considerable expense and leisure time required (often several months) sharply limited the range of people likely to make the journey. In the late 1850s, for example, the total cost for a two-month Nile cruise for two might cost £200, which equaled almost half the average annual income of a middle-class professional, putting travel to Egypt beyond their reach.[36] Many visitors in the first half of the century were not leisure travelers, but rather merchants, officials, and archeologists traveling through or with other business in Egypt. A rough picture of the growth of travel to Upper Egypt in this era comes from Lucie Duff-Gordon, who suggested that while in the 1830s five to six boats made the journey each winter, by the 1860s she was seeing 70 to 120 boats.[37]

Within decades, the number of leisure travelers visiting Egypt would rise to the thousands.

Thomas Cook and the Invention of Organized Tourism

As western travel to Egypt slowly increased, in the English Midlands leisure travel was being revolutionized, becoming a popular middle-class activity and leading to the expansion of commercial opportunities in tourism-related enterprises. The "discovery" of these opportunities, however, was in part an indirect effect of one man's effort to create spectacles in the service of his moral crusade. A printer by trade and temperance advocate by conviction, Thomas Cook was a large force in creating tourism as a modern industry. In the summer of 1841, Cook arranged a railway excursion from Leicester to a temperance meeting in Loughborough. He negotiated with the Midland Countries Railway Company and secured much-reduced fares for the trip. After selling tickets to about 500 members of his temperance society, Cook turned the excursion into a memorable affair, thus gaining publicity for his battle against drink.[38]

While Cook was not the first to organize a railway excursion, he was the first to use the idea to generate a social phenomenon. Much of his initial success followed from his ability to draw upon an existing social organization, his temperance society, as a ready client base. He quickly expanded beyond temperance meetings to other events, including seaside holidays on the English shore and tourist trips to Scotland, viewing these as promoting "rational recreation" for the working class and providing an alternative to the pub.[39] More broadly, Cook sought to democratize the benefits of rail travel, for "to travel by train is to enjoy republican liberty and monarchical security."[40] Cook's greatest early success was organizing discount travel for more than one hundred thousand visitors to the 1851 Great Exhibition at London's Crystal Palace. The exhibition represented the world as collections of commodities on display, while tourable components allowed visitors to see and experience foreign "places."[41] To help advertise his fares and build interest in the exhibition, Cook created a magazine. *Cook's Excursionist*, as it would later be called, became the firm's main publicity vehicle.[42] Four years later, Cook led a tour of the European continent, ending at the Paris Exhibition of 1855, and thus opened international venues for popular tourism.

Before the 1840s, travel by train was complicated and expensive. Railway companies saw their main function as serving the needs of industrialization, chiefly hauling freight and business-related persons. The railway operators had often looked upon working-class travelers with suspicion,[43] but Cook helped the rail companies "realize the economic potential offered by the mass, low-income market."[44] Eventually, rail companies across Britain and Europe began selling economy fares and coordinating their schedules to expand the accessibility of rail travel and the mobility of broader sections of the population.

Thomas Cook became well known for his personally conducted, all-expenses-included group tours; later they would be led by guides employed by the firm. These exposed broader elements of British society to the sights and cultural offerings of cities like Paris and Florence, which had long been enjoyed exclusively by the wealthy.[45] While Cook took pride in his "Working Men's Excursions," for the most part his travelers were middle-class professionals—such as doctors, lawyers, accountants, shopkeepers, clergymen, and professors—with an income in the £300–600 range.[46] Cook's trips were popular not only for their affordability, but more so for the convenience they offered in coordinating what would have been a complex set of purchases in generally unfamiliar contexts where travelers felt vulnerable to being exploited. By organizing these tours, Cook developed and operationalized the concept of what came to be called the "package tour." The package tour was a revolutionary business concept that created a new "commodity" through organizing consumption rather than production. This profoundly transformed the experience of popular leisure travel, which had been confined—excepting religious pilgrimage and the Grand Tour—to vacationing in a single "resort" location such as the shore or at a spa. In sum, "the design of the tour as a 'total experience' was Cook's invention."[47]

During the firm's early years, creating this total experience was largely a result of Cook's meticulous organization. He exploited the opportunities offered by new technologies to prearrange transportation, accommodation, meals, and itineraries. Using his promise of a large volume of sales, and often playing rival firms off each other, Cook secured discount prices. Travelers, in turn, could purchase tour tickets, with their packages of services, ahead of time as a single bundle. With his costs predetermined, Cook could bank prepaid tour ticket receipts while paying the establishments only after they rendered their services. This arrangement, which helped ensure cash flow, defined the core business model that enabled the birth of what would later be called the "tour operator."

These practices generated the disciplined, fast-paced nature of Cook's guided tours. Cook's tourists traveled by rail and often crammed in as many attractions as possible into a day's itinerary. This mode of travel flattened out the touring experience and limited the forms of cultural engagement that visiting foreign destinations could yield. The operation of Cook's popular tourism was often likened to the efficient running of a factory, and Cook is generally credited with applying "the production principles and techniques of the Industrial Revolution to tourism."[48] The company organized packaged tours as a closed system of economic transactions much like a factory conveyor belt connecting dedicated workstations of fixed operations. This structure fosters creating a large quantity of standardized products in the fastest time at the cheapest price through minimizing transaction costs and achieving economies of scale. At the same time, while a few tourists might occasionally stray from the group and its rigid itinerary, such a structure generally restricts tourists to prescribed spaces and precludes agency on their part. Unlike the independent traveler, package tourists have no control over their itineraries, limited autonomy, and little time or opportunity to interact spontaneously with local people, places, and businesses.

Instead of mechanical parts, this "factory" organization of tourism relied on Cook's organizational skills: "Standardised, precisely timed, commercialized and high-volume tour packages heralded the 'industrialisation' of the sector."[49] For many Cook supporters, this mechanical analogy confirmed Cook as an agent of industrialization and rational progress.[50] Critics of popular tourism complained about the crowds Cook marched through museums and archaeological ruins. The more snobbish were most offended by such intrusions into their own aristocratic spaces, whereas more romantic critics doubted whether Cook's tourists could appreciate, let alone understand, the art and history on display when viewed at such speeds.[51] Many Cook tourists, however, particularly appreciated the experience of mobility that the tours offered. While aristocratic travelers viewed their journeys as personal experiences of discovery, Cook tourists developed a new style of travel which exchanged depth and reflection for broader exposure to new sights and the social experience of group travel.

Tourism Networks and the Structuring of Tourism Economies

While package tours played a central role in Cook's "invention" of popular tourism, one cannot fully understand the rise of tourism as an "industry" and the development of tourism economies—nor Cook's role in these processes—by focusing exclusively on them. Cook's development of the package tour was one of many factors that expanded opportunities for nineteenth-century tourists, transportation companies, and entrepreneurs in diverse tourism-related businesses. This in turn led to the rise and global expansion of a *heterogeneous* international tourism industry. Following "actor-network theory"[52] we may view the development of tourism economies in terms of "a *dispersed* and *distributed* understanding of agency by directing attention to the variable power conferred upon actors by virtue of their enrollment in *heteroge-*

neous networks."[53] In their studies of science and technology, Bruno Latour, John Law, Michel Callon, and other developers of actor-network theory refer to "heterogeneous networks" as consisting of both human and non-human elements: "they are made up of a host of elements we tend to label technical, social, natural, political and so on."[54] In doing so, these theorists make the radical suggestion that nonhuman elements—such as material objects, technology, and nature—should be accorded agency since "what counts as a person is an effect generated by a network of heterogeneous, interacting, materials."[55] They argue that any stable pattern of social behavior or any organization that appears to act as a structure relies not only on social interaction and socially constructed meaning, but also on associations between diverse human and nonhuman elements. Moreover, actor-network theory highlights how the consequences of any statement, action, or technological change are shaped through a process of repeated interaction and adjustment among the actors who form heterogeneous networks.[56]

The development and popularization of tourism as practice was not simply an extension and replication of Cook's packaged tours, but involved diverse agents who operated within and across other networks.[57] These various agents included not only Cook and his firm, but hotel owners, tour guides, regional promoters, and local governments. The rise of tourism as an economic activity, that is, as a source of income, spawned these agents who in turn shaped the industry's expansion and the increased commercialization of tourism experiences. A broad range of other agents also influenced the various networks in which these actors operated. They included, for example, engineers whose inventions led to the development of new transportation technologies, archaeologists whose research projects created new tourist sites, and novelists who wrote about locations that travelers sought as destinations. We could also, of course, include material features such as distance, natural geography, the location of tourist attractions, and routes and speeds of various transportation technologies which, following Latour, can be understood as interacting with tourists and tourism firms to structure and stabilize the patterns of activity that constitute tourism economies.

Moreover, we also need to consider the agency of tourists themselves. The general increase in convenience and decrease in price expanded tourist demand in the second half of the nineteenth century. While these tourists operated in structures shaped by the industry, the physical geography of tourism sites, and existing transport technologies, the tourists interest in seeking out attractions—especially when they traveled independently—was a major force shaping the structure of tourism economies. These factors operated together in the context of U.S. tourism development: It was more than the speed of the railroads and the convenience of new hotels that made touring popular. Indeed, the touring infrastructure, at least in part, expanded to serve the needs of the increasing number of people with the desire to tour. The two, in effect, fed each other: more tourists clamored for more facilities and more sights to see, and the owners and operators of new hotels and attractions increasingly promoted tourism.[58]

As we begin to consider the influence of these various agents, the rise of tourism as an industry no longer looks like the spread and replication of the tours Cook offered, but rather a process in which diverse forms of tourism developed across the globe along with a heterogeneous tourism industry. A critical aspect of this argument is built on the contrast between the *nature of the networks* enabled in the development of popular tourism across Europe and those developed in Egypt under the direction of Thomas Cook & Son. This divergence is reflected in the limited *forms of tourism* developed in the Egyptian context.

In order to explain the relationship between the nature of tourism networks and forms of tourism, it helps to reduce the diversity of tourism economies to two simplified models of tourism development: enclave and integrated. In the *enclave* model an exclusive network governed by a dominant agent manages tourists' movement, their gaze at sights, and their consumption of services. In the package-tour version of this model, a fixed itinerary prearranged by a tour operator defines tourist activity. The resort version confines activity within a bounded space designed by a tourism developer. In either version, the enclave model resembles the structure of the exhibition; it limits what we might call tourists' agency, because their choices and behavior do not influence or redefine the structure of the tourism economy. At the same time, social and cultural interaction with the indigenous society is restricted, as tourists are not required to navigate independently within local communities. As a result, the social impacts of enclave tourism will be limited and tourists can easily be steered through "exotic" territories and societies. The enclave model thus facilitates expanding tourism volume and extending travel to new, unfamiliar territories despite little prior development of tourism facilities. Enclave tourism relies on a dedicated tourist infrastructure, which is easier to build than a public one but is generally used only for tourism purposes. While costs and revenues are more concentrated and stable for the tourism developer, the enclave model "greatly restricts the diffusion of industry profits" across the local economy.[59]

In contrast, the *integrated* model refers to tourism economies generated by an interactive back-and-forth process between tourists and diverse local entrepreneurs. Integrated tourism economies are constructed by heterogeneous networks of actors in which the outcome of the process is indeterminate and only stabilized through associations between diverse human and non-human elements and after a process of repeated interaction and adjustment between these actors. As one scholar explains: "The integrated option generally means a very gradual development of tourism . . . where tourism's relationship to the society evolves with increased interaction."[60] This approach limits tourists' and operators' insulation from the local economy and society. It functions best when there is less social, cultural, and/or economic distance between hosts and guests, as tourists must learn to negotiate their own paths though the foreign environment.

Cook's packaged tours, viewed in isolation, clearly resemble the enclave model.[61] His firm deserves credit for the invention and popularization of the model. It was critical to the expansion of the overall tourism market as it made tourism cheaper and more convenient for more people. The firm's subsequent activities, however, did much to promote mechanisms to support tourist travel outside of resorts and package tours. Through this expansion of tourism activity, tourism economies across Europe and North America came to be shaped not simply by tourism developers and tour operators, which tended to build enclave tourism, but by heterogeneous networks—including government agencies, local entrepreneurs, regional "place-myth" makers,[62] various types of tourists, and so on—which sustained patterns of integrated tourism development.[63] In the first decades of his firm's expansion, Cook interacted with railway operators, guidebook writers, and hotel owners, who eventually were able to promote tourism independent of his business. Moreover, as tourism demand expanded across Europe and North America, the firm introduced many tools, such as prepaid ticket coupons and traveler's checks, to facilitate independent travel.

Cook's early excursions helped lead to transformations in British and European rail networks. The railways themselves began coordinating their routes, allowing advance purchases of tickets, and printing timetables.[64] Cook both enabled and had to adapt to the changing railway economy. Beginning in 1868, Cook gained the right to sell single tickets at excursion fare prices and thus could begin to service the growing number of independent travelers.[65] By the 1870s, the firm issued circular tour tickets that came as a bound set of vouchers for ship, rail, and coach, allowing tourists to travel on their own schedules.[66] These tickets could be prepaid in one's own currency. The firm, increasingly under the direction of John Mason Cook, developed into a massive ticketing agent; having sold 200,000 tickets in 1868, it rendered more than three-and-a-half million tickets by 1890.[67] These ticket sales became one of the largest sources of income for the firm.[68] In the process, J. M. Cook sought to increase the rail ticketing system's flexibility. In an early company history, W. Fraser Rae suggested that after hearing about travelers who, during the outbreak of the Franco-German war in 1870, found themselves unable to use their Cook's tickets to cross Germany since the rail lines were shut to civilians, "The firm became convinced of the advantage that would accrue to travelers if they were supplied with tickets which would give them a choice of routes, and render them independent in the event of one route being blocked."[69]

Cook also learned to negotiate with hotels to make a block of rooms available over a set period of time, which could ensure his clients a fair price at an establishment he had evaluated. In 1868, he increased his clients' flexibility by issuing prepaid hotel coupons for accommodations and meals.[70] The Cooks might have stolen this idea from their rival Henry Gaze, but unlike Gaze, they were able to extend its functionality. By 1880, Cook had signed up four hundred hotels across Europe for inclusion into this system.[71] For independent travelers who made their own arrangements, Cook would often "publish a list of accommodations he had inspected with their prices and a brief description, noting where English was spoken and where 'plain English' food was served."[72] Once Cook had pioneered the market for middle-class hotel accommodations, hotel owners began independently to cater to such travelers, while entrepreneurs built hotels to tap into this growing market, which soon was no longer exclusively British. At the same time, tourists began booking their accommodations on their own, aided by guidebooks that reduced uncertainty about hotel prices and quality. Eventually, guidebooks would complete the loop, relying on readers to verify basic information and help keep it up to date. Travelers thus both acted as consumers of services and played a role in producing knowledge about the tourism economy, which reciprocally reshaped that economy.[73]

J. M. Cook was also responsible for launching in 1873 the development of the circular note. It came in various denominations and could be cashed in for local currencies at various hotels and banks.[74] Such use spread the prepaid coupon idea. This practice would lead the firm eventually into the banking and finance business. The note was one of the precursors of the traveler's check developed by the U.S.-based firm American Express, which helped launch its worldwide travel business after World War I.[75]

These changes in the firm's business practices were not simply technological inventions unleashed by Cook, as Thomas Cook's "invention" of the excursion tour is often portrayed. Rather, the firm under J. M. Cook was seeking to find ways to cater to shifting tourist tastes and practices, which, in turn, were adjusted to take advantage of each innovation. These advance planning tools offered convenience and reduced uncertainty for the more independent traveler. They also helped sustain Cook's cash flow, since the traveler paid in advance for the coupons and the firm only later paid the service providers when coupons were redeemed. More important, these practices had a greater impact beyond Cook's company and its tourists. By making more forms of tourism more affordable for more people, Cook helped create a much larger market, in terms of volume, class background, and geographic reach, for technologies of independent mobility, such as traveler's checks, leading to their wider acceptance and increasing convenience for independent travelers. Overall, Thomas Cook "created a new system, a technology, which took account of all the tourist's needs. Its system offered a wide range of services. . . . It was a complex scheme which could satisfy the needs, the tastes and the purses of a mixed clientele."[76] In developing this system in the 1860s and 1870s, Cook set the pattern for other firms.[77]

Cook generated further far-reaching effects. By acting as ticket agent, it created opportunities for small firms, such as smaller rail lines and hotels, to become part of tourist circuits. Together with other agents—guidebook writers, the railways, hotel owners—the macro impact of leisure travel's popularization in the 1860s and 1870s and the development of technologies for independent travel created economic opportunities that shaped heterogeneous tourism economies across Europe. Travel agencies, guidebooks, and railway companies "attempted to free customers from all material shackles . . . the effect was to render the tourist's task as easy and agreeable as possible. . . . In a sense the object was to organize a technical and commercial response to a socially determined demand."[78]

Travel to "the East"

In contrast to Europe and North America, where package tours developed by Cook were giving way to diverse forms of independent travel, in Egypt, Cook found a large territory that could be developed as a closed-enclave tourism economy. Thomas Cook began expanding the firm's operations to Egypt in 1869, when he conducted a tourist party to Egypt and Palestine which included witnessing the Suez Canal's opening. It was, he exclaimed, "a great event in the arrangements of modern travel."[79] The canal made Egypt the British Empire's main artery and its draw as a tourist destination only expanded with Egyptology's development, the wave of published travelogues, and proliferating images of ancient Egyptian monuments, all made possible with the development of photography and the stereoscope, an early form of virtual tourism.[80]

Soon, Cook's business practices would be the main driving force behind expanding Egyptian tourism.

Cook began building his Egyptian operations, as elsewhere, by making arrangements at each location while traveling the season before. His first tours, however, encountered problems Cook could not control out on this new frontier.[81] Cook's travelers were mobbed while disembarking in Alexandria. Some travelers complained that the rented steamers were not very clean and one took off without its passengers on board. On the voyage back down the Nile, the river level was low and the steamers' pilots kept running them aground. Thomas Cook himself, on one occasion, even came close to drowning.

While Cook could arrange very affordable passage from London to Alexandria, £20 first class, transplanting his model for popular tourism inside Egypt required more extensive planning, more complicated arrangements and negotiations, and a larger staff. Cook could soon offer his tourists an itinerary similar to those of the travelers of years past—landing in Alexandria, a stay in Cairo, and a journey up the Nile to Luxor or Aswan to see the ancient antiquities along the banks—but as a cheaper, quicker, and more convenient journey.

Overall, Egypt was a relatively expensive destination in comparison to Europe, and the clients Cook attracted were generally more wealthy, marking a contrast to the popular continental tours offered working-class clients in the company's early years. For many travelers a prearranged, prepaid, personally conducted tour eliminated the fear and inconvenience of independent travel. Earlier travelers, using their Murray or Baedeker guides and helped by a dragoman, could negotiate each step of the journey. Cook, however, could eliminate the need for making these choices and the bargaining routinely required for setting prices. With Cook, the total experience of Egyptian tourism could be purchased as a single commodity. The entire journey could be arranged months ahead of time, often by selecting an itinerary featured in *Cook's Excursionist*. Prices would include coupons for transportation and accommodations from Europe and across Egypt as well as all the expenses for donkeys, porters, guides, bakshish, and provisions, with the exception of drink.

Constructing Tourism Spaces in Egypt

Within their dahabiyyas and traveling with their dragomans, travelers to Egypt even before Cook viewed themselves as passing through a separate, anachronistic space apart from contemporary Egypt. The travelers' racial attitudes, ignorance of the local language, and negligible interest in contemporary Egyptian society shaped this space, as did their focus

on ancient Egyptian ruins. Florence Nightingale, for example, explained that "Egypt to the European is all but uninhabited. . . . The present race no more disturbs this impression than would a race of lizards,
scrambling over the broken monuments of such a star. You would not
call *them* inhabitants, no more do you these."[82] To the degree that travelers interacted with contemporary Egypt, they gazed upon Egypt through
mental maps and lenses shaped by the Bible, images from the "Arabian
Nights" (*A Thousand and One Nights*), and Orientalist texts such as
Edward Lane's *Manners and Customs of the Modern Egyptians,* which "transformed Cairo into an open-air [museum] gallery."[83] These mental maps
might have shaped how travelers viewed Egypt, but the practicalities and
logistics of travel often interrupted this gaze. For some travelers the
museum gallery could seem disorganized, rather like a zoo with all the
cages opened. Writing in 1857, a special correspondent from the *New
York Daily Times,* while praising the service of his dragoman as a "guide,
informant, and interpreter," noted that "Men who wish their thinking
done for them—who want to be carried about the world as a sort of visit
to a panorama, and have it move before them in the same way—may
need something more in a dragoman."[84]

This "something more" is what Cook came to provide. While many
early visitors had labored so as to view Egypt as an exhibition, Cook created a tourism infrastructure that would allow anyone to travel to Egypt
and reliably experience it in this way. Beginning in the 1870s, Cook
transformed travel in Egypt. The firm organized and mechanized it,
erecting a system that could carry travelers though Egypt as if visiting a
panorama. J. M. Cook accomplished this by insulating the tourist. To
facilitate his clients' journeys, Cook established offices in Cairo and Jaffa
in 1873 and later developed regional suboffices. The firm worked to
build a network of easy to identify dragomans, guides, porters, and servants across Egypt. John Ward exclaimed that "the very name Cook
becomes in Egypt a magic talisman securing all who trust in it immunity
from fraud and protection from rudeness, incivility [and] petty annoy-
ances of any kind."[85] Thereby Cook constructed a nearly contiguous
envelope through which the tourist could travel with ease and security,
isolating the tourist from having to interact with the local culture and
economy. In the process the tourist delegated his or her agency to the
structure of this tourism economy. For example, given the firm's control
over river transportation, Cook could create along the Nile a branded
tourist space with porters whose uniforms sported the firm's name, ships
docking under Cook banners, and eventually guests spending the winter
at company-owned hotels in Luxor.

Egypt, together with Syria and Palestine, provided a territory where
the firm developed an exclusive network of tourism-related services,

gaining a near monopoly across the region. Their early efforts quickly made an impact on the Eastern travel market. In 1874 a group of eighteen dragomans in Syria and Egypt, with the help of an unnamed traveler, published a letter in *The Times* of London complaining that "during the last few years our living has been almost taken from us by English agents monopolizing the conveyance of tourists to this country in large companies."[86] They accused Thomas Cook & Son of scaring off independent travelers by saying that there were no good dragomans or not enough travel supplies available. They argued that not only were their own charges cheaper but that they also allowed travel in small self-organized groups at a more flexible pace. Travelers with them were "free to arrange and alter their route at pleasure, to encamp and stop when and where they like."[87] The Cooks replied, denying that they had made such negative claims—although most of the firm's literature did repeat such charges about guides—and explaining that the dragomans failed to calculate the price of Cook's trips correctly.[88] Concerning travel to Palestine, they took credit for introducing competition into the market, noting that travelers had them to thank for the fact that "dragomans are at last prepared to accept reasonable rates for their services." The Cooks repeatedly suggested that questions about whether their package-tour customers were pleased with the firm's service and prices were best answered by any of the 240 passengers on their most recent tour. They took special pride in noting that they had brought rational and efficient organization and management to the travel industry, for "we have worked the steamers to a profit instead of a loss, as was invariably the case before we undertook the agency."[89]

The Mechanization of Nile Tourism

Nile travel, via any means, provided a space for a separate, voyeuristic tourist experience. Elizabeth Butler, who traveled in the winter of 1885–86, recounted: "Travelling thus on the Nile you see the life of the people on the banks, you look into their villages, yet a few yards of water afford you complete immunity from that nearer contact which travel by road necessitates; and in the East, as you know, this is just as well."[90] A major factor for Cook's in decreasing the cost and length of the journey, while enhancing this effect, was making the steam-powered boat the major vehicle for Nile tourist traffic. The first steamers appeared on the Nile in the 1830s, but most travelers continued to use the leisurely dahabiyyas.[91] By the late 1850s steamers were emerging as an alternative, but such ships only made a voyage when there was sufficient demand.[92] In 1870 Cook became the agent for the Egyptian government–owned steamer fleet, which he soon improved and expanded. By the mid-1870s,

Cook had transformed travel on the Nile by introducing steamers running on a regular schedule throughout the winter season, November to March.

Steamers could transport larger numbers of passengers more quickly and on precise schedules. Unlike the dahabiyyas, they were not vulnerable to delays caused by lack of wind.[93] A trip from Cairo to Aswan and back via dahabiyya might take fifty days at a cost of £150 for two, while Cook could offer a steamer trip taking twenty days at a cost of £50.[94] In 1886, Cook introduced tourist and express steamers "which have been the means of throwing open the wonders of Egypt and the Nile to thousands of people who would otherwise have been debarred by expense from seeing one of the most wonderful countries in the world."[95] By 1897 Cook offered "popular tours" from London to Egypt, lasting four weeks and priced under £35. Soon the firm also advertised a forty-five-day version, which included rail and express steamer trips on ships that delivered the mail up the Nile for £42.[96] As its fleet expanded and more travelers ventured to the Nile, Cook could offer a wider range of Egyptian tourist products, including luxurious, privately conducted parties, as well as sail and mechanized dahabiyya trips.[97] Thereby, the firm captured both scale and scope economies and dominated the market (Figure 1.1).

As its transportation infrastructure and wide client base solidified, Cook's Egyptian tourist business began expanding dramatically. Whereas in 1872, Cook escorted 400 tourists to Egypt,[98] F. M. Sandwith reported in 1889 that Cairo saw 6,000 visitors that winter with about 1,500 venturing up the Nile on Cook's ships.[99] *Cook's Excursionist* claimed that in the 1889–90 season, more than 11,000 visited Cairo.[100] Ten years later, George Steevens wrote that Cook was "opening up Egypt as a holiday-land to all the world" and "some say there have been 50,000 visitors," adding, "though that seems impossible."[101]

In 1892, Rae argued that Cook's tourists "make a trip in the Nile, not to learn anything about the condition of the country or the people, but to see ancient ruins. . . . A sort of ruin-mania is one of the maladies to which American and European voyagers on the Nile are subject."[102] Steamer travel, which transported larger tourist groups at a faster pace, further isolated travelers from Egyptian society. Once Cook controlled his own fleet, he soon upgraded the vessels to a luxurious standard so that they became floating hotels and increasingly insulated social environments, as if transported directly from Europe. Their speed and independence from the wind helped produce a standardized experience. Steevens remarked that the trip floated through "Rural Egypt at Kodak range."[103] A present-day scholar stresses that this observation "was typical of the late-nineteenth century culture of Orientalist travel, conjuring

Figure 1.1. Cover of Thomas Cook & Son's "Egypt and the Nile" brochure, 1904. Reproduced by kind permission of the Thomas Cook Archives, Peterborough, UK.

up the security of a modern viewing-platform and the exhibition of Egypt as a succession of fleeting and exotic images to be captured in film."[104] Nile tourism's panorama effect improved when the Egyptian government cleaned up the sites and began charging a visitor tax.[105] At that point, "Egypt [was] an open-air museum where temples and tombs [had been] arranged like shop windows for public inspection."[106]

Egypt as a Resort

As early as 1862, W. M. Thompson complained about Cairo's transformation, writing that the city was becoming "more and more the resort of Europeans in the pursuit of commerce, of health, or of pleasure."[107] Between 1860 and 1880 the number of Westerners living there expanded from 6,000 to 100,000.[108] While antiquities-based tourism remained a strong segment of the tourism market in Egypt as European colonial control over Egypt increased, new forms of leisure activity developed. In the wake of the British occupation during the early 1880s, Egypt received growing numbers of visitors and long-term residents. These Europeans set up not only shops and schools, but also sports and hunting clubs, luxury hotels, and other institutions of high society. Many came because an Egyptian tour or residence marked high social status.[109] During the winter, especially in the towns along the upper Nile, visitors came to Egypt for health reasons. This demand propelled the building of hotels in Luxor and Aswan by Cook and others. Eventually Egypt became a winter resort, or as Cook's literature claimed, "no more than a winter suburb of London."[110] By 1925 passengers would set off down the Nile from Cairo in train carriages cooled with blocks of ice hidden in false ceilings, with blinds on the windows to shade the passengers. The blinds "obscured the view, but the banks of the Nile held little interest for most of the passengers who were simply going to winter in the sun at Aswan."[111] As Egypt's tourism and tourism-related economies became more complex and interconnected, drawing on European visitors as well as long-term residents to sustain business, with less and less direct connection to Cook, the spaces these businesses created became yet more isolated from indigenous Egyptian society.

John Mason Cook's Business Empire on the Nile

The expansion of tourism networks across Egypt and the intensified commodification of Egyptian travel marked a critical era in the international tourism industry's development. The Egyptian market was essential to the success and business growth of Thomas Cook & Son. As early as 1872 J. M. Cook noted that Egypt and Palestine were "the two greatest features in our present programmes."[112] By 1890, of Cook's 2,692 employees worldwide, more than a third (978) operated in Egypt and Palestine.[113] In 1894, nearly half the firm's profits came from its Nile steamers.[114] With the profits from its dominance over tourism and Nile transportation, the firm became and remained into the twentieth century a global business that defined how tourism was practiced and how tourism firms operated. Moreover, Cook's experience in Egypt had global implications. Egypt was the first territory outside Europe and North America to become accessible to popular tourism, heralding the reach of international tourism industry to regions that generations later would be referred to as the "developing world." In the 1960s and 1970s, international tourism from wealthier industrialized societies to poorer, developing ones, following the mold of Cook's enclave model in Egypt, would become a major hard currency earner and, to many policy officials, a new engine for economic growth.

The acceleration of Cook's Egyptian operations coincided with the transfer of management authority from Thomas Cook to his son. John Mason Cook joined the firm in 1865 and became an equal partner in 1871. By 1878, after a bitter dispute with his father, J. M. Cook operated as the sole managing partner. Thomas had been driven by a belief in the ethical benefits of travel and often referred to opening Middle Eastern travel in missionary terms. His profit margins were "razor thin," and he continued to provide Holy Land tours even when they produced losses.[115] John, in contrast, was an ambitious businessman driven to promote the firm's pecuniary interests. Thus, the 1870s marked a transition from "commercial philanthropy to imperial entrepreneurship," as John "transformed his father's rickety mission of good will into an efficient and profitable commercial enterprise."[116] Egypt played a critical part in this transition and it is plausible that J. M. Cook would have found it difficult to forge such a successful and prosperous global tourism business without the opportunities Egypt offered the firm.

Although most European travel occurred in summer, winter was the Egyptian tourist season, allowing the firm to book income throughout the year, which nicely helped sustain cash flow. Moreover, while Cook's grew in the 1870s, it was losing many of its competitive advantages in Europe and North America. More travelers proved capable of traveling independently and did not need or want Cook's personally conducted group tours. New hotels now catered to independent tourists, and railroad companies, by simplifying their routes and schedules, facilitated their journeys. Increasingly, such enterprises sought to sell their services directly to the growing tourist public and did not need Cook as an agent, thereby avoiding paying him commissions. At the same time, a new set of firms, including Pullman and Ritz, were creating luxury tourism options across Europe and North America.[117] Many travelers in this segment sought leisure spaces free of the "common" tourists Cook had helped mobilized. Cook's firm, even though it assisted many independent travelers with hotel and travel coupons, still had a reputation defined by its personally conducted tours and its early emphasis on opening the travel market to the British working class. J. M. Cook saw this reputation as limiting the firm's opportunities and often felt compelled to remind the public that conducted tours were only a small part of the firm's business. Early on he strove to shift the firm's client base and reputation to wealthier travelers.

In Egypt, J. M. Cook found this opportunity and more. Egypt had not yet seen the full commercialization of tourism. Meanwhile, it represented a relatively exotic, exclusive destination that only attracted wealthier clients, as well as those who sought places off the beaten track. In Britain and Europe, "central governments and local powers were developing huge stakes in the new resorts, not only because of the revenues they represented, but also because of the need to establish control over the developing industry."[118] By contrast, Egypt was ruled by the descendants of Muhammad Ali, an Ottoman governor, who had formed an independent dynasty in the wake of Napoleon's evacuation.[119] Eventually claiming the title of *khedive*, these rulers had autonomy from Istanbul and control over much of the land and economic resources of the country. Yet in their effort to promote "defensive modernization," which included building, with the help of European advisors, munitions factories and a standing army, and the "Europeanization" of its urban spaces, they found themselves deeply in debt and increasingly subject to external European control. Under Khedive Ismail, the Egyptian government went bankrupt in 1875 and by 1882 the British invaded the country both to repress the nationalist Urabi revolt and to ensure Egyptian debts was repaid by "rationalizing" its economy. During this period, private businessmen from Britain and elsewhere sought economic opportunities in the country as it became increasingly integrated into the world capitalist system.[120]

Much of the firm's success in Egypt depended on J. M. Cook's close ties to both the Egyptian ruling dynasty, who valued Cook's ability to provide them with critically needed income, and to British officials, who viewed his effort as supporting their project of colonizing Egypt and, as they saw it, helping to "rationalize" the country's finances. In Egypt, J. M. Cook would build a vertically integrated tourism business based on its control over Nile transportation, several hotels, and hundreds of guides, porters, and servants across Egypt. The critical center in this business empire was Nile transportation, which provided the main artery of the tourism economy; only later would it be challenged by railways.

Thomas Cook & Son had not previously managed a transportation network. In Europe, Cook acted as an agent, selling tickets on commission or using rail services as part of his excursion trips. Egypt, however, was a different context, allowing for the invention of a new, "rent-seeking" business model. As a revisionist scholar of Egyptian development argues, much political conflict between rival business groups centered on access to guaranteed revenues (rents). "In practice, investors turn to the state to create monopoly rents" by granting exclusive concessions and limiting competition. Overall, "from the point of view of nineteenth century investors, colonialism in Egypt was a rent seeking project on a vast scale." J. M. Cook was one of those investors who eventually gained a rent-providing (near) monopoly over Nile steamship traffic.[121]

Using his political influence with the Khedive Ismail, in 1870 J. M. Cook was able to get himself appointed as agent for the Egyptian government's passenger traffic between Cairo and Aswan.[122] Pleased with the income J. M. Cook was providing his government, the Khedive extended the firm's business down to the Sudanese border, near Wadi Haifa, and was "given exclusive right to transport government mail along the Nile."[123] By 1877, "Cook was being challenged by others trying to get into the Nile cruise business, including his old rival, Henry Gaze," but was able to fend off competition and hold onto his monopoly, in part, by "arguing that the Nile was becoming overcrowded [and] that there was not enough coordination of services."[124] J. M. Cook prevailed and in 1880 "signed a ten-year contract with the Khedive which gave him complete control over the Nile steamers."[125]

The firm's ties to Britain's colonial project became even tighter in the wake of the 1882 British invasion and occupation of Egypt. With the tourism market disrupted, J. M. Cook helped transport the British military to help suppress the Urabi revolt and after the British triumph at Tell al-Kabir he delivered the wounded from Cairo to Alexandria. The following year, J. M. Cook delivered to Khartoum General Charles Gordon, who was sent to organize the withdrawal of Egyptian troops after they were defeated by the Mahdi revolt against Egyptian rule in the Sudan. These conveyances were conducted at cost.[126] In 1884–85, with the Egyptian tourism season ruined, J. M. Cook engaged in a more extensive operation that was a precursor to the use of private military contractors in the United States' occupation of Iraq. The British War Office commissioned Cook to convey an expeditionary force of 6,000 British and 7,000 Egyptian soldiers and their considerable supplies from Alexandria to Khartoum to rescue Gordon; he, however, had been killed before they arrived.[127]

Through his monopoly over passenger traffic along the Nile, J. M. Cook was able to bank considerable profits leading "to a take-off of tourism on the Nile."[128] Forced to replace the Egyptian government's steamers damaged in the military operations, and having funds to do so, J. M. Cook set about buying and building a new fleet. These new steamers, wrote a member of the firm's staff, "will be floating palaces and will be finer than anything that has floated on the grand old river since the days of Cleopatra. They will cause a sensation and I hope will prove a great attraction."[129] By the 1890s "the Cooks were operating six tourist steamers, four mail steamers, five old fashion paddle steamers, two steam dahabeahs, five steam launches, and fifteen dahabeahs on the Nile."[130] With this fleet, valued at a quarter-million sterling, "passenger traffic on the river" rested "virtually in the hands of the firm."[131] In 1895, the steamers' profits for tourist passage, local passage, and Egyptian government mail and personnel transport surpassed £17,000, while total expenses were £12,000.[132] This virtual monopoly continued until 1896 and only in 1906 did "keen" competition arrive threatening to undercut Cook's command over the Nile transportation.[133]

"For the Prosperity of Egypt"

At Thomas Cook & Son's fiftieth anniversary banquet in 1891, Khedive Tawfiq officially decorated J. M. Cook for his long-term service to Egypt. In a message to mark the occasion, the Khedive thanked Cook for his "most valuable" endeavors to facilitate tourism, make Egypt known to the world, transport troops and baggage, and give assistance to public schools.[134] The transcript of Major General Sir Francis Grenfell's remarks is telling: "I feel in mentioning the prosperity of Egypt I am mentioning the name of Mr. John Cook (Cheers). I know few people who have assisted in producing prosperity in Egypt more than Mr. John Cook (Cheers)."[135] Other speakers also emphasized the firm's services to the Egyptians living in the villages along the Nile. Egyptians, Cook's admirers asserted, often referred to him as "King of Egypt."[136] Indeed, the firm described itself as the largest employer of labor in the country.[137] In 1889 the *Excursionist* estimated that "Cook's tourists spent 2.5 million dollars a year in Egypt" and that "this figure increased almost fourfold over the next twenty-five years."[138] Near the end of his 1898 travelogue, Steevens exclaimed: "Mr. Cook is a blessing to Egypt . . . It is not only the vast amount of money he brings into the country, nor the vast number of people he directly employs. Besides that, you will find natives all up the Nile who practically live on [Cook]. Those donkeys are subsidised by Cook; that little plot of lettuce is being grown for Cook, and so are the fowls; those boats tied up on the bank were built by the sheikh of the Cataracts for the tourist service with the money advanced by Cook."[139] While these accounts celebrate J. M. Cook and his business for funneling tourist spending to Egypt and creating jobs for Egyptians, more sophisticated observers viewed Thomas Cook & Son acting as agents for "progress" and modernization. Not only did J. M. Cook rationalize the organization of Nile transportation—making it at last a profitable operation—but Cook's ships also provided Egyptians with faster transportation, taught them the value of time,[140] and introduced Egyptian pilots to the use of a wheel for navigation, replacing the less efficient tiller. Thus, J. M. Cook not only increased tourist flows and income but his firm also initiated a modern form of tourism in Egypt that led to structural changes in the local economy.

Rae, who studied the firm's operations in the early 1890s, suggested that J. M. Cook's reorganization of tourism along the Nile delivered its economic impact by seemingly converting a system that operated through traditional modes of exploitation into one that operated through fair prices leading to local prosperity:

In bygone days the villagers along the Nile were in dismay when a boat was moored near their dwellings and a demand made for supplies. The steward landed and the Sheikh met him and learned his requirements. After a little delay the articles were produced, and they were paid according to an arbitrary scale which the steward had prepared. The sum of the money due to the villagers was handed to their Sheikh, who put into his pocket what he considered a proper percentage, and gave the remainder to those who furnished the articles. This system satisfied the village Sheikhs, but it did not commend itself to the villagers. Nowadays all the provisions are paid directly to those who supply them, the sum is calculated by Mr. J. M. Cook and his agents among the Fellaheen has tended to render them prosperous.[141]

Cook's firm did employ hundreds of workers in Egypt—and claimed to have always hire a native where possible—contracted for the services of countless local merchants over the years, and brought tourists who spent millions while in Egypt. Thus many Egyptians in Cairo and along the Nile found their economic well-being dependent on Cook's tourism industry. Rae's own comments, however, undermined the suggestion that Cook's tourism brought structural change, modernization, and economic independence to Nile villagers. He concluded with the following warning: "If the tourist traffic on the Nile were to cease, and it will certainly fall off when British influence or example wanes, the lot of the toiling villagers along the river's banks from Cairo to Wâdy Halfa will again be as hard as it was in the bygone days of abject poverty and intolerable oppression."[142]

Crucially, not only did Rae associate British firms and colonial influence with the positive benefits of tourism, he suggested that tourist flows required "British influence or example" to sustain them. Cook's Egyptian tourism operations thus clearly constituted a closed enclave tourism economy, in which any agents—guides, ship pilots, porters, and so on—Cook associated with remained exclusively dependent on his organization of the tourism economy. Egyptians working in the tourism sector, we might suggest, were servicing a life-sized exhibition of Egypt built by Cook. In contrast to the integrated tourism model or patterns of tourism development in Europe and North America, the Egyptian venture failed to promote forming a heterogeneous tourism sector built through the interaction of diverse agents, businesses, and touristic forms. In particular, J. M. Cook failed to promote growth for independent Egyptian businesses or cooperatives in trades such as handicraft manufacturing or taxi service. Most of the independent agents the company contracted with operated in the informal sector, rather than being organized in unions, guilds, or cooperatives then just beginning to assert their power, as would be demonstrated in the broad 1919 nationalist uprising. Businesses in Cook's tourism economy—hotels, railways, or photography studios—were foreign-owned and catered to visitors, expatriates, and colonial officials, in addition to a very small slice of the westernized indigenous elite. The other "entrepreneurial" opportunities sustained by tourism lay in relic hunting and tomb plundering.[143] Far from having positive effects on economic vitality, these activities also robbed Egypt of aspects of its national heritage.

While American newspaper editorialists may have condemned relic hunting and romantically oriented critics of Cook, such as Pierre Loti, lamented the destructive impact of Cook's mechanized tourism,[144] a full assessment of tourism requires incorporating Egyptian voices. Those who gained employment might praise Cook, but such views would not in themselves depict the full history of towns near Egyptian tourism sites nor tourism's socioeconomic and cultural impact on Egypt. Many of the Egyptians who "worked" for Cook did so for little reward. William Charles Maughan, for example, recounts how the coal for the steamer he rode was supplied:

A dirty disagreeable operation it was. . . . The work is performed by a number of the poor peasants, chiefly women and children, who were forced to do this without any remuneration from the authorities. The unfortunate *fellaheen* . . . carried the coals on their heads in small baskets, and they ran up and down the bank in Indian file, urged on by one or two men with whips, who superintended the work. . . . When it was over, they all congregated on the bank and looked with interest upon the steamer and its passengers who, on such occasions, appear on deck, and occasionally fling copper coins and oranges among the dusky throng.[145]

A rare Egyptian view is presented by the Egyptian writer Muhammad al-Muywaylihi, whose turn-of-the-century novel *A Period of Time* depicts a group of European tourists at a Cairo nightclub: "They're tourists from

Western countries . . . and regard Oriental people with utter contempt. . . . Their activities are evil and their knowledge is pernicious. They're the people who rob others of their wages. . . . They're beset by the twin diseases of listlessness and boredom."[146] Historian Donald Reid suggests that "Western exploration, archeology, and tourism were immensely destructive of local customs and economies,"[147] but elsewhere notes that the histories of these processes remain unwritten, largely because "many Egyptians involved in the growing tourism industry were illiterate, and most Egyptian authors of the day wrote of other things."[148] This is both a problem and a challenge.

The Politics of Heritage and Tourism

Not only did Egyptian firms and skilled professionals—as well as labor—play almost no role in shaping the structure of Cook's tourism economy in Egypt, Egyptians and other nonwestern "tourists" and travelers were absent as well. J. M. Cook's approach did not lead to the leveling of social barriers or the "democratization" of travel among Egyptians in the way his father's efforts sought to in England and the continent. While economic barriers might have limited the ability of most Egyptians and other Arabs to travel as tourists with Cook, in the context of nineteenth- and early twentieth-century Egypt, most Europeans *did not even imagine native Egyptians as potential tourists.* Cook's 1906 Egypt handbook, written by the British Egyptologist A. Willis Budge, explained:

The Egyptians in general, until quite recently, have . . . never been accustomed to travel, and they look upon those who wander from country to country as beings who are possessed of restless though harmless devils . . . they believe that the ancient Egyptians were idolaters and very wicked people, and that God destroyed them and . . . buried their palaces and temples. . . . That anyone should wish to make excavations for the love of learning or the advancement of science is more than they can understand. The younger generation, though not fanatical, is as skeptical about the traveller's motives as his elders, only, seeing that money is to be made out of the "Frangi," he conceals his doubts, and devotes himself to making money out of him.[149]

Budge here presented an inverted history of the relationship between tourism and commerce—or, as noted above, rent extraction—portraying the western tourist as a knowledge seeker whom native Egyptians exploited, taking advantage of the traveler's lofty modernist virtues, which the locals would never understand, given their devotion to "making money out of him."

Budge also ignored the diverse but critical role travel historically played in Muslim practice. These include the *hajj* pilgrimages to Mecca, the popular tradition of visiting of shrines, and the practice of *rihla* or travel for purpose of seeking knowledge.[150] While Cook once organized a hajj trip for a group of South Asian pilgrims,[151] his firm played little role in the extensive travel networks developed across the Muslim world to assist this annual flow. Medieval cities across the Islamic world long had their own "hospitality" sector made up of mosques, guest houses, and khans built to cater to pilgrims, merchants, and traveling scholars. These, however, never evolved to provide an infrastructure for commercial leisure travel across territories which in the nineteenth century had their transportation infrastructures reshaped by and for colonial interests.

J. M. Cook's commercialization of western tourist travel not only shaped much of the transportation infrastructures of Egypt, but it also helped promote a vision, set out in *Description de l'Égypt,* which defined the terms for contemporary Egypt's incorporation into modernity and possible independence under western tutelage.[152] In line with this Orientalist framing of Egyptians' history (*viz.* Edward Said), J. M. Cook viewed appreciation of the ancient monuments as critical for Egyptians if they were ever to rule themselves. In 1892 Cook sponsored a trip up the Nile for a group of fifty Egyptian teachers and selected pupils in order for them to acquire "a knowledge of the country."[153] He told them, "On making inquiries of well-to-do and well educated natives, I have found that hardly any of them have visited Upper Egypt, with the exception of Government officials who have chanced to be sent up the river on duty. . . . But if Egypt is ever to be governed and controlled by her own children every one of you should see all the famous places in the land, and strive to understand its history and special requirements in the far past as well as in the more recent times; it is in this way that you may become able to deal intelligently with important problems in its commerce and administration."[154]

Cook's definition of "all the famous places in the land" relies on a construction of history written by western Egyptologists and Orientalists, rather than on indigenous Egyptian discourses that, while diverse and contested, were dominated by referents from Arab and Islamic history. Thus, few Arab/Islamic heritage sites surfaced on Cook's itineraries. A museum of Arab art opened only in 1903, and by the 1914 edition of Baedeker's guide, it garnered but one-tenth the coverage of the "Egyptian Museum" that housed the Egyptology collection.[155] J. M. Cook, however, was not averse to generic "Islamic theming." Loti writes of Cook's Cataract Hotel: "Cook & Son (Egypt Ltd.) have even gone so far as to conceive the idea that it would be original to give their establishment a certain *cachet* of Islam. And the dining-room reproduces (in imitation, of course . . .) the interior of one of the mosques of Stamboul."[156]

At the same time, while Budge righly noted that, much as in the Old

Testament, the "Quranic image" of the pharaohs presented them as "tyrannical and idolatrous," Egyptian scholars such as Rifa'a al-Tahtawi as well as ones within the Coptic Christian community were in this era developing an "alternative vision of ancient Egyptians as illustrious ancestors all the world might envy."[157] By the 1920s and 1930s—once Egypt had attained a degree of independence from Britain and Cook began to lose his monopoly over Nile tourism—a range of Egyptian scholars, writers, and politicians would seek to incorporate pharaonic elements into Egyptian national identity.[158] These have never displaced popular attachment to Egypt's Arab and Islamic heritage within constructions of Egyptian national identity, just as Nile tourism would to this day continue to cater to Western tourists.

Other Views of "the Orient"

A close reading of late nineteenth-century travelogues to Egypt reveal traces of this desire to see beyond the ancient Egyptian temples and stereotypes portrayed in Lane's *Manners and Customs*. Rae, for example, notes that he "was more interested in the lot of the people which are now living than in the ruins left by an extinct race."[159] Such concern, however, was rooted in a notion, described above, that British influence and example was imperative for improving the lot of these people. Sidney Low also ridiculed the focus of Cook's pleasure-seekers. He admired the technological sublime of the Aswan dam more than ancient temples there, "as it was 'modern Egypt,'—colonial Egypt, more emphatically *Britain's* Egypt—that captivated Low."[160]

To discover other, potentially post-Orientalist, gazes requires reading alternative, generally indigenous travelogues and representations of "the East." While it would be misguided to conceptualize an Islamic "mode of tourism" to contrast with some notion of a modern western culture of tourism, archives do document cases of Arabs and Muslims who visited cities such as Cairo with a different eye. These travelers explored the "sights" not as leisure tourists looking for the picturesque or examples of Orientalist motifs, but in terms of how they related to Arab, Muslim, or Egyptian history and culture.

For example, we may contrast how the nineteenth-century French political journalist Gabriel Charmes and the Egyptian administrator and author Ali Mubarak Pasha understood the al-Azhar mosque at the center of old Cairo. Charmes was one of the few European travelers to say much about al-Azhar, one of the most important religious and educational institutions in the Islamic world. This near silence was a product of European "preoccupation with Egypt's ancient monuments, the unattractive appearance of al-Azhar, and the underdeveloped state of al-

Azhar as a tourist site." Charmes' discussion of al-Azhar's history was culled from previous treatments and developed through his own visual observation. He viewed the institution as decaying and "lacking an openness to new ideas of science and social progress," and thus a symbol, it seemed, for the whole of Islam.[161]

Ali Mubarak, by contrast, viewed al-Azhar as a living center of Islamic learning with a long history of change and a cosmopolitan body of scholars and students. In his text, the institution was "related implicitly, not to Islam as a religion, but to Egypt as a national community."[162] He observed that like the rest of Egypt, it was in transition, undergoing a period of much needed, but not fully adequate reform. By being able to relate the specifics about al-Azhar, Ali Mubarak could critique the limits of reform within the mosque while remaining "firmly convinced of the essential rationality of Islam."[163] Given that Said's critique of Orientalism is widely viewed as having erased the nuances and active negotiation that shaped many representations of the Middle East—especially by nonwestern artists, photographers, and scholars[164]—portrayals such as Ali Mubarak's never had any influence over what remained Orientalist cultures of travel governed by enclave tourism economies.

Legacies of "Enclave Orientalism" and Beyond

In January 1915 a London *Times* correspondent in Egypt reported: "There is, to speak strictly, no Egyptian season this winter. . . . Most of the hotels are closed."[165] That winter the tourism-related economy of Cairo was animated not by European leisure travelers, but by soldiers serving in the British army and by resident colonial officials. The tourist economy of upper Egypt became "defunct."[166] The steamers had stopped running in 1914 and were taken over "for war purposes" and the military used Cook's hotel in Luxor as a hospital, while Aswan was "like a city of the dead."[167] J. M. Cook had passed away in 1899, and while his sons continued to run the firm, Thomas Cook & Son eventually lost its dominance over the Egyptian tourism economy as the era of empire came to a close in the Middle East. Globally, the firm shrank and international tourism, like much of the interwar economy, began an era of decline.

When the global tourism economy launched its rebirth during an era of explosive growth after the end of World War II, Thomas Cook—nationalized during the war—stood as but one among many international tour operators developing new forms of organized tourism, exploiting not the railway but the large airplane. Egypt spent much of this era seeking to rid itself of the remaining British troops on its soil, claiming sovereignty over the Suez Canal, and promoting an inward-oriented experiment in socialist-style industrialization. Tourism development only became a priority with its turn toward economic liberalization in the 1970s.[168]

During the 1980s and 1990s, with the expansion of the Egyptian tourist economy, a new incarnation of Thomas Cook & Son sought to "revive" its Nile excursions for a new generation of tourists.[169] The firm would never, and could never, rebuild its near monopoly over Egyptian tourism, but its legacy can be seen in the generalized structure of tourism in Egypt and elsewhere, which fashions spaces resembling exhibitions. In the postcolonial era, tourism in developing countries such as Egypt is not shaped by colonial policies but by states in search of hard currency, states that organize their tourism economies—including their transportation sectors, cultural monuments, and even various forms of cultural self-representation—to cater to foreign visitors. Nile archaeological cruises, luxury Cairo hotels, coastal beach resorts surrounded by walls, and the layout for tourism development in Luxor—built to "minimize unregulated contact between tourists and the local community"—continue to be modeled along the lines Cook first established.[170] Today, upgrading tourism along the Nile has even required the "de-development" of villages near tourism sites "to preserve the touristic quality of the villages and Pharaonic sites."[171] Meanwhile, most non-Muslim visitors, with the aid of Egyptian tourism officials, continue to sightsee in Egypt through lenses focused on timeless images of ancient Egypt.[172]

Alternative modes of tourism development are possible, but require the development of alternative business practices, and with them, alternative modes and cultures of touring that challenge and dissolve the imaginative geographies of colonial-era travel. One path toward this goal is anchored by taking the agency of Egyptian as well as other Arab and Muslim tourists more seriously. Tourism developers have long avoided catering to this poorly articulated, uncertain market, but today the possibilities for seeing a shift are more robust, given the rise of regional Arab tourism and Islamic tourism. Not only have such flows expanded since September 11, 2001, whereas many other destinations have seen declines, but efforts are also underway to define a new form of "Islamic tourism."[173] These projects are "reorienting tourist destinations towards less consumption and 'western-culture loaded' sites [and] towards more Islamic historical, religious, and culture sites." A central challenge is the development of "new 'touristic' interpretations of pilgrimage and efforts to merge religious and leisure tourism in joint programs."[174] Now needed are, first, new business strategies, and then entrepreneurial talent and visions of people such as the Cooks, to bring finally the "democratization of travel" to the Middle East.

Chapter 2

The Compagnie Générale Transatlantique and the Development of Saharan Tourism in North Africa

KENNETH J. PERKINS

Tourism in North Africa Before World War I

The highly subjective process of distinguishing among foreign explorers, adventurers, travelers, businesspersons, and tourists in nineteenth-century North Africa makes it difficult to date with precision the origins of Western tourism in the Maghrib (Algeria, Tunisia, Morocco, and Tripolitania). As early as 1849—less than two decades after the French landings that set in motion the conquest of the Algerian coastal plain and only a year after the surrender of Abd al-Qadir, the leader of the most effective resistance to the occupation—the Algiers Municipal Council pointed to the city's mild winter climate and its striking venue as reasons to anticipate that two recently concluded public projects, a new theatre and the Chemin de Télemly, a promenade through the wooded hills above the city offering splendid views over Algiers and its bay, would serve not merely the local population, but substantial numbers of visitors as well.[1]

As in European cities around the Mediterranean that developed into tourist centers during the nineteenth century, many of the earliest visitors to Algiers were in poor health. European physicians and other advocates of the curative powers of climate—climatotherapy—prescribed seasonal travel to the south for patients with pulmonary diseases and other illnesses believed to be ameliorated by the abundant sunshine and relative dryness characteristic of Mediterranean winters.[2] By the mid-1860s, ailing northern Europeans in search of experiences more exotic than Nice, Malaga, or Naples had to offer were beginning to venture across the Mediterranean. For their security and comfort, they gravitated to places over which a European power exercised a measure of influence and which had undergone some degree of Westernization.

For the French, Algeria was a logical destination. An 1848 law incorporating Algeria's three *départements* into the *métropole* meant that French citizens traveling there were on a domestic journey unaffected by the intricacies of crossing international borders. The presence of visitors in failing health amidst the thousands of soldiers garrisoning Algeria and the hardy settlers populating its cities, villages, and farmsteads signaled the extent to which France had brought the territory into its orbit. Moreover, the sojourns of these seasonal guests—usually in or around Algiers—exposed them to countless manifestations of France's self-declared *mission civilisatrice*. Their firsthand observations of the application of French rule and the dissemination of French culture enabled them to supplant imagined notions of imperial France with (a version of) reality. Other Europeans also made therapeutic winter visits, drawn to Algiers not only by its attractive physical setting and mild winter climate but also by the juxtaposition in the city of Western appearances and an aura of Oriental mystery and intrigue that lingered—albeit less threateningly than in the past—under French rule. Britons who crossed the Mediterranean in search of healing warmth tended to congregate in Egypt, even before its unofficial absorption into the empire in 1882. Even so, enough British subjects found their way to Algiers to constitute the second largest contingent of northern European visitors there between the 1880s and World War I. By the turn of the century, Algiers had an Anglican and a Presbyterian church built in 1868 and 1886, respectively, two English language newspapers during the winter season, an English grocery store, and, as a melancholy reminder of the original lure of the region, a small cemetery.[3]

Throughout the last quarter of the nineteenth century, quite vigorous French citizens, other Europeans, and a small number of North Americans with interests that went beyond the sedentary pleasures of the Algiers winter season followed in the footsteps of the infirm. Several developments at the time underscored the growth of Western tourism not only in Algiers but in other parts of the country as well. Nothing so clearly anointed a location as a suitable tourist destination than its inclusion in a tour organized by Thomas Cook and Son. The first Cook's tour of Algeria left London on February 15, 1875, traveled through France by train, and sailed from Marseilles to Oran, reaching there on February 21. Relying on trains, steamships, and stagecoaches, the group spent three weeks visiting the cities, the countryside, and the sites of Antiquity in northern Algeria.

The vestiges of Roman civilization provided graphic reminders of the role of peoples from the northern shores of the Mediterranean in North Africa's past and naturally invited analogies with the present. To many tourists, the Westernized urban quarters built by the French appeared as contemporary counterparts to the cities of Roman Africa, while settlers' modern farms seemed poised to revive the region's ancient importance as a granary. As a result, the ruins that crowned the visits of many educated tourists immersed in the classics also validated French colonialism. The tour organizers, who had shaped its itinerary to satisfy the curiosity of their clients, had not consciously cultivated this political by-product, but French officials were quick to appreciate its value in linking tourism and the promotion of colonial endeavors.

Moving east to Tunisia, Cook's pioneers spent four days in and around Tunis, including the nearby site of Carthage. Just under a month of additional sightseeing in Sicily and mainland Italy followed their departure from North Africa, with the group returning to London on April 15. The two-month length of the tour and its cost—£77 for first class, £67 for second at a time when the annual wages of a British craftsman approximated £75[4]—suggest that such a trip was the preserve of those with substantial reserves of both money and leisure time. Nevertheless, this tour, or variations on it, including one that returned to Europe via Spain rather than Italy, became regular Cook offerings. In 1880, the United States' edition of the company's newspaper, *Cook's Excursionist and Tourist Advertiser*, began promoting the same tour departing from New York.

A second certain indicator of tourism growth was the appearance and proliferation of guidebooks. For the first time in 1862, the Parisian publishing house Hachette issued, in its Guides-Joanne series, *Itinéraire historique et descriptif de l'Algérie, comprenant le Tell et le Sahara* by Louis de Piesse.[5] Later editions, which also contained information on Tunis and Tangier, appeared regularly until 1885. Responding to the establishment of a French protectorate over Tunisia, Hachette replaced the older volume with *Algérie et Tunisie*, also by de Piesse (1883). Shortly after the turn of the century, a new edition on which the North African scholars Augustin Bernard and Stephane Gsell collaborated took its place as the standard French language guide. By 1911, five editions had appeared. A 1916 volume revived de Piesse's inclusion of Tangiers and further expanded the scope of the guide with material on Malta. Complementing these general guidebooks were others of a more localized nature, perhaps the best known of which was Charles Desprez's *L'Hiver à Alger*, which, for four decades after its original 1864 publication, was esteemed as "the indispensable vade-mecum of the winter resident,"[6] or at least of those able to read French. Among the more successful English guides to Algiers were George Harris's *The Practical Guide to Algiers*, which went through no fewer than ten editions between 1891 and 1903, when it was acquired by Thomas Cook & Son and reissued as *Cook's Practical Guide to Algiers*, and Joseph Hyam's *Illustrated Guide to Algiers: A "Practical" Handbook for Travellers*, first published in 1899. Hyam, the editor of the *Algerian*

Advertiser, one of the English-language winter weeklies, contrasted his volume, which contained many of his own photographs, with its "*un*practical, dull, exhaustive, and decidedly uninteresting" competitors.[7] No doubt Harris was the primary target of this attack, but because Hyam's book included lengthy sections on other regions of Algeria, it might also have been aimed at the highly regarded *Handbooks for Travellers* series published by John Murray. A *Handbook for Travellers in Algeria* written by Sydney Courtauld had appeared in 1873, but was so riddled with errors that the company commissioned R. Lambert Playfair, the British consul-general in Algiers, to produce a new volume the following year. A second edition in 1878 added *and Tunis* to the title. Three new versions appeared between then and 1895, with the last reissued periodically until 1902, by which time Cook's was publishing, along with the former Harris guide, another which combined Algeria and Tunisia.

A third marker of tourism growth was the formation in Algiers of a Comité d'Hivernage Algérien in 1897. Hopeful of elevating Algeria to the status of "la reine des stations hivernales de l'Univers entier,"[8] the committee enjoyed the patronage of high government officials and members of the business community. It maintained an office in the Algiers city hall, which assisted visitors with practical information about local facilities and the services of English, German, Italian, and Spanish translators. An adjacent reading room stocked local newspapers and a selection of books of regional interest, making it a popular meeting place for winter visitors. The committee also sponsored walking tours of the city, including the *qasba*, or Arab quarter, weekly concerts from November through April, and other occasional activities such as fantasias, falcon hunts, and balls.

Increasing numbers of tourists followed the French flag into the Tunisian protectorate. The practice of visiting Tunisia in conjunction with a more extensive tour of Algeria remained the norm in the years preceding World War I, but Tunisia's attractiveness, especially for Europeans intrigued by the Carthaginian and Roman vestiges littering its landscape, is apparent from the steady growth and greater regularity of tours, the conclusion of an agreement between the city of Tunis and the Compagnie des Stations Hivernales Africaines in 1900 to construct a hotel and casino in the capital, and the 1902 decision of Thomas Cook & Son to open a second North African office in the city—the first had operated in Algiers since 1887.[9]

In Morocco, which preserved its independence until 1912, tourism preceded the flag by many years. Beginning in 1891, Cook's invited travelers on its tours of southern France and Spain to extend their journeys into Morocco with a selection of a dozen options lasting between three days—to Tangier and Tetouan—and two months—a true "Cook's Tour" of the country that ventured as far south as Marrakesh. Advertisements for several of the tours lured sportsmen with descriptions of wild-boar hunts and streams teeming with fish; others appealed to a more sedentary audience, featuring travel by steamer to ports along the Atlantic coast as far south as Mogador (Essaouira). Still others advised prospective travelers to expect daily horseback rides of as many as twelve hours. The company's publicity assured readers that visiting Morocco entailed "no question of danger or annoyance, and Europeans, especially English, are received with cordiality and respect." Nevertheless, a frank statement cautioned that a month-long trip into the Middle Atlas mountains was "not recommended for ladies, as extra care has to be taken when crossing the independent tribes of Zair and Beni Mtir." The uncertain security situation in parts of the Sharifian Kingdom at this time, the primitive internal transportation system, and the recommendation that "travelers . . . take their own saddles, with crupper and breastplate, as the gear is bad"[10] gave even the least ambitious of these initial ventures in Morocco the look of late nineteenth-century "adventure tourism."

From an early date, European tourists' fascination with a starkly different and unfamiliar environment drew them to those desert locales that were relatively easily accessible and safe for casual visitors. Principal among them was Biskra, an eastern Algeria oasis whose rail link to Constantine after 1888 made it a popular destination for visitors who wanted a quick and comfortable introduction to the desert, as well as for those who spent the entire winter season there. At the western end of the country, a second railway line penetrated the desert as far south as Colomb-Béchar, near the frontier with Morocco, in 1905, but its raison d'être was almost entirely military. Thomas Cook & Son's awareness of the possibilities of desert tourism predated the arrival of the railroad in the Sahara, however. Cook's organized its first desert excursion in 1886, shortly after the inauguration of regular stagecoach service to Ghardaia. In the 1888–89 season, it offered more elaborate tours that gave "a taste of camp and desert life, which must be experienced to be fully appreciated, and which cannot fail to leave a marked and lasting impression upon the traveler." Participants in a five-week "Grand Excursion and Sporting Tour to the Desert of the Sahara" traveled by camel, mule, or horse over a U-shaped route from Laghouat to Biskra that took them through the oases of Ghardaia, Ouargla, and Touggourt, spending their days hunting the abundant game that made the area "a real paradise for sportsmen" and passing at least a few of their nights at "some convenient spot" in the desert.[11] Spartan expeditions such as this and the more genteel surroundings of Biskra, whose hotels and casino established it as a "ville d'hiver or a ville d'eaux on the lines of Nice, Pau,

Lucerne, or Aix,"[12] offered fin-de-siècle tourists a wide range of desert experiences.

In every locale where the tourist trade evolved into a significant aspect of the economy, the commodification that inevitably ensued of the place, its people, their history, and their culture affected local Arabs and Berbers who, at first unwittingly, but then more intentionally, constituted the human scenery of tourism. Nowhere was this more evident than in desert communities such as Biskra, as local economies underwent a more dramatic restructuring with the advent of tourists than occurred in any larger cities, even those most frequented by foreign visitors. Prior to the popularization of the oasis as a tourist destination, its 7,000 or so Algerian residents depended for their livelihoods on agriculture, the caravan trade, and Biskra's role as an administrative center.

Thereafter, the steady November to April influx of transient and semipermanent visitors created new jobs directly serving tourists and exponentially increased the number of potential consumers for local artisans' products. In the early 1890s, each of the five hotels in Biskra employed Arab and Berber men in menial jobs. Others worked as guides, carriage drivers, cameleers, or stable hands. Shops owned and managed by Europeans catered to Western tastes, figuratively and literally, by supplying everything from "tinned meats, vegetables, [and] Huntley and Palmer's biscuits . . . down to dog chains and walking sticks."[13] Some also sold souvenirs, but enterprising Algerians stocked stalls around the marketplace with items sure to appeal to tourists: jewelry, knives, antique weapons, household goods, slippers and other leather products, baskets, animal horns and skins, and stuffed lizards. Perhaps the most notorious example of commodification in Biskra and elsewhere involved the women of the Ouled Naïl tribe. Known throughout Algeria as singers and dancers, and widely assumed by foreign visitors to be prostitutes—which many were—the Ouled Naïl's sensual dancing figured salaciously in numerous tourist descriptions of the Algerian Sahara. Postcard images showing them and other Algerian women bare-breasted, in provocative poses, or engaging in forms of behavior that shocked Western sensibilities became a scintillating staple of desert tourism.[14] The cultural chasm separating residents of the oasis from foreign visitors reinforced the antipathy some Biskrans had harbored for westerners, whose arrival in the region had cast a shadow over their way of life that the economic benefits of tourism did not at all brighten. Persuaded that Islamic values were at risk in an environment so zealously given over to the pursuit of non-Muslims' pleasures, some pious families fled from Biskra and other Saharan regions in emulation of Muhammad's *hijra* from the sinful environment of Mecca.[15]

Biskra's celebrity had a trickle-down effect on the oases of Touggourt and El Oued. By the turn of the century, improvements to the roads had brought these less Europeanized centers within a four- or five-day carriage drive of Biskra, some of whose winter residents began turning to them in a search for more authentic examples of desert culture. Despite the increasing interest in the Sahara—the French writer Charles Lallemand said that going to Biskra without including Touggourt was tantamount to visiting France but failing to go to Paris—it was only after World War I that tourism in the region truly took off. Algeria, with vast stretches of desert and already well known as a tourist venue, figured significantly in a process, one driving force in which was the Compagnie Générale Transatlantique (CGT).

The Compagnie Générale Transatlantique and North African Tourism

One indispensable ingredient for the success of tourism in North Africa and, more importantly at the time, for the region's general economic well-being was the availability of frequent, rapid, efficient, and comfortable sea links with Europe. In 1879, after winning a government contract to provide service to Algerian ports, the CGT enlarged its existing fleet by commissioning the construction of ten new steamers and purchasing others from a financially troubled competitor. In the summer of 1880, its nineteen vessels inaugurated a schedule of two weekly sailings from Marseille to Algiers, two more to Philippeville (Skikda), and one departure a week to Bône (Annaba), Tangier via Oran, and Tunis. The CGT also served North Africa from two other Mediterranean ports. A weekly steamer to Algiers departed from Sète, some one hundred miles west of Marseille and almost due north of Algiers. Two ships a week, one bound for Algiers, the other for Oran, left Port-Vendres, whose location only a few miles east of the Spanish border made it the closest point to Africa on the French coast.[16] The city's promoters claimed that traveling from Port-Vendres ensured not only the shortest, but also the calmest, crossings.

Although the CGT faced competition on its Algerian and Tunisian routes—most notably from the Compagnie de Navigation Mixte and the Société Générale de Transports Maritimes—it controlled the lion's share of the traffic between France and North Africa from the inception of its trans-Mediterranean services. At the turn of the century, Marseille boasted six weekly CGT sailings for Algiers and three each for Oran and Tunis, while its rivals offered only weekly or, in the case of Algiers, twice weekly, departures. The fastest, largest, and most luxurious CGT steamers plied these flagship routes, with some able to complete the Marseille to Algiers run in twenty-four hours. The speed of the company's ships, coupled with the coordination of their sailing times with the schedule of the Paris-Lyon-Marseille (PLM) Railroad assured the company more efficient service than its rivals. Throughout these early decades, most CGT passengers were government officials, businessmen, or settlers and their families, with only a small number of tourists. From the outset, however, company management recognized the potential importance of leisure travel to North Africa. In 1882 it offered special tourist fares of 205 francs for first class and 105 francs for second class for combined rail and ship passage from London or Paris to ports in Algeria and Tunisia.[17]

The good name acquired by the CGT in Algeria and Tunisia helped the company to gain entrée into Morocco ahead of other lines and even before the installation of the protectorate. In 1911, as he prepared for the occupation of Morocco, General Hubert Lyautey requested the CGT to inaugurate a line between Bordeaux and Casablanca. In view of the potential profitability of this appeal, the company lost no time in complying. Thus, it secured its first Moroccan port of call outside the Strait of Gibraltar, initiated its first service from a French Atlantic port to North Africa, and laid the foundation for an excellent relationship with Lyautey when he became France's first resident general in Morocco in the next year.

By the time the August 1914 war ended tourism, French officials in the North African dependencies had come to appreciate its value as both a source of revenue and a public-relations tool. Although some pre-war French tourists arrived in the Maghrib unfavorably disposed toward colonialism and left with their convictions reinforced by what they witnessed in their travels, their influence on public opinion was more than offset by glowing assessments many empire proponents offered, using their personal experiences in the dependencies to enhance their credibility as colonial advocates. Even some skeptics who saw the results of their countrymen's labors in North Africa underwent a change of heart and became enthusiasts of *la mission civilisatrice*. Similarly, tourists from elsewhere in Europe and from North America generally formed positive impressions of French North Africa, although their judgments derived as much from the mild winter climate, the varied and unusual landscape, the abundance of sites preserved from Antiquity, and the novelty of Arab-Muslim society as from any serious analysis of the merits or demerits of colonial rule. Not surprisingly, some British travelers made a point of enumerating the shortcomings of French policies and practices in comparison with those of their own empire, but even these chauvinists usually enjoyed themselves and returned home acknowledging the virtues of French rule in the region.

Anxious to again reap the benefits of tourism, French officials rushed to promote North Africa as a tourist destination for both their fellow citizens and other Europeans and North Americans as soon as hostilities had ended. Prospects for an increase in the number of Anglo-Saxon tourists in the immediate postwar years appeared especially promising. The expectation of a surge into France of North American visitors eager to end their enforced isolation from Europe prompted government officials and *syndicats d'initiatives* (tourist bureaus) in North Africa to find ways of persuading some of them to expand their itineraries by crossing the Mediterranean. A second circumstance with the potential to attract an Anglo-Saxon clientele to the Maghrib was the nationalist revolution in Egypt in 1919. The attendant violence naturally dampened the enthusiasm of many British subjects who had been visiting and wintering there for decades. French North Africa offered these displaced vacationers a setting similar in climate and culture to Egypt, one closer to Great Britain and long a popular winter retreat for many of their countrymen.

Even as the Maghrib prepared to benefit from British tourists' reluctance to expose themselves to Egypt's gathering anticolonialism, the Algerian and Tunisian authorities knew that similar, if as yet less militant, forces were coalescing in their own territories. The resumption of a steady flow of French tourists seeing for themselves the "civilizing" effects of colonialism would, they calculated, win them valuable allies in the looming struggle with the nationalists. Not content to rely only on the traditional allure of climate or exoticism to attract these visitors, the Algerian governor general made a connection between tourism and the memorialization of World War I—one already in place in Europe with organized tours of the battlefields. Recalling the wartime contributions of Armée d'Afrique soldiers—French, Arab, and Berber alike—to the defense of France, he asserted that touring North Africa was a unique means for citizens of the *métropole* to express their gratitude and honor the sacrifices of the colonial troops.

The governor-general's allusion to the service of the Armée d'Afrique cultivated the image of the Maghrib as a region of which France was justifiably proud. Even more than before the war, Algeria, Tunisia, and Morocco merited the understanding and appreciation of the people of France. Not only were they the crown jewels among the overseas dependencies that held the economic key to the nation's postwar recovery, they were also the setting in which France might supplant the trauma and devastation wrought by the war with a vision of a global community in which the dedicated pursuit of *la mission civilisatrice* would ensure harmony, prosperity, and progress. French tourists continued to visit North Africa and other colonies and protectorates for the pleasurable recreational experiences they offered, but in the interwar period their travels also manifested, even if unconsciously, their patriotism and identification with the ideals implicit in the concept of *la plus grande France.*[18]

In order to encourage tourism in the colonies, a 1920 Semaine du Tourisme Colonial took place in Bordeaux, including a working conference at which metropolitan and colonial officials discussed such techniques for developing tourism as the formation of a confederation of Algerian, Moroccan, and Tunisian syndicats d'initiative. Two years later, Marseille hosted a wider-ranging Exposition Coloniale that, while not specifically aimed at increasing tourism, nevertheless helped to keep the concept of colonial tourism in the limelight. By underscoring the enduring nature of the colonial endeavor, the exhibitions affirmed the recent French rejection of demands for independence made by nationalist representatives in conjunction with the peace negotiations at Versailles. They also reinforced overseas administrators' hesitancy to implement reforms promised as rewards for the loyalty of Algeria and the protectorates during the war. Bordeaux and Marseille, the two French ports with the longest histories of commercial and maritime connections with the colonies and the ports of embarkation for almost every traveler to the overseas dependencies, were logical venues for exhibitions that made the prospect of traveling to them both more plausible and more appealing.

Among the earliest and most influential promoters of postwar tourism in the region was John Dal Piaz, chief executive of the Compagnie Générale Transatlantique. At the Bordeaux meetings, Dal Piaz told representatives of North African syndicats d'initiative that his company intended to increase the number of vessels bringing tourists to Algeria and Tunisia, develop more extensive links between French North Africa and Italy and Spain, and press for the extension of passenger railway lines on to the quays of North African ports to expedite movement from ship to shore.[19] As the most important shipping line between France and North Africa, the CGT had an obvious part to play in the renewal of tourism, but Dal Piaz envisioned a broader role for the company in North Africa. He planned to move CGT well beyond its traditional maritime services and to lead it into two new ventures: hotels and land transportation. The engagement of private corporations such as the CGT in the North African tourist trade rounded out a web of interwar participants—metropolitan and colonial business interests; government officials in Paris, Algiers, Tunis, and Rabat; settlers; and tourists—all keen to enhance the accessibility of the Maghrib, burnish its reputation as a hospitable tourist venue, and keep its public image positive, even in the face of mounting nationalist invective.

The CGT's entry into the hotel business initially focused on Morocco because that country, which had been drawn into the European sphere later than the rest of North Africa, lagged behind its neighbors in the availability of satisfactory western-style accommodations. Through a subsidiary, the Société des Grands Hôtels Nord-Africains, the CGT bought existing hotels in Casablanca, Marrakesh, and Rabat and refurbished them to bring them up to luxury standards. In Fès, the company purchased the urban mansion of the aristocratic Jamaï family, built in 1879 just inside the walls of the old city. After an extensive overhaul that preserved aspects of the original artisanal work, the company opened the building as the Palais Jamaï in 1933. This elegant hotel and the sumptuous La Mamounia in Marrakesh—one of whose architects, Henri Prost, served as Lyautey's chief adviser for urban planning—took pride of place in a chain that soon spread across North Africa. Although they did not bear the Hôtel Transatlantique name by which most of the others were known, the Palais Jamaï and La Mamounia quickly achieved fame as world-class establishments, a status they have continued to enjoy through the present day.[20]

Between 1920 and 1925, when the company merged its twenty-eight regional hotels with its land transportation network to form the Société des Voyages et Hôtels Nord-Africains (SVHNA), the CGT spent 29 million francs building, purchasing, and enhancing hotels; amassing a fleet of motor vehicles; and publicizing its services.[21] The SVHNA continued to acquire new hotels and by the end of the decade, the Transatlantique name graced forty-four properties in Algiers, Batna, Beni Abbès, Beni Ounif, Biskra, Boghar, Bône, Bougie, Bou Saada, Constantine, Djemila, El Golea, El Oued, Fort MacMahon, Ghardaia, Ksabi, Laghouat, Michelet, Ouargla, Taghit, Tenès, Timgad, Timimoun, Tlemcen, and Touggourt in Algeria; Les Chênes, El Hamma (Gabès), Tozeur, and Tunis in Tunisia; and Casablanca, Fès, Marrakesh, Meknès, Oudjda, Rabat, and Taza in Morocco.[22] To be sure, these locations included the main political and commercial centers of North Africa, but almost half were Algerian towns in the desert or on its fringe where adequate accommodations (by Western standards) had not previously existed or were in short supply.

In 1923, the *Traveller's Gazette*, the magazine of Thomas Cook & Son, which worked closely with the CGT in North Africa, noted that "until comparatively recently the Anglo-Saxon has been a little nervous of exploring the hinterland of North Africa owing to the inadequate hotel accommodation. This drawback no longer exists, however, for, thanks largely to the splendid organization of the CGT, some two dozen commodious hotels—always first class and often luxurious—have been established throughout Morocco, Algeria, and Tunisia. It is due to them that the very finest cuisine and the maximum of European comfort and hygienic efficiency are now available on the very borders of the desert."[23] By making comfortable, well-appointed lodgings available even in remote regions, the CGT encouraged more tourists, both French and foreign, to come to North Africa and to spend more time exploring Algeria and the protectorates. Because the records maintained by shipping lines, port officials, and hotels—aside from their registers—did not distinguish tourists from other travelers and because public and private organizations dedicated to facilitating tourism (such as the Touring Club de France and the Fédération des Syndicats d'Initiative) compiled only fragmentary statistics, the number of tourists visiting Algeria during the 1920s is extremely difficult to assess. The 1926–27 winter season, with its approximately 50,000 visitors—a figure roughly equating to a quarter of the 190,630 disembarkations throughout Algeria in the calendar year 1927—was, however, fairly typical of the decade.[24]

Rounding out the CGT's tourist infrastructure was a network of overland routes operated from 1920 to 1925 by a subsidiary, the Société des Auto-Circuits Nord-Africains, and thereafter by the SVHNA. At the end of the 1920s, 285 vehicles, some of them specially equipped for traversing desert terrain, provided service on twenty-two itineraries throughout North Africa. Local government officials welcomed this boon to tourism, the more so since the CGT sought no subsidy to support its new venture, even at its inception. Resident General Lyautey, who grasped what tourism could do for Morocco but also understood the difficulties the protectorate government faced in competing with an established tourist trade in Algeria and Tunisia, lauded the CGT's "fine example of private initiative and its decisive contribution to opening Morocco, a country of great natural and esthetic beauty, to tourism."[25] Although tourists always constituted the bulk of the passengers on auto-circuits, when the company inaugurated its first route, from Algiers to Marrakesh, it made a point of reminding businessmen who were "ready for new enterprises, [that] the tour offers a rare opportunity for examining a new country, full of promise, and rich in the powers of production."[26]

A multilingual guide escorted group tours whose passengers traveled in vehicles with ten armchair seats. The company also arranged private tours in smaller vehicles for which guides were also available. Overnight stays were at Transatlantique hotels that, in the words of the company's advertising, provided "excellent cuisine, fine wine cellars, great cleanliness, bathrooms, a warm welcome, and a restful atmosphere."[27] The extension of the Marrakesh to Algiers auto-circuit, which traversed almost 1,400 miles in twenty-seven days, to Tunis in 1921 and, soon afterward, southward to Sousse and Sfax, made it possible for visitors to travel the breadth of French North Africa, or to tour various segments of the main east-west route, seeing the sights in the major urban centers, studying

Roman and Carthaginian ruins, and exploring the coastal plains and mountain ranges. The subsequent addition of new routes into the south during the 1920s—to Laghouat from Algiers; to Biskra from Constantine; and to Tozeur from Tunis—stimulated Saharan tourism and accounted for many of the patrons at the more remote Transatlantique hotels.

As greater numbers of tourists journeyed to these oases in search of the mystique of the Sahara, the company offered a variety of excursions deeper into the desert either by camel caravan or in six-wheeled Renault automobiles specifically designed for desert use. Some of them revived successful specialties of an earlier era—expeditions from Laghouat that catered to hunters, for example—while others made available to typical visitors what had previously been rather extraordinary journeys. In contrast to Biskra, Touggourt retained a more traditional atmosphere, even after the extension of the railroad there from Biskra in 1922 facilitated tourists' access. In the 1920s, the town became the staging point for overnight camping trips into the desert and for week-long treks to Biskra, both by camel. Starting in 1925, a longer jaunt to Tozeur via El Oued and Nefta—ten days by camel, only four in a Renault—permitted tourists, for the first time, to travel between Tunis and Algiers across the desert rather than along the coast. Touggourt had connections to Algiers both by road and rail and the same was true of Tunis and Tozeur, which lay at the end of a spur of the railway on which phosphates were shipped from southwestern Tunisia to the port of Sfax.

In a parallel to the use of this industrial railroad by tourists, the lessening of tensions opened the military railroad along the southern Moroccan-Algerian borderlands to tourists traveling to the oasis of Figuig, most of which lay in Moroccan territory under the control of the French army, but some parts of which, notably Beni Ounif (in which there was a CGT hotel), were Algerian. By far the company's most ambitious and adventurous desert tour used the specially equipped Renaults to cross the mountainous dunes of the Grand Erg Occidental in the southernmost reaches of the Algerian Sahara. Undertaken first in 1926 and offered regularly thereafter, this three-week journey provided a unique experience for those who had time, money, and a spirit of adventure. Starting or ending at either Ghardaia or Figuig, it passed through the oases of El Golea, Fort MacMahon, Timimoun, Adrar, Ksabi, Beni Abbès, and Taghit, all of which had CGT hotels. In most of these locations, winter tourism supplemented the French military presence as the basis of the impoverished local economy.

Across the Sahara to French West Africa

As the CGT combined its transportation and accommodation resources to advance tourism in the Saharan regions of the Maghrib, other French companies experimented with the development of motor transport across the desert. An overland route linking North Africa with French West Africa would have surefire appeal to wealthy and adventurous tourists, but its real merit lay elsewhere: primarily in the economic value of expeditiously moving goods and military personnel from the Mediterranean to sub-Saharan areas, yet also in its ability to showcase French technology overcoming previously insurmountable obstacles in the service, and for the glory, of *la plus grande France*. Soon after World War I, the automobile manufacturer André Citroën developed a vehicle capable of operating in deep sand as well as able to maintain a relatively high speed on hard surfaces: a six-passenger car with caterpillar treads in place of the rear wheels. Using this equipment, an exploratory mission made the trek from Touggourt to Timbucktu in three weeks during the winter of 1922–23. In the following winter, after similar vehicles blazed a more westerly route from Colomb-Béchar to Bourem on the Niger River in only six days, the Compagnie Générale Citroën (CITRACIT) was established to carry passengers and freight on regularly scheduled trips across the desert.[28]

Effusive articles in Thomas Cook & Son's French and English language publications in January 1925 heralded the approaching inauguration of biweekly five vehicle convoys from both Colomb-Béchar and Gao, the southern terminus on the Niger. At Gao, passengers would have the option of proceeding overland to Niamey or transferring to river transport to Timbucktu. Promotional literature presented the trip as a rare opportunity for tourists captivated by the history, archaeology, and scenic beauty of the desert. For reasons of both time and cost, however, only the very wealthy could afford so extraordinary a journey. The roundtrip to Timbucktu would require three weeks—fourteen traveling days of between 200 and 500 kilometers each and a week in the Niger Valley. Its all-expenses-paid price was 40,000 francs, but continuing from Gao to Niamey added another five days, 450 kilometers, and 5,000 francs. Sportsmen who could spare a total of five weeks and wished to push still farther south to the best big-game hunting areas could arrange a ten-day safari from Niamey, which included everything except weapons and ammunition, for a supplement of 15,000 francs.[29] CITRACIT solved the problem of accommodations en route by building small hotels in the style of desert military architecture at Colomb-Béchar, Beni Abbès, Adrar, Gao, and Timbucktu. At these *bordjs* (literally, forts), tourists would find "every modern convenience: comfortable rooms, toilets and bath rooms, and clean and abundant food."[30] Large campgrounds with spacious tents were planned at seven other locations.

To publicize the inauguration of the venture, Citroën secured the participation of two prominent figures, King Albert of Belgium and French president Philippe Pétain, in the January 1925 maiden crossing. In the last weeks of 1924, however, both the military commander of the Colomb-Béchar region and the governor-general of French West Africa warned that the volatile nature of the tribes in these remote and loosely administered territories made it impossible to guarantee the safety of either the route or the company's property. A deadly raid by Moroccan tribesmen into Algerian territory just south of Colomb-Béchar in late December reinforced persistent rumors that plans were afoot to attack the first convoy. The Belgian monarch canceled his plans and CITRACIT postponed the initial departure. In a matter of weeks, Citroën abandoned the entire enterprise, repatriated his staff and equipment, and put the hotels up for sale, sustaining a loss of some 15 million francs in the process.[31] The automaker, sniffed the pseudonymous commentator "Un Saharien" in the colonialist *Bulletin du Comité de l'Afrique Française*, "had shown all the qualities of an old Saharan hand in this venture except for tenacity."[32]

The powerful economic and patriotic urge to link the French possessions north and south of the desert meant that Citroën's failure would not bring down the curtain on attempts to organize regular trans-Saharan motor services. Even before the collapse of CITRACIT, Louis Renault had supplied six-wheeled vehicles similar to those CGT already used on its desert circuits to Gaston Gradis, a Moroccan entrepreneur determined to blaze a commercially viable route to French West Africa. Gradis and Renault founded the Compagnie Générale Transsaharienne, naming as its president retired general Jean-Baptiste Eugène Estienne, who had acquired his expertise in tracked vehicles designing and building tanks during the war. Believing that Citroën had attempted to launch his company with insufficient preparation and planning, the Compagnie Générale Transsaharienne waited several years before starting a monthly Saharan crossing from Colomb-Béchar to Gao in the winter of 1927–28. Security along the route had improved in the interim, but the influx of travelers utterly unfamiliar with the Sahara and its perils placed additional demands on the French forces charged with maintaining order in the desert, prompting the lieutenant-governor of French West Africa to observe that "the increase in trans-Saharan tourism poses a problem for *Méharists* [camel patrols] who are barely able to protect themselves."[33] A later increase in service to a weekly basis brought more tourists to the desert, although the monetary and temporal costs of trans-Saharan leisure travel kept their numbers small. Nonetheless, their heightened presence at Timbucktu and Gao necessitated the administrative reclassification of those communities in 1931 so as to qualify them for additional funds earmarked for the promotion of commercial and touristic pursuits.[34]

Long-distance driving into and across the Sahara required a set of specialized skills that few tourists possessed, but westerners' fascination with the barren landscape and its inhabitants tempted some visitors—and some European residents of North Africa—to undertake more limited desert jaunts in their private vehicles. In 1930, the Algerian governor-general enacted a Code Saharien de la Route, which regulated automotive traffic in the Territoires du Sud. With an eye toward assisting and safeguarding these independent tourists, the Directeur of the Territoires du Sud, General Octave Meynier, and an officer in the Service des Affaires Indigènes, Captain A. F. Nabal, compiled a *Guide Pratique du Tourisme au Sahara* in 1931.[35] In addition to extensive material on the environment and history of the Sahara, the book provided thirty-two detailed desert itineraries, each of which included a description of the terrain, kilometrage between points, and information on facilities and services along the route. Another indication of the popularity of desert travel was the establishment, in 1927, of the Société des Amis du Sahara whose primary goal was to facilitate its members' trips into the Sahara and across it to the French Sudan by arranging special prices and other concessions for their travel and lodging. The society also supported infrastructural and other projects aimed at making desert travel safer, more convenient, and more comfortable.

From Celebrations to Collapse: North African Tourism in the 1930s

To mark the 1930 centennial of French rule in Algeria, the government allocated some 80 million francs for commemorative events[36] that not only celebrated the occasion, but also stimulated tourism. In January 1929, CGT president Dal Piaz—hardly a disinterested party in the matter of North African tourism—contributed an article to *La Revue des Voyages* entitled "The Second Conquest of Algeria," by which, he explained, he referred to "the peaceful conquest of Tourism."[37] In the century since the heroic military exploits of the conquest of Algeria, the mother country had

rendered its great colony not just accessible to visitors from all over the world, but marvelously welcoming and easy to travel through. Such is the case not only along the coast, but in the heart of its mountain ranges, on its high plateaus, and all the way to the desert fringes of its territory, constantly pushed southward first by the audacity of explorers, then by the curiosity of tourists.

Now, all of North Africa, but especially the Queen of the Colonies [Algeria], is a land that is easy to explore in every way, perhaps even more comfortably than the Métropole itself.[38]

Similar essays sang the praises of Algerian tourist destinations in both the English and French editions of Cook's travel literature and in the mainstream French press throughout 1929 and 1930. Other pieces, such as one that appeared in *La Revue des Voyages* a few months after the centennial, reiterated the important connections between colonial tourism and patriotism, national pride, and identification with the imperial mission that inspired so many postwar travelers to the Maghrib. "To visit Algeria from the sea to the desert," it proclaimed, "is today a . . . national duty for French tourists . . . that they more and more clearly recognize. . . . They have profoundly understood that the road from France to Africa passes through Algeria. . . . The voyage to Algeria is, for them, like a pilgrimage to pay appropriate homage to those who have accomplished this work [of colonization]. It is also an expression of great joy and deep pride in the energy and generosity of France."[39] In the same vein, an article in *La Revue TCF* (Touring Club de France) described the conquest of France in Algeria as "a transformation . . . of a beautiful country oppressed under the yoke of barbarism." The author described it as a duty "for all French people of some culture and a certain social rank, dilettante or *homme d'affaires*, to know the beauties and economic resources of this Second France."[40]

Also in 1930 the Catholic Church convened a Eucharistic Congress in the Tunis suburb of Carthage. No sooner had these events ended than did the observance of the semicentennial of the Tunisian protectorate begin, albeit on a smaller scale and with considerably less fanfare than the Algerian anniversary. Nevertheless, the two occasions increased the flow of visitors to Tunisia. Some were delegates to the congress, but many others were individual tourists attracted by the spate of publicity about the country, much of which emphasized Tunisia's history as a center of Christianity in the fourth and fifth centuries, the site of the Crusade of the king-saint Louis IX in the thirteenth century, and, in the twentieth century, the home of dedicated missionary orders furthering *la mission civilisatrice* in the dependencies. Like the postwar exhibitions, these celebrations put the empire on display and encouraged travel, not merely to join in the festivities or see the sights, but to better appreciate France's colonial venture. Not surprisingly, nationalists in Algeria and Tunisia regarded the commotion surrounding these anniversaries as humiliating. In later years, some credited the insensitivity and arrogance embedded in these spectacles with intensifying their distaste for colonial rule. In all likelihood, however, few metropolitan visitors grasped the depths of the resentment harbored by so many of the Algerian and Tunisian bystanders to the colonizers' exultant parades and haughty oratory.

By far the most extravagant "colonial advertisement" of the interwar period—an undertaking designed "to make the colonies known, in all their beauty, attractions, and exoticism"—was the Exposition Coloniale Internationale held at Vincennes from May to November 1931.[41] Eight million visitors, all but a million of them French, toured Parisian pavilions representing the various colonies, purchased artisanal work in replicas of indigenous markets, and sampled unfamiliar foods in restaurants serving African and Asian cuisines. The exposition organizers intended that visitors' simulated journey would whet their appetites for a trip to one of France's dependencies. To further encourage such a journey, exhibitors from the travel industry—steamship lines (including the CGT), hotels and tour organizers (including the SVHNA), and overseas syndicats d'initiative (including many from North Africa)—promoted their products and services. The Touring Club de France also had a major presence at the exposition, during which it formed a Groupe Colonial et Cynégétique within its Comité du Tourisme d'Outremer et Colonial. The new unit arranged group trips to the colonies and promoted tourist-oriented economic development.[42] Of all the overseas territories, Algeria, Tunisia, and Morocco almost certainly gained the most substantial benefits from the exposition. Their proximity to Europe (the voyage from French to North African ports now required between twenty-four and seventy-two hours, depending on the points of departure and arrival, while air travel reduced the time to as little as twelve hours); the relatively modest cost of traveling to them (as opposed, for instance, to Indo-China); and the well-developed and widely publicized infrastructure awaiting tourists (unlike the situation in French West or French Equatorial Africa) made the Maghrib a destination accessible to many of the exposition's visitors who left Vincennes with a thirst for seeing the colonies.

The interest in North African travel generated by the Algerian and Tunisian anniversaries centennial and the Exposition Coloniale Internationale offset any decline in the number of visitors attributable to the depression that was devastating economies around the globe. Through the mid-1930s, the annual tally of tourist entries in Algeria did not significantly deviate from the 50,000 figure attained during the 1920s, although more now came from countries other than France. In 1937, tourist disembarcations at the port of Algiers climbed to a new high of 68,000, or almost a quarter of all arriving passengers.[43]

Air service to and within North Africa expanded dramatically during the 1930s. Air France, created in 1933 by the merger of five companies, offered service between Marseilles and Algiers (via the Balearic Islands) or Tunis (via Corsica) in eleven-passenger hydroplanes. A third Air France route linked Toulouse and Casablanca, with stops at Barcelona, Alicante, Tangier, and Rabat. Well-timed connections made it possible to leave Paris early in the morning and arrive in North Africa by the late afternoon or early evening. In 1936, Air France carried 3,400 passengers to Algiers.[44] Many were businessmen, government officials, and other Europeans resident in Algeria, but some indeed were tourists. The airline had begun promoting opportunities to see "L'Afrique en quelques jours" by taking one of several "circuits de l'air" that began in Algiers and visited French West Africa, French Equatorial Africa, the Belgian Congo, Nigeria, or southern Sudan. In addition to these routes crossing Algerian territory, the presence of 200 "tourism planes" in the country by 1937 made domestic air transportation, if not yet routine, certainly commonplace.[45]

The allure of the desert for Westerners ensured that most tourists in the Maghrib at least traveled to its fringes and that some continued to spend extended periods of time in the Sahara. To add to the region's appeal, business and commercial interests did not hesitate to innovate. An aviation pioneer and entrepreneur in Touggourt, for example, used a mail plane to give tourists rides over the dunes of the Grand Erg Oriental and the El-Oued oasis, thus enabling them to "see" the desert in safety and comfort.

Perhaps more than any other community in the Algerian Sahara, Touggourt worked aggressively to capitalize on the tourist trade in the 1930s. To distinguish itself from neighboring oases, all of which enjoyed the same climatic assets that had first brought places such as Biskra to the attention of European visitors, Touggourt's syndicat d'initiative experimented with organizing a festival in spring 1936. Entertainment at the "Grandes Fêtes Sahariennes," which became an annual event for the next several years, included performances of traditional tribal dances, songs, and music; fantasias; military parades; camel races; and an air show sponsored by the local Aero-Club. In addition, there were organized excursions to Touggourt's souks and its palm grove; to several neighboring villages, including Tamelhat, where Sidi Ali Tidjani, founder of the Tidjaniyya sufi order, was buried; and into the desert to see the dunes. Exhibitions of regional agricultural products and artisanal goods were on display and local residents staged a mock wedding. Organizers arranged a gazelle hunt for which they provided both transportation and guides. In the evenings there were fireworks and the public gardens, syndicat d'initiative, and Hôtel Transatlantique were all illuminated. The festival ended with a grand ball in the hotel. Travel literature described the Touggourt festival as the "most curious attraction that the Algerian south had to offer to the tourist" and praised it for exposing European visitors to the "living ethnography . . . of a world unknown to them."[46]

In 1936, Thomas Cook & Sons organized a special twelve-day Algerian tour that included the Touggourt festival, then offered 50-percent reductions on Mediterranean crossings and on travel on the Algerian railway system for tourists en route to the 1937 festival. Such discounts were becoming common—one promotion in 1936 offered tickets at two-thirds the regular rate to honeymooners sailing to Algeria, with the railroads allowing them to travel inside the country for only one-third of the usual cost.[47] The mounting of festivals such as the one in Touggourt and the practice of offering travel discounts to encourage attendance at them in the latter half of the 1930s may have been driven by a concern that tourists who would once have come to Algeria were now choosing to go to Morocco instead. The southern reaches of the protectorate, which offered experiences similar to those of Algeria and Tunisia, had become less dangerous destinations than in the past following the repression of the last vestiges of tribal resistance to the French in 1934. In any case, the outbreak of war in Europe reduced the flow of visitors to a trickle in the winter of 1939–1940, bringing to a melancholy end two vibrant decades during which the number of tourists visiting North Africa had steadily increased and the resources and facilities available to them had expanded and diversified.

In no part of the region had this been more evident than in the Saharan oases of Algeria. For the first time in the 1920s and 1930s, the desert, which had long fascinated Europeans, became quickly, easily, and safely accessible to tourists unwilling to forego the comforts and conveniences available to them in the urban centers of the coastal plain. Without the CGT's pioneering work in building hotels in the Saharan oases and maintaining them at high European standards, few tourists would have risked going beyond Bou Saada and other towns on the northern fringes of the desert. Without the CGT's auto-circuits, those same towns would have been "the end of the line" for regular motorized transportation, preventing tourists with limited amounts of time at their disposal from exploring more remote parts of the desert. The chain of CGT hotels in the Sahara and the auto-circuits that linked them to each other and to the remainder of Algeria as well as Tunisia and Morocco superbly complemented each other both from the company's point of view as business ventures and from tourists' perspectives as facilitators for seeing the sights. The remarkable efficiency of the CGT in enabling tourists to immerse themselves in the extraordinary landscapes and exotic atmosphere that lured most of them to North Africa—exemplified by its coordinated scheduling from the heart of the Sahara to the center of Paris and by its interlocking advertising of sea routes, land transportation, and accommodations—greatly contributed to its success in the tourist industry. Even without the intervention of the CGT, a few oases—Biskra, for example, which had gotten a head start in attracting visitors because of the early arrival of the railroad—would have evolved into important tourist destinations and experienced the economic and cultural consequences that went with that designation, but such an outcome would not have occurred in most desert communities without the impetus provided by the CGT. Thorough scholarly assessments of the economic and cultural impact of tourism in most of the Saharan communities into which it was introduced by the CGT are still lacking. Future research designed to elicit a better understanding of what difference tourism made in the lives of the oasis dwellers and in the worldview of their visitors would significantly enrich our comprehension of Saharan tourism.

The importance of generating a positive image of French colonialism in North Africa amid growing expressions of nationalist sentiments during the interwar years prompted officials on both sides of the Mediterranean to embrace tourism in the dependencies as a valuable tool to heighten public support of the colonial enterprise by cultivating pride, not only in what tourists witnessed as the political and economic accomplishments of their countrymen living and governing overseas, but also in what they observed of the natural beauty and ethnographic richness of *la plus grande France.* Not surprisingly, the tourist industry enthusiastically endorsed this concept and strove to encourage ordinary French men and women to explore the dependencies. Tourism in *la plus grande France* thus became an expression of patriotism and a virtual obligation of the good citizen who could afford to travel. The Maghrib, as the closest colonial region and the one with the oldest, strongest, and most prolific connections with metropolitan France, was the most obvious location for the manifestation of tourism as patriotism. The CGT and other companies that provided for North African tourists' needs benefited accordingly and its president spoke out frequently and forcefully on the theme. For those lacking the means or time to indulge in a tour of the colonies, exhibitions and fairs in the cities of France provided opportunities for a vicarious experience of colonial tourism. Although scholars have recently begun to examine the connections between French national identity and colonial tourism, much work yet remains to be done to understand fully the importance of these linkages.

A few years after the end of World War II, small numbers of intrepid travelers began to return to prewar tourist haunts,[48] but the growing militancy of nationalist movements in all three North African countries in the 1950s, capped by the outbreak of a brutal rebellion in Algeria in 1954, robbed the region of the air of insouciance that had so appealed to visitors. Casual travel to and within North Africa all but ceased until independence (in Morocco and Tunisia in 1956, in Algeria only in 1962). The new governments quickly recognized the economic value of tourism and two of them set to work almost immediately to resuscitate it. Tourism rapidly took its place as a crucial component in the development plans of Tunisia and Morocco. Ironically, this did not happen in Algeria, the country that had led the way in the development of tourism during the colonial era. Algeria's abundant petroleum reserves made it unnecessary for it to cultivate tourism to any appreciable degree, while memories of the violence of the independence struggle and the anti-Western rhetoric of the country's subsequent leaders compromised it as a tourist destination in the eyes of many potential visitors. Even in the early twenty-first century, when Tunisia and Morocco enjoy reputations in Europe as prime vacation spots, the political climate in Algeria and its petroleum-based economy have given it little opportunity or incentive to imitate its neighbors' evolution into world-class tourist destinations.

Chapter 3

"Food Palaces Built of Sausages [and] Great Ships of Lamb Chops"

The Gastronomical Fair of Dijon as Consuming Spectacle

PHILIP WHALEN

> *The Gastronomical Fair of Dijon is but a savory way to make direct and complete contact with one of France's most generous regions.*
>
> —*Gaston Roupnel, "La Somptuosité de Bourgogne,"* L'Alsace Francaise *(1925)*

The celebrated food critic M. F. K. Fisher came into her culinary awakening in Dijon circa 1930: "We lived for almost three years in Dijon, which the Burgundians called without any quibble and with only half-hearted contradictions 'the gastronomical capital of the world.'"[1] It was there she witnessed and recorded the transformation of a sleepy provincial capital into a referent of modern French gastronomy. Fisher declared, "the streets were narrow and crooked, in the district around the *Faculté,* and at that time of the year rich with a fruity odor of cellars, dog dirt, and the countless public urinals needed in a wine town."[2] *Serve It Forth* and *The Gastronomical Me* describe her experiences as a newlywed learning to negotiate the imperatives of romance and gastronomy simultaneously. Indeed, to discuss cuisine in Burgundy is to invoke the romance of that region's cultural identity (Figure 3.1).

For all her colorful anecdotes, insights into French provincial manners, and resourceful culinary itineraries, Fisher's texts (re)produced a preferred reading of Burgundian gastronomical identity.[3] Her descriptions of making and consuming "authentic" meals were set within the tour of the city's obligatory gastronomical icons such as famous restaurants (snails *chez* Crespin), the pedagogical ministrations of a sympa-

Figure 3.1. Cover from the 1934 Gastronomical Fair's official catalogue,
Archives Municipales de Dijon, series 2F "Foire (1934)."

thetic waiter at Aux Trois Faisans, "loud-mouthed stall-keepers" in the
covered market (*les Halles*), aged pâté de foie gras at the Buffet de la
Gare, and the discoveries of a grouchy but well-stocked wine merchant.
These iconic incidents underscored a familiar tale about the centrality
of gastronomy to Burgundy—as though the entire region were united in
the production, promotion, and consumption of the one and the same
(ideologically encoded) menu.[4] Indeed, this refined gastronomical tradition was internationally recognized, for example, when Gertrude
Clark Powell first translated the Burgundian Brillat-Savarin's epicurean
The Physiology of Taste into English.

In contrast to this well-publicized "tradition," the commercialized food fairs and wine festivals of interwar Dijon reveal that gastronomical regionalism generated multiple cultural openings for different popular ideological investments through the middlebrow aesthetics of gastronomic spectacle(s) in an age of emerging mass culture. Following Guy Debord's theorization of "spectacle" as "the acme of ideology,"[5] art historian T. J. Clark has defined "spectacular society" as "an attempt—a partial and unfinished one—to bring into theoretical order a diverse set of symptoms which are normally treated . . . as anecdotal trappings affixed somewhat lightly to the old economic order: 'consumerism,' for instance, or 'the society of leisure'; the rise of mass media, the expansion of advertising, the hypertrophy of official diversions."[6] This understanding of how cultural choices become organized and promoted has particular salience where M. F. K. Fischer's Rabelaisian vision figured ideologically in Gaston Dery's authoritative 1930 *Dictionary of Jovial Gastronomy*: "Burgundian cuisine is worthy of the wines of that admirable province. All things savory are abundant there. . . . Dijon offers gaiety, playful irony, snails, mustard, cassis, spice bread, saddle of rabbit à la Piron, parsleyd ham, lark and woodcock paté, jellied milk piglet, stuffed carp, and Chablis shrimps, what cheeses. . . . [and] the best wines in the world!"[7]

In an era of increasing mass marketing and democratic political choice, the preferred ideological register invoked by regional cuisines acquired a popular tone and middlebrow aesthetic. This tone countered the elitist claims made by cosmopolitans such as Raymond Badouin, editor of the all-important *Revue du Vin de France*, who "want[ed] to be the preferred guide for those who wish to find good succulent French cuisine on their plates [and] those who seek distinguished wines."[8] Informed by the labors of cultural intermediaries such as Gaston Gérard and Gaston Roupnel among others, the Gastronomical Fair of Dijon became, instead, a paradigmatic model for marketing a republican culture of economic and cultural regionalism through middlebrow spectacles calculated to "captivate all spirits, all intelligences, and interest all competences."[9]

Making and Marketing Burgundy

> We won't be content to see splendors through store windows. We will touch them in ways to better appreciate them: by eating and drinking.
>
> —*Gaston Gérard*, Dijon, Ma Bonne Ville (1959)

In 1927, Dijon's visionary and indefatigable mayor, Gaston Gérard, who served the city from 1921 to 1935 and whom *L'Opinion* dubbed "the ambassador of French wine and advertising," argued that new times required decisive action and new methods.[10] He bemoaned the sight of French cities plastered with posters designed to induce the French to travel abroad while local opportunities remained underdeveloped. As the first High Commissioner of Tourism (1930), first Under-Secretary of Tourism (1931), Under-Secretary of Public Works and Tourism (1932), and Governor of the Rotary Club (1933), Gérard was instrumental in implementing some of interwar France's most innovative marketing strategies and lasting tourism developments. He believed the solution to contemporary economic stagnation lay in the use of aggressive "American" marketing strategies calculated to stimulate sales by enhancing product identification. The gastronomical fair he launched in Dijon in 1921 would promote regional production and culture whose diversity would support the overarching national economy and identity. "We possess a firm called Burgundy," he declared, "and our interest is to valorize it and made it bear fruit (*fructifiée*)."[11] This entailed, as Xavier Aubert, General Secretary of the Committee for the Fair prosaically elaborated, the ability to "absorb yesterday's enemies and stay today's competition" in all matters relating to "liquid and solid alimentary products" through Gérard's coordinated combination of private and public interests.[12]

In 1934, a local journalist observed that "Ardent defenders of Burgundy" were "convinced regionalists" who "revived a spirit whose work ethic, intelligence, and common sense has, after numerous setbacks with the central government, become one of the foundations of our nation."[13] When it came to marketing the region, as Albert David stated, "Success Comes to Those that Dare."[14] Gérard wanted his province to stand on its own economic feet under limited direction from the national state.[15] He plotted a Burgundian cultural agenda along the axes of decentralized economic regionalism and republican political principles that served as paradigmatic model of sustainable economic growth for early twentieth-century France.[16] Its coordinates were regional leadership and economic productivity as a means to sustain consensual national unity through regional diversity—"Unity Without Uniformity," said the conciliatory regionalist Jean Charles-Brun.[17] The success of this project depended on its implementation as an uplifting cultural phenomena liable to economic exploitation through modern marketing strategies that could exploit the catalogue of preexisting tropes, symbolize residual values and beliefs, reflect contemporary cultural concerns, and mobilize current political interests.

Drawing civic leaders and regionalists in his wake, Gérard sought events that "radiated publicity." He rallied the Burgundian cognoscenti to stage cultural revivals, organize civic events, found erudite associa-

Figure 3.2. Dijon's cultural intermediaries attending a conference in the State Room, inside Dijon's City Hall, 1932. Photo courtesy of Jean-François Bazin.

tions, and establish regional journals designed to promote "an ideal representation of local cultural life."[18] They collaborated to promote regional economic and cultural interests by marketing an essentialized, uplifting, and recognizable cultural identity packaged in the form of regional products such as wine, mustard, sweet bread, and cheeses. This marketing strategy was most successful where it sustained immediate regional cultural interests (Figure 3.2).[19]

The Burgundian interwar cultural agenda exploited familiar images and idioms to articulate a rustic version of French modernity. Carefully orchestrated spectacles (re)classified notions of rustic traditions into provisionally stable social, cultural, and political phenomena through representations of an idealized Burgundian community. The various gastronomical registers in which Burgundian culture was scripted onto regional products and into civic events created the possibility that Burgundians could inhabit both real and imagined social and cultural spaces through different patterns of consumption. They provided overlapping templates through which contemporary Burgundians acquired self-understanding, fashioned self-identities, scripted their own heritage, and defined their role within the national culture.[20] By participating in elaborately staged and choreographed fairs and festivals, consumer/participants positioned themselves (one to another) in a community in which subjective political preferences were embraced, negotiated, and/or displaced through market mechanisms. A "magnificent" revival of fairs and festivals—"clearly reflecting post-war economic activities," noted Roger Thiblot—allowed Burgundy to (re)claim its desire prestige.[21] "Burgundy banished by the pens of revolutionaries," writes Jean-François Bazin, "was reborn and resplendent . . . she inspired and federated new ardors. . . . It was recognized that the name alone was worth gold."[22] Even Colette, who wrote sentimental novels while living in Paris and the Côte d'Azur, reclaimed her Burgundian accent and identity; "I belong to a pays that I left," she lamented.[23] Their "collective dreamworld" (ur-phenomena), "imagined community," or project of collective imagination, collaged regional "traditions" and industrialized modernity into a lasting social, cultural, and political phenomena. This process made it possible to collectively debate, define, (re)produce, or contest the dominant or preferred Burgundian cultural identity.

An Enriching Agenda: Dijon as Gastronomical Epicenter

The destiny of nations depends on the manner in which they nourish themselves.

—*Brillat-Savarin,* Aphorismes du Professeur *(1940)*

Although the city of Lyon claimed to be gastronomical center of France under Edoaurd Herriot's mayorality, this status was quickly rivaled and surpassed by Dijon under Gaston Gérard's administration.[24] His most notable accomplishment was the founding of the successful gastronomical fair in Dijon in 1921.[25] As president of the Federation of Burgundian Regional Syndicats d'Initiatives, Gérard was ideally positioned to coordinate competing and diverse local interests into cogent regional strategies. "Fortunately," he reminded his constituents, "we retain and will make the most of our most important pretext for drawing tourists to our region: our gastronomy."[26] He noted how tourists at British International Exposition of 1900 were not merely "comical characters . . . [who] often paid more than things were worth." He learned that it was thanks to them that "budgets could be balanced."[27]

Following Paul Léon's precepts concerning passive and active tourism (*vente sur place*), Gérard wanted ordinary fairgoers to spend and consume Burgundian "place" as much as they looked.[28] His overall strategy was to promote regional economic and cultural interests simultaneously by marketing recognizable regional products. These included: Burgundian wines (more than 1,200 vintages in 1925); mustards (Amora, Mack,

Dumont, Truchot, Guyenot, Fagart, Fauroy, and Grey-Poupon); choco-
lates (Lavin and Duthu); sweet breads (Philbée, Mulot, Petitjean,
Michelin, Guilleminot, and Rouard-Pernot); candies, pralines, and *patis-
series* (Renardiet, Georges Aymé, and Bonnet); liqueurs (Legay-
Lagoutte); biscuits (Bossuet); cheeses (Citeaux and Gachot); dried
meats (Julien Rambaud and Sellenet); snails (Carnet and Thabard);
jams and condiments (Citeaux, Goldité, du Chalet, Duband, and Pari-
zot); honey (Bertrand and de Lantenay); and even bicycles (Peugeot).[29]
Gérard intended for Dijon to host "a complete exposition of all alimentary and more especially Dijonnais and Burgundian specialties that constitute the most interesting manifestation of the culinary arts and
gastronomy . . . such that it would be embarrassingly difficult to say that
anything was left out."[30]

Gérard described his initial meeting with Dijon's "commercial and
industrial notables" to discuss the possibility of a future gastronomical
fair in his autobiographical *Dijon, Ma Bonne Ville* (*Dijon, My Fair City*).
The group was not initially receptive to his ideas. Only seventeen of
thirty invitees arrived bearing "severe expressions," which he read as
indicating: "talk all you want but you might as well take a hike than
count on me."[31] Undaunted, Gérard outlined an ingenious plan that
would showcase both regional products and industries while minimizing
capital outlays. Seeking to create an environment in which tourists
would do more than ogle showcases and store windows, the mayor suggested that visitors consume—eat and drink—those very same wares
seated in a stimulating and comfortable environment. Following the presentation, Lucien Richard, the modernizing president of the Pernots bis-
cuit factory and leader of Dijon's Chamber of Commerce, finally agreed
the young mayor's idea might be good after all. Although only five others concurred, Richard's stature was preponderant and his opinion
determining.

Building on the memory of Dijon's fair of 1858 as well as other annual
industrial events such as the Paris fair; extensively borrowing marketing
strategies from the Universal and International Expositions held in Paris
in 1855, 1867, 1878, 1889, 1900, and 1925 that so effectively promoted
French notions of prestige, pleasure, progress, and profit;[32] and emulat-
ing Eduoard Herriot's highly successful Silk Fair in Lyons, competing
with Beaune's annual Wine Exposition since 1863, Gérard's Gastronomical Fair of Dijon successfully linked cultural novelty and sociopolitical
inclusion. He diplomatically included as many private agricultural,
industrial, commercial, and tourist interests as would participate. These
highlighted Dijon's alimentary industries, colorful history, and accessible communications to create a fair that would position Dijon on the

map of French gastronomy; the Foire Gastronomique would highlight and sell samples of Burgundy's culinary arts.[33]

The coordination of this annual spectacle illustrates Gaston Gérard's flair for marketing. Different fair days highlighted specific industries or fields of interest ranging from local agriculture to novel kitchen gadgets and from amateur sports to the fine arts. Each day's theme was marked by a parade, musical performances, an evening ball, and citywide banquets produced by Dijon's many restaurants. Rather than allowing the fair to compete with existing restaurants or having them compete among themselves, the mayor drafted their participation and resources by having them all prepare in a spirit of professional competition and serve the same meals—lunch and dinner—twice each fair day in their own establishments, which also spared the municipal budget an imponderable cost. Indeed, the gastronomical fair was so successful that the first fairs of France conference was held in Dijon in 1925 to examine questions concerning fair organization, exhibitor interests, local infrastructure, and "multiple questions relating to fairs."[34]

Evidence of Dijon's pioneering use of up-to-date media practices to market Burgundian identity, culture, and commerce may be gleaned from the existence of two promotional films commissioned by Gaston Gérard and directed by Henri Cruchetel for the Agricultural Days at the Gastronomical Fair of Dijon in 1926.[35] "The Production of Wheat" (La Production de Blé) and "The Vine and Wine in Burgundy" (La Vigne et le Vin en Bourgogne) were advertised as "representing the best modern advertising methods."[36] An estimated eight hundred persons watched what one critic judged should be shown to "the most enraged prohibitionists." Designed in three parts, "The Vine and Wine in Burgundy" depicted modern techniques and technology, the *vigneron*'s "noble" work, and "an amusing" description of how Burgundians drink wine in the course of a "real" meal. The film ended with "four reputable gourmets" touring landmarks associated with the history of wine—all in Burgundy.[37] Half a decade later, Gertrude Clark Powell noted the spectacular results of Gérard's vision(s): "on our arrival we found the annual Gastronomical Fair in full swing. . . . Every year in November thousands of people are drawn into town to attend the Fair. . . . A central avenue, leading off the Place Wilson, about a mile in length, is covered over and lined with booths exhibiting everything from pottery to peanuts. There are beautiful exhibits of food palaces built of sausages; great ships of lamb chops. Burgundy is the gourmet's paradise. Preparing food here is an art."[38]

Never at a loss to exploit an opportunity for promotion, Gérard claimed "the Fair resembles no other. For five years, imitators have tried to steal its title but the Gastronomical Fair of Dijon remains incomparable . . . never-ending crowds, informed by visitors from previous years, hasten toward the odors of prepared meals and fragrant wines."[39] By the end of the second fair in 1922, local opinion underscored the obvious success of this "local and regional manifestation." Come the success of the eighth fair in 1928, one well-fed critic remarked that Gérard "had turned himself into the apostle of the restoration of French cuisine."[40] Dijon was "literally overwhelmed by tourists: hotels and restaurants were taken by assault and early on circulation slowed" to the benefit of all merchants, "Dijonnais, Burgundian, and some from without."[41] Although examining the profits of individual merchants is beyond the scope of this study (and remains to be charted), increased attendance and entry fees regularly generated a net gain until the economic downswing starting in 1935 and lasting until the suspension of the fair between 1940 and 1949.[42]

The first Gastronomical Fair of Dijon was an immediate success. If we can believe Gérard's neat formula, the 1921 fair drew 80,000 visitors to a town of 80,000 and netted more than 80,000 francs.[43] More precisely, Christelle Guilard has tabulated, for example, that the 1926 fair grossed 828,977 francs and netted 92,722 francs after expenditures, salaries, free tickets, and taxes; a considerable success that confirms Gérard's recollection.[44] While the fair would not always generate the profit hoped for, especially during the late 1930s, attendance doubled annually, peaking in 1925 when 600,000 visitors came to see the wares of approximately 900 merchants.[45] The number of exhibits grew from 220 and—with great fluctuation—leveled off at 500, while attendance shrank to an average of 175,000.[46] While Dijon's gastronomical fair also drew exhibitors from around the world, it never ceased promoting Dijon's gastronomical importance. Nor did the influx of national, Parisian, and international vendors mean that the fair was losing its regional character.[47] The preponderance of scheduled events and daily menus continued to reflect the Burgundian agenda. Indeed, Christelle Guilard's tabulations show that local and regional participation actually increased into the 1930s.[48] This increased participation ensured that local and regional wares and products were centrally positioned within a national, colonial, and international economic and cultural context.

At the height of its success the fair started building a new and unique "monumental entrance" each year to impress visitors young and old with the most exotic sight in Dijon. Speaking for the collected mayors of the Côte-d'Or who, despite competing agendas and economic itineraries, became Dijon's "attentive and cultivated vassals," the mayor of Beaune—Dijon's nearby and most important competitor—M. Labet thanked Gérard for creating a fair that "gives such a powerful boost to the economic life and revival of our province and region."[49] Similarly, the president of the Côte-d'Or Commercial and Industrial Union, Albert David, applauded the "splendid success" of Gérard's "magnificent manifestation" by contrasting the new Dijon with its former sleepy self: "for those who remember Dijon of before, when the days disappeared into a perfect calm from one end of the year to the other, the contrast is striking and, according to everyone, presents the advantages of the modern times."[50] Dijon's city hall circulated the following communiqué explaining the aims of the event as part of the preparations for the 1921 gastronomical fair: "the Fair will consist in the wholesale and retail of not only consumables of all kinds but also of everything connected with food; production, manufacture, packaging, transportation, preservation, cuisine, the art of hotel management, gastronomical tourism, and the different details that, more or less, relate to food and gastronomy."[51]

Within several years of its inauguration, even the mayor of Beaune—who had held a rival wine festival—conceded the general benefits his nearest competitor had conferred onto the entire region: "your fair gives a fecund and powerful boost to the economic life of our region and province. The mayors of the Côte-d'Or give you their recognition and appreciation for this support."[52] Although they continued to develop their own gastronomical events, they participated as the fair promoted their collective interests.[53] When the mayors of 630 villages assembled for the 1931 gastronomical fair's Banquet of Mayors, Gérard's benefice was delivered in the form of a speech on the traditional interdependences between Dijon and the region's villages. Since the hinterland needed outlets for its products, it was no great sacrifice for the city, he magnanimously asserted without apparent irony, to tax itself "a few centimes" to electrify and develop the countryside so that it could ride the new tramways to attend the fair.[54]

An Enticing Recipe: "Dijon My Fair City"

> He who has never attended the Gastronomical Fair of Dijon doesn't know what a real feast is, a veritable celebration, an explosion of popular joy.
>
> —Marcel-E. Grancher, Denise Mène Les Boeufs (1953)

When Stefan Zweig traveled to Dijon in November 1931 to visit the tombs of the Dukes of Burgundy, he hadn't expected to find the city decorated with "thousands of little flags dancing like miniature flames." Although familiar with the sleepy provincial capital through his friendship with Romain Rolland, nothing had prepared the morose German author for such excitement. Zweig determined that the Gastronomical Fair of Dijon was in full swing from banners spanning the streets.[55]

Indeed, residents of Dijon annually anticipated the days when "all the streets were superbly festooned and illuminated" and the merchants "competed by tastefully and humorously decorating their stores and artfully arranging their shelves to draw the admiration of visitors."[56] "Once a year, in November for the Foire Gastronomique," recalled M. F. K. Fisher, "[Dijon] recaptures for those days all its old glitter. . . . full of gourmets from every corner of France, and famous chefs twirled saucepans in its kitchens, and wine buyers drank Chambertins and Cortons and Romanée-Contis by the cave-ful."[57] Even local newspapers noted the extent, variety, and color of street decorations.[58]

Among the cultural intermediaries who shaped Burgundian tourism and placed Dijon's fair on France's gastronomical map, Henri Charrier, president of the Academy of Arts and Sciences and Letters of Dijon and general secretary of the Regional Committee on Tourism, singled out the "historical authority, poetic seduction, and philosophic intuitions" with which Gaston Roupnel persuaded contemporaries that "each corner of Burgundy . . . sings for the soul of the human past."[59] The editor of the regionalist La Bourgogne d'Or Gustave Gasser also judged Roupnel's eight-page "Burgundy and Burgundian Art" catalogue for the Jean Charpentier Gallery exhibit in Paris on March 8, 1936[60] as providing a succinct and balanced overview of the region's history, arts, and people.[61] Roupnel celebrated Burgundy's culinary traditions in articles such as "The Sumptuousness of Burgundy," "The Cook's Truce," "Burgundy and Gastronomy," "Praise for Family Cuisine," "Burgundy, Types and Customs," and in the preface to Max Cappe's Les Chants du Terroir, Poèmes Bourguignons as well "The Jérémie Affair" in the gastronomical fair's twelfth official guide.[62] These writings drew attention to the historical links between the newly incarnated Foire Gastronomique and traditional Burgundian agriculture. In his preface to Cappe's Les Chants du Terroir, for example, he explained that "to good wine, in fact, corresponds good food. One cannot go without the other. The entire spirit (génie) of Burgundian gastronomy comes from this delicious fatality that produces intoxicating (énivrante) and savory consequences. In the pays of Chambertin or Corton, a mouthful is a mouthful."[63] His "The Sumptuousness of Burgundy" further reminded readers that "the [1925] Gastronomical Fair of Dijon provided the most direct and complete encounter with France's most generous and tasty cities."[64]

Rather than simply the occasion for a "sumptuous snack," Roupnel promised readers that the gastronomical fair would provide a holistic experience: "it invites one to experience . . . and to glorify the vast production of a privileged land. It promises visits to museums and conferences, walks along the streets, artistic pilgrimages, the pleasures of the table, and the stirrings of memory."[65] He also promised fairgoers the opportunity of discovering the entirety and uniqueness of the "Burgundian spirit" (*génie bourguignon*) through winetasting.[66] Indeed, Stefan Zweig reported:

visitors munched fresh waffles in the streets. In front of stores were stacks of thousands of delectable snails that, with wine, disappeared from the same vineyards they previously inhabited. The chefs—in white uniforms, red faces, and ceremonious airs—are the object of unlimited admiration and the incontestable masters of ceremony. As happens at wine fairs, shoppers from different countries, their eyes slightly anxious . . . amble along the streets tantalized by the prospect of another wine tasting. Not a little boisterous, these copper-faced and voluminous gentlemen are happy, content, and joyous. They compose a petulant tableau of Sileniuses in smocks.[67]

Pierre Léon-Gaithier described the fair as "fifteen days of celebration and feasting."[68] Lasting six to fifteen days depending on the economic climate, the fair was scheduled from mid to late November. This date dovetailed with the Saint Martin Farmers Fair held around mid-November—typically on the tenth—since its inception in 1666.[69] Remotely associated with early modern Burgundian markets through renaissance trappings, the Saint Martin Fair had, by the early 1920s, mostly devolved into a flea market replete with tinkers, cobblers, and various vendors selling foodstuffs, bric-a-brac, candies, and "recent" antiques.[70] Exploiting the same agricultural calendar, the gastronomical fair was scheduled for after regional harvest and local wine festivals and before the annual wine auction in Beaune and Roman Catholic Advent: "the peasants come in from the country and hold market at the fair, selling livestock, vegetables, flowers. The country folk at the fair go about all stiff and uncomfortable in their Sunday best" (Figure 3.3).[71]

Within less than one week before the grand opening of the first Gastronomical Fair of Dijon in 1921, a local booster anticipated "never before" would Dijon be so attractive and animated as during a "complete exposition of all the alimentary products and more particularly Dijonnais and Burgundian specialties." Within luxuriously decorated salons for the "pleasure and profit" of merchants and visitors, the event promised to constitute "a most interesting manifestation of culinary and gastronomical arts."[72] There was also a strong emphasis on spectacle through "attractions of all kinds . . . for everyone." Most memorable perhaps was the annual construction of a gaudily opulent monumental gate that served, in the parlance of World's Fairs, as the event's "spike." The monumental gate of 1931, designed by Georges Parisot, was described as "following simple, elegant, and imposing principles of modern architecture" to harmoniously produce an "impression of balance and lightness." Standing twenty-five meters high with sides draped in "luminous cascades" of water, the entrance's gold and blue ornamen-

Figure 3.3. Postcard of the Monumental Gate at the Gastronomical Fair of Dijon, early 1920s.

Figure 3.4. Entrance to the 1931 Gastronomical Faire in Dijon. Archives Municipales de Dijon, series 2F, "Foire (1931)."

tation on white background and red doorway were set into relief each evening with "impressive clarity from the velvety-dark and somber skies" by hidden lights.[73] Through this and lesser gates, visitors entered to wind their way around hundreds of merchants' stalls and on to the fair's principal attractions: the "food courts," "industrial chambers," and "artisan salons" (Figure 3.4).

Following Gérard's inclusive policy of offering "something for everyone," Dijon's mid-November festival offered all the attractions usually found at general *fête foraines* (fairs). The *Progrès de la Côte-d'Or* reported that crowds along Dijon's Place Wilson observed various mechanized rides in which "delirious couples were thrown one onto the other on a rotating platform" or the "amateurs of violent emotions" aloft a centrifugal platform. Further on, the "clamor of spirited youths and the sharp cries of young girls" could be heard coming from the bumper cars. Children and grandparents "gave themselves to heartfelt joy" as they "went up and down" on the carousel's wooden horses. Past the lure of feats of strength and accuracy, crowds shuffled between jugglers and clowns through the covered alleys to see the wax museum's skeleton of "a man who died of hunger" and Arnisio, the daughter of Ramses III. Elsewhere, "funny mirrors" deformed one's reflection into grotesque shapes, making their victims "laugh uncontrollably." Others clamored to have their caricatures sketched and silhouettes cut. A great success was the water-chute sustained by "gigantic scaffolding" in front of City Hall. "Crazily exuberant" youths, it was reported, rode down its sides in wooden wagons at "vertiginous speeds." Occasionally the atmosphere might be overwhelmed by the cries and laughter of swarming schoolchildren on a loosely monitored class outing.[74] Closer to the Place Darcy, fairgoers were treated to more exotic sights. Amidst a discussion of the foot races between the waiters of Dijon's cafés, Gertrude Clark Powell recalled that "every square in town is filled with sideshows, fakirs, itinerant merchants, 'instantaneous' photo stands, hurdy-gurdy men, merry-go-rounds, [and] Arabian villages guarded by mangy camels."[75] One tent contained a "Freak Show" where one could see an octopus with a young woman's head or another woman with three feet. Another act offered acrobatic fleas towing miniature chariots in hops and leaps. After visiting the vast exhibition halls, the crowd, to "augment its truculent trepidation," jostled past "charming young girls selling medallions to raise money for *familles nombreuses* (large families)" to conclude "an incomparable day of popular animation" with an evening of "fantastic festivities" at Wilson Square.[76] Nocturnal tourists coursing beneath a "polychrome ceiling" of multicolored lights were welcomed by directional banners guiding them past the freshly decorated restaurants, stores, stalls, games, and bars. Blasted by amplified directives, jostling crowds squeezed through the Monumental Gate and wiggled into the Court of Honor.[77] These were merely preludes and sideshows, however, to the fair's gastronomical centerpiece: "after the eyes have feasted on the many spectacles to the glory of Burgundian gastronomy in the Hall of Honor, once through the entrance doors, they are suddenly arrested by a series of succulent things."[78]

An impressed reporter described how the 250-square-meter Court of Honor (Salon d'Honneur), designed by the Parisian architect Gaston Paris and built and garlanded by the city of Dijon, was a "veritable altar to gastronomy." Its grand scale and kitschy decor awed and delighted fairgoers.[79] Green brocaded walls covered with black netting rose according to the "clean lines" of "svelte columnettes" toward a ceiling dressed in "an elegant cascade of flowers." From its center fell an "amusing" and "stylistically contrasting" string of cherubs and other mythological figures. Trees and flowering plants filled the corners of the room while broad sheets of white vellum rose from the center of the room to create a pyramidal chamber within the hall. This "curious motif" was lit separately so as to set it off from the rest of the hall. Invoking the vocabulary and imagery of the spectacular to describe the experience of visiting the fair's gastronomical "courts," reporters employed formulations such as "like a Gargantuan dream," "an enticing phantasmagoria," "a vision followed like dream," and "the drunken impression of having undertaken an apotheosis" to describe the experience of entering the 1925 Hall of Honor.[80] The gastronomical reporter Marcel Grancher described a grandiose Court of Honor resplendent with decorations illustrating and jumbling territorial motifs and historical themes from different epochs. "An immense fresco" painted by the students of the Beaux-Arts school depicted the ancient city of Dijon surrounded by the Legion of Honor and the region's succulent riches: "vintners carry bottles of fine wines, cooks dress boars' heads, roast piglettes, pluck fowl, grill meats, and prepare snails and shrimp against a background of vines and decorative nudes."[81]

Over-the-top marketing stratagems could put off supporters when they threatened the moderate sensibilities of conventional aesthetics. "What can one say of minced meats, soufflés, and towers of paté that cease to be real roasts and proper poultry. Married to the contorted styles and convulsions of art they become [architectural] cornices, capitals, and full arches," quibbled Gaston Roupnel.[82] Disquieted, he observed "venerable lobsters that a bold chef had erected into an Eiffel Tower with Turkish minarets. I would have preferred a little less effort [*préféré du poil aux pattes*] than Persian art. That is no longer cuisine; it is architectural and monumental art. They build in Renaissance or Louis XIV styles; the nougat is naturally Rococo and the ice palaces are made of strawberries. I don't envy those who have to do it all in a colonial vein . . . !"[83]

For most, however, accustomed as they were to a regimen of seventeenth-century architecture, an occasional clearance sale (*baderie*), and "café sitting [as] the only diversion," the gastronomical fair was easily the most memorable, exciting, even marvelous event of the year in "painfully bourgeois" Dijon.[84] "The visitor is seduced as his eyes draw him to the next stand and his admiration continuously grows." Where else could the Dijonnais admire a three-layer pyramid made from a cubic meter of glistening giant shrimp in rows alternating with colorful Burgundian fruit, all supporting an "enormous" bottle of red wine aloft? On the steps of this monumental pedestal, strawberries were sculpted to represent both wild and familiar barnyard animals. Here, rows of wares were framed by the smiles of young salesgirls wearing folkloric skirts and headdresses. There, tucked into a bower of green plants, a butcher surrounded by whole lambs and cows. Elsewhere, a giant mound of butter against a backdrop of chrysanthemums keeping company with an active beehive covered by an enormous glass bell.[85] Grancher described the "prodigious" Table of Lucullus displayed across from the entrance of the Court of Honor:

imagine . . . an extraordinary spectacle . . . that hits the visitor right in the stomach so that he remains dumbstruck: knees weak and saliva running from the corners of his mouth. It's a matter of a huge, brightly lit rotating table covered with flowers and greenery to display all that the region produces that is good and beautiful. . . . It is something prodigious; wild pigs stuck with silver forks, jellies trembling with luminescent transparency, motifs out of saindoux, cascades of shrimps, medieval towers made of truffled medallions topped by boats of shrimp with their red tails in the air. . . . Here a plane made of calf bones, hazel hens, and woodcocks stacked and topped by a royal pheasant, his tail sprightly deployed in whose dazzling gold, purple, and red feathers is reflected the prestigious memories of the courts of days of old, the parades of the Dukes of Burgundy dressed in gold and of lords in their finest robes—a heroic feast painted by Breughel and touched up by Jan Van Looy![86]

Not to be outdone, the wine stalls, which could easily have constituted a fair on their own, might draw the gaze of visitors with "coquettish installations" calculated to invoke particular vintners, grower's associations, and brand names. Memorable stalls included Victor Morot and Company's spiraling glass staircase made entirely of colored liqueur flasks and Antoine Rodeo's electrical windmill with wings covered in wine bottles. The most successful innovation was the *buvette-restaurant* where visitors could rest, listen to music, and continue sampling the regional products they had just seen or tasted.[87]

The Quarrel of the Dishes

> *Gourmets are nothing more than gourmands who lost their appetites.*
> —*Roupnel, "La Trêve du Cuisinier,"* Dépêche de Toulouse *(1921)*

The fair's promoters espoused a gastromony of popular "family recipes." The merits of "good family cooking" were also regularly touted in the Automobile Club of Burgundy's monthly newsletter to "gastronomades."[88] While this provenance has been attributed to the Burgundian chef Alfred Contour and the publication of his *Le Cuisinier Bourguignon: Nouveau Livre de Cuisine Pratique* in 1891, the official catalogue for the 1936 gastronomical fair pointed, instead, to Pierre Hugenin's *Les Meilleurs Recettes de Ma Pauvre Mère* (n. d.), where one could find short, simple recipes for vegetable soups, pot roast, lamb scrapple, carp meurette, and pineapple flan as the basis of "Burgundian cuisine."[89] Even the famed Curnonsky promoted a "practical gastronomy" that "gather[ed] only the champions of simple cuisine, this real French cuisine in which the sauces do not mask the flavors of the dishes and in which 'things have the taste of what they are.' "[90] In 1922, the *Revue de Bourgogne* contrasted "old Burgundian cuisine," identified in terms of vegetable potée, pot roast (Boeuf bourguignon), snails, and *meurette*, among others, to the architectural *"gastrotechnie"* of the 1900 Paris Exposition.[91]

Gaston Roupnel echoed this gastronomical populism when he responded to the "pernicious pretensions" of the "intrusive nouvelle cuisine" of new culinary "experts" such as A. Escoffier, Philéas Gilbert, or Emile Fetu. Asserting such "erudition has always been indigestible," Roupnel argued that "real cuisine" was closer to hand: "after all, good cuisine, real cuisine is nothing more than a simple pot-au-feu [roast]. The pot-au-feu . . . I don't know why it has become so unappreciated! In the bottom of a good round pot, trusting like a good man, murmur the delicate harmonies of a simmering broth slowly cooked over a low fire. Leeks and cloves add the aromas of the garden and tropics and abandon themselves to the bubbling juices of a loin that spent its life ruminating on the subject."[92] He further charged that in matters of culinary art "the Best is the enemy of the Good . . . for cuisine has become an art, a refined art, too refined. One prepares without a philosophy; without understanding the origins of dishes"[93] and sarcastically concluded that "new fangled gourmets [were] nothing more than gourmands who lost their appetites." His pages on the salted hams, raw sausages, and local wines of the vintners' mid-afternoon snack remain one of the best thick descriptions of the period—encrusted as they are with the use of regional patois.[94]

Roupnel's revaluation of Burgundian cuisine also included a public lecture on Jean-Anthelme Brillat-Savarin's gastronomical legacy at the 1929 Gastronomical Fair of Dijon.[95] The significance of Roupnel's interpretation of Burgundy's most famous eighteenth-century epicure and author of the gastro-philosophical tract entitled *La Phisiologie du Goût* (1848) lay in the popular and inclusive spirit he attributed to his Burgundian legacy. In fact, he made little effort to hide a certain disdain for what the fair was becoming: "there is a Gastronomical Fair in happy Dijon. . . . By habit, however, good cuisine is generally available a little everywhere. Across precipitous staircases that lead to the true Paradise of Beatitude waft deadly aromas from timbered dining rooms . . . where Lucullus would die for never being able to leave."[96]

Against the rapturous celebration of a French gastronomy that imposed itself internationally in the eighteenth and nineteenth centuries as a symbol of privilege and exaggerated wealth, Roupnel, perhaps thinking of Pierre Ronsard's poem "Salad" or Aimé Piron's rustic culinary verses, offered a more appealing, accessible, and populist interpretation of Burgundian gastronomy.[97] Following the popular journalist Curnonsky's efforts to make French gastronomy both more bourgeois and democratic,[98] Dijon's two left-leaning populist mayors, Gaston Gérard and Robert Jardillier, revalued Dijon's gastro-political role accordingly.[99] Gérard, for instance, interpreted Piron's theatricals and verse as reflecting an amiable and popular Burgundian "character" in a series of talks organized by the Librarie Hachette on the "glories of Burgundy" during the seventeenth gastronomical fair in 1937: "more than others, Burgundians understand Piron whom they must love as much as he resembles them. He reflects their finesse, realism, and common sense as much as their faults; a sharply critical eye ["discerner la paille dans l'oeil de son voisin"] . . . that is the principal trait of our amiable character."[100]

This was also the time and place when the food critic M. F. K. Fisher first discovered the joys of indulging in simpler cuisine at the expense of gastronomic prejudices she judged "foolish . . . pretentious, often boring, as well as damnable expensive."[101] Had not Léon Daudet, "who knew how to make everybody hate him," also written "The Rehabilitation of Garlic," Pierre Descaves an homage to "Red String Beans," Anatole France on "The History of a Plate of Macaroni," and Gabriel Paysan "The Sausage" in the same "down-home," populist vein? Even the neo-Baroque Maurice Edmond Sailland, self-styled Curnonsky "Prince of Gastronomes," noted that it was Brillat-Savarin's clear, plain style that made him a "classic."[102] As late as 1949, Georges Rozet, the official historian of the Knights of Wine Tasting, insisted that "true and pure Burgundian cuisine is certainly rich (robuste) and flavorful (relevée) but neither overly complicated (tarabiscotée) nor pretentious (recherchée): all told, a relatively simple and rustic cuisine" [code for bourgeois].[103]

This tradition survived through the 1930s in regular paeans to "the pot-au-feu of the French farmhouse" and other dishes in recipes frequently offered, for instance, in the culinary column of the *Progrès de la Côte-d'Or*.[104] Gertrude Powell recalled being invited to the home of Professor Georges Connes in Dijon, "charming people" and a bourgeois couple if there ever was one: "the dinner table was laid under a spreading cherry tree in the back of the garden; a regular French dinner" built around a roast chicken and tomato salad![105] On another occasion, she and her husband were invited by their host family, the Rigaulets, "for a family dinner" consisting of "roast beef, a dish of potatoes, and cabbage boiled with bacon. All very good. Madame told me the cabbage was in my honor."[106] No Escoffier recipes in the homes of Dijon's bourgeoisie. At mid-century, Waverly Root was able to assert, "Burgundy is still renowned for good food. Probably no other comparable area in the country, not even the Ile-de-France, can boast of so uniformly high level of good eating throughout the territory."[107] Colette Willy made sure that Parisians knew as well. She informed them, on the authority of her pedigree as having been "born in a province [Burgundy] where we ate well without knowing that we were gourmand," that "true cuisine" could only be "simple, ancient, and considered."[108] Even *Le Monde* diplomatically recognized the pot-au-feu, even as it "makes the happiness of more than a few chefs," as the "emblematic dish of household cuisine."[109] As this interest served to pique interest and appetites, it remained to get the people to Dijon.

Frenchmen into Tourists: Getting Gourmands and Gourmets to Dijon

> *Gastronomy is the craze and passion of the day . . . like puzzles, yo-yos, dances, crosswords, cubism, and Freudism before . . . restaurants, inns, and hostels grow like mushrooms. With the help of automobile tourism, the French have gone off to discover the magnificence of our provinces.*
>
> —*Curnonsky and Gaston Derys,* Anthology of French Gastronomy *(1936)*

It took Dijon's foremost gastronomical booster to recognize that "the city of 100 steeples" was blessed with resources that could be more profitably exploited. Gaston Gérard listed the city's attractions— museums, divers monuments, evening musical and theatrical performances, attractive parks, an "illustrious" history, a ducal palace, and most importantly a regional cuisine—in a promotional article in 1922. France, as he saw it, would discover Burgundian culinary traditions and regional products on the back of the national rails, as reduced-fare trains pulled in and out every five minutes during Dijon's fair days: "Dijon, Gastronomical Capital. It's the word. It's the thing. It is only in Dijon that one savors a cuisine never to be equaled. . . . Come and you will return annually if you are, as I hope, joyous and gourmand" (Figure 3.5).[110]

In 1925, a reporter for the *Progrès de la Côte-d'Or* covered a public conference on the theme of tourism and hygiene offered in one of the University of Dijon's large amphitheatres. The speaker reminded readers that Burgundy could easily profit by exploiting its "coquettish" villages to situate stunning centers for rest and relaxation (villégiature et repos). He added that individual localities (pays) wishing to promote the reputations of their "natural, local, and built riches" needed to "organize themselves in order to better welcome and retain visitors."[111] Along these lines, Gérard credited his political patron André Tardieu for making tourism an important element within national domestic policy:

He made it official. And, for three years and through five successive ministries, established a politics of tourism to which we owe the complete repaving of our

Figure 3.5. Crème de Cassis advertisement, 1920s.

roads, the coordination of land, sea, and air transportation, the interpenetration of all organizations responsible for creating and promoting tourism: Chambers of Commerce, the Touring-Club, the Club-Alpin, the Automobile-Club, hotel industry—now benefiting from a system of credit, tourist exchanges abroad, the evaluation of the nation's cities in terms of their tourist amenities, an entire reorganization of thermal spas, the protection of historic sites, the organization of great folkloric festivals . . . etc.[112]

With Tardieu's exit from government, the onset of the Great Depression, and reduced national subsidies, local and regional governments were increasingly forced to mostly fend for themselves. They continued to lobby Paris and local initiative. "The state," Gérard argued, "must at all costs support this endeavor, not by taxes but, rather, through tourism revenues."[113] Accordingly, Gérard promoted the sales of French wines and foodstuffs by traveling to 32 countries—from Indochina to Canada—and attending more than 600 conferences during his political tenure.[114] His efforts were such that Prime Minister André Tardieu noted that "everything [Gérard] wants, he gets. Everything he thinks, he advocates . . . whether in a brief concerning wine, roads, or tourism, he affirms a visionary zeal."[115]

Challenging a two-hundred-year-old trend in which the French sought sophisticated, complicated, and difficult dishes accompanied by mediocre wines,[116] the rapid development and expansion of modern transportation and communications technologies—trains, planes, automobiles, bicycles, radio, chambers of commerce, booster societies, and tourist magazines—during the first decades of the twentieth century made travel to "la France profonde" (literally "deep France") to indulge in regional gastronomy more accessible, affordable, sager, and desirable.[117] Historian Patrick Young has shown how a burgeoning turn-of-the-century tourism industry provided "the foundations for the potential economic revitalization of the [French] provinces."[118] Travel clubs, hotel associations, resort entrepreneurs, gastronomy societies, railway companies, and *syndicats d'initiative* (local booster associations) emerged to assist and profit from "internal" tourism.[119]

In contrast to nineteenth-century travel to religious shrines, chaste "centers of recuperation," or the historical "sites and monuments" reproduced on postage stamps, new destinations were more akin to the spas frequented by upper-class patrons during the mid- to late nineteenth century, yet they were within postwar budgets. These new vacation sites provided "stimulating" leisure in the form of "authentic" food, wine, and cultural entertainment to middle-class clients. In 1935, Raymond Baudouin, the editor of *La Revue du Vin de France* told assembled members of the Agrarian Party (Le Partie Agraire) that rural areas should develop tourist economies. "Rural communes," he insisted, "must have the ambition to create tourist stops distinguished by original cachet, veritable temples of regional dishes and local wines in a rustic or picturesque décor."[120] The Touring Club of France noted in 1929 that "the preferred cuisine of tourists is regional: each terroir possesses original resources and savory recipes."[121] Even the Duchess d'Uzès insisted on a visit to Dijon with a reception at City Hall in 1931 for her Automobile-Club Féminin's "caravan."[122] By the late 1930s, the francophilic gastronome and correspondent for Paris edition of the *Chicago Tribune*, Waverly Root, could report that the Michelin guide, "which gourmets never fail to carry with them when they sally into the provinces, lists just seven three-star restaurants outside of Paris; four of them [in Burgundy]."[123] Such gastronomical enticements were reason for Côte-d'Or's Flying Club to zoom in locals and their guests for a Grand Burgundian Wines Rally in 1935.[124]

Burgundian tourism found a ready ally in the Touring Club of France, whose principal objective was to "popularize the use of small tourist vehicles and generally enhance automobile circulation."[125] Its monthly journal lured tourists along France's roadways with detailed and picturesque narratives about the sights, meals, wines ("Burgundy, when it is authentic"), and accommodations travelers could find in "the country of Larmartine," "along the Cluniac trail," "through 'unknown' Burgundy," and around "the Churches of Mâcon and Farms of Bresse."[126] The Automobile Club of Burgundy, whose radiator seal was the image of a Burgundian vigneronne, went one step further. It organized contemporary desires for "gaiety, vivacity, and honesty" into provincial tours with an eye to finishing in time for nine-course meals accompanied by a "vin d'honneur."[127] It organized events such as "The Rail and Road: the Gastronomical Fair" in 1932, the "Morvan Circuit" in 1935, and the "Gastronomical Dijon Rally" in 1937 to promote and benefit from the festivities at Dijon's annual fair.[128] Covering 150 kilometers per day for five days, the automobile club's 1937 "Excursion in Burgundy" sought authentic regional cuisine.[129] From touring in Burgundy, the author Robert Desnos recalled how he and companions feasted like Olympic gods: "we made numerous toasts, drank a quantity of wine, and sang with deserts."[130]

"J'ai Découvert a Dijon," a promotional brochure designed by Georges Rozet, provided budding gastronomes seeking the "ideal travelers' *rendez-vous* in Dijon" with a sample itinerary. Addressing his readers as "[his] brother tourists," Rozet described how neophytes could lodge at the conveniently located Hotel Terminus. There, following a day touring the monuments or the casino at the cinema-theatre, they could dine at La Grande Taverne restaurant. Whispering to readers "worthy of the confidence," Rozet promised a fine regional cuisine and "authentic vintages" of "pure and high lineage" at prices no longer expected "after so many years of gastronomical inflation." The "Hotel Terminus menu prix fix," he noted, provides dishes descended from a long culinary tradition reaching back to the Dukes of Burgundy set off by a modern decor."[131]

The Touring Club of France published a three-page report on tourism, "In the Burgundian Region," in 1925 in which the reviewer, following a discussion of the region's history, topography, tourists, and infrastructure, concluded that it was the region "where one ate well . . . better than one slept!"[132] By 1930, general services had improved such that the gastronome Gaston Derys invoked a culinary contest organized by the Touring Club in Brillat-Savarin's Burgundy.[133] Gaston Roupnel provided a fictional account of the annual banquet of a fictional scientific society ("*agapes amicales de l'année*"). Members of the "venerable and erudite" Helium Club convened "in one of those good old restaurants in Dijon . . . where pure genius operates through pots and pans." The establishment's most modest dish was so admired that "rajas and maharajas left their elephants in India simply to discover its tripe. The house paté was terrestrial spirit en croûte! . . . A cup of coffee was an ode to Moka; simply smelling it made one delirious with tropical thoughts. . . . As for the fine champagne, the barrel was said to have known Napoleon I in earlier days."[134]

The link between a commodified gastronomical culture, where all aspects of the experience are packaged, scripted, valorized, marketed, and sold, and the development of Burgundian tourism is revealed in the experiences of tourists themselves. As a member of the Club Alpin of the Côte-d'Or, M. F. K. Fisher recalls the "energetic but agreeable" outings to "carefully planned feasts at little village inns" where members consumed as "many courses and as many wines" before walking them off along the Route des Crus to see "castles and convents and wine caves that were seldom bared."[135] Her most orgiastic eating was with the Club Alpin where "the schedule was always the same: a brisk walk from the station and the little train that had brought us from Dijon, four or five hours of eating and drinking, and then the long promenade, the climbing, the viewing of monuments and fallen temples. The real reason, though . . . was that every time we spent half a day plugging doggedly across muddy fields and shivering in bat-filled slimy ruins, we spent an equal amount of time sitting warmly, winily, in the best local restaurant, eating specialties of the village or the region more ardently than ever peak was scaled or Gothic arch gazed on."[136] Indeed, the gastronomical impulse provided an education in wine, cuisine, manners, and suitable topics for conversation in provincial society. According to Fisher, "the Club secretary always tried to arrange our sorties so that after we had studied a regional cuisine with the thoroughness it deserved, and had made solemn notes both physical and spiritual on the vintages that flourished there, or there, or there, we could devote ourselves with equally undivided zeal to the promenade itself."[137]

The Touring Club, for example, organized a "gastronomical pilgrimage" around a Concours de Cuisine (Cooking Competition) among various restaurants in Brillat-Savarin's native Bresse in 1930. Famous for its slowly cooked and aromatic lamb, boar, and fowl stews, this region was recognized as a "gastronomical paradise."[138] By 1936, France's reigning gastronomes—Curnonsky and Gaston Derys—were equally seduced. They dedicated a volume of their series of guides to the nation's "culinary marvels and reputable French inns" to Burgundy.[139] Highlighting the region's "delectable cuisine" and "incomparable wines," they dubbed Dijon "a rare terrestrial paradise."[140] Simon Arbellot repeated this evaluation in his *Gastronomical Guide of France*. The Côte-d'Or chapter drew attention to the Gastronomical Fair of Dijon where tourists could find "great cuisine and great wines everywhere. From the Palace of the Ducs of Burgundy to the vineyards along the slopes, enchantment is the voyager's most constant companion . . . [and] royal tradition exists between the old establishments and our daily tables."[141] Four-day roadtrips were organized to bring Parisians to visit Burgundy's "Four Glories" the Paulée in Meursault, the Gastronomical Fair of Dijon, Beaune's wine auction, and the Caveau Nuiton.[142]

The region's gastro-tourist attributes were seductively deployed through lavish menus such as the one served to the National Union of Reserve Officers for their annual banquet in Nuits-St.-Georges on July 24, 1932. Much as diversity was nationally heralded as promoting unity, the Hotel de la Côte-d'Or's menu drew on the region's diverse offerings to create a sequence of courses that represented a unified gastro-political experience: warm paté Côte-d'Or, Morvan ham with creamed mushrooms, Charolais filets with Burgundian peas, Bressian chicken in a Mâconnais white wine, and cheese from the Abbey of Citeaux, not to mention the thirty-three regional varieties of reds, one white, and seven liqueurs.[143] Such orchestration was the happy result of complex and calculated marketing alliances that linked the culinary high and low. This "recipe" was calculated to merge local and national agendas within a gambit aimed toward gaining tourism market shares. "Rather than be satisfied with an international cuisine with neither conscience nor flavor, opined Gaston Gérard, "the gastronome . . . desires honestly prepared and savory dishes [found in the Côte-d'Or]."[144] The popular Burgundian family dishes tempered restaurant fares and resulted in "a regional cuisine prepared with love."[145]

Evidence of the mutually beneficial link between tourism and gastronomy was prominent, for example, in contemporary marketing strategies and pedagogical techniques employed to promote gastronomical tourism at the Pavilion of Tourism at the 1931 Gastronomical Fair of Dijon.[146] The success of the Burgundian project for regional economic growth was showcased, most notably, at the 1937 Paris International Exposition's Regional Center. The administrative director of the exposition's regional committee declared that "with each regional pavilion, the Regional Center will be like a 'Little France' [comme une Petite France] directly produced by the regions and remaining in regional hands." He believed visitors who experienced Burgundian gastronomy in an appropriately rustic setting would take home a powerful memory (souvenir) of Burgundy's artisan, aesthetic, and folkloric riches. Replicating the Burgundian wine festivals and gastronomical fairs developed in the 1920s and 1930s, the exposition's Rural Center featured a 600-square-meter "Burgundian Cellar" modeled on Camille Rodier's popular caveau (cellar) in Nuits-Saint-Georges, Burgundy where the pseudo-folkloric Order of the Knights of the Wine Cups (Chevaliers de Tastevin) convened. Mindful of tourism interests, the administrative director fully expected visitors to the pavilion would leave with the strong desire to visit Burgundy "to better appreciate its charms within their original scale and setting."[147] An annex further offered tourist information in the form of documentary films, enlarged photographs, wall maps, dioramas, and commercial brochures "glorifying the well known cities, tourist attractions, thermal spas, historic sites, monuments, as well as seasonal sports" of Burgundy. The organization of the exposition's sixteen restaurants further underscored the ascendancy of regional cultural intermediaries over Parisian restaurateurs. The Burgundian Pavilion's self-guided tour terminated with a visit to a restaurant where, we are told, the "high priests of gastronomy officiated with dignity."[148]

Conclusion

> *The Gastronomical Fair of Dijon radiates and illuminates Burgundy with its immense publicity and distributes its benefits to all.*
>
> —Gaston Gérard, Le Bien Public *(1927)*

The success of the Burgundian gastronomical agenda lay in its ability to create a shared cultural space for diverse economic interests in terms of inclusive aesthetic registers. Unable, unwilling, and most likely not eager to resolve the *querelle des recettes et mets*, Gérard invoked and mobilized multiple traditions without irony or difficulty in *La France à Table*'s volume on Burgundian gastronomy, tourism, and folklore in 1954. He located Burgundian culinary excellence as residing both "on the table of the most modest inn of the most humble village" and in "our hotels" where "the most reputable chefs create the most celebrated dishes in the world."[149] Could this have been what Gaston Gérard envisioned when he hoped the Gastronomical Fair of Dijon would "allow everyone to escape reality, chase away grey thoughts, and combat monotony" and "find their own happiness?"[150] Hence the Gastronomical Fair of Dijon had the singular merit of simultaneously staging popular, elite, rustic, and urban spectacles with a crowd that reflected the social, political, and economic divisions that wracked greater France. The result was an important and lasting experiment with a directed economy resting on popular support and participation. Consider that the gastronomical fair has continued to attract an average of 195,000 visitors and 1,000 merchants through the 1980s and 1990s.[151]

Seen in broader perspective, the Burgundian cultural movement sought to mediate the seemingly irreconcilable demands of modern and traditional practices through sophisticated cultural stratagems more often associated with postwar, postmodern commercial culture. This project (re)negotiated Burgundian identity (inclusive—via semiotic conflation—of all levels of society) by manipulating emerging patterns of consumption that required the coordination of both productive forces and patterns of consumption. This provided contemporaries with new critical templates necessary for negotiating political tensions and cultural contradictions inherent in a region experiencing uneven economic development during a period of rapid modernization. By marketing gastronomical products within a popular and reassuringly middlebrow aesthetic, the shapers of the Burgundian cultural project showed how regional practices, values, and investments could be promoted through modern economic strategies. Economically speaking, Gaston Gérard's gastro-political "firm called Burgundy" had arrived.

Part II
Engaging Religion

Chapter 4

Consuming Simple Gifts
Shakers, Visitors, Goods

BRIAN BIXBY

In just over two centuries, the term "Shaker" has been transformed in popular culture. Originally, it was the conventional designation for an odd religious sect that formally called themselves the United Society of Believers. Today, it is more commonly used to label a variety of commodities. Instead of being the focus for life and worship, Shaker villages have been turned into tourist destinations. People who want more Shaker experience can buy authentic Shaker furniture, reproduction Shaker furniture, furniture said to be inspired by Shaker styles, and many other goods with the label "Shaker" attached, often on tenuous grounds. Few will ever come into contact with the remaining Shakers, and fewer still discuss religion with them.[1]

In this chapter, I identify three major stages in the transformation of the label "Shaker." After recounting how the early Shakers interacted with religious seekers, I will describe how the relationship between Shakers and visitors became commercialized in the early nineteenth century. Then we will see how the popular image of the Shakers was gradually romanticized and detached from contemporary Shakers, starting in the mid-nineteenth century. Finally, I will discuss how the human qualities of the Shakers in popular culture were transferred to objects during the late nineteenth and twentieth centuries. "Shaker" came to mean a type of artifact or replica thereof, leading one twentieth-century Shakeress to complain that she did not "want to be remembered as a piece of furniture."[2]

Shaker Origins and Early Interactions with Visitors

The Shakers were originally of English origin. They emerged in the late 1740s among the dissenters to the established Anglican Church in Manchester, England. Like Quakers and other Pietist movements, they recognized a spiritual inner light as a source of religious wisdom. Like certain Anabaptist and other radical groups, they believed in an imminent second coming of Christ and the Millennium. By way of the Camisards, a French Protestant group of the late eighteenth century, they inherited the practice of spirit possession. Armed as they believed with superior spiritual knowledge, the English Shakers openly confronted Anglican priests and congregations during services, leading to their prosecution as heretics and disturbers of the peace. In the face of this persecution, nine Shakers under the leadership of Ann Lee fled to New York in 1774. Subsequently the English branch of the Shakers died out.[3]

The Shakers in America began their first major effort at proselytizing from their base in Watervliet—near Albany, New York—during the years 1780–83. This period was just after the "New Light" and Free-Will Baptist revivals had swept through back-country New England. Many revivalists had not found spiritual peace, however, and were searching for new answers. Ann Lee and two other English Shakers spent much of this time crisscrossing southern New England, spreading their beliefs among these seekers and making converts.[4]

Shaker interactions with visitors already followed a pattern that would persist, with some changes, into the nineteenth century. Whether at Watervliet or on the road, the Shakers welcomed interest and invited people to attend services with them. These services often involved spirit possession, in which worshippers would be overcome by the spirit and begin to shake, twirl, dance, and exhibit other phenomena typical of a Christian revival meeting. Thus, the Shakers acquired their popular name from these activities. After worship, the Shakers would invite their guests to partake of a meal with them, with members and their local sympathizers supplying the food. They encouraged hopeful recruits to come away from the World, and to spend time among the Shakers to reinforce their faith. Overall, this experience was a wholly religious one, with no commercial overtones.[5] In the aftermath of Ann Lee's death in 1784, however, the Shakers underwent a profound transformation. The Shaker leadership called for the gathering of believers into their own villages, where they would live with fellow Shakers and apart from "the World," as the nonbelievers were called.[6]

Once gathered into villages, Shakers committed themselves to an intertwined religious and economic order radically different from that of their neighbors. Their villages were dually organized, having male and female spiritual leaders, elders and eldresses, alongside male and female secular leaders, deacons and deaconesses. Believers accepted the dual nature of God, the incarnation of the Christ spirit in the female aspect in the person of Mother Ann Lee, the practice of celibacy, and the need to confess to their spiritual leaders. Contact between the sexes was strictly limited and carefully supervised by the leadership. Shakers rose, worked, worshipped, ate, and relaxed almost always in the company of other Shakers, at the orders of their dual hierarchy of leaders. They worked primarily for their own use and consumption. Visitors, trips into the World, and outside reading material were forbidden except by permission of the spiritual leaders. In general, theirs was a closed community. The Shakers even stopped proselytizing for most of the 1790s.[7]

However, the demands of the religious and economic orders required the Shakers keep some contact with the World. No Shaker village could be fully self-sufficient; thus Shakers had to produce surpluses to trade with the World for what they lacked. Since they were celibate as a matter of faith, they needed new members just to keep from dying out, to say nothing of the glory of gaining new believers. They also sought a constantly renewed supply of young, able-bodied members to carry out the heavy work of the Shaker community and to support the children, the aged, and the infirm. Finally, Shakers had to engage in publishing and lobbying state governments to react to attacks in the press and in legislatures against them. Not everyone was happy with wild millennialists whose conversions broke up families and who looked to gobble up surrounding farmland when their community successfully competed against local family farms.[8]

The Shakers carried forward their tradition of inviting religious seekers to their worship. Usually, one of the first buildings constructed in each Shaker village was the meeting house. Because it was one of the few places the public was admitted by design, it was routinely located on the edge of the village, as at Canterbury, New Hampshire, or along the main road, as at Pleasant Hill, Kentucky, to limit the intrusion of the World. There on Sundays, the Shakers invited the public to sit as guests and watch a Shaker religious service. No doubt they hoped to attract new members this way. The meeting also naturally served the Shakers' spiritual needs, but it was not their only religious service; they met among themselves for worship several times each week.[9]

The Sunday public meeting became the first Shaker tourist attraction. It was not just the event, but the publicity about it, that raised interest in the World. Early visitors to village Sunday meetings seem to have been driven by curiosity, when not by faith. Once the meetings had been sufficiently publicized, through newspaper reports or travelogues, they became a well-known destination. Accounts from the last few decades before the Civil War indicate that writers knew what to expect before going. For example, when Captain Marryat, a British traveler, published his account of a visit in his 1839 travelogue, he did not bother to describe Shaker theology because he thought that it was too well known. Visitor numbers kept climbing, at least into the 1840s, and probably into the 1850s. Shaker villages started appearing in tourist guidebooks. Some villages gained additional visitors thanks to fortuitous locations. Tourists going to Lebanon Springs, New York, as part of the typical northern tour in the early nineteenth century could easily swing by Mount Lebanon, the Shaker headquarters. Similarly, tourists heading to Mammoth Caves in Kentucky could stop by Pleasant Hill.[10]

To judge from visitors' accounts, antebellum Sunday public meeting generally followed the same pattern. Visitors walked or rode to the meeting house, a sizable structure with separate entrances for men and women, then lined up by sex and entered through the appropriate door. Inside was a great hall, without walls or columns interrupting its extent. The hall was plain, with only windows for light. Along each side rested benches for the visitors from the World to sit upon. The Shakers arrived, like the visitors, each sex having its own door. After hanging their hats and cloaks, they sat in ranks facing each other, on benches in the middle of the room. Usually a Shaker speaker would offer a sermon that often was directed to the visitors, expounding on their sinful state and explaining the virtues of Shakerism. (The Shakers were aware of the effect a good speaker could have, and had designated speakers at least as far back as 1807.) Other Shakers might rise up and testify to their faith, as the spirit moved them. Before they began a dance, they carried their benches to the sides of the room, leaving a large open space in the middle. They would then draw up in formation, still segregated by sex, and proceed to execute one of their elaborate group dances, such as the Square Order Shuffle. The group dances had been devised in the years following the gathering into villages, and gradually replaced the more spontaneous ecstatic dancing by individuals. Since all Shakers were expected to attend Sunday meeting, if there was sufficient room, these dances might involve hundreds of worshippers. One contemporary likened them to theatrical exhibitions (Figure 4.1). The Shakers in the picture are engaged in a lively ring dance in the center of the meeting house, while visitors watch from their benches along the side. At various times during the service, the Shakers would sing a song, typically one of their own, for they were vigorous composers. Finally, the service would come to an end, a Shaker speaker would thank the visitors for their good behavior—although disruptions by jeering visitors did happen—and all would exit.[11]

Printed accounts of Shaker worship tended to be published in one of two forms, as articles in newspapers or as part of a travelogue. Newspaper stories typically appeared in local weeklies with limited circulation, though some were reprinted elsewhere. Travelogue books, in contrast,

Figure 4.1. Shaker group dance with spectators. Reproduced from "The Shakers in Niskayuna," *Frank Leslie's Popular Monthly* 20 (December 1885), courtesy of the Sophia Smith Collection, Smith College.

often had national and even international distribution. The travelogue quickly became a popular form of literature in nineteenth-century America, so much so that later writers freely corrected earlier ones. Along with the Shakers' own publications and those by apostates, they must rank as among the most influential accounts in the antebellum years.[12]

Travelogue writers who mentioned the Shakers, such as Basil Hall, Harriet Martineau, and James Fenimore Cooper, tended to be wealthier and better educated than the average American, with the means and contacts to travel for months or years and to see their accounts into print. Indeed, many were not Americans at all, but foreigners such as Hall and Martineau, out to discover what the New World could show the Old. These writers described the other visitors much as they saw themselves: curiosity seekers, fashionable people of means. They viewed the service with the "tourist gaze": the pursuit of extraordinary sights, labeled and categorized as a particular type of memorable experience. In this case, the experience involved watching the mysterious sectaries and their unusual forms of worship. Several of these accounts emphasized the Shakers' lowly social status in implicit contrast to the writer's.

Some described the female Shakers as wan in appearance, implying that their deviant sexuality—celibacy—harmed their health and spirits. Others condemned Shaker doctrine as nonsense, directing particular ire against the practice of celibacy and the role of Ann Lee as the "Pope" of Shakerism. Most of all, writers described Shaker dances as extraordinary, not just in their complexity, but because the Shakers danced as part of their worship. In the early nineteenth century, dancing was regarded by many as an empty diversion from more profitable pursuits at the very least, if not an enticement to sexual sin. The Shakers had to offer Biblical citations in their attempts to justify the practice. Many visitors were not convinced, and described the dancing as disgusting. Mrs. Basil Hall, less reserved in her private correspondence than her husband was in his published travelogue, captured the critical perspective when describing the dancing Shakers flapping their hands "in a penguin motion."[13]

Still, travelogue writers found some things to admire about the Shakers. They admitted that Shaker villages were clean and neat. On her visit, Harriet Martineau observed that there were no stones in the roads, no weeds in the gardens, and the "floors were as even and almost as white as marble." Shaker villages in the early nineteenth century occupied the frontier: first the most recently settled parts of New England and New York, and then the newly settled West—Ohio, Kentucky, and Indiana. The American frontier has rarely been noted for orderliness, but Shaker villages were different: cleaning and setting things in order were regular parts of Shaker work. Indeed, the Millennial Laws, the internal rules first devised by the Shakers in 1821, required that the village be cleaned up every Saturday, the day before visitors came. Account writers also acknowledged the industriousness and honesty of the Shakers, who were soon known for the quality of their seed sold to farmers and gardeners across the United States.[14]

A curious common thread runs between foreign travelogue writers' praise of the Shakers and their admiration for such institutions as penitentiaries and asylums. Many writers came to visit the new institutions Americans were developing, and were impressed by their order, cleanliness, and benevolent intent. Although none to my knowledge ever said so explicitly, their language in praising Shaker villages implies that there, too, they had found values and practices comparable to those evident in penitentiaries and asylums.[15]

While accounts by relatively wealthy, educated people dominated the antebellum press, they are surely not representative of those who visited Shaker public meetings. An analysis of the visitors' register at the Enfield, Connecticut, Shaker village for June–August 1856 shows that 64 percent of visitors came from nearby communities. While some traveled from the cities of Hartford and Springfield, many were probably from farming families not much different from the Shakers, except in religion and community organization. This is not surprising. In antebellum times, roads were often poor and travel accommodations dismal. One had to be wealthy to travel long distances, for such a journey could take weeks or months. Other Shaker villages would probably also show a preponderance of local visitors, if they had kept registers that survived. The Ohio and Kentucky villages had been founded in the tradition of camp meeting, where neighbors came from miles around for a revival service. No doubt Shaker meetings continued to draw visitors on that basis. Such neighbors visited to see the odd Shaker worship, perhaps even to be converted, but they came also to see relatives and transact business with the Shakers. Many of these neighbors would write letters matter-of-factly mentioning their visits to Shaker villages, yet few published accounts. That they could write so simply about the Shakers implies an acceptance of them as neighbors, if peculiar ones.[16]

One fair indication of the common perception of the Shakers comes from the play *The Shaker Lovers*, first produced in 1849, and performed many times thereafter. In the play, two Shaker couples wish to wed, and therefore contemplate leaving their celibate sect. Conspiring against one of the couples is an elder who embezzles money and attempts murder and seduction. In the denouement, the elder is exposed as a criminal, and the Shakers, with a wink, let the two couples leave. The play's primary target for criticism was the Shaker practice of celibacy, condemned as against God's will. Indeed, the play implied that many Shakers might be glad to cast off that practice, a theme that has recurred in fiction to the present day.[17]

The theatrical *Shaker Lovers* differed significantly from the short story of the same name on which it was based. Daniel Pierce Thompson, its author, had had to struggle for an education and took great pride in his personal freedom as part of his Revolutionary heritage. While he structured his story around the melodramatic romance of the young couple threatened by an elder, much of his criticism was directed against the Shaker rules demanding absolute obedience to the leadership and forbidding outside reading. Both of these critiques vanished from the play. Instead, its author introduced a second couple in order to reinforce the critique of celibacy by making it explicit and separating it from the melodrama. Presumably, the playwright altered the story to emphasize the more popular message and seems to have been successful.[18]

In sum, the play condemned the Shakers only when they committed misdeeds, such as preventing lovers from marrying or allowing corruption. This mirrored the general attitude toward Shakers by their neighbors, once the communities had become firmly established. The only mob attacks on Shaker villages, all in the antebellum era, occurred when non-Shakers alleged that their spouses or children were being held by the Shakers against their will. The mobs acted to right a wrong, to restore a family they saw as severed by the Shakers.[19]

Toward midcentury, the advent of railroads made transportation speedier and cheaper. Some Shaker villages benefited greatly from this, and began to draw more tourists from the cities. By 1850, Harvard and Shirley Shaker villages became a convenient day-trip from Boston, as was the Enfield, Connecticut, Shaker village from both Albany and New York City. More remote locations, such as South Union, Kentucky, and Enfield, New Hampshire became much more accessible when railroads ran within a few miles of each village. Indeed, in selling land to the railroads for a right of way, the Enfield Shakers cannily demanded that the trains always stop at Enfield any time they passed through it.[20]

As a spectacular tourist attraction, the Shaker public meeting was a success. Offering the chance to see the odd sectaries and watch their elaborate dances, they could attract hundreds of visitors on a Sunday, so many that some could not be accommodated in the Shaker meeting houses. So popular were the dances that troupes of apostate Shakers toured cities demonstrating them. As an inducement to religious conversion, though, the public meeting was not very successful. Indeed, no recruiting tool, whether meeting, missionary, or printed work, proved very successful. Apart from the aftermaths of three religious revivals— the "New Light" revival in New England circa 1780, the Great Awakening in Ohio and Kentucky circa 1800, and the Millerite revival in the early 1840s—the Shakers were never able to gain young adult members faster than they lost them, due to death or apostasy. One good month's worth of visitors, had they all converted, would have easily doubled Shaker numbers, but nothing close to that ever happened.[21]

The Shakers must have realized early on that they would not secure many converts from the Sunday public meetings. Already in the 1810s, one Hancock Shaker referred to the visitors at meetings as "spectators," certainly not a hopeful label for prospective members. This reference was an exceptional one: typically, early journals did not refer to the visitors at all. After their initial successes, the Shaker leadership confronted a period of slow growth from 1820 to 1850. They realized that they would not convert all the world any time soon. There was no danger of mankind becoming extinct from becoming Shakers: too many were choosing marriage and the generative world rather than celibacy in the regenerative world of Shakerism. Already, the leaders knew that the demographic trends were undermining the future of their communities. They were not recruiting enough young adults, while their existing membership aged and their children rarely remained. Moreover, the

Shakers fulfilled some of their own social and spiritual needs in the Sunday services. Hence, they continued holding public meetings.[22]

The Shakers' economic order inadvertently encouraged the tourist trade by making high quality goods available for sale in their villages. The combination of a strong, religiously inspired work ethic—encapsulated in the Shaker maxim, "Hands to work, hearts to God"—and the economies of scale of a community of workers under central control made Shaker villages financially successful in the early nineteenth century. The Shakers became known for high quality agricultural and manufactured products such as seeds, chairs, flat brooms, wooden ware, and baskets. Initially, the Shakers had expected only to sell their goods wholesale in exchange for goods they needed. They constructed a building on the main road in each village called the Office, where their external business representatives, the Trustees, dealt with the World's businessmen. However, their goods' reputation and the increase in their unintended tourist business gave rise to a retail trade. A visit to the Shakers was no longer complete until one stopped by the Office to buy some Shaker goods; for example, Harriet Martineau mentioned doing so in 1837. This trade grew in importance until Office buildings were remodeled specifically to create room for a retail shop geared to tourists, before the Civil War in some villages. Marianne Finch, yet another English traveler, thought the Office building was nothing but a store when she visited in the early 1850s.[23]

Partaking of a Shaker village meal became another part of the tourist experience. It had long been traditional for Shakers to offer visitors a meal, a practice encoded in the Millennial Laws, the Shakers' regulations, when first formulated by the leadership in 1821. The Shaker reputation for quality food followed their reputation for other goods, encouraging tourist interest in dining. Too, the physical distance separating Shaker villages from "the World" meant that a visitor was not likely to get a meal anywhere else nearby. Yet feeding for free the hundreds who came to Sunday public meeting was beyond a Shaker community's capability. Thus Shakers began to charge these tourists for meals, while still providing free food to those in need. The regulation requiring a meal to be offered was dropped when the Millennial Laws were revised in the 1840s.[24]

In much the same way, the Shakers found themselves running boarding houses. Traveling businessmen, workers with skills the Shakers lacked among themselves, and no doubt visitors stranded by weather had to be put up somewhere overnight. Since the Shakers required all outsiders except Sunday worshippers to stop first at the Office, each community added rooms to its Office buildings for boarding visitors. These rooms also housed outside day laborers, an increasing need as the

number of able-bodied Shaker men declined. Because the Office building lay within the village, the Shakers enforced rules of conduct compat-
ible with their beliefs, including men and women sleeping apart from
each other. In sum, the relationship between Shakers and visitors
became commercialized by the 1850s. The visitors were primarily tourists, consuming Shaker worship as a spectacle, and paying for their
meals, their stays, and the Shaker goods they purchased.[25]

On other fronts as well, the Shakers could not stay apart from "the
World." After 1787, the leadership and the majority of Shakers were
Americans, drawn from the very "World" the Shakers were trying to
escape. Despite their new faith, they brought some of the World's goods
and attitudes with them. The archaeological work at Canterbury Shaker
village has turned up many fragments of fancy ornamental china, which
may have been carried in by new members or even purchased by resident members. This was but one indication of how Shaker simplicity in
decoration gradually gave way to Victorian ornamentation, culminating
in the lavish "Marble Hall" Office building at Union Village in the
1890s. The introduction of outside values caused even more substantial
changes. The Shakers had initially provided only practical schooling for
children and restricted the circulation of newspapers and magazines to
the leadership. These measures were out of step with American ideas
about education and freedom of thought, a point several critics noted.
The Shakers had to upgrade their schools repeatedly to satisfy parents
and retain children upon reaching adulthood. The ban on outside periodicals, although restated in the 1860 Millennial Laws, had collapsed by
the early 1870s.[26]

The visitors attending Sunday worship helped sustain contact with the
World. Those services may well have represented the most extensive contact many Shakers had with the World on a regular basis. The Shakers
could observe, understand, and possibly envy some of the changes going
on in the World by watching their visitors. They became sensitive to the
World's opinions. When spirit possessions and elaborate spiritual theater became a major part of Shaker worship during "Mother's Work" in
the 1840s, the Shakers temporarily closed Sunday meetings to the public, fearing that the content of worship would provoke jeers or puzzle-
ment. In this they were not entirely successful, as one journal reveals
that spectators watched some of the outside services of the early 1840s
from a distance.[27]

The result was an erosion of the barriers between Shakers and the
World. Shaker treatment of visitors demonstrates this. By the 1840s, visitors' accounts no longer focused only on public worship, but extended
to Shaker-led tours of their villages. By the 1850s, the Shakers invited a
magazine reporter to spend time in a Shaker village. Also, how the Shak-

ers thought of visitors changed. Early Shaker records about "visitors" did not normally describe visitors from the World; they concerned visits of Shakers from other communities. Gradually, the Shakers gave formal recognition to the tourists, for example, in 1840 starting a record of visitors to Union Village, Ohio. They originally intended to document only potential converts, but soon extended the accounts to include visiting relatives and the occasional traveling businessman. By 1856, the Enfield, Connecticut, village had a visitors' register similar to those seen today at many tourist stops. In the 1890s, the Shirley register included Shakers and the World alike, with no distinction drawn between them. This change all came at a price: the commercialization of the relationship between Shakers and tourists. Most outsiders were no longer guests, but sightseers.[28]

Not every Shaker approved of this growing accommodation to the World and its tourists. Elder Freegift Wells argued in 1850 that visitors corrupted the Shaker youth. After buying goods at the Office store, visitors went sauntering in mixed company through the village, showing off their fine clothes and lustful behavior. Communities were having problems disciplining and holding on to young believers, and Wells feared these activities would encourage disobedience and departure for the World among them.[29]

Shakers who disapproved found a powerful means to attack these changes during "Mother's Work" in the late 1830s and early 1840s, a time of intense spiritualism. Shakers believed the manifestations of the period to be under the guidance of Ann Lee, the "Mother Ann" of their faith. Mother's Work has been interpreted as a revival of Shaker fervor and as a rebellion against hierarchical authorities. It was also a purification movement: an attempt to restore Shakerism to what the Shakers believed it had originally been. The spirit-possessed individuals laid down many new regulations for Shaker behavior, so much so that, to include them all, the leadership had to revise and expand the Millennial Laws in 1841, and again in 1845. Among those spiritual gifts were new regulations about the presence of outsiders in Shaker communities. One sacred writing, said to be from the spirit of Father Joseph Meacham, an early leader, criticized the Shakers for feeding visitors too elaborately, and called for no more "than eight or nine different kinds of food upon [the table] at once." The same writing specifically demanded an end to all visitors trampling through the village, and their confinement to restricted areas at the leadership's direction. As mentioned, the Shakers did close Sunday public meeting for a few years in the early 1840s. This may well have been to obey the spirits, not just to prevent ridicule from the visitors at the extravagant spiritualism of the period.[30]

These new rules demonstrated a split between Shakers willing to accommodate and even engage the World and those who wished to return to their religious and communal roots. Yet the new stringent rules in the Millennial Laws of 1845 were considerably pruned when revised in 1860. Certainly the restrictions on visitors apparently did not survive long past the end of Mother's Work, as Freegift Wells's remarks in 1850 indicate. The traditional Shakers lost ground to the progressives after Mother's Work was over, but the struggle between the two groups continued. After the Civil War, Elder Frederick Evans served as the Shakers' chief spokesman to the World, offering it the lessons of Shaker socialism. Others, such as Isaac Youngs and Elder Hervey Eads urged an inward turn to revive the old Shaker spirit of yore.[31]

The Romance (and Business) of Shaker Decline

The Shakers began a long, slow decline during the Civil War era. According to Federal census records, their peak population of 3,489 was in 1850, spread across eighteen villages. By 1900, it was 855 in fifteen villages. Historians have offered a number of reasons for this decline, blaming both internal and external causes. Millennialism fell out of favor in mainstream religion after 1844 with the failure of the Millerites' predictions. To some, the Shakers' claim that the millennium had already started in 1747 seemed equally absurd. Clara Endicott Sears, the first non-Shaker to create a Shaker museum, dismissed Shaker millennialism in that vein as primitive and old-fashioned when writing about the Shakers in 1916. Perhaps the collapse of eschatology's appeal is one reason why the Shakers were unable to capitalize on revivals after 1850 in any major way. The few new converts could not stem the gradual aging of the Society, which increasingly consisted of the elderly, particularly elderly women. The village economies also suffered. Some businesses failed because they could no longer compete with the farms of the west and factories of the east. Others ended because the Shakers no longer had sufficient able-bodied workers, particularly men. The seed, broom, and clothing businesses all declined after 1870. Archaeological evidence indicates that the Canterbury village, once one of the most industrialized communities, had ceased manufacturing anything but fancy goods by roughly 1900.[32]

Closely related to this decline was the World's development of a romantic interpretation of the Shakers. This romance redefined what Shakers were by how the World regarded them, rather than by what the Shakers themselves did and said. Benson John Lossing's 1857 article from *Harper's New Monthly Magazine* offers an early example. Lossing provided a picture of the Shakers as odd but successful farmers. His introduction set the Shakers apart in a pastoral environment, in explicit counterpoint to the busy urban America outside. Though Lossing described several Shaker industries at Mount Lebanon, they well fit a rural community: making up herbs, extracts, and seeds. The chair industry was not mentioned, though it was an important part of Mount Lebanon's economy.[33]

Lossing also minimized the Shakers' controversial differences with the World. In his view, the old antagonisms had died out. He treated their theology factually, without warmth or condemnation, as if it was indeed uncontroversial. If he still objected to a few particulars of their faith, such as celibacy, he described their worship sympathetically and praised the sincerity of their faith. By contrast, antebellum accounts had emphasized the Shakers' differences from other Americans in terms of theology and religious practice.

Lossing's contribution to a romantic Shaker image was to emphasize their distinctive lifestyle, making the Shakers out to be a pleasant, successful religious community, while downplaying the significance of religious differences. Lossing was fortunate that his main contact was Elder Frederick Evans, the leading advocate of closer relations between Shakers and the World. The internal controversies about how close the Shakers should be to the World, and the increasing demographic problems, played no role in his article. Lossing's account also signaled a shift in published assessments of the Shakers. Previous accounts had been written primarily by travelers, but increasingly, the Shakers would be profiled by reporters and professional writers.

William Dean Howells, the noted American author, composed several works about the Shakers that exemplified these changes in authorship and tone. Like so many cultured visitors before him, he summarized his visit to a Shaker village, Shirley, around 1876. Howells followed in Lossing's footsteps, describing the Shakers as simple, honest believers living in a bucolic setting, ignoring Shirley's Phoenix cotton factory as Lossing had ignored Mount Lebanon's chair factory. Like Lossing, he also described their theology simply and factually, while denouncing their practice of celibacy. By Howells's time, the decline in Shaker numbers was evident, giving his account a bit of poignant nostalgia. The Shakers were no longer what they once were, and those who remained were increasingly elderly women. Howells even tied the Shakers' decline to the perceived degeneration of the old Puritan stock of rural New England, a notion that had become popular among urban New England elites in this period. Thereby he asked his readers, no doubt other urbanites of old New England stock, to imagine the Shakers' fall as their own.[34]

Howells also published at least two novels in which Shakers and Shaker villages played an important role. He depicted the Shaker village as an Arcadian refuge from the world in *The Undiscovered Country*. Vardley, the fictional Shaker village of the novel (presumably based on Harvard, Massachusetts, and Shirley), was a refuge both in being a place to rest and recuperate, and a place one must eventually leave to go back into the world, as the young woman Egeria does to be married. The Shakers, by staying in their refuge, remain separate from the greater world. In *The Vacation of the Kelwyns*, written much later, Howells brought the Shaker refuge into the world, with dire results. The relationship between the Shakers and the World was commercialized when the Shakers rented out a vacant building in their village. The Shaker village was supposed to serve as a vacation refuge for the Kelwyns, but the commercial relationship, absent in *The Undiscovered Country*, put the Shakers, the Kelwyns, and the local help hired to serve the Kelwyns at odds with one another.[35]

Howells's work illustrates how much the interaction between Shakers and visitors was changing. The late nineteenth century featured a veritable explosion of tourism, as the rising middle class, especially office workers, secured regular paid vacations from their employers. But the Shakers could capitalize on this rise only in limited ways. They could no longer offer a spectacle. Fewer of the aging members could or would dance, so that Shaker tradition began to die out. Besides, dancing had become more respectable. Even the Sunday public meeting died out at the end of the nineteenth century. What the Shakers could offer was a retreat from the World. Experts of various kinds argued that "brain workers," whom today we would call white-collar workers, required regular rest and relief from their jobs. This the Shakers could offer. Indeed, in the years following the Civil War, two Shaker villages added taverns, by construction or purchase, just beyond their limits. There people of the World could come to stay, living leisurely in the World while having the Shaker village within walking distance. Howells, for one, did just that at Shirley. The Harvard Shaker village went so far as to rent out one North Family dwelling for the same purpose for a brief period. Some visitors, such as the historian and former Boston mayor Samuel A. Green, returned year after year, making friends with Shakers. Clearly the remaining members no longer maintained such a distance from visitors as they had done in antebellum times. Accounts from the late nineteenth century onward frequently refer to visitors being greeted by elderly female Shakers like old friends. The Shakers even allowed marriages to be celebrated on their property.[36]

Clara Endicott Sears took Howells's nostalgia for the Shaker past and reworked it into a myth of a Shaker golden age. Sears, a wealthy Boston Brahmin, moved out to Harvard to be close to the idealized New England past about which she wrote. She discovered the Shaker villages in Shirley and Harvard and became a frequent visitor to them in the years before they closed, in 1908 and 1918, respectively. In *Gleanings from Old Shaker Journals*, she reinterpreted Shaker history as a golden age leading to decline. The golden age was that of the founders and the antebellum Shakers up to 1840. More than two-thirds of her book covered that golden age, retelling the early days of the Shakers as legendary tales. Readers could thrill to accounts of early Shaker persecution in Harvard, or be amazed by the spiritual marvels of "Mother's Work," or even sigh to the poetry of the mysterious Leoline. Since those wonderful days, the Shakers had come to grief: their religious fervor had died down and their membership shrank to a few old women. Sears turned a sympathetic eye to this decline. Rather than write about it in detail, she used allusions to contemporary Shakers as a nostalgic framing device for defining the golden age. Like rural New England generally, the Shakers had had their era of greatness. Now all that was left, Sears wrote, were the quaint worshippers of a decaying faith, soon to follow Brook Farm and the Millerites into oblivion.[37]

Not every writer succumbed to lure of romanticism. Charles Nordhoff toured almost all the Shaker villages in the early 1870s as part of a larger project to assess the possibilities of communal living in the United States. Nordhoff celebrated the economic and social success of the Shakers, without romanticizing or ignoring their problems. His description of the settings of villages lacked Lossing's charm, consisting of discussions of acreage and buildings. Unlike Howells's fictional treatment, Nordhoff's reviews of Harvard and Shirley emphasized their character as working villages, covering past and present agricultural and manufacturing production in detail. Nordhoff wanted to understand how and why Shaker villages worked, as he thought communal living would help farmers and laborers with little capital. Romanticizing the Shakers would have defeated his purpose, which was not shared by Lossing, Howells, or Sears, who sought wealthy and genteel readers, uninterested in using the Shaker as a lesson in helping to elevate the laboring class.[38]

The romantic interpretation of the Shakers spread into newspaper and magazine accounts unevenly, depending on the style of magazine and the specific topics covered. *The New England Magazine*'s 1897 coverage of Union Village praised the Shakers with restraint, while noting that "the total extinction of the community will only be a question of time." Moreover, the article did not portray a Shaker village as any sort of refuge from the world. In contrast, the very next year the *Ladies' Home Journal* offered an article entitled, "A Wonderful Little World of People," which positively gushed over the Shakers. "Here are men and women, intelligent beyond the average, who have found a life of good works." This article stood controversies of the past on their heads. The

Shaker creed, far from being unusual, was "based on the simple precepts of Jesus." Celibate women did not pine for love, rather "the Shaker girls typify the poet's ideal of maidenhood." A picture showing Mount Lebanon sitting in the country complemented the text describing the Shaker village as "a palm tree and fountain in the desert." Perhaps one reason this article was such a glowing one was that the author, hiding behind a pseudonym, had a Shaker sister. It certainly celebrated in emotional language many features of Shaker life that had been condemned as deviant a century before.[39]

The mass-circulation magazines of the twentieth century often followed Sears's path by fixing on the contrast between a golden age and the contemporary decline. Articles in *Life* or *Yankee* offered a version of Shaker history emphasizing the legendary tales from the early years of the sect's history. However, photos would show a few elderly women, carrying on with chores and worship while quietly awaiting the end. It became routine to announce the imminent demise of the Shakers, so much so that many people today believe they have died out. *Life*'s 1949 article was more negative than most, ending with a stark picture of the Shaker monument in the Canterbury cemetery. By the middle of the twentieth century, the golden age myths of a Boston Brahmin had become mass-media truisms.[40]

Meanwhile, Americans' increasing interest in their history and cultural identity, symbolized by the Philadelphia Exposition of 1876, created an interest in antiques and fine handmade goods. Among elites, this interest was part of a broader rejection of machine-made products and a desire to find authenticity in artifacts. For the Shakers, it was a fortuitous turn. The rising interest in fine handcrafts meshed both with the loss of many of their old industries and with the increasing percentage of their members who were elderly women. Toward the end of the nineteenth century, Shakers began to emphasize production of fancy goods and foodstuffs, items that would appeal to the tourists visiting their villages. In an exception to the general decline in clothing manufacture, the stylish Dorothy cloak became a famous Shaker product during this period. The Shakers also adapted more to the World's tastes by making goods more in the World's styles. Chairs developed Victorian flourishes. Boxes sported ribbons. The Shakers added such items as dolls to their goods for sale. The Shaker store began to look like a modern museum gift shop; indeed, Hancock's store was called a "gift shoppe" in the early twentieth century (Figure 4.2). If a box or doll was sold by a quaint woman dressed Shaker-style, all the better. Shaker women went out into the World by the 1890s to sell their fancy work, an activity that would have been hardly imaginable under the 1821 Millennial Laws.[41]

Figure 4.2. Hancock fancy goods gift shoppe, from the Collection of Hancock Shaker Village.

With greater economic dependency came a further breaking down of barriers between Shakers and visitors. In antebellum times, visitors staying at the Office had had to abide by Shaker regulations, most notably the separation of men and women. As mentioned above, two villages acquired taverns just beyond their village limits in the years shortly after the Civil War, where guests could stay as if in the World, as they indeed were. Now Shakers went out into the World, too. At the Sabbathday Lake, Maine, village Shaker women went over to the Poland Spring Hotel to sell their wares from the 1890s through 1920, as a perfectly natural thing to do. Complaints about the World intruding too much still existed; William Dean Howells mentioned in 1876 that some Shakers still did not like tourists wandering through the village as if it were public property. Yet by and large those willing to accommodate and go out into the World except in matters of faith predominated among the Shakers. Shakers even began vacationing in the World, visiting such well-known spots as Lake Winnepesaukee in New Hampshire.[42]

The Shakers' reaction to their increased economic dependency on tourists—and on collectors, as we shall see—is hard to gauge, because it was related to so many other issues they faced in this period. Even a fervent advocate of engagement with the World such as Elder Frederick

Evans could worry about getting too close. As early as the 1870s, he regretted measures that made the Shakers economically reliant on the World, such as buying clothing rather than making it. More traditional members felt all the different capitalist relations the Shakers had entered into were the cause of their decline, a view shared by some of the romantic outsiders such as Sears. Yet their demographic and economic situation was otherwise so dire, with membership dropping and the old businesses failing. At least one village, Pleasant Hill, Kentucky, decided to stop taking in unproductive members in 1900, for fear their community would collapse otherwise. Even so, Pleasant Hill closed and was sold in 1910. Still, traditionalists might well have envied those Shaker villages that could capitalize on the tourist trade. Those Shakers who did engage with tourism seem to have done so whole-heartedly, if the Sabbathday Lake Shakers are representative. They established a special relationship with the local Ricker family and their Poland Spring House that endured for many decades. Of course, changes in the tourist business could cut against a Shaker village as well; Mount Lebanon suffered from the decline of Lebanon Springs as a resort in the late nineteenth century.[43]

In some respects, the twentieth-century romantic interpretation of Shaker history and life was accurate: the Shakers were not what they once were. But the romantic interpretation departed from reality on two points. First, it treated the golden age of the Shakers as a legendary heroic time, without considering how social and economic forces had shaped the Shakers then, as at the present. Shaker history became discontinuous. Second, it treated the golden age as the norm, as the way Shaker life properly was. This view may have been excusable in Howells's day, when the decline had only been evident for a few decades. By the time of the 1949 *Life* article, however, the Shakers had been in decline far longer than they had prospered in their villages. By continually referring to the present-day Shakers as a remnant, the romantic interpretation indicated a preference for viewing Shakers in idealized rather than historical terms.

Shaker Goods Acquire Shaker Virtues

Early purchasers of Shaker goods bought them for their quality. The Shakers successfully pioneered the sale of packaged seeds by guaranteeing their freshness; their traders recalled unsold packets at the end of each year. Likewise, Shaker medications set a standard of quality for the patent medicine industry, due to the care members took in preparing them consistently. The Shakers certainly realized the value of this reputation for quality. They used visual markings to identify their products as authentic, to protect them against fraudulent competition, and to successfully realize the higher prices their quality could command. This included distinctive packaging for their seeds and medicines even in antebellum decades, and trademarks for their chairs in Victorian times.[44]

Before 1900, Shaker goods began to acquire nontangible values because they were handmade. The rise of cheap machine-made goods provoked a reaction in American culture. The arts and crafts movement, originally British in origin, linked the quality of the worker to the quality of the object produced. It spread to the United States in the wake of the Centennial Exhibition, where British examples and Shaker furniture stood out compared to the machine-made furniture there. Owning handcrafted products soon implied that one had the good taste and judgment to appreciate how the craftsman expressed his values in his work. It also meant that one had the extra disposable income to pay higher prices for handmade goods. Thereby handcrafts became evidence of what Thorstein Veblen called "conspicuous consumption." People with income and leisure began to prefer such objects, including antiques.[45]

The Shaker maxim, "Hands to work, hearts to God," fit nicely with the ideology of the arts and crafts movement. By its logic, Shaker goods must embody and express their makers' strong religious beliefs and character. Not surprisingly, Shaker furniture influenced the work of some members of the arts and crafts movement in the period from 1890 to 1910, such as Gustav Stickley and Ernest Gimson.[46]

The Shakers' fate assisted in this transfer of Shaker qualities from people to goods. Shaker membership declined throughout the twentieth century, from 855 in 1900, to fewer than 10 by 1992, which caused villages to close. Tyringham, Massachusetts, founded during the gathering at the end of the eighteenth century, emptied as early as 1875. The Shakers sold twelve more villages between 1889 and 1938. Mount Lebanon, the Shakers' headquarters, closed in 1947, leaving only three remaining villages. Visiting Shakers became a less likely activity because there were simply fewer of them in fewer places. Conversely, the closing of villages meant that more Shaker furniture and antiques entered the market, sometimes, as at South Union and Shirley, sold off in massive auctions.[47]

Shaker goods became souvenirs. One way to look at souvenirs is as articles that remind one of experiences that are no longer present, because they have become remote in either time or space. A souvenir is equivalent to a material memory: both souvenirs and memories recall and connect to a past experience; vacation photographs, for example, serve the same function. Now, anything bought at a Shaker village *could* have been a souvenir. But in the early days, this normally would have been unimportant. Visitors from the World did not see Shaker goods as distinctive, even though they were well made. There was little reason in antebellum times to memorialize the Shakers: they were both disturbing and easy to visit. However, once cultured people like Howells and Sears romanticized the Shakers, an object they produced could easily become a souvenir for people who accepted that romanticization. It could represent an image as well as could the actual Shakers, perhaps even better, because of the difference between the charming Shaker image, rooted in the past, and the sad Shaker reality of the present. The ideology of the arts and crafts movement assisted in turning goods into souvenirs by providing a rationale for the attribution of Shaker qualities to Shaker goods. With the decline of the Shakers, it became easier to find Shaker goods than to meet actual Shakers. A Shaker object became something one could display to indicate a connection to those rare folks.

Valuing Shaker goods as souvenirs was related to the first wave of Shaker object collectors at the beginning of the twentieth century. If a souvenir is a material representation of a visit, collectables such as Shaker furniture can be thought of as souvenirs from visits that never occurred, but that someone wished for. Wallace Cathcart's interest in Shakers began when he heard about North Union, Ohio, a Shaker village that had already been bulldozed to make way for a suburban development called Shaker Heights, outside Cleveland. Cathcart became one of the early twentieth century's great collectors of Shaker documents, amassing the core of the Western Reserve Historical Society's unsurpassed collection.[48]

Other people with connections to the Shakers, or Shakers themselves, also realized that the Shakers were disappearing, and tried to memorialize them through their history and their objects. John Patterson MacLean, another Ohioan at the Western Reserve Historical Society, wrote articles and books between 1900 and 1907 on the Ohio Shakers' history. In the waning days of the Shirley community, Eldress Josephine Jilson used a spare shed at Shirley, and then the Square House at Harvard, to set up what may have been the first Shaker museum, but it did not survive Harvard's 1918 closing. Clara Endicott Sears set up the earliest Shaker museum that endured until 1920; she had published her history of the Shakers four years before. Significantly, she acquired the Shaker building and the goods to fill it as the Shirley and Harvard Shaker villages closed. Some items she got from Eldress Josephine Jilson, trying to save for posterity what she could.[49]

Despite this activity, few people visited Shakers before World War II. In general, tourism was on the increase: the availability of cheap automobiles in the 1920s and the extension of paid vacations in the 1930s meant that many working Americans could travel great distances for leisure. Yet they saw few reasons to visit a Shaker village. Nothing there was terribly interesting to see, for Shakers looked more and more just like the World's people. Neighbors came to buy goods; as a child, cybernetic-ist Norbert Weiner used to purchase peppermints from the Shaker store in Harvard. Otherwise no reason existed to see the Shakers unless one was attracted by the romantic image. Judging from reportedly declining visitation, the romantic image remained confined to elites. Few workers evidently shared Clara Endicott Sears's view of the Shakers, for her historical novels sold poorly.[50]

Similarly, Shaker furniture became a popular collectible only gradually. The Shackletons, writers on furniture collecting for the popular press, mentioned having Shaker furniture in 1906, but it was a minor part of their "colonial" furniture collecting. William Dean Howells did not suggest that Shaker products were distinctive and valuable until *The Vacation of the Kelwyns*, published in 1920. In keeping with the ironic tone of that novel, the genteel Mrs. Kelwyn hoped to find their vacation property furnished with old-fashioned Shaker handicrafts, only to discover that the Shakers had filled it with contemporary furnishings from the World to make the Kelwyns happy. Wallace Nutting's enormous *Furniture Treasury* (1928–33), one of the largest antique furniture catalogues published in that period, has no mention of "Shaker" in its index, despite the fact that, like Sears, Nutting romanticized old New England. Many other books on furniture collecting ignored Shaker furniture, or gave it a cursory mention, as late as 1940. Yet that would change with the work of Edward Deming Andrews.[51]

Andrews well represents the modern transformations of Shaker identity. According to his own account, he first became interested in the Shakers in 1923 when he stopped to buy a loaf of bread from them. His initial relationship with them was a commercial transaction. Already antique dealers and collectors, Andrews and his wife began to gather Shaker artifacts, often buying them directly from the Shakers themselves. Andrews mounted his first public exhibitions of Shaker products in 1932. In his exhibitions and writings on Shaker goods, Andrews combined the romantic image of a Shaker golden age with the ascription of personal qualities to these handmade objects. The title of one of his books sums up his approach: *Religion in Wood*. He interpreted Shaker objects in terms of Shaker values: Shakers were simple, spiritual people; therefore Shaker chairs were simple, spiritual objects. By the end of his career, he had inspired many others to take the same approach. In his introduction to *Religion in Wood*, Thomas Merton wrote, "Indeed, one is tempted to say that [Shaker furniture form] is a better, clearer, more comprehensible expression of their faith than their written theology was."[52]

Andrews also recast Shaker history in the romantic image. *The People Called Shakers*, published in 1953, was a genuine work of historical scholarship, but it was heavily shaped by his own interpretation. Andrews structured his book in line with the golden age myth. Ten of the eleven chapters covered either the founding of Shakerism or its "normal" antebellum state. Only one chapter treated the century-long decline. Thereby, Andrews constructed a heroic image of the Shakers' early history by taking their own accounts at face value, much as Sears had done decades before. He added a holistic perspective to the golden age by explicitly treating all facets of Shaker life as closely interrelated: "Before the Civil War eighteen prosperous colonies proclaimed the vitality of a unique system of thought and life."[53]

Andrews was very effective in shaping Americans' perceptions of the Shakers and Shaker goods, and his history is still in print today. Its initial publication stimulated a great wave of interest in the Shakers. Mount Lebanon Shaker Village's closing had almost gone unnoticed in 1947, six years before *The People*'s release. By 1960, two groups were buying Shaker villages to make them over into museums, and others would soon follow. Granted, Andrews was not the only one popularizing the Shakers; the photographs of Charles Sheeler and the music of Aaron Copland, among the works of many others, contributed to this popularization. Yet it was quite fitting that the curator of the first Shaker museum village to open was Edward Deming Andrews.[54]

The Shakers' tourist trade, which had been declining through the early twentieth century, now revived. The major Shaker museums began receiving tens of thousands of visitors each by 1970. Air travel and the development of the interstate highway system, combined with the extension of paid vacations to most Americans during the century, made Shaker village museums accessible even to workers of modest means. Today, many schools take their students to Shaker villages as part of their education in American history.

Published accounts of the Shakers' reaction to these developments convey mixed feelings. On one hand, the Shakers have fought against what they perceive as misrepresentations of their faith, or making it a thing of show. They have protested attempts to restage their dances as professional theater. Nor do they want to be remembered as chairs. On the other hand, the Shakers owed a good deal of their fame and tourist trade to the reputation of their goods, and they cooperated with some of the early collectors. Their involvement with the tourist trade continued in the twentieth century. However, not all Shakers have been happy with tourism and its commercialization, and the remaining Shaker village places close limits on where and how many tourists can visit Sabbathday Lake. Yet without reenactments, which have declined at the museum villages, the only way most tourists and collectors can connect to the Shakers is through objects and books they acquire through commercial relations. Shaker things are far easier to reach than Shaker people.[55]

Conclusion

The meaning of the term "Shaker" has changed as Americans' perception of what was important about Shakers changed. Shaker religion and dancing, Shaker rustics, and Shaker furniture: each image supplanted the one before, without ever quite eradicating the earlier images. These changes were also closely connected with Shaker history. For example, had not the closing of so many Shaker villages led to the release of so many Shaker goods, Shaker furniture collecting would be a much different business today.

At present, the major museum villages help foster the romantic Shaker image, although the museum staffs know their limitations. Site interpreters offer a history that still in the main follows the lines set down by Sears and Andrews, a story of legendary beginnings and a long, slow decline. This version is what the public wants to hear, and it makes for a good story. Because the Shakers tore down many buildings as they lost members, the museum villages are only a fraction of the size of the Shaker villages at their height. Their attractive country settings give them a restful appearance. Lossing, back in 1857, found them a refuge from urban America; no doubt many tourists still do. A visitor to the Canterbury museum village today can stand at the edge of a chain of ponds and look up the hill at a small, quaint, peaceful village (Figure 4.3). The visitor is unlikely to be reminded that the ponds were actually formed to power mills that have long since disappeared, as have the Shakers themselves.[56]

The idea that Shaker goods have Shaker qualities has become a commonplace; it can be found in most books about Shaker furniture. Few expressed it as elegantly as Thomas Merton when he observed, "The peculiar grace of a Shaker chair is due to the fact that it was made by someone capable of believing that an angel might come and sit on it." The mystique can even be extended beyond Shaker goods, as the Shaker song "Simple Gifts" was at one time used to sell automobiles.[57]

Romanticizing the Shakers and attributing Shaker virtues to Shaker objects has been unfolding over about 150 years. In my view, the process speaks to a deep need among some Americans to find a past that can help them cope with the present. Howells offered Arcadia; Sears a lost golden age; Andrews an idealistic society. The question that remains as to whether people are inspired enough by Shaker history and objects to

Figure 4.3. Canterbury Shaker Village from the artificial ponds, from the author's personal collection.

incorporate their attributes into their own lives, or whether having an object representing "faith" or "simplicity" just pays lip service to those values. If the former, then the Shakers can take satisfaction in knowing that the goods they made extend their values, as understood by the World, to those who now own them.

Chapter 5

"I Would Much Rather See a Sermon than Hear One"
Experiencing Faith at Silver Dollar City

AARON K. KETCHELL

Since its inception in 1960, the Silver Dollar City theme park in Branson, Missouri, has offered patrons a sometimes anachronistic fusion of the Missouri frontier, preindustrial craftsmanship, and simple faith. In a 2003 interview, Pete Herschend, co-owner and vice chairman of the Herschend Family Entertainment Corporation (Silver Dollar City's parent body), discussed the ways his attraction seeks to inculcate visitors with a sense of Christian ethics and values. Vocalizing the experiential nature of his park's piety, he declared, "I would much rather see a sermon than hear one." This statement keenly speaks to the visual and pragmatic character of a site that currently draws more than two million guests per year to its presentation of late nineteenth-century Ozark culture, purportedly timeless "family values," and unique rendering of religiosity. Silver Dollar City has continuously appended thrill rides and artisan demonstrations, but even such seemingly secular updates are designed to satisfy the values of their producers and consumers, and thus subtly support more overt exhibitions of Christianity.[1]

For more than forty years Silver Dollar City has been the leading tourist destination in Branson, Missouri. Branson began attracting vacationers as early as the 1910s, with most coming to visit sites made famous in Harold Bell Wright's place-defining novel, *The Shepherd of the Hills*, or to venture into the cave that now lies below the theme park. When it opened in 1960, Silver Dollar City was joined by two other important tourist offerings that debuted that year. Only a few miles down the road, the Shepherd of the Hills Farm began a nightly enactment of Wright's novel that has welcomed as many as 250,000 guests annually and has often ranked as the number-one outdoor drama in the country. In addition, Table Rock Lake, also adjacent to Silver Dollar City, was created by the Army Corps of Engineers and provided access to nearly one thousand miles of shoreline for recreational activities.[2]

In the 1960s and 1970s, Branson was primarily a regional destination for families looking to partake of water sports, outdoor drama, "hillbilly" musical acts, and the various offerings at Silver Dollar City. By 1980 it was drawing perhaps two million visitors per year principally from the Midwest and mid-South. The town began to gain national recognition, however, in 1983 when country legend Roy Clark opened a variety show theater on Highway 76—the "Branson Strip." Other stars of the genre such as Boxcar Willie and Mickey Gilley soon followed suit, and by 1989 more than twenty theaters lined the Strip and attracted a total of nearly four million patrons.

All observers of Branson's tourism history mark 1991–94 as the city's "boom years." During that period, the number of lodging rooms and restaurant seats both increased by nearly ten thousand, the number of indoor theater seats swelled from 22,788 to 50,065, and construction values skyrocketed from roughly $20 million to nearly $140 million. In 1994, 5.8 million guests came to the area to participate in a host of entertainment offerings and were welcomed by a number of new stars, including Andy Williams, Tony Orlando, the Osmonds, Kenny Rogers, and Wayne Newton. Through a variety of attractions that blended nostalgic retellings of a premodern American culture and an unwavering, popularly arbitrated devotion to Christian theology and precepts, a city of less than four thousand residents had become a national phenomenon.[3]

In 2004, Branson hosted an estimated 7.3 million visitors. The senior market, fueled by a cadre of aging country and pop stars, was a vital component of area tourism. Roughly 35 percent of guests that year were over sixty-five, with the average tourist being fifty-seven years of age. However, families constituted 20 percent of vacationers, drawn not necessarily for theater entertainment but instead for a wealth of go-carts, miniature golf, boating, and theme park entertainment. During a typical summer season, which amounts to half of overall visitation, four-fifths of all Silver Dollar City guests arrive with children. Once exclusively a regional draw, Branson now has a national tourist base. In 2004, nearly 50 percent of all visitors came from outside a three-hundred-mile radius. Although Silver Dollar City does not allow the public access to its demographic data, it can be safely assumed that its millions of annual patrons diverge somewhat from the local market by attracting more families than seniors. Still Branson's main attraction, its myriad craft displays and musical acts do appeal to older individuals. However, the park's core constituency remains parents and children—an emphasis constantly invoked through the use of nondistinct "family values" rhetoric to promote the site and its similarly nebulous religious product.[4]

Not all contemporary visitors to Silver Dollar City arrive expecting to be blatantly inculcated with Christian values. In 2005, a $43.65 single-day adult admission offered access to many ostensibly worldly offerings. There were five yearly festivals ranging from World-Fest in the spring to Old Time Christmas in the winter; twenty attractions and rides, including some of the nation's best roller coasters; sixty specialty shops and hundreds of craftsmen; forty musical shows per day; and a host of dining opportunities. However, according to Pete Herschend, these attractions were built upon a supernatural foundation—one that is encountered on different levels by different patrons. As he stated, "Sometimes people will never know why they feel good about this place. There are people who are Christians who spot it rather readily in the feeling of the park—you do not hear swearing, or the Lord's name taken in vain. People who are not Christian say this place has a special feeling. People often write back and say this is where they met the Lord." An investigation into the popular brand of Christianity offered at the site requires an unearthing of the various ways that this imprecise sense of faith is conveyed through the theme-park medium. As tourist S. T. Lambert commented by paraphrasing an interpretation of enigmatic parables offered in Matthew 13:16, Silver Dollar City's devotional aspects are available to all who have "eyes to see and ears to hear."[5]

Silver Dollar City was built atop Marvel Cave, a site that for nearly one hundred years welcomed visitors who regularly observed an indefinite yet palatable godly presence within a subterranean world. When the theme park was constructed above the fissure, its founders envisioned an attraction that approached guests with the Golden Rule—"In everything do to others as you would have them do to you" (Matthew 7:12)—as a guide and honored divine creation through the stewardship of nature. Employee guidelines since the 1980s have codified these initial dictates by compelling staff members to handle their work in a fashion that is consistent with Christian values. Missionary sentiments, while present, have intentionally merged with the site's thematic attempts to create a seamless presentation of religion and recreation. Sometimes one must even look to more explicitly sectarian organizations and initiatives associated with Silver Dollar City to realize how thoroughly it has been linked with proselytizing impulses.

Ever-growing attendance and revenues indicate that this melding of faith and frivolity has been a successful strategy. The Herschend family took ownership of Marvel Cave in 1950 by investing $7,000. That summer they welcomed 8,000 guests for tours. By 1959, 65,000 vacationers visited the site, generating $200,000 in revenues. The company opened Silver Dollar City one year later and, with only a dozen employees, served 125,000 visitors. By 1966, nearly 500,000 people visited the park, and it brought in $3 million in revenues. In 1967, several episodes of *The Beverly Hillbillies*, who purportedly hailed from Silver Dollar City, were filmed on site. This notoriety produced the park's greatest one-year increase in visitation and inspired a national interest. By the early 1970s, more than one million guests visited. By 1977, "the City" welcomed 1,500,000 patrons and employed more than one thousand individuals. In the early 1990s, revenue totals approached $40 million, and by the end of that decade attendance surpassed the two-million tourist mark with approximately 2,500 full-time and seasonal staff working on site.[6]

Silver Dollar City's success allowed its proprietors to add additional sites to their tourism holdings. As of 2005, the Herschend Family Entertainment Corporation owned and operated Celebration City in Branson, a theme park that nostalgically remembers various "golden eras" of twentieth-century American history; Dollywood in Pigeon Forge, Tennessee; a southern-themed attraction within Stone Mountain State Park in Georgia; a showboat on Table Rock Lake; an additional Ozark cave; various water parks; and a shopping center. Although Silver Dollar City is the best illustration of the company's relationship with popular Christianity, each site has tried to integrate Christian values into leisure activities. All these attractions generated well over $100 million in 2005, collectively earning brothers Pete and Jack Herschend a spot in the Theme Park Industry Hall of Fame in 2004.[7]

The foundation of Silver Dollar City arose hundreds of millions of years ago and grew out of the region's unique geology. The area surrounding Branson, Missouri, can be categorized as a karst landscape, one in which the underlying limestone has been partially dissolved by ground water. Throughout time, rain moving in cracks and crevices has caused large amounts of rock to soften and created nearly seven thousand Ozark caverns. In *Sacred Places*, a work that explores the relationship between nineteenth-century American tourism and religious sentiment, historian John Sears described how natural attractions such as Mammoth Cave in Kentucky possessed the ability to inspire a sense of sublimity. In his assessment, vacationers considered the site to be a type of "axis mundi" (or meeting point between heaven, earth, and hell) and so bestowed upon it a variety of ritualistic meanings. A 1992 promotional video for Silver Dollar City described the origins of their cave and park in a fashion that resonated with ideas of sublime transcendence: "The story begins with the Creator. It was he who fashioned a land of calm that would attract those of adventure, retain people of enterprise, and spawn fruits of vision." Though associations between Branson area caves and the divine would remain indistinct for the first half of the twentieth century, Silver Dollar City is underscored both figuratively and

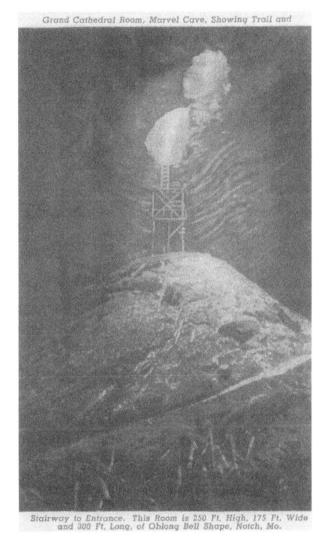

Figure 5.1. Cathedral Room, Marvel Cave, about 1950. Postcard from the author's collection.

literally by a fissure entrenched in numinous rhetoric since its discovery (Figure 5.1).[8]

The formation now known as Marvel Cave was originally dubbed Devil's Den by Osage Indians who inhabited the Ozarks prior to the Louisiana Purchase and demarcated both the physical and mystical dangers of the site with V-notches cut in nearby trees. Frequently compared to Mammoth Cave by early explorers and visitors, Marvel's Cathedral Room is the largest cave entrance in the United States and its passages and chambers have never been challenged as the grandest of Ozark natural wonders. Still, the first arrivals to Missouri caves came in search of mineral deposits rather than spiritual insights. In 1869, a St. Louis speculator bought the property from railroad interests hoping to discover lead. Finding no minerals, Henry T. Blow did mistakenly believe that much of the cavern was lined with marble and thus re-titled his property Marble Cave. Blow's interest in the cave quickly waned and he abandoned his undertaking within the year. Evidence suggests that the cavern then remained undisturbed for thirteen years, except for occasional visits by vigilantes who purportedly used its opening as a repository for murdered bodies. Knowing this and that the cave was populated by thousands of bats, locals avoided the grotto because, in the words of long-time guide Ronald L. Martin, they were convinced that "the Almighty had not intended man to enter."[9]

In the 1870s Marble Cave changed ownership a number of times, and in 1884 it was acquired by T. Hodge Jones of Lamar, Missouri. Jones and members of his fraternal organization, the Lamar City Guards, formed a mining company in hopes of extracting bat guano—a natural fertilizer and important ingredient in gun powder—that then sold for $700 per ton and could be found twenty-five feet deep in many portions of the cave. In 1884, the Marble Cave Manufacturing and Mining Company developed a small town at the mouth of their holding and investors hoped to further their profits by capitalizing upon a late nineteenth-century boom in tourist spas and health resorts through exploiting the "healing waters" available at their site.[10]

In the first published piece to detail the cave's formations, stockholder Capt. J. B. Emery described its surroundings in 1885 as "a bracing, invigorating atmosphere" of "springs of pure water, and medicinal springs, chalybeate, sulphur, etc." Water cure, or hydropathy, was popular at the time and individuals throughout the United States sought healing baths and springs as treatments for a wide range of ailments. Moreover, individuals such as Phineas P. Quimby, a celebrated mid-nineteenth-century mental healer, promoted the eradication of physical ailments through the cultivation of healthy attitudes rather than topical remedies. A great influence upon those who championed ideas of faith-oriented treatments such as Mary Baker Eddy (founder of Christian Science) and Julius A. Dresser (a leader in the New Thought movement), Quimby joined promoters of homeopathy in acknowledging the power of suggestion and the workings of nature as viable means for encouraging wellness.[11]

The best-known healing waters in the nineteenth-century Ozarks were at Eureka Springs, Arkansas, a town one hour south of Branson. When incorporated in 1879, Eureka Springs had a population of only four hundred clustered around more than sixty local springs. After a series of accounts claimed that consumption of the city's water could cure ailments as diverse as hay fever, insomnia, and paralysis, however, the population grew to an estimated fifteen thousand residents by April 1880. Shortly thereafter, Eureka Springs' water was bottled and shipped nationally and investors constructed the elegant, Gothic-styled Crescent Hotel to house a massive influx of visitors. Closer to Branson, Panacea Springs in Cassville, Missouri, and Eau de Vie and Reno Springs in Christian County also flourished briefly as summer resorts in the 1880s by promising natural treatments for rheumatism, kidney disease, dyspepsia, and bowel troubles.[12]

The Marble Cave Manufacturing and Mining Company intended to draw upon these regional success stories for its own resort community. Initial plans called for a housing development and a number of parks, but by the mid-1880s the only businesses were an ordinary general store, a one-room school (predominately used to train aspiring cave guides), a blacksmith shop, and a saw mill. With their dream gone, the company dissolved itself in 1889 and sold the property to Arthur J. Lynch, a businessman from Jackson County, Missouri. A month later, Arthur sold Marble Cave to his brother, William Henry Lynch. Lynch, a Canadian miner, dairyman, and amateur archaeologist, bought the property primarily as a place to hunt for prehistoric animal bones. After five years of futile searching, he, along with daughters Miriam (an opera singer) and Genevieve (a nurse and poet) decided to develop the site as an Ozark attraction.[13]

The Lynch family allowed tourists access to the cave via wooden ladders that descended two hundred feet into the Cathedral Room, a huge chamber two hundred feet high, four hundred feet long and two hundred and twenty-five feet wide. Though their attraction possessed many breathtaking qualities, transportation was problematic at the turn of the century. For instance, in a recollection by Miles H. Scott, the author described a harrowing fifty-mile journey from Marrionville, Missouri, to the cave that took his party over some of the "roughest hilly roads" in the state. His 1922 visit was undertaken with twenty others who traveled to the Branson area in the flat bed of a Model T truck. Along the way, multiple stops were made to refill the radiator, patch tires, and push the vehicle up steep hills. Upon arrival the group was outfitted with coveralls, equipped with candles, and led down a steep slope via "rickety ladders and wooden steps." Despite the dampness, mud, narrow passages, and "long strenuous climb" to the surface, Scott concluded his narrative by invoking the "awe and admiration" felt by the tourists amidst "the beauties of the magnificent works of nature beheld." Considering the travails necessary to both arrive at and tour the cave, it is not surprising that the Lynches were lucky to welcome ten or twenty visitors per day during the summer months.[14]

Over time, Henry Lynch took steps to make the cave more accessible and urbane. In the 1920s, he and nine-year-old Lester Vining blazed a winding trail with a gas-powered saw that would eventually become the Branson Strip. He was also a primary lobbyist for the rail line that reached the town in 1906. At the cave itself, he replaced wooden ladders with scaffolding, constructed gracious cabins, built an auditorium inside the Cathedral Room (said to be able to seat 10,000 spectators), and equipped this subterranean theater with a grand piano so Miriam could showcase her operatic talents for guests. Through such an incongruous merger of leisure opportunities, boosters attempted to imbue a vacation in the wilderness with the sophistication of Victorian culture and thereby offer an image of a rustic past nevertheless replete with modern comforts. After traversing rocky hills, dressing in coveralls, and plunging two hundred feet on treacherous steps, guests could then relax in temperature-controlled surroundings and partake of arias from a classically trained singer.[15]

By the 1920s, the Lynches' cave had become a heralded Branson-area tourist draw. Visitors increasingly proclaimed the other-worldly qualities—both terrifying and astonishing—of the site, which had aptly changed its name to Marvel Cave in 1913. An account from that period detailed vacationers' concerns over "hobgoblin perils" that gripped "the soul with a dread that precludes passage into the unventured beyond." Another guest recalled that her tour in 1920 produced "the kind of feeling that one might experience upon a visit to another planet." Scientists joined tourists in extolling the cave's ability to produce of a sense of "mysterium tremendum." In 1893, representatives from Missouri's World's Fair Commission and researchers from the state geological survey declared the cave a "new wonder of the world." G. Kingsley Noble, a curator at the American Museum of Natural History, recorded his experiences in an article for *Scientific American*. Though primarily interested in the cavern's blind salamander, Noble nevertheless was "spellbound" by the "inky blackness and perpetual coldness" he found. Visitors thus departed with emotional imprints, not at all dissimilar from those available at more traditional grottos, cathedrals, and sacred spaces.[16]

Little evidence suggests that the scholastic and scientifically minded Lynch ever envisioned his holding as a location where tourists could encounter the divine or the sublime. When he died in 1927, however, the property came under the ownership of his daughters and the mood changed. These women began to employ their training in the arts and humanities to vest the cavern with spirituality and sentiment. For the next twenty-two years, the "Misses Lynch" worked to cloak their attraction in transcendent language that allied the cave with other piously grounded Ozark destinations.[17]

Miriam and Genevieve Lynch sought to merge the refined and luxurious elements of early twentieth-century America with the bucolic quaintness of the "frozen-in-time" Ozark hills. In an account offered by visitors from Chicago, Genevieve is described as a stylish proprietor clad in "tight fitting jodhpurs, a tight little woolen bodice, and a colorful scarf bound round her head." Miriam, in contrast, is depicted "as picturesque as a character doll." During this visit, the guest was not only awed by the cave, but also amazed by the property's hundreds of flowers and the Misses Lynch's knowledge of botany. After only a few short paragraphs devoted to cavern exploration, this missive instead focuses upon the owners' impeccable decorum, a post-cave meal of chicken and asparagus served on rare English china, and a cache of items from Rose O'Neill—local creator of the Kewpie Doll—displayed with reverence and "devotion" in a large glass case. This report suggests that Miriam and Genevieve sought not only to valorize Marvel Cave's attributes, but also to showcase a variant of progressive culture. By augmenting their attraction with a tea room, an antique shop, and a spacious lodge, the sisters celebrated and sanctified a vision of overly sentimental modernity within a locale supposedly immune to modern change.[18]

Marvel Cave's popularity grew in part because of the writings of Harold Bell Wright. Wright's novel *The Shepherd of the Hills*, which is said to have been outsold only by the Bible in the early decades of the twentieth century, tells the story of a messianic city-dweller—the Shepherd—who travels to an isolated Ozark mountain village populated by simple country folk. Prior to his arrival the community is in turmoil, with residents plagued by unreconciled familial misfortunes, a sense of malaise in relation to the ever-encroaching elements of modernity, and an overall perception that traditional ethics and practices were rapidly waning. After moving onto a piece of land purportedly haunted by a malevolent spirit and proving to his superstitious neighbors that moral purity triumphs over even the nastiest demons, the Shepherd systematically heals all the ills of the Mutton Hollow residents. Throughout his work, Wright valorized both the physically and spiritually curative qualities of the Ozark hills, praised the simple yet virtuous character of their residents, and legitimated the promotion of Christian principles in a variety of forms and lived contexts. Glorifying the inherent holiness of Branson and its environs, the book's protagonist stated, "There is not only food and medicine for one's body; there is also healing for the heart and strength for the soul in nature. One gets very close to God . . . in these temples of God's own building." Numerous visitors to Marvel Cave echoed Wright's sentiments in the early decades of the twentieth century.[19]

Guests did so, in part, because shortly after the publication of *The Shepherd of the Hills*, a local industry emerged to provide tourists with access to the sites and people described in the novel. Most heralded was Old Matt's Cabin—the central focus of the work, home of its main characters, and locale where Wright actually penned a portion of the book while vacationing in the Ozarks at the turn of the twentieth century. The author often toured Marble Cave while sojourning at this homestead. By 1904, the proprietors had even named his favorite grotto the "Harold Bell Wright Passage." Because of his frequent visits, local lore began to hold that the cave was the model for the one mentioned in *The Shepherd of the Hills*. By the 1930s, its ties to the book had been cemented as promotional brochures subcaptioned it, "The Famous Shepherd of the Hills Cave," and advertised cabins at the Marvel Cave Lodge named after Wright's characters. The site's operators thus joined all attractions and personages of early Branson tourism history in implicating themselves in the production of regional folklore—or "fakelore"—to entrench their cavern within a master narrative that sanctified Ozark people and places.[20]

In a tourist pamphlet from the 1930s, Miriam and Genevieve Lynch wrote that visitors to their cave would encounter a "veritable doorway to adventure, recapture youth, and in the almost endless welter of common things behold a star-like vision of sublimity." Here, familiar Branson area promises of untamed nature, recaptured virility, escape from urban drudgery, and encounter with spiritual forces all merged around this subterranean attraction. When tourists guided by the sisters dipped tin cups into a natural spring christened the "Fountain of Youth," they may have reckoned the experience as merely fanciful participation in a time-tested legend of American exploration. However, Marvel Cave's advertising and reminiscences by visitors suggest that interpreting the cave through a religiously based lens was possible and often probable for guests. Though no explicitly Christian themes found their way into early promotional materials, the Misses Lynch certainly couched their attraction in general pious language and symbolism that pointed to a godly presence. For example, in a poem that memorialized the cave's Cathedral Room, Genevieve wrote: "Here, something lingers, subtle, fine, / Irradiations, veiled, devine [*sic*]; / God's temple and the age's tomb." Such poetics thus seem to promise psychical and spiritual wellness to those with "eyes to see and ears to hear."[21]

When Chicago-area residents Hugo and Mary Herschend first visited

Marvel Cave in 1946, it was drawing roughly four thousand visitors per year. They, like many urbanites, had come to the Ozarks to fish, hunt for wildflowers, and vacation at Mac and Annabelle McMaster's Rockaway Resort. The Herschends returned to Branson for four consecutive springs and were introduced to a wide variety of local attractions by their hosts. During one trip, they met Miriam and Genevieve Lynch and toured Marvel Cave. Now both in their seventies, the sisters were looking to sell the property. The Herschends and McMasters entered into a partnership, brokered a 99-year lease for the cavern, and became its proprietors in April 1950. Because tour revenues were initially unable to support the Herschends and their two sons, Jack and Pete, Hugo kept his job with the Evanston, Illinois, vacuum manufacturer, Electrolux, and left operation of the property to Mary and the boys. Although they doubled previous totals by hosting eight thousand visitors during their first summer, no one could have predicted the amazing future of the enterprise.[22]

The McMaster-Herschend partnership lasted only two years before the latter family assumed sole management. During the winter of 1950–51, the Herschends replaced wooden stairs and walkways with concrete and installed electric lights. However, they were not content with a solely underground focus. Tourists often asked for something to do while waiting to visit the cave, so Hugo negotiated with Marlin Perkins, a Carthage, Missouri, native, to install a small zoo in the early 1950s. When this proved successful, Hugo dreamed further. According to Pete Herschend, his father believed that "visitors coming to the cave would like to see men and women of the hills . . . doing their own thing." Not content merely with gimmicks such as subterranean square dances and séances, the Herschends decided to purchase 640 acres around the site to showcase local culture. Silver Dollar City developed on this land—originally named "Marvel Cave Park"—and an additional 1,600 acres.[23]

Hugo Herschend died of a heart attack on November 14, 1955. But prior to his death, he laid the groundwork for an attraction that would come to define regional mythmaking and heritage marketing. Under his management, cave guides developed tall tales about the cavern and the surrounding country's local history. Devoted not only to the manufacture of legend, Hugo also envisioned an area-wide valorization of Ozark craftsmanship via cottage industries that showcased the arts of the blacksmith, basketweaver, or potter. While researching his plot of land, he encountered the short-lived history of the guano company's Marble City (or as he preferred to call it, "Marmaros," Greek for "marble"). The former existence of this actual nineteenth-century village on the grounds inspired him further. Though Hugo failed to see his plans realized, Silver Dollar City—described by one *St. Louis Post-Dispatch* writer as

Figure 5.2. Silver Dollar City, about 1960. Courtesy of Curt Teich Postcard Archives, Lake County (Illinois) Discovery Museum.

"a mixture of fantasy, history, and just plain 'hillbilly fun'"—would be the fruition of his aspirations.[24]

Silver Dollar City opened on May 1, 1960. A frontier-style blacksmith shop, general store, ice-cream parlor, doll shop, inn, and two reconstructed, late nineteenth-century log buildings made up the village. One of these latter structures was the Wilderness Church, a house of worship that continues to serve as an emblem of spirituality within the park. Guests were treated to local music performed by the Mabe brothers (who would later open Branson's first music show) and entertained by staged "feuds" between the stereotypical Hatfields and McCoys. Later that year the park would append its first rides—a tilt house called Slantin' Sam's Old Miner's shack and a stagecoach/mule ride. The overall aim, declared in a press release, was that "The Ozark Village is not a museum or a ghost town, but a living, working village" (Figure 5.2).[25]

Though early promotional materials adamantly proclaimed the park's authenticity and boasted that "everything about the City remains just as it was nearly a century ago in the Ozarks," promoters consciously elided problematic historical happenings. For instance, although the site did recognize and portray the existence of Alf Bolin, the regions' most notorious post–Civil War bushwacker, it benignly restricted—and continues to restrict—his murderous ways to a jovial attempted train robbery as patrons circumambulate the grounds. Reflecting upon this reworking of the past, park historian Crystal Payton wrote, "Frontier bad behavior was recycled into good entertainment. History, bloody and painful the first time around, is enacted as playful amusement." Thus, although Silver Dollar City owners, directors, and administrators have, since the attraction's inception, stressed its accurate portrayal of history and its ability to educate patrons about the Ozarks' past, the locale has continually offered only a sanitized and refined variant of earlier days that coincides with its equally genteel vision of proper ethics.[26]

Throughout its history, everyone involved with Silver Dollar City's management has resolutely stated that the site is a theme park, not an amusement park. Though the difference is seemingly small, this distinction is important for understanding the ways that the locale integrates promotion of Christian ethics and values with craft presentations, variety acts, and thrill rides. The creator of the theme-park genre, Walt Disney, spent his boyhood in the northwest Missouri town of Marceline, which subsequently served as a model for his quaint enactments of heartland America. Like Branson boosters who have followed his lead, Disney hoped to offer a leisure space quite unlike the existing models of Coney Island or Riverside in Chicago—attractions he characterized as "dirty, phony places, run by tough-looking people." When Disneyland opened in 1955, its proprietor perceived American society as troubled by failing families, a lost sense of community, and a mounting disregard for moral principles, courtesy, and decorum. Thus, at Disneyland, and later Disney World, guests were offered a nostalgic portrait of what once was. (Or more suitably, an imagined past grounded in the staging of sociocultural cohesion that lacked the messy elements of postindustrial America.) A stroll down each park's Main Street USA was to be a re-embrace of a fabled public square prior to civil-rights battles, ethnic divisiveness, or the muddling of conventional gender roles. For a hefty fee, patrons are offered psychical reassurance that there is still one spot where things are uncomplicated and "traditional"—a strategy described by E. L. Doctorow as the production of "abbreviated shorthand culture."[27]

Commentators on the Disney experience have continuously described the parks' presentations of stereotypes, archetypes, and historical pastiche in religious language, thereby more firmly indicating the sites' desired ideological functions. Terms such as "pilgrimage," "national shrine," "Disney rites," "New Eden," and "secular mecca" find their way into descriptions and critiques. Though elements of sacred space, ritual, and clergy can be teased out of an analysis of Disney's properties, his "imagineers" have chosen to interpret their version of core values as shaped, sanitized, and sanctified recollections of the past rather than using any overt reference to divinity. Silver Dollar City undoubtedly drew inspiration from this model upon its opening in 1960, but it went beyond Disney by augmenting its brand of utopia with the workings of popular Christianity.[28]

Though no accounts of Silver Dollar City's development indicate that Hugo and Mary Herschend were strong advocates of institutional religion, Pete Herschend remembers his stepfather as one who always sought to embody Christian precepts in daily life and to ensure that such a worldview pervaded his business practices: "If there ever was an embodiment of the Golden Rule, Hugo was it. . . . I never, ever knew that man to compromise his values." Additionally, Mary had an abiding concern for conservation motivated by a belief that she was protecting divine design. The park's official history claims that this "almost obsessive reverence for the things of God's creation" manifested itself sometimes antagonistically through the firing of people who harmed trees, but was more often gently evidenced by her protection of the locale's abundance of wildlife and natural features.[29]

When Silver Dollar City opened, the Wilderness Church was its one unambiguous religious space. The church was an abandoned log sanctuary designed to seat approximately eighty. It was found by Mary Herschend near a local creek in 1959, dismantled, and brought piece by piece to the park. The site chosen for reassembly was occupied by a massive sycamore. Ever-reluctant to fell such specimens, Mary acquiesced when the tree's trunk was hewn into a pulpit. Shortly thereafter, she insisted that a huge picture window be installed so that worshipers could draw inspiration from its scenic vista. To reinforce this relationship between geographic place and transcendence, a placard quoting the King James Version of Psalm 121:1, "I will lift up my eyes to the hills from whence cometh my help," was stationed prominently above the outlook (Figure 5.3).[30]

Touted as a site for spiritual refreshment amidst the frequent disarray of the vacation experience, the Wilderness Church has, since the early 1980s, been conducting services for employees and guests with the aid of an on-staff parson. Sunday ceremonies are offered to staff prior to the park's opening and visitors are invited to the church for both formal worship and hymn singing. In keeping with the interdenominational thread that courses its way through the park's presentation of Christianity, these events are billed as free of creed. Nevertheless, despite such ecumenical attempts, it is easy to characterize the brand of religiosity offered at the site as Reformation-derived and often Manichaean. Referencing a classic Protestant contempt for the prioritizing of church tradition over the injunctions of scripture, former Wilderness Church pastor Bob Burton stated, "If I have a theme, it is that the message has to get out to Christians that we have tended to put religion over relationship

Figure 5.3. Wilderness Church, Silver Dollar City, about 1970, from the author's collection.

with Christ. . . . We've talked about faith, sin and about being yielded vessels, about total surrender to his [God's] service. We're all ministers of the Word." As a former Catholic priest turned member of a nondenominational fellowship, Burton was a good fit for Silver Dollar City's brand of evangelical Protestant nondenominationalism.[31]

Currently, the Wilderness Church offers three Sunday morning services, including an 8:30 A.M. event for staff. When this practice began, administrator Don Richardson claimed that the theme park was the only one in the nation that offered worship services, weekly Bible study, and an on-staff minister to its employees. Research indicates that this is still the case and thus demonstrates Silver Dollar City's distinctive focus and unique place within the wider industry. After the park opens, it offers two other morning rites for visitors. Both services are usually full. Additionally, hymn singing occurs five times daily. The singing is often led by employees who have left the ranks of institutional evangelism for the more popular variant offered at the park. For instance, Linda and Bob Friedel are retired missionaries who work on the grounds and frequently spearhead the hymns. Their efforts regularly inspire sizeable crowds who had not ostensibly come to the site for devotion, with upwards of one hundred people gathering at the church for song. Wedding-vow renewals are also offered in the afternoons, and more than two hundred couples annually have their nuptials performed in the sanctuary.[32]

As the site is within the confines of a theme park, it must tailor its religion to conform to tourist expectations of the frontier past. According to Bob Deeds, who had a thirty-four-year career as a Methodist minister before becoming pastor of the Wilderness Church in 1986, this message is extraordinarily straightforward: "We just preach Jesus Christ and the love of God. And once in a while we tell them there's a Hell." Fielding vacationers from across the Christian spectrum, the locale must serve a double function by putting forth a brand of spiritual succor that has appeal to millions of vacationing devotees and showcasing the religious intentions of the park at large. Such authenticity is evidenced by the lack of bulletins distributed to congregants, a simple presentation of both theology and liturgy, and a populist ceding of song choice to attendees. Though not professing to be an attraction with an explicitly religious theme, Silver Dollar City's proprietors still feel that their holding must demonstrate Christian epistemology. As Pastor Deeds asserted in a 2003 interview, "If you really want to know the truth, this church is the basis for this park."[33]

Mary Herschend underwent surgery for cancer in 1963. Though she continued to be active in the park's management until her death in 1983, administrative decisions were gradually ceded to her sons, with Pete fronting public relations and Jack overseeing day-to-day operations. Throughout these early years, the attraction continued to grow. In 1963 it became Missouri's foremost tourist destination. In the latter 1960s and early 1970s it added other craft displays such as glass blowing, metal-smithing, candle-making, and a print shop. Regionally themed rides such as Jim Owens Float Trip, named in honor of a longtime promoter of Ozark rivers and multiterm mayor of Branson, and Fire in the Hole, a ride that invoked the tumultuous post–Civil War period in the region, were also added to the site. By the mid-1970s the park was one of the nation's most popular tourist attractions and garnered more repeat business than any other similar locale. Throughout the 1980s and 1990s, Silver Dollar City became more high-tech: state-of-the-art roller coasters joined its offerings alongside craft displays and musical acts.[34]

This period also saw the birth of many yearly festivals on site, such as a summer event for children, a Christmas festival, and a global folk-culture fair. Yet despite this growth and embrace of contemporary technologies, Mary Herschend was ever cognizant of offering predominantly urban Midwesterners a glimpse of fabled premodernity. As she told a reporter amidst the park's expansion, "My job is to keep the modern from creeping in." Pete and Jack Herschend followed their mother's lead. For them, avoiding the modern meant not only a supposed allegiance to late nineteenth-century artisanship and material culture, but also a thorough yet muted integration of Christian morality into the park's attractions and tone. Although raised by parents who looked to religious precepts for business guidance, the sons were not exposed to institutional faith in their youth. As self-described "baby Christians" in 1960, they sat down behind the Wilderness Church on a log bench for a "board meeting" that solidified Silver Dollar City's future direction. Pete recalled that during that session they decided "to look our Lord in the eye in terms of our business" and subsequently coined the term "'Making decisions with Christ in the room.'" Pete Herschend married in 1966. In 1969 he and wife Jo Dee were "baptized in the Holy Spirit" while at a meeting in Springfield held by Episcopal renewal leader Dennis Bennett, and they began to attend Shepherd of the Hills Episcopal Church in Branson.[35]

Pete Herschend's religious journey reflects a critique of theological liberalism within mainline American Protestantism that has been underway since the early twentieth century. This opposition was inaugurated by seminarians engaged in an ongoing fundamentalist versus modernist battle over issues such as evolution and biblical Higher Criticism, and continues to simmer via a contentious "culture war." American Protestant "renewal movements" began in the early 1960s as efforts within individual denominations to combat the perceived threat of women's leadership, homosexuality, ecumenism, and theological diversity. First implemented by the Presbyterian Lay Committee in 1965 and followed shortly thereafter by the United Methodist Good News Movement, these associations promoted schisms within the most progressive mainline churches.

The Episcopal renewal movement has roots in John Stott's Evangelical Fellowship in the Anglican Communion, which established an American branch in 1961. Since that time, liberal congregants and clergy within the Episcopal Church have faced opposition from a wide variety of right-leaning organizations, including Charles Fulton's Episcopal Renewal Ministries, an association that formerly had Pete Herschend as its vice president, and Pat Robertson's Regent University, with Pete Herschend serving on its board in the early 1990s. Ultimately, a central strength of renewal movements is their ability to integrate conservative religious stances into other sociocultural spheres, a tactic certainly utilized by Herschend when molding Silver Dollar City's "public face" and organizational directives over the past forty years.[36]

In the late 1990s Pete and Jo Dee Herschend abandoned spirit-filled Episcopalianism to join the heavily charismatic Assemblies of God, whose world headquarters is only forty miles from Branson in Springfield, Missouri. This change reveals an ambivalent yet palatable interplay between institutional and popular religiosity. According to Father Richard Kellogg, current rector of Branson's Shepherd of the Hills Episcopal Church: "They left here not because of any difficulties with this parish but because of the liberal attitudes of the entire Episcopal Church—the national church. But I would say they tend to be toward charismatic and probably a very conservative attitude. Part of what went on is that their charismatic tendency was almost divisive. This congregation, as far as Episcopalians go, is little more conservative than I anticipated. It's kind of a subtle conservative." Concomitantly, the promotion of a subtle yet transformative experience of Christianity is indeed the modus operandi at Silver Dollar City. According to Pete Herschend, "A friend once told me, 'Preach the gospel always, using words only whenever necessary.' We go out of our way not to be preachy, but if people leave here feeling good or a little closer to God, then I feel like maybe we've done our jobs."[37]

Although often posited as adversaries of modernity, numerous prominent Pentecostals have undertaken a similar melding of religious message with popular and mass culture. Revivalist and founder of the International Church of the Foursquare Gospel Aimee Semple McPherson opened the nation's first Christian radio station in Los Angeles in the 1920s. Drawing inspiration from McPherson, Fundamentalist Charles E. Fuller's California-based *The Old-Fashioned Revival Hour* was carried on 575 stations and reached twenty million homes in the mid-1940s. In 1953, Pentecostal minister Rex Hubbard bought time on a local television station in Akron, Ohio, and set the standard for later manifestations of televangelism, including a faith-healing ministry inaugurated by Oral Roberts in 1954. In 1961, Pat Robertson, an ordained Southern Baptist minister who nevertheless espouses Pentecostal theology, began airing programs over his Christian Broadcasting Network (CBN) and eventually launched the first privately owned communications satellite in the world. CBN featured the popular *700 Club*, which was originally cohosted by Robertson and then unknown Jim Bakker. Bakker left the network in the early 1970s to host the equally popular *PTL Club*; fellow Assemblies of God minister Jimmy Swaggart commenced his own show in 1973; and Paul Crouch founded the Trinity Broadcasting Network that same year. Scholar of Pentecostalism Grant Wacker has accounted for the success of the movement by detailing its ability to blend a "primitivist" focus on returning to a more pure and spiritual past with a "pragmatic" impulse that encourages the use of modern methods to facilitate the spread of religious messages. In light of Silver Dollar City's emphasis upon a semimythical history and its creative methods for evangelism, this paradigm seems apt for understanding the park's connections to a larger Pentecostal history.[38]

Pentecostals have also been active in the realm of religious theme parks. Most notably, Jim and Tammy Faye Bakker's 2,300-acre Heritage USA in Fort Mill, South Carolina, ascended to the nation's third most popular park—only trailing the two Disneys—in the mid-1980s. In 1986 it attracted six million visitors who came to enjoy a 500-room hotel, 2,500-seat church, five-acre water park, gable-fronted "Main Street USA," and enclosed mall. During its tenure, evangelical and charismatic Protestantism was blatantly evidenced as lifeguards occasionally shut down their pools to perform baptisms and secular variety acts transformed themselves into Passion plays at Eastertide. Such moves led a writer for *Time* to characterize the overall experience as "the triumph of born-again nice." Jim Bakker's legal difficulties beginning in 1987 provided a warning to other planners of religiously motivated theme parks. Interestingly, in 2002 Bakker chose Branson as the place to revitalize his ministry after serving a prison sentence for fraud and conspiracy. In January 2003, he began broadcasting a daily television show from the Studio City Café on the Branson Strip and has recently acquired a 590-acre parcel of land just outside of town for a Christian-themed residential community.[39]

As Bakker's experience demonstrated, Christian-based leisure can be volatile and perilous when stripped of its perceived ethical underpinnings. However, industry experts also agree that Calvinistic and transparently proselytizing recreational offerings do not result in profits. As Tim O'Brien, an editor with *Amusement Business*, stated, "No one wants to go on vacation and be preached to. Just imagine the kind of rides you'd see. I think a 'Fires of Hell Funhouse' would be a bit too much to take on vacation." Silver Dollar City boosters seem to have gently negotiated all these examples, caveats, and injunctions to offer a product that is perceived as sincere yet unassuming. As Pete Herschend has explained: "The phraseology my brother and I have long time used is, 'What would we do if Jesus were in the room?' It's the guiding principles, the moral values that make a difference in the business." Adding biblical precedent to this notion of Christly emulation, he has also asserted that Matthew 25:35, "For I was hungry and you gave me food, I was thirsty and you gave me something to drink, I was a stranger and you welcomed me," offers a template for the park's approach to customer service.[40]

The religious path of Jack Herschend, though institutionally dissimilar to that of his brother, has exhibited a comparable focus upon methods of popularly mediated evangelism and religious instruction. Jack and his wife, Sherry, drew upon the consecrated nature of their attraction when they married in the Cathedral Room of Marvel Cave. For more than thirty years they have been active congregants at Branson's First Presbyterian Church. In 2002, their longtime service to the congregation was recognized when they were awarded the Sunday School Teachers of the Year Award by Gospel Light Publishers, a distributor of children's curricula and resources. Throughout this period, the couple has emphasized the motto, "Being a Christian is fun," a maxim that is certainly at the root of Silver Dollar City's approach. This delicate mix of prudent proselytism and entertainment within the theme-park context was recently framed by Jack through the analogy of a spiritual feast: "Witnessing is like seasoning a meal. Too much spoils the meal. We don't want to cross the line from what is tasteful and appropriate."[41]

Sherry Herschend has also been involved with a more explicitly religious theme park venture. Nazareth Village in Israel, which opened in April 2000, is a re-creation of the first-century town where Jesus grew up, replete with authentic crafts and guides in period costumes. Existing as a site where the life and teachings of Jesus can be conveyed in a manner true to biblical text, Nazareth Village also hopes to bring people to Christ via multisensory exhibits of his ministry that are exciting and engaging. Throughout the past twenty years, Sherry has led more than twenty tours of the Holy Land. She is on the Miracle of Nazareth International Foundation, Inc.'s Board of Trustees and donated $1 million for the building of the attraction. Via this project, she hopes not only to offer a glimpse of ancient Hebrew history, but also feels that the site can help to facilitate Middle Eastern peace by stressing Christly emulation. As she stated, "Regardless of their [Jewish or Muslim] cultures, they all know that Jesus was the great peacemaker."[42]

In the late 1980s, Silver Dollar City Inc.—now Herschend Family Entertainment Corporation—codified its approach to religiously inspired tourism by crafting a mission statement that compelled employees to provide experiences "All in a manner consistent with Christian values and ethics." According to Jack Herschend, the company recruits and trains its thousands of employees, religious or nonreligious, "based on Christian values." Each is thereby expected to provide a "Christian witness" to the park's guests without "wearing faith on our sleeves." Evidence suggests that this obligation is welcomed by employees. Many staff members have been with the enterprise for multiple decades and 70 percent of all promotions come from within.[43]

Verbalizing this mandate to missionize and allying Silver Dollar City's Christian underpinnings with the historical period it seeks to represent, current employee Orville Conrad stated: "Christianity is integral to the Ozarks way of life in the late 1800s and cannot be separated from the theme. Many of us are really offended by non-Christian attitudes and behaviors of a few of our guests but the only Christian way to deal with these is to provide an appropriate example for them with gentle suggestions of what might be more appropriate without making any accusations. We can show the evedence [*sic*] of god's love in non offensive ways just as the early settlers of this area did." Alicia Bolin, a singer at one of Silver Dollar City's many shows, added that the park "supports God in a lot of things" and claimed that a majority the site's guests visit because it is a Christian-based attraction. As she wrote, "I know this because I sing at SDC and over half my audience comes up to me and the rest of the cast after the show and tells us how much they love the fact that there is a dress code, and that they play Christian music threw [*sic*] the entire park all the time."[44]

To further substantiate the ways that employees are compelled to provide Christian witness, Jack and Pete Herschend frequently have told stories about longtime street cleaner Luke Standlee. Jack recalled one instance when he was watching Standlee in action as he talked to a disabled and distraught girl visiting the park with her parents. As the child cried, Luke's attention and efforts to cheer her up became more resolute. After the family departed, Jack inquired about the circumstances. In his rendering, "Luke aw shucked, then said, 'Whenever I see youngsters who have had a hard road, I try to get them to smile. Then I ask them to do things that would make their mom and dad happy and to please the Lord.'" Luke had apparently been utilizing this approach daily for many years and sealing each promise from a child with a shiny silver dollar. Marking Standlee as an exemplar of Matthew 25:35, Pete Herschend held that this is only one instance of a pervasive method used by Silver Dollar City "citizens": "It's simply living out what we as Christians are called to do. Our people know what it is to share love."[45]

Additionally, an endorsement of Christianity has not been limited to on-site employees. Although Pete and Jack Herschend are often listed as co-owners and are unquestionably responsible for the site's spiritual impetus, Pete currently serves as vice chairman of the board of directors and Jack as chairman emeritus for the Herschend Family Entertainment Corporation. Since 1972 the still-private company has been run with the assistance of a board that is given formal say on strategic decisions and sizeable capital expenditures, and now has more than thirty owners with varying stakes in the enterprise, though the Herschend family retains the majority share. Individuals active within the realm of conservative Protestantism have been part of this leadership structure from its instigation. For instance, Sam Moore, head of Bible publisher Thomas Nelson, Inc., was an original board member. In the late 1980s, the company received frequent consultation from Harry Hargrave, the chief operations officer for PTL Network, who claimed that his first job priority was to "glorify God." Upon his retirement in 1998 as president and chief executive officer of the corporation, Cary Summers claimed that the Lord led him to service at the park. Finally, in 2003 Joel Manby was named CEO. Among Manby's many credentials was the founding of Family Wise, a nonprofit Christian ministry focused up offering tools to corporations, public schools, and churches that can facilitate the rediscovery of wholesome family time, trust in God, and behaviors guided by the Golden Rule.[46]

Although Silver Dollar City's millions of guests are not fully privy to the ways that the Herschends ideologically position and justify their property, it is easy to identify these techniques. Though the park has featured a saloon since 1973, visitors are not able to imbibe Ozark moonshine, or any alcoholic beverage for that matter. In fact, the on-site "saloon" has roots in an embrace of physical restraint rather than drunken revelry. According to Jack Herschend, a park tavern was planned because one was included within the site's original mining town. However, not wanting to promote inebriation, he discovered that Carrie Nation, the ax-wielding leader of the nineteenth-century temperance crusade, was born in nearby Eureka Springs, Arkansas. To showcase this regional connection, Silver Dollar City's saloon show once started in a typical can-can girl fashion only to be interrupted by a Nation impersonator who broke whiskey bottles, called sinners to the stage, and closed down the business five times daily. A century after Nation's campaign, temperance is still a calling card for the park. As stated by Ron Farris, a trucker who delivers supplies to the site and frequently visits as a guest, "It's an incredible place . . . I can bring my family and never have to worry about drunks because there aren't any." Further equating the attraction with Christian-based social and cultural decorum, visitors can enjoy bloodless bouts between law enforcement and outlaws, re-created nineteenth-century miners with sparkling hygiene and profanity-free dispositions, and stand-up comedians who resist the risqué jokes that exemplify their trade. In this manner, aspirations of wholesomeness fuse with a recent stockholder statement of objectives that mandated a "Christ-centered company" to produce a variant of "family fun" firmly entrenched in popular religiosity.[47]

Although an amorphous translation of decency finds its way into all entertainment venues at the park and easily meshes with the upright brands of country, bluegrass, and "hillbilly" tunes continuously featured, a guest can also easily locate traditional gospel performances. Each day (except Sunday) concludes with a showcase of religious music at the site's amphitheater. As a capstone to the week, a program currently entitled "Gospel Jubilation" is offered after the park closes. Gary McSpadden, who holds credentials as a former Southern Baptist minister, member of the Oak Ridge Boys and the Gaither Trio, and inductee into the Gospel Music Hall of Fame, has frequently hosted this Sabbath-day event. In addition, McSpadden also operates a ministry out of Branson that hopes to bring gospel music and biblical truths to Europe and Latin America. Silver Dollar City has also made devotional melodies ubiquitous throughout its acreage. As one strolls the winding paths, such songs are always heard though speakers shaped as rocks. These devices, which demonstrate the site's commitment to fusing religion with the greater theme-park experience, perfectly embody the dictum to preach while not being "preachy."

The performing of Christian precepts at Silver Dollar City is not exclusively aimed at adults. In 2002, animated Veggie Tales characters joined the park's annual National Kid's Festival. The creation of Phil Vischer and Mike Nawrocki, Veggie Tales cartoons feature fun-loving vegetables that entertain children with Bible stories and help their parents teach Christian values. A remarkable business venture in its own right, the Veggie Tales enterprise began in 1993 and has never been supported by a cable TV network or syndicated show. Nonetheless, it is currently the most popular children's video series in the world with more than twenty-five million copies sold. Prior to their arrival, Pete Herschend labeled the pious plants as a "glove fit" for his property. Considering that Veggie Tales has prospered from presenting easygoing moral lessons in inventive ways, it is not surprising that Vischer declared, "Most parents want their kids to be more forgiving, more kind, more compassionate. It's the same thing Silver Dollar City's been doing for 40 years." Attesting to ways that Veggie Tales conjoined with the restrained religiosity of all the locale's offerings, tourist Shelby Sears stated, "It's not a direct message. They [her children] don't even get it that they're getting preached at."[48]

The Herschend Family Entertainment Corporation often reiterates that its goal is not proselytism. As Pete Herschend maintained in 2000, "This is not Billy Graham. We're not trying to convert anyone." Still, although the park may not station preachers on its street corners, it is undeniable that the site and associations sponsored by its parent company engage in evangelism by broadcasting their variant of Christian values to the larger society, with its proprietors claiming that many people have "met the Lord" during their visits. Central for this mission, each spring the company sponsors "Young Christians Weekend," an event that draws up to sixteen thousand teens for a combination of entertainment and dating, self-image, and sexuality seminars. Christian artist-ministers perform for youths, and despite attempted missionary restraint, Pete Herschend claimed that "We've seen a lot of lives changed through these weekends" and that many attendees have "accepted Jesus" as a result of their stay. At the 2001 event, for instance, teens attended a sermon by Ryan Dobson, son of Focus on the Family founder James Dobson, who told them that they are loved by God despite their flaws. Minutes later, Christian boy-band Plus One took the stage to the delight hundreds of junior-high girls. The park also used this occasion to unveil the eighteen-million-dollar looping rollercoaster, Wildfire. Beyond braving the ride, attendees gathered on Sunday morning for a rousing service at the Wilderness Church. After this weekend of faith and fun, Pete Herschend received calls from a bevy of youth leaders and estimated that nine hundred kids made a commitment to Christ as a result of these activities.[49]

Furthermore, all Herschend Family Entertainment Corporation holdings are required to give a percentage of their yearly profits to Christian ministries, and Jack and Pete Herschend have been active as board members with a variety of these groups for more than a decade. Organizations supported by Silver Dollar City donations include: Habitat for Humanity; Lives Under Construction Boys Ranch, an association that offers alternative programs and homes for troubled boys; the Young Life/Discipleship Focus Program, a discipleship training and Bible study initiative for youth group members; and Ozarks Food Harvest, a mission intended to alleviate hunger in southwest Missouri and northern Arkansas. Supplementing these endeavors is the Silver Dollar City Foundation, formed in 1996 to serve as a grant-giving umbrella entity for Branson-wide community programs. By offering funds that assist needy Ozarkers in paying their utility bills, "adopting" impoverished families at Christmas time, and providing conflict management classes to schools and community organizations, the Foundation utilizes, according to President John Baltes, a "grass roots approach to growing a community centered in Christian values" and hopes to ultimately lead "people into a personal relationship with Jesus Christ."[50]

In addition to his business enterprises, Pete Herschend has engaged in a variety of political pursuits that inform the tenor of Silver Dollar City and signal his importance outside of the Branson area. A life-long Republican, Herschend avowed, "I am a conservative, both philosophically and politically." This claim was solidified in 1992 when President George H.W. Bush chose Silver Dollar City as the place to emphasize his "family values" message and celebrate his nomination to a second term of office—an event that attracted 10,000 people in the August heat to a brief rally. Also notable is Herschend's long-term relationship with John Ashcroft. Ashcroft, a fellow member of the Assemblies of God, served as both senator from and governor of Missouri before taking office as the U.S. Attorney General in 2001. This religious and political like-mindedness led Herschend to contribute tens of thousands of dollars to Ashcroft's campaigns of the early 1990s—generosity that was rewarded by an appointment to the Missouri State Board of Education in 1991. He still sits on this board, and in 2005 he assumed the office of president for the second time. Herschend has often used this political station as a vehicle for his opposition to gambling in the Ozarks, something he has vigilantly campaigned against for more than a decade.[51]

The possibility of gaming in the area has caused consternation among many residents since it was first proposed by a New Jersey–based company and the Eastern Shawnee tribe in 1994. Word of these plans inspired a range of negative reactions from residents and vacationers, many of whom phrased their objections in religious language. Although the planned casino was to be erected north of Branson in Christian County, it would have still been easily accessible by the town's millions of travelers. Numerous responses posited Branson as the antithesis of America's gambling citadel, Las Vegas, and contrasted that city's Sodom with the Ozarks' consecrated terrain. Amidst a decade of battles over this issue, Silver Dollar City has indeed led Branson's charge against what Herschend has termed the "cancer of gambling." On several occasions, the company has paid employees to conduct studies of its effect upon local economies and to assist those combating its influences with fundraising and resource gathering. In an attempt to defeat 1998's Amendment 9 to the Missouri Constitution, which legalized gaming in artificial moats, it donated more than $25,000 to a lobbying group. Illustrating the union of tourism boosters and clergy people around this and other social matters, Howard Boyd, pastor of Branson Hills Assembly of God Church and opponent of local gambling, praised Silver Dollar City's efforts when he stated, "I probably will not know until I get to heaven just how much the Herschends have influenced this community."[52]

The most sizeable challenge by gambling advocates arose in 2004 when Rockaway Beach, a tiny town twelve miles from Branson, proposed the construction of a casino that promoters claimed would bring year-round jobs to its depressed economy. In a now familiar refrain, Pete Herschend voiced his opposition by claiming that the enterprise would damage the "image" of Branson—one that relied upon its orientation as "wholesome, family-oriented, good entertainment." To counter roughly $12 million spent by the pro-gaming coalition, the Herschend family and their corporation bankrolled the "Show Me You Care" campaign. Finance reports showed that Pete Herschend contributed $125,000, his brother and sister-in-law added another $125,000, and the Herschend Family Entertainment Corporation donated $970,000. These three gifts amounted to nearly 90 percent of the campaign's overall budget. On August 3, 2004, Missouri voters defeated a constitutional amendment that would have made Rockaway Beach's plans legal. While money and grassroots political effort certainly aided the anti-gambling cause, Pete Herschend also suggested divine intervention led to victory: "The Lord's on our side. I have such a tremendous prayer group working. I have consciously sought out prayer groups around the nation to be in prayer about this."[53]

No contemporary visitor to Silver Dollar City would find evidence of the Herschends' opposition to gambling or to any other hot-button political initiative that is part of the larger evangelical "family values" agenda. While placards do not adorn the ground in protest of abortion or homosexuality or in support of school prayer, a religiously derived focus on families is thoroughly commented upon by guests. Although the American "culture war" is thought by most to be a product of the 1980s, it has a century-long history in the Branson area. Throughout the past one hundred years, area attractions have promised an escape from the ills of modernity via retreat to a changeless and pristine environ. Many technological transformations and other progressive innovations arrived on Ozark soil during this period, but boosters, including those at Silver Dollar City, continued to tout the area as an escape from ethically bereft aspects of the country at large. Here was a place where one could leave car doors unlocked without fear of theft; where children could safely play without constant parental supervision; where vulgarity was an infrequent occurrence rather than a way of life; and where the seeming chaos of contemporary existence was calmed by a core group of amusements focused upon God, country, and the traditional nuclear family.

In contemporary exit surveys, Silver Dollar City patrons frequently extol the site's "safe, family atmosphere," "friendly" employees, "clean" and "orderly" environment, and overall "Christian values" Often these attributes are juxtaposed against competitors within the tourism market said to have a less welcoming, mannerly, and pious disposition. As one tourist commented within a recent online review of the park:

During our June trip my mother lost track of my 4-year-old son. The staff not only kept him entertained, they sent someone out to find my mother. Later in the day she decided to buy the kids some ice cream, not thinking she left her billfold sitting on the counter. When we returned to the cabin she had rented we called the park, they had her billfold. I would like to add that there was nothing missing, not even a dollar, do you think that would happen anywhere else? . . . I went to Six Flags St. Louis recently and was really grossed out by the conditions of the park. Since they added the water park all you see is half naked women, running around half drunk, and trash all over the park. I may never go back there.

Thus, the nonthemed, urban, lascivious, and unrestrained competitor paled in comparison to its diametric Ozark opposite. Another internet review perhaps summarized Silver Dollar City's aura most succinctly by labeling the site "clean (in all ways)."[54]

Each of the aforementioned "family values" elements is integral to the vision of appropriate religiosity represented by the park and subtly preached to its guests. As Pete Herschend explained: "The greatest ministry that we have is the operation of the company properties. The greatest witness we have to who Jesus was and is, is how we operate day in and day out." Although not every guest may ally characteristics of decorum, integrity, and modesty with imitation of Jesus, the link was apparent to a tourist from North Carolina, who wrote:

At so many amusement parks the attendants are all young people who could care less about their job and they let it show. SDC has mostly older people as attendants and they were so friendly. They also had some young people working for them, and they too were very nice and friendly. Also you didn't see immodestly dressed people like you do at some parks, where you have to pray your children don't see their lack of clothes. The entertainment was wholesome, we loved Chapter 6 [a Christian a capella ensemble], and the Veggie Tales show was so fun for the kids. We are Christians and this was a fabulous wholesome place to take my children.

Through such an account, one therefore becomes even more privy to the ways that the park's unwritten (yet thoroughly scripted) "sermons" are enacted within the everyday workings of the site and interpreted by patrons through a religious lens.[55]

In the minds of many visitors, Silver Dollar City has served as the antithesis of other American recreational locales. Moreover, the consciously crafted culture of the place, solidified within the park's motto, "Creating Memories Worth Repeating," has often resisted the cultural inclinations of America at large. The site's attendance surged in the late 1960s not only because of its national exposure through episodes of *The Beverly Hillbillies*. Instead, as administrator Brad Thomas explained, "With Vietnam and other uprisings . . . a lot of people were purposely looking for ordinary people and simple themes that they could relate to. . . . Places like Silver Dollar City offered families a chance to escape from those turbulent times and get back in touch with their roots." In the latter twentieth century, Silver Dollar City has employed its brand of antimodernism to combat a perceived severing of morals from daily life, the ever-increasing degeneracy of popular culture, and the decline of wholesome leisure opportunities for families.[56]

At first glance, the amusements historically offered at Silver Dollar City appear merely to be part of a larger valorization of a mythical Ozark past that has underscored and continues to provide a foundation for the region's tourism industry. Although this is undeniably a primary impetus for Branson leisure, close examination reveals that for more than a century, such nostalgia, premodern longing, and whitewashed rusticity have been thoroughly informed by a variant of evangelical Christianity that seeks to inspire memories of and prompt a return to a less complicated and profane era. Out of this amalgamation has been crafted what cultural theorist Pierre Bourdieu labels a "habitus," or a "system of dispositions" that comprises a symbolic universe and helps individuals cope with unforeseen and ever-changing situations. In this manner, Silver Dollar City may ostensibly represent the turn-of-the-century Ozarks, but on a larger level, it has always sought to enact an alternative culture for those able to see and hear its message.[57]

The history of Marvel Cave has always had a spiritual dimension. Under the proprietorship of the Lynch sisters, the stress was on divinity. Contemporarily, nearly one-half million people still take the cave tour while visiting Silver Dollar City and its mystical nature remains palpable to many. As a recent guest from Illinois wrote, "It is amazing the treasures that our earth holds that God has created that are just waiting for us to discover." Since the Herschend family bought the site, the cavern's mystique has become part of a thorough, above-ground embrace of amusement-oriented Christian evangelism. A thread of piety indeed winds its way through park employees, guests, and attractions alike. As a chief catalyst for local tourism, Silver Dollar City has provided an often-imitated leisure model for other Branson attractions. In a place that now annually draws more than seven million vacationers, the vitality of the industry is reliant upon a continued consecration of pleasure and consumption of faith. Silver Dollar City has always framed itself as a simple place populated by plain folk who provide glimpses of a trouble-free age. However, its experiential brand of remembering, imagining, and worshiping has spoken to the complexities of culture for many decades and offered tourists unique reaffirmations of the place of faith within American life.[58]

Chapter 6

"Troubles Tourism"
Debating History and Voyeurism in Belfast, Northern Ireland

Molly Hurley Dépret

In the summer of 2005, following the Irish Republican Army's commitment to disarm, a flurry of news articles began to fill newspapers: "Belfast Regains its Charm,"[1] "Troubles Hot Spots Warm to Tourism,"[2] " 'Vibrant, Virginal' Belfast Lauded,"[3] and "Destination Belfast? Tourists Flood In."[4] These articles homed in on visitors' interest in Belfast's recent history of state and paramilitary violence and Belfast's aura of mystique, since most visitors have shied away since "the Troubles" began in the late 1960s. Despite these hopeful headlines, in early September 2005, riots shook West and North Belfast when police refused to allow a Protestant Orange parade to pass through a largely Catholic area. Some leaders of the Orange Order demanded its members stage a sit-in and incited violence, especially against police; the rioting injured sixty officers, and sixty-three rioters were arrested.[5] Despite efforts to promote Belfast as a renewed city, these riots highlighted for many the tensions that have emerged after the 1998 Belfast Agreement, particularly between the city's working-class Protestants and the historically Protestant police force, who must police and regulate Orange parades in the summer and early fall.

Such tensions have spilled over into city and community attempts to market Belfast as a tourism destination. In a recent article, "Belfast Is Ready for the Party to Begin," *New York Times* travel editor Stuart Emmrich ambled about the city sampling new hipster attractions in the city center: fusion restaurants, nightclubs, and pricey boutique hotels filled with young Londoners on a weekend break. Emmrich praised a restaurant or two, but for the most part dismissed Belfast as a new spot of "cool." Before leaving, however, he hopped aboard a red double-decker bus for a tour of the Falls and the Shankill Roads of Belfast—where the recent riots began—and noted,

As we rumbled through the neighborhood, the mood turned somber, and idle conversation ceased. . . . At one point the guide casually pointed out a 70-foot-high fence that she said ran the length of the Catholic and Protestant neighborhoods and kept each side from crossing into each other's territory. . . . Seeing it now, on a Sunday morning, shut tight and heavily barricaded, it stood as stark a symbol as the Berlin Wall, now fallen. It was a chilling moment, one whose force caught me by surprise. For it is one thing to have read all about "the Troubles" and yet another to actually witness firsthand the legacy of this conflict. As the bus turned back toward town, and the spruced-up city center came back into view, my attitude toward Belfast began to change. Yes, the "new" Belfast—the Belfast of outsized ambitions, and perhaps unrealistic expectations—clearly had far to go. But it had already come an awfully long way.[6]

The "new" Belfast, according to Alan Clarke, chief executive of the Northern Ireland Tourism Board, will place little emphasis the city's divisions, however. Despite the fascination with "political tourism" or "Troubles tourism," Clarke recently insisted that "It's the reason people have heard of Northern Ireland but that doesn't mean it's the reason they necessarily want to visit. . . . Our research hasn't shown that political tourism, murals and such things are big motivators. We recognise that when people get here they may, and on many occasions do, want to experience that side of things. That's a fact of life. We're not in any way trying to be defensive about this. We are trying to respond to what our customers tell us they want and at the moment they are not telling us that this is a prime motivator."[7]

Belfast's official tourism Web site, www.gotobelfast.com, tells a slightly different story, with numerous independently operated political tours on offer by taxi companies, youth hostels, groups of former paramilitary members and prisoners, and Belfast City Sightseeing Tours tours, the cherry-red double-decker bus company.[8] Since 1994, the year of an important IRA ceasefire, tours of the vivid historical and paramilitary murals painted on the sides of homes, the Crumlin Road jail, and the Peace Wall, the aforementioned towering fence running through parts of West Belfast, have regularly meandered through working-class Belfast neighborhoods, particularly on the Falls Road and the Shankill Road in West Belfast. Fáilte Feirste Thiar/Welcome to West Belfast, a predominantly Catholic/Republican/nationalist umbrella group promoting tourism, not only includes political tours in its annual Féile an Phobail/ Community Festival—the largest community festival in Europe—but has also implemented its own tourism strategy, a strategy differing from that of Alan Clarke (Figure 6.1).

With the proliferation of political tours in Belfast, and some city officials' attempts to promote the less sensational "heritage" sites, such as Cathedral Quarter, the Laganside waterfront, or the developing "Titanic Quarter," a series of questions emerge: why has tourism—

Figure 6.1. "Peace Line" Springfield Road, Belfast, August 2003. Photo by Molly Hurley Dépret.

either with a political flavor or not—become a source of economic hope for some? In presenting the city to visitors, who controls or attempts to control the story of the city's past? How do official and unofficial histories coexist, conflict, and reinforce one another?

Finally, tourism brings ethical issues to the surface, particularly voyeurism. Questions of voyeurism are clearly central for the tourism of Belfast, where many of its citizens have long suffered from sectarian divisions, military and paramilitary violence, and economic inequalities. Can a history of violence contribute to a revitalization process for communities within the city? How are the marketing and consumption of the city's contested past fraught with debates over voyeurism, and can this be mitigated? Engaging with these questions of historical representation and the ethics of tourism will, I hope, generate a nuanced and provocative discussion of tourism's relationship with Belfast's fractured and factional history.

A Brief History of Belfast's Troubles

Questions of history pervade this essay, yet for the sake of contextualizing the emergence of tourism in Belfast—and the sites toured—a more general sense of the debates concerning the Troubles is called for. Commentators on Northern Ireland—academics, journalists, politicians, activists, ordinary residents—have extensively debated the roots of the Troubles. Is, or was, the recent sectarian and military conflict rooted in primordial ethnic divisions and tribal loyalties? Is it religious, as the labels "Protestant" and "Catholic" seem to imply? Or did it emerge with the colonization of Ireland, and particularly the northeast, in the early modern period? Does this conflict stem, rather, from long-standing inequalities in the institutions of Northern Ireland, which mostly Catholic civil rights marchers protested in the mid-1960s? Is this a continuation of "the Troubles" of the 1920s that led to the independence of all but the six northern counties—a battle to either unite with Ireland or remain a part of the United Kingdom? Was Ireland supporting and inciting nationalists in the north, or was the British influence the source of the problem?

The questions above reveal some—if not all—of the assumptions or arguments regarding the origins of the Troubles. Yet none of them wholly explain how this conflict came about, why it lasted so long, and why the residents and leaders of the city are divided still. Assuming one of the above stances as well often relegates a person to one "camp" or another. John Whyte, in *Interpreting Northern Ireland*, outlines the multiple interpretations of its history. He relates, for instance, the traditional Unionist or Nationalist points of view, both of which interpret Northern

Ireland's history of conflict as a result of outside involvement, be it, respectively, English or Irish. He also discusses another common interpretation, the "two communities" argument, whose proponents argue that the source of the conflict comes from within, not from without.[9] These interpretations of history are not the only ones that exist, however; these interpretations may intermingle and overlap, despite their inherent contradictoriness.

In thinking about Northern Ireland, the oft-debated distinction between history and memory[10] is less pertinent to my discussion here than the weight or authority given to a particular narrative, whether it is called "memory" or "history." As Michel-Rolph Trouillot, a Haitian-born historian and anthropologist of his country, has argued in *Silencing the Past: Power and the Production of History*,

> Between the mechanically "realist" and naïvely "constructivist" extremes, there is the more serious task of not determining what history is—a hopeless goal if phrased in essentialist terms—but how history works. For what history is changes with time and place or, better said, history reveals itself only through the production of specific narratives. What matters most are the process and conditions of production of such narratives. Only a focus on that process can uncover the ways in which the two sides of historicity intertwine in a particular context. Only through that overlap can we discover the differential exercise of power that makes some narratives possible and silences others. Tracking power requires a richer view than most theorists acknowledge. We cannot exclude in advance any of the actors who participate in the production of history or any of the sites where that production may occur.[11]

How do narratives about Belfast's history get produced in the context of tourism? When, how, and by whom is a narrative produced? Which narratives are possible? What silences are imposed? Trouillot's final sentence above points to the fact that history may be produced in unlikely sites—in taxi cabs and big red buses, in unrealized proposals and in a tourism board's corporate plan.

Why Tourism, Why Now?

The recent reemergence of tourism in Belfast, and particularly city officials' and community leaders' investment in this reemergence, is deeply connected to a broader process: deindustrialization and the emergence of postindustrial cities. Postindustrial cities once had manufacturing bases, but have since turned to the cultural domain and a service economy as their primary economic engines. The transition from an industrial city to a postindustrial city stems from processes of globalization that have shifted industrial production to developing countries; Western European cities have become sites of cultural production. Recent stud-

ies have focused particularly on the role of tourism in these cities' economies.[12] Postindustrial cities in England and Scotland serve as points of
comparison; one needs only to review the literature on—and debates
over—heritage tourism in the United Kingdom to grasp the significance
granted to cultural attractions in these cities' revitalization.[13] Situating
Belfast in this context sets the stage for city leaders' recent emphasis on
cultural tourism, that is, tourism emphasizing museums, heritage, theatre, dance, and music.[14] The hopes invested by some leaders in political
tourism—a specific form of cultural tourism—seem to stem partly from
Belfast's status as a postindustrial city.

Belfast's history as a city is enmeshed deeply in Britain's rise to manufacturing greatness in the nineteenth century. Belfast became a center
of shipbuilding and the engineering of linen-making machinery. These
industries reached their high points by the late nineteenth century, and
the linen industry was increasingly facing foreign export tariffs and paying its workers less and less.[15] The housing that workers lived in was
located near large mills in the city. The Falls and Shankill Roads, now
frequently toured working-class areas that have been affected deeply by
the Troubles, were developed originally as residential areas for workers,
and various quickly constructed, inexpensive homes called "parlour
houses" were built up in the north and the west around the mills.[16]

Nineteenth-century Belfast's growth paralleled that of cities such as
Manchester, Leeds, and Liverpool in the North of England. In 1717, for
example, Manchester had a population of 8,000 people; by 1850, there
were at least 250,000.[17] In 1757, Belfast had 8,500 residents, and by 1851
there were more than 87,000.[18] The incredible growth of Belfast—30
percent between 1830 and 1840—was also partly due to its busy, productive port. Channels were cut, allowing for more docking; in 1837,
288,143 tons were being shipped, while by 1867, 1.3 million tons were
shipped.[19]

Belfast's economic base was further bolstered by World War I, when
the Harland and Wolff shipyard was in great demand, aircraft were
being built, and linen and rope were utilized in great quantities. Following World War I, however, many workers in the linen and engineering
industries became unemployed and one shipyard closed permanently.
Though these industries later regained some momentum, the service
industry was emerging as the new basis of employment.[20]

This drastic shift from the industrial city to the postindustrial city in a
span of only 60 to 70 years is linked inextricably with current debates
over these cities' futures. In the *Christian Science Monitor*, Christopher
Andrae noticed the trend toward cultural tourism. He commented that
"times are such, in this post-industrial period, that 'culture' has assumed
a major importance in the thinking of city councils searching for new

urban identities, money-spinning ventures that might bring in the tourists."[21] Such "money-spinning ventures" in Belfast have centered recently on the land surrounding the Lagan River. Where canals once transported rope, linen, and machinery, a Hilton Hotel and the Odyssey, an entertainment complex in the Laganside area, now stand. Alan Clarke, the aforementioned chief executive of the Northern Ireland Tourism Board (NITB), has great hopes that the Titanic Quarter, which will focus on Belfast's industrial heritage, will aid Belfast's reputation as a postindustrial heritage city.

The postindustrial nature of West Belfast's tourism efforts are most vividly related through the example of the Conway Mill. The mill was once where flax was spun and linen was woven from the mid-nineteenth century to the mid-twentieth century. In 1969, houses surrounding the mill were burned to the ground when Catholic residents were violently expelled from their homes at the start of the Troubles. In the early 1980s, the derelict buildings "were leased to a group of community activists for the purpose of stimulating, promoting and supporting community economic development."[22] The mill now employs local residents primarily in cultural activities, such as creating ceramics, jewelry, and art projects and exhibitions. Some guides who give political tours, particularly taxi drivers based in West Belfast, stop here and allow visitors to browse the crafts. A community once based around an industrialized economy has now reformulated their economic efforts with an emphasis on the cultural, and with an eye toward attracting tourists. Through this example, one can see the ways in which tourism—both political and cultural—has become central to specific communities in Belfast.

The very existence of tourism is new even to the NITB. For twenty-five years they were in relative hibernation, not daring to market Northern Ireland to fearful travelers from overseas. Yet in just the last ten to fifteen years, the tourism board has envisioned the possibility of a "new," or renewed, Belfast, thanks to the real beginnings of the peace process in 1993 with the Downing Street Declaration and the 1994 IRA ceasefire. Most of the developments in tourism—including the black taxi tours and the now-annual West Belfast Festival—date to the early days of peace agreements. So for slightly more than a decade, Belfast NITB officials, tourism promoters in city hall, and community groups have been confronted with the opportunities and dilemmas provided by tourism.

The NITB has not been alone in its efforts to rebuild the image of the country. Northern Ireland received millions of pounds from the European Union specifically for tourism—£34.1 million, to be exact—under the Community Support Framework 1989–1993, as well as £58.3 million since.[23] Since the 1994 ceasefire, the tourism boards have promoted all-island tourism, as opposed to marketing holidays in solely in the Republic of Ireland or Northern Ireland. These efforts had political implications, though both boards have flirted with such marketing since the 1960s. Since the late 1990s the tourism industry has experienced substantial changes in its makeup, such as the merging of Bord Failte, Ireland's tourism board, and CERT, the hospitality training industry into "Failte Ireland."[24] The NITB and Failte Ireland allow Tourism Ireland Limited (TIL) to market the island internationally.[25] These two bodies now promote themselves solely within the island and focus more on "at-home" matters.

With the broader picture of Belfast's place in Ireland and Europe in mind, below I will discuss some of the on-the-ground efforts to envision and reenvision Belfast as a postindustrial city. The Crumlin Road Gaol (Jail), which dates to the Victorian period and is known for holding early prisoners of the Troubles—closed its doors in 1996 and the Maze/Long Kesh, though not in Belfast, freed all its prisoners in 1998. Entrepreneurs started black-taxi tours in the early 1990s, and the West Belfast Festival, or Feile an Phobail, sought to attract tourists in the summer months with concerts, historical and political tours, and Irish-language lessons. Presently the Crumlin Road Gaol is being touted by its developer as a "criminal justice trail" that will rival Alcatraz, and various factions argue over whether the Maze/Long Kesh should be a museum to the Troubles, a sports stadium, or a police training center. Not all sites of conflict are being preserved: in Andersonstown, a Catholic area of Belfast, there is currently talk of tearing down the unused former Royal Ulster Constabulary barracks—"the most bombed barracks in the history of the conflict"—and replacing it with a youth hostel. If anything is emblematic of the fundamental changes going on within Belfast and Northern Ireland, it is the transformation of prisons and police barracks into tourist attractions. Yet these changes bring new and difficult questions to the surface.

The Question of History: Who Can (Or Will) Tell the Story of the Belfast's Past?

As tourism has become central to postindustrial Belfast's economy, the stories of Northern Ireland and the Troubles are mired in competing historical interpretations and in the production of silences. These competing interpretations are interwoven into major political changes and the revival of tourism. In a city with a clearly fractured history—though what history is not fractured or contested?—the "official" story of the city is not readily apparent. The reemergence of tourism reveals the ways in which divergent "tourisms" articulate coexisting official and unofficial histories. When searching for Belfast tourism information online, most likely one will discover Gotobelfast.com, "Belfast's Official Tourism Website," maintained by the Belfast Visitor and Convention Bureau. Under the heading "Belfast's Top 10 Things To Do!" shopping, dining out, family activities, and partying at nightclubs all make the list. Scattered among these activities are assorted "historical" activities; visitors are encouraged to "Visit Historic Belfast," "Discover the Story of Belfast," "Take a Walk," or go on a "Historical Pub Walking Tour," better known as a pub crawl. In each of these categories, typical "heritage" points of interest are emphasized: the architecture of City Hall, the Cathedral Quarter, walking tours of the Old Town, Titanic Trail, or the City Centre, the Ulster Museum's exhibit on early Ireland.

Visitors are also entreated to "Tour Belfast": "By boat or black taxi, open top bus or mini-coach . . . to discover the best of Belfast, old and new, take a tour." The mention of "black taxi" and "open top bus" clearly point to the political tours. In contrast to Alan Clarke's statement that Belfast's tourism strategy will not emphasize prospective visitors' interest in the city's political and military history, "Belfast's Top 10 Things to Do!" includes it at number six.[26] As well, clicking the "Heritage" button leads one to choose between "History" and "Future." Under "History," the final paragraph focuses on the Troubles: "[w]hatever its scale, history here still has the power to touch. The great exhibitions at the Ulster Museum reveals the bigger picture of Belfast's heritage but at Culturlann, the Irish arts centre on Falls Road, and Fernhill House in the Shankill, you get the people's story, too. And while you're in the area, join the crowds of tourists queuing to be photographed at those world-famous Troubles icons, the political murals. In Belfast, history is all around you."[27] Contrasting the city's tourism Web site with Alan Clarke's statement suggests that the city is, at its core, ambivalent about marketing of Belfast's political history.

While marketing the unique "feel" of the city's landscape (e.g., "the curiosity factor") has crossed the mind of tourism board members more than once,[28] the NITB and city hall generally promote the ordinariness of Belfast's history. Brochures rarely allude to the city's recent history of violence, though several studies have noted that political murals potentially draw tourists. In a recent study, the City Council's Tourism Development Unit noted that political murals are potential draws, and even used the term "Troubles Tourism" to describe this type of tourism.[29] As further evidence of the ambivalence toward the city's contested history, publications often emphasize the future. The Tourism Development Unit of the City Council has recognized that Belfast has experienced a lot of violence in the recent past, but they deem Belfast's problem an "image issue."[30] Their recognition of Belfast's recent violent history looks toward the future, however: if Belfast has an image issue, then the future consists in changing outsiders' judgments of the city through marketing and development of a "'cultural tourism' product" within the city. The NITB's Corporate Plan, 2002–2005, likewise emphasized the future. The words "Moving On, Moving Forward" grace the cover, and within the authors note that "Northern Ireland conjures up a set of images, ideas, and perceptions—both positive and negative—that are personal to each individual. Our difficulty over the past number of years has been the global media preoccupation with our problems. This has had profoundly negative effects on tourism. When we undertook our strategy review during 2000, it was very clear that we were entering an era of change and the challenge to us as a Tourist Board was to harness that change for the good of tourism."[31]

The ambivalent attitude of the tourism authorities toward the city's contentious past is situated in debates over how to represent it. No one agrees on how—or whether—to discuss it with visitors, though it is a pressing question. By avoiding a discussion of the Troubles, they certainly avoid ugly debates and further division, yet how do they expect visitors to understand the city's past? Furthermore, what does this say about the state of divisions within Belfast? To cite Michel-Rolph Trouillot once again, "any historical narrative is a particular bundle of silences."[32] Belfast authorities' silence on the years of conflict, and their on-going repercussions, opens a space for competing historical narratives, while at the same time performing the operation of silencing. The conflictual past goes undiscussed for the most part in the 2002–2005 Corporate Plan, and is only partly answered by directives on the Web site. Visitors are encouraged to discover the past for themselves, yet given little direction regarding what they might find. The question, "who can tell the story of Belfast's past?" is then answered by a cacophony of voices, and chief among them is the politically and socially active who reside in Catholic/Republican/Nationalist West Belfast, one of the primary areas where the military and civil conflict of the Troubles occurred.

The West Belfast Economic Forum, "an independent information, monitoring, research and lobbying resource concerned with social and economic justice issues" launched a tourism strategy in the late 1990s. In the strategy outline, "Fáilte Feirste Thiar/Welcome to West Belfast," their tourism branch focused on political tourism, cultural tourism, and the establishment of an arts and culture center. In their discussion of the significance of political tourism—listed first—they noted that

West Belfast's reputation creates a curiosity factor which can be harnessed by providing organised tours of its murals, and explanations of its political ideologies. As a potential tourist destination, it has a unique social context to complement its more overtly political background. Its places of interest, when set against their historical perspectives, produce an unusual picture of a people from two distinct communities, with differing aspirations, surviving under great pressure, in close proximity to each other. Already part of the Loyalist perspective on Belfast's political development is provided by the military exhibition at the award-winning Fernhill House Museum in Glencairn, but there is ample scope for other interpretations of West Belfast.[33]

The "curiosity factor" echoed earlier Northern Ireland Tourism Board studies. Throughout the description, it is clear that the promoters of political tourism in Catholic West Belfast felt more at ease discussing the history of sectarian division than the promoters of tourism in Belfast as a whole. They raised questions of historical interpretation, social context, and politics. They contended that Loyalist history was already represented within the Fernhill House Museum. In this assertion, the West Belfast Economic Forum argued that the Loyalist perspective—Loyalist being a term that many Protestants do not ascribe to, as it often connotes paramilitary support—was dominant, and that their perspective was the alternative.

In the West Belfast Economic Forum's statement, the group explicitly attempted to offer an interpretation of Catholic West Belfast's past, an engagement that does not yet exist for the city as a whole. Still, it should be noted that they wrote this tourism strategy "with support from Making Belfast Work and [the] Belfast City Council, and with funding from the Northern Ireland Tourist Board."[34] The Northern Ireland Tourism Board and Belfast City Council have actually both been supportive of what they term "community tourism" through Partnership Boards. In fact, in 2003, the Tourism Development Unit of the city council noted that "community tourism is said by some to be the next stage of development in cultural tourism." Yet simultaneously, they commented that "where community tourism developments are attempted, revenue streams back into the community must be clear for all to see. Initiatives will succeed best if they are developed so that they co-ordinate with the citywide offering. This also provides an opportunity for linkages to be created."[35] In their comments, one can sense the tensions surrounding localized tourism developments; they were encouraged, yet they must not diverge too far from "the city-wide offering."

Support for community tourism raised the question of whether the leaders in the NITB and the City Council preferred to allow communities to address their histories separately from the city as a whole. If so, what are the implications of this possibility? Does it imply that Belfast's history—and its future—is hopelessly fragmented? Could it mean that responsibility for the past lies solely with communities? Does it further entrench one-sided interpretations of history? Or might it open the door to alternative histories that crisscross sectarian lines?

Three Tours and Three Histories of Belfast

In exploring the role of alternative histories in the promotion or concealment of sectarian interpretations, I now turn to histories of Belfast collected while conducting research in the summer of 2003. In three different "living history" tours I meandered through Belfast to the murals on the Falls Road, the Shankill Road, the Crumlin Road Jail, the offices of Sinn Fein, and desolate areas where houses were boarded up. A popular youth hostel developed the first tour I took, the second was created by a taxi company, and the third was produced by Belfast City Sightseeing Tours.

The youth hostel tour proposed to take us to the "hardest hit areas that you've seen on t.v." The hostel was located on Donegall Road, in a working-class Unionist enclave in South Belfast, best known as the university area. As I strolled from my housing at Queen's University down Donegall Road on an untypically sunny Saturday at midday, there was a marked visual shift. Union Jacks hung in front of homes, many curbstones were painted red, white, and blue—both symbols of political loyalism to the United Kingdom. The youth hostel, itself neither Protestant nor Catholic, sat amidst this little Unionist stronghold, just off the busy main artery of South Belfast. As we loaded onto the mini-bus parked out front, our guide was in no hurry to get started as he smoked outside the mini-bus. The passengers were primarily young—and, unsurprisingly, staying at a youth hostel; some were couples, while others were traveling by themselves. The tour followed the path of Donegall Road to the Falls to Shankill, then from there to Antrim Road and the Belfast Castle; at the end we had a brief tour of the city center. The mini-bus was the only tour that traveled up to the scenic Belfast Castle, from which one can supposedly see Scotland on a clear day, but many of the other spots were well trodden by almost every tour.

Though the route is a popular one, the stories along this path were not the same. We drove past the old Crumlin Road jail, the closed-circuit television cameras along Antrim Road in North Belfast, and murals of heroes—or criminals, depending on who one is talking to—who have died during the Troubles. Bobby Sands's memorial mural—one of the most visited murals in Belfast—covers the entire side of a building; he was the leader of a series of protests for political status by Republicans in Long Kesh prison in the late 1970s and early 1980s. He died in 1981 during the final protest—a hunger strike—along with nine other men. We passed by murals of loyalist paramilitary heroes as well; by crisscrossing West Belfast, and parts of North Belfast, the guide professed to give a balanced history of Belfast.

Yet while he certainly included a number of agreed upon "facts"—that joyriding youths create problems, that the Milltown cemetery was the site of murders during a funeral for IRA members—there was a mythic quality to his storytelling. He weaved pulp-fiction stories about Belfast's underworld with hopeful comments about the progress of the peace process or integrated education. The most sensational stories from the "hardest hit areas that you've seen on t.v."—drug and cigarette smuggling, murders by "the Shankill Butchers," and gory punishment attacks for moral offenses meted out by paramilitaries—punctuated his commentaries on the changes within Belfast. The mythic landscape of Belfast's political history emerged, a landscape dotted with bombings and shootings, clandestine peace talks and public protest. To evidence the progress of Belfast, he claimed that "they can't get [integrated schools] opened quick enough," there is so much demand. Yet if one looks at the actual schools in Belfast, segregated ones are completely dominant, and the few unsegregated schools have severe problems with sectarian divisions among students. As well, he mentioned the plans for the Police Service of Northern Ireland (formerly called the Royal Ulster Constabulary) to step up recruitment of Catholics as police officers. The force is historically Protestant—and still is, for the most part. This guide, however, was the only one who discussed the continued violence and tensions that plague many neighborhoods and traverse North Belfast, the area of the city with the most "interfaces," the built or implicit borders between Protestant and Catholic neighborhoods.

Was the guide creating an alternative vision of Belfast's history? Is this too much to ask from a two-hour tour? This tour was clearly for entertainment and for basic information regarding Belfast's recent history, but despite the tour's emphasis on entertainment, it stands as a site of historical production, a tale of history that offers a partial view of Belfast. In many ways it avoided any sort of over-arching idea about why the Troubles began or why joyriding, segregated schools, and police forces persist. It consisted of a series of vignettes, which are perhaps the only history that can be told in the midst of fragmented histories.

The black-taxi tours of Belfast—my second example of alternative narratives—are the example *par excellence* of a tourist experience that arose not from a bureau of cultural tourism, but rather from entrepreneurs in the early 1990s who saw a way to make extra money during the summer months while entertaining those interested in the darker points of Belfast's recent history. These tours generally cost about twenty-five pounds and take visitors for a one-hour tour of West Belfast, though they are generally flexible about their itinerary. Upward of eight taxi companies operate these tours, and they are not exclusively Catholic, though the black taxis originated in Catholic neighborhoods during the 1970s (Figure 6.2).

According to one source, who grew up with the black taxis when she lived in West Belfast, the taxis were actually old, broken-down taxis that were imported from London, thus the distinctive style of the vehicle, with a driver in the front and a huge backseat that fits six or more people. These taxis were dangerous to ride in since they often did not fit safety requirements, with floorboards that were nearly falling out and passengers squeezed in past capacity. Though they were called "taxis," the "black taxi" of West Belfast functioned much more like a bus, since they were used as a replacement for the Belfast bus system. During the most turbulent and violent period, the buses in West Belfast had been set on fire and used as blockades between Protestant and Catholic areas. The bus-like black taxis follow certain routes: from Falls Road to City Centre, for example. The taxi driver stops for everyone who flags him down until he has a full load; the cost is about ninety pence.[36]

The taxi tour guide had much in common with minibus tour guide. He followed most of the same route and offered some similar stories. The difference between the two, however, is that the taxi tour guide is interactive. In fact, several of the companies propose that the tourist can tell the driver where to go, but this strategy has its limitations. If the tourist knows where he would like to go, it is probably already on the driver's itinerary. For my tour, I called the number on the brochure and met the driver in front of the City Hall in city center. I almost missed him: I was looking for a black taxi; it turned out his was white—a tourist's hopes were dashed for the authentic black taxi *sans* floorboard. I hopped in the front seat of the taxi with Roger, a thirty-eight-year-old man from East Belfast who had been driving for fourteen years and giving tours for ten. A no-nonsense fellow, one of the first things that he told me was that he grew up during the Troubles and that the conflict was "a load of crap." He was definitely a Protestant in terms of his voting but saw the paramilitaries as "generals lining their own pockets," especially in the Loyalist paramilitaries, who make their money through racketeering, tax rackets, drug dealing, and cigarettes. At the same time, however, he commented that young men who joined paramilitaries "thought they were doing the right thing." Furthermore, he noted that the residents of Falls Road and Shankill Road—"working-class neighborhoods"—were "entitled to be bitter." As we stopped in the lower Shankill to regard the murals, there were at least six cabs with more than twenty tourists like myself. The area was utterly desolate aside from these tourists wandering through empty lots, where homes had stood until the early 1990s; the few houses still standing around us were mostly boarded up, partly to prevent young people from breaking in. The significance of this empty

Figure 6.2. Black taxi driving through Republican-Nationalist West Belfast, August 2003. Photo by Molly Hurley Dépret.

space—an "interface area"—is that three Loyalist paramilitaries control the lower and upper Shankill; the Ulster Defense Assocation and the Ulster Freedom Fighters control the lower Shankill, while the Ulster Volunteer Force controls the upper Shankill. More than one hundred families had to move because they lived in the "wrong" area; this empty space is now a buffer zone between the two territories, which reveals that there are divisions *within* communities, as well as between communities.

Since he drove me past the Bobby Sands mural, I asked him what he thought about its meaning. The mural has one of Sands's quotes painted beside his smiling picture, "our revenge will be the laughter of our children." For Roger, this was a sectarian threat; he interpreted it to mean that the IRA will defeat the British and unionists and laugh in their faces. For him, "it brings back memories of '81," the tense time of the hunger strikes, as well as the time when he decided to leave school. The fact that he drew a parallel between leaving school and the hunger strikes revealed how the wounds of the past continue to affect people's lives today, as well as the loss of opportunities for all young working-class people during these years.

He gave me his own opinions to the questions I asked, though these were tempered by his boss's directions. He doubted if I would get a different perspective from anyone at his taxi company, which indicates that they are given training in how to give the tours. A friend separately took a taxi tour with a West Belfast driver, a former Republican prisoner, who took her inside the Milltown Cemetery, where many Republicans—including Bobby Sands—are buried. Yet when I asked Roger to go there, he said they used to, but "don't do Milltown Cemetery [anymore] out of respect," though they "used to visit it." The withdrawal of this site from his company's itinerary reflects that there must have been orders for Protestant taxi companies to stay out of Milltown Cemetery, especially since it is frequently toured, during the West Belfast Festival, by Republican taxi drivers and by independent visitors.

This tour offered more opportunities to ask questions and to interact with the tour guide. This interaction affected the content of the tour; Roger rarely seemed to give an entirely prepared speech like the minibus driver, even though the route was preplanned. In this way, both driver and visitor were producing the history that was being told. This Protestant taxi driver's tour was an alternative narrative, particularly in terms of his conflicted feelings regarding paramilitaries, his interpretation of the Bobby Sands mural, and his own reflections on his life in the early 1980s.

A third tour atop a Belfast City Sightseeing Tours bus engaged much less with the city's political history. This absence of detail, however, is a significant silence. According to one of the originators of the tour, Joe

Lavell, "We steer away from anything really political. . . . We might talk about 'the Troubles' in general, but we will avoid talking about episodes like the Shankhill Butchers. We try to be as evenhanded as possible—we don't spend any more time on the Falls than we do on the Shankhill, for example."[37] The lack of engagement with the city's political history indicates a reticence to attempt a narration of the city's past, similar to the position of the Northern Ireland Tourism Board and the Belfast Visitor and Convention Bureau. In a positive sense, though, this disengaged quality can potentially allow anyone to ride the tour bus without feeling alienated.

As we piled into the crowded bus near a McDonald's in the city center, I was reminded of the Grey Line tours of New York City, since a guide sat in the open-air area of the bus with a microphone, reciting an dizzying mix of fact and fiction—often indistinguishable—as we drove through the city. This tour was the only one that traveled extensively to other areas of Belfast; we circled the building where the Titanic was constructed, a largely desolate area of former shipyards, and we drove down Malone Road, past Queen's University. Our tour of West Belfast was abbreviated—we only passed through the Falls Road and the Shankill Road. Perhaps most disconcerting was the tour guide's lightheartedness in describing the history of the Troubles. Unlike the tour taken by *New York Times* travel editor Stuart Emmrich, there was no hushed silence among the passengers, and there was certainly no gravitas from the tour guide. As we drove along, the guide told absurd stories, commenting with a poker-face that Kentucky Fried Chicken was a key supporter of Loyalist paramilitaries, going into an elaborate—albeit incredibly silly—history of KFC's secret ties. He ultimately commented that he was only teasing us. His story was fascinating, however, in its concoction of a faux conspiracy theory that plays with the abundance of Troubles conspiracy theories. A writer for the *Irish Times* noted the "breezy tone" of the tour guides in a recent article: "Passengers huddle up beneath the city's customary leaden skies while tour guides provide a running commentary, full of jokey bonhomie. Presumably intended to put nervous tourists at their ease, the breezy tone sometimes jars. Passing the Royal Hospital on the Falls Road, tour guide Saoirse describes how—during the Troubles—doctors from all over the world came to the hospital to train in dealing with gunshot trauma. 'It's nice to be famous for something,' she laughs nervously."[38] The nervous laughter of the tour guide and the joking tone, in part, reflect the tensions surrounding this subject matter. Though the company's silence on the contentious political history and the jovial tone of the tour might seem disrespectful to some, the silence in some ways has allowed this tour to cross boundaries and achieve wider acceptance through its absence of partisanship.

All three tours contained silences, in their own ways, as did the government documents and Belfast's tourism Web site. Collecting all the different tellings—or absence thereof—of history will not produce a clearer picture of Belfast's history. What it can do, however, is help us detect where the silences occur, and which silences pervade multiple tellings. In these three tours, the most significant silence was the lack of discussion about Belfast's present state, and the divisions that continue to exist in all of Belfast. The September 2005 riots reflected continuing and emergent divisions, such as the relatively recent division between the police and Protestants. Some of the violence in areas of North and East Belfast has developed only since the 1998 Belfast Agreement.[39] Crimes against ethnic minorities, such as residents from Hong Kong, underscore new tensions that have emerged in Belfast in just the last five to ten years. The emphasis on past violence tends to distance violence and division and ignore ongoing and new forms of division within the city.

Unfinished Plans; Unfinished Histories

The histories described here—of taxi drivers, youth hostel minibus operators, and double-decker bus guides—differ from one another and articulate histories that either fit with, or diverge from, the silences of the city government. What they share in common is that most often they discuss history in terms of the past and rarely mention current developments and debates. But the unfinished plans for a "criminal justice trail" through the Crumlin Road Gaol, a Victorian prison where, in the 1970s during emergency legislation, Diplock Courts sentenced people according to one judge's pronouncement, provide additional insights into the role of history in tourism in the postindustrial age. Anthropologist Ann Laura Stoler has noted the significance of paying attention to plans that are incomplete, unfinished, set aside. The incomplete plans— and the debates along the way—can reflect tensions involved in envisioning futures for now "historic" buildings.[40] In this case, the visions are expressed, alternately, by the residents of a community, a developer, and the government.

In April 2002, a conference was held by The North Belfast Tourism Project Advisory Group, which is a collection of various businesses, community agencies, and tenant's associations in North Belfast as well at the NITB.[41] The conference sought to examine the future of the Crumlin Road prison. It was organized because "the Crum" has been sitting idle since 1996. Built in 1846, the jail had existed since Belfast began to emerge as a central industrial city. In her introduction, Geraldine Wilkins, coordinator of the North Belfast Tourism Project, commented that people were beginning to ask questions about the jail, such as how it would be preserved or how it could be used to attract tourists. There was also the question of to whom the jail belonged—eventually it was awarded to the Northern Ireland Executive by the Prime Minister and the Chancellor. As for the potential of the prison—where convicts awaited deportation to Australia in the nineteenth century and IRA members protested on the rooftops—she noted that "It is clear that old prisons museums around the world have massive appeal as visitor attractions. A million people a year visit Alcatraz. Melbourne Gaol—from where Ned Kelly was hanged—is the city's biggest tourist attraction. Where does their appeal lie? Perhaps, to quote the keynote speaker of the morning, Jim Arnold [restorer of New Lanark Mills in Scotland], they allow the visitor 'to connect emotionally' with the story. The story we have to tell is unique—the story of Belfast."[42]

The ambition to attract tourists was clear. And the selection of keynote speaker Jim Arnold, from New Lanark Mills, made it clearer. Arnold told of the sucess story of a restoration of the mills as an industrial heritage tourist attraction, as well as "a resident population of 180 . . . rented space for enterprises, a 60-bed youth hostel, an award-winning visitor centre." Approximately 400,000 visitors tour the village and preserved mills each year.[43] From the workshop report, the participants also agreed that they should create a "mixed-use" facility within the jail and the now-unused courthouse, which connects by underground tunnel.[44]

Once a number of ideas were voiced, the participants agreed on the two strongest ideas: a museum of the jail and a backpacker's hostel. Three other priorities were to "create an education and training facility for local youths and adults," especially in trades such as brick-laying. Secondly, the jail should employ "ex-prisoners to work with young people." They emphasized that the jail should not "be a 'Museum of the Troubles'" and were concerned with funding and ownership of the site.[45] Throughout the report, there is definitely a tension between making the jail "belong" to local people (e.g., through creating jobs and creating public meeting space) and meeting the requirements of developers and tourists. Also, when looking at the conference participants' list, the "community" the jail might serve would primarily be Catholic, even though North Belfast has the most Protestant/Catholic interfaces in the city. At the bottom of the conference participants' list, it states, "Greater Shankill Partnership attended in the capacity of observers";[46] the Shankill area is a Protestant working-class area, and this notation highlights the divisions within the area.

Developer Barry Gilligan was awarded the contract to develop the Crum in September 2003.[47] The original plans included "65,000 square feet of new office space. The rest would then be allocated to what the developer referred to as a 'criminal justice trail.'" Workers dismantled railings and gates built during the 1970s to prevent paramilitary attacks on the courthouse.[48] Gilligan expected the project to cost ten million pounds and, at the time, commented that it could potentially be completed within a year. He has since founded Crumlin Road Courthouse Ltd. They proposed to attract businesses and government offices that plan to relocate, such as the Public Records Office in south Belfast. Gilligan himself is the former chief executive of Dunloe Ewart and Carroll, a venture-capital firm in Belfast. His former group criticized his purchase of the Crumlin Road Belfast Courthouse from them for the low price of 57,518 Euros. Gilligan shot back that the building "is now derelict and is costing stg [sterling] 25,000 pounds a year to insure it against public liability and there is no income off it. I bought it as a punt." In terms of funding the renovation of the building and making it productive, "it must also have an Urban Development Grant of many millions to do anything with it and I'm working with some conservation architects on a plan. We want to insert new offices and retain some of the historic character."[49] The Crumlin Road Courthouse and Gaol was eventually granted more money from the government in 2003 and 2004: "The Gaol was transferred to the Office of the First Minister and Deputy First Minister (OFMDFM) in August 2003. In January 2004, Government announced that the proceeds (around £3.8 million) of the sale of the former army barracks at Malone Road, Belfast would be used for the social and economic regeneration at the Gaol site."[50]

The courthouse and jail opened to visitors in September 2005—the same weekend as the riots in West and North Belfast—it has thus far been a limited, though successful, engagement. According to a BBC article, "Belfast's Crumlin Road Jail Is to Take Inmates Again Next Month—But Only for the Weekend," the jail opened for one weekend as part of "European Heritage Open Days," special days in the United Kingdom, the Republic of Ireland, and forty-eight other countries during which historical buildings and other sites are free and open to the public.[51] The day following this successful temporary reopening, the Department for Social Development issued a press release citing the Social Development Minister, David Hanson, who remarked that "the imaginative and sensitive development of the Crumlin Road Gaol and Girdwood Barracks [now-closed army barracks next to the jail and courthouse] has the potential to create a regeneration project of international significance which can bring maximum benefits to the community in North Belfast and the wider city. . . . The future development of these sites will be subject to a full public consultation. . . . I am confident that this process can lead to decisions on the future development of the sites which have the full support of the whole community."[52] The tour guide Web site www.inyourpocket.com has noted the potential of these buildings to become a tourist draw:

> These foreboding buildings are connected by an underground tunnel which was once used to spirit prisoners from the Jail to the Courthouse for trial. The Neo-Palladian Courthouse is topped by a scales-free figure of Justice and was opened in 1850. Since its official closure in 1998 the building has been used as a makeshift theatre, film location and cinema. Throughout the Troubles the Jail witnessed many breakouts, bombings and rooftop protests and today it, too, stands empty. If a multi-million redevelopment plan gets the go-ahead, both the Jail and Courthouse could become an unlikely tourist draw. The Alcatraz of Belfast?[53]

The future of the Crumlin Road Gaol and Courthouse is hardly settled. Though the Department for Social Development has proposed a "public consultation," the fact remains that so many different parties are interested in the redevelopment of these buildings, there are inevitably a wide range of opinions. The developer is much less likely to be concerned with how local residents are benefiting from a "criminal justice trail" than the North Belfast Community Action Unit or the local government. Despite public discussions about the buildings' future, the question of how to represent the past in such a museum is problematic; will it become a museum of the Troubles? A recent BBC report noted that "historians, archivists and museum curators will no doubt welcome a debate about a Troubles museum. But they warn that there is more to creating a museum than just picking a building to house it in. There are the technical realities of ensuring any building has the right conditions for the preservation and display of historic artifacts. There is also the difficulty of telling the story of the Troubles in a way which is accessible to outsiders and acceptable to those who were touched directly by the conflict."[54] The unfinished quality of the museum in the Crumlin Road Courthouse and Gaol allows us to clearly see how this one place is filled with debates over who should tell the story, which story should be told, and who should benefit. It is interesting to note, in this case at least, that few have openly contested the transformation of these buildings into museums, perhaps because all the parties involved see a potential benefit, either for the whole city or for the neighboring communities.

The Roots of "Tragedy Tourism"

The debates over the future of the Crumlin Road Courthouse and Gaol leads directly into questions about visitors to Belfast's murals, its Peace Wall, or cemeteries: even if this tourism ultimately brings financial gain, is it ethical? Is it inevitably voyeuristic, or is it possible to visit respectfully places where the Troubles occurred? As Carolyn Strangea and Michael

Kempab have commented in their writing about tours of Alcatraz and Robben Island, "the refashioning of punishment as a tourism product raises ethical questions about the commodification of suffering and its evident entertainment value, as some scholars have warned."[55] A *Wall Street Journal* article addressed the question of respect and voyeurism in tours of troubled neighborhoods of large cities, such as the *favelas* of Rio de Janeiro or New York City's South Bronx: "Beyond issues of basic safety, there are more complicated questions of cultural voyeurism and respect. Tour organizers say they're doing a public service by exposing people to places they wouldn't otherwise have seen. But some see it as ripe for potential misunderstandings, if not outright exploitation." Such tours in the U.S.—of the South Bronx and North Philadelphia, for example—have been created and promoted by residents of the neighborhood or by the local government, which adds yet another layer to the problem of such tourism.[56] Though the problematics of voyeurism are particularly obvious in poor neighborhoods in a "wounded city,"[57] where military and civil violence have deeply affected the lives of its residents, voyeurism is nonetheless an issue common to all types of tourism. Are tourists watching "tribal dances," going on a romanticized African safari, or ignoring locals while tanning at Club Med any more ethical than a tourist interested in a city's turbulent political history? Should everyone simply stop traveling to avoid any possibility of exploiting people during their travels?

Malcolm Foley and John Lennon, coauthors of *Dark Tourism: The Attraction of Death and Disaster*, claimed in a news article that present-day tourism of Pearl Harbor has its roots in pilgrimages to Canterbury.[58] Though it may have its roots in such pilgrimages—a point noted first by Dean MacCannell in the early 1970s—such travels have their own distinctive character in the twentieth and twenty-first centuries. Toni Holdt, one of the originators of battlefield tours in Great Britain in the 1970s, has argued that visits to sites of war and tragedy have their origins in practices of World War I. During the war, "widows journeyed on pilgrimages to visit the graves of their dead. The same phenomenon followed the Second World War, but then veterans also began returning to the battlefields to relive the experiences of their youth."[59] Holdt argues that the self-conscious visitation of sites of national or political importance by nonmilitary citizens is peculiar to the twentieth century and generally connected to the processes of tourism and the commodification of history (or living history, as it is dubbed by some Belfast tour operators) that has emerged so visibly in the postindustrial age seems especially suggestive.

When thinking about Belfast, one must also consider other sites of tragedy that are mired in the processes of tourism and consumption.

Some of the most toured sites are Treblinka and Auschwitz, Hiroshima and Nagasaki, Oklahoma City and New York City.[60] The tragedies and losses that occurred at each of these sites are historically unique, yet a common feature is that all have witnessed traumas over the course of the last 60 years and are now commonly parts of tourist itineraries.[61] Yet Belfast is more akin to Sarajevo, Beirut, or Jerusalem as they are all "polarized cities"[62] that have been split by ethnonationalist sentiments. The tourism of Belfast is also similar to political tourism, such as tours to Nicaragua that focus on the Sandinista revolution,[63] or tours of Alexandra, South Africa, that tour Nelson Mandela's former home and the headquarters of "'Vlakplass'—'death squads' which operated in the 80s."[64] Zijad Jusufovic started a tourism company in Sarajevo to lead a "Mission Impossible Tour," where he "take[s] people to the old siege lines around the city, to the secret tunnel under the airport and sniper positions."[65] Bosnia political tours, like those in Belfast, emerged following a protracted civil war and an upsurge in postconflict tourism. Beirut, which has also seen more tourists in the last fifteen years, is part of an Explore! Worldwide package tour. This British company notes in their itinerary that "when people think of Lebanon and Beirut they still seem to think of war, terrorism and Hizbollah but the country has been at peace since 1991. . . . They have kept some of the shelled, bullet marked buildings as a reminder to foreigners and residents alike, and despite the current political situation in the region there was no anti-western sentiment. Explore Trips include a walking tour of Beirut and expert guides take you through the city's recent history and war."[66] Global Exchange, one of the forerunners in catering to politically minded tourists, promotes "Reality Tours" on their Web site. "Syria & Lebanon: From Beirut to Damascus—Crossroads of the Middle East," offered in October 2005, proposed meetings with journalists, political leaders, and NGOs, a visit to the former Al-Khiam detention camp and the border between Israel and Palestine, as well as hikes among Roman ruins and tea-drinking in Aleppo's bazaar. Through these examples, one can see that political or historical tourism in Belfast is hardly an isolated phenomenon; these sorts of tours have been created throughout the world.

The Ethics of Troubles Tourism

In 2003, more than 710,000 tourists from outside of Northern Ireland stayed overnight in Belfast, and 5.3 million people visited as part of a day trip. In September 2005—one day after the riots—the Belfast Visitor Centre celebrated its one-millionth visitor. According to the Tourism Development Unit of the Belfast City Council, most visitors to Belfast travel there by sea, have been to Northern Ireland before, travel as a couple, are between the ages of twenty-five and fifty-four, and tend to stay in a bed and breakfast or with friends and family.[67] Numbers of European visitors had grown by 27 percent by 2000, and North American visitors' spending constituted 10 percent of the annual revenue from tourism.[68]

Carolyn Strangea and Michael Kempab discuss some of the ethical questions raised by tourism to Alcatraz near San Francisco and Robben Island in South Africa: Is suffering simply used to entertain? Yet they note in their conclusion that

historic penal sites may be gloomy, but their interpretation provokes debate when frames of remembrance, forged by external political pressure and internal policies, illuminate disturbing practices and institutions. Preserved prisons are stony silent witnesses to the things former regimes were prepared to do to people who violated laws or who seemed threatening or suspicious. The murkiest project of all would be to close them to tourists rather than to confront the ongoing challenge of interpreting incarceration, punishment, and forced isolation.[69]

Ignoring such spaces of tragedy—silencing these histories, in effect—then, is as problematic, if not more so, than encouraging visits to these sites. Dr. Neil Jarman, an anthropologist and noted researcher of murals and Catholic/Protestant neighborhood boundaries, has commented that the tourism of murals can actually have positive effects for residents of Belfast:

There is a certain sense of opportunism as the tourist operators move into the working-class areas, but these tours also offer an opportunity to see the city in a different light. These routinised repetitions help inscribe new and distinct routes around the city, they help to link up and reconnect many areas that have long been separated. . . . This is particularly poignant for those residents of Belfast who take the tour. In daily life, routes and journeys to and from the city centre, and between different residential areas, become hardened by routine. Avoiding "the other side" people remain in the known areas, among their own. . . . As the tours cross between Protestant and Catholic areas they are able to focus on and emphasise the commonality of experience over the past 30 years for those living, for example, in the two west Belfasts. The images on the murals may serve to symbolise the differing aspirations of the two communities, but their presence as artefacts also helps to indicate something of the shared history which may in the future provide the base for shared understandings.[70]

Though the tours may be primarily for tourists, they have given some residents of Belfast their only opportunity to see "the other side" safely. In a 1999 BBC article, "All Aboard Belfast's Terror Tour," the operator of the Belfast City Sightseeing Tours (originally Citybus Tours) commented that "when we started we found that we had a lot of local interest. There were areas of the city that some people had never seen. The tour was the only way that many people felt able to cross a peace line."[71] This positive effect of tourism problematizes any attempt to simply dismiss these tours as unethical and voyeuristic.

The locals taking tours of Belfast also highlights the variety of people who visit the murals and reveals that their reasons for taking such a tour can vary widely. Tourists may come to West Belfast as explicitly "political tourists," such as those from Basque Country who visit as a sign of solidarity with Northern Irish Republicans.[72] Even before tour operators began to give "living history," or Troubles tours, in the mid-1990s, people were visiting Belfast independently and walking through the Falls Road area.[73] In fact, even in the mid-1970s, locals were giving visitors informal tours of their neighborhoods.[74] Recent literature in tourism has attempted to counter John Urry and Dean MacCannell's ideas about a singular "tourist gaze," an effort that reflects a move away from assuming homogeneity among tourists. In this vein, Betsy Wearing and Steven Wearing

posit tourism as individual experience and interaction in a space apart from that of the everyday life of the tourist. In this sense tourism is not an escape *from* the workaday world as suggested by Rojek but an escape *to* a social space which allows for learning and growing. Nor is it "sightseeing" or the passing gaze at objects either authentic or unauthentic as argued by MacCannell or Urry. Rather, the analysis we suggest is feminized in that it critiques previous male oriented theories of tourism which assume a subject/object relationship to the tourist destination and a bounded conceptualization of the tourist place. Following the feminist geographer Massey, we wish "to confront the gendered nature of our modes of theorizing and the concepts which we work" and to argue for a conceptualization of space which incorporates the dynamic social relations of the place and the multiplicity of experiences which imbue it with meaning for the people who interact within it.[75]

The singular view of a "gaze," they argue, does not reflect the variety of gazes that can occur in tourist encounters. As well, theories of a tourist "gaze" rarely reflect that tourists are themselves *gazed at* in their travels. Their perspective brings out the intersubjectivity of any tourist encounter. The ethics of tourism of a "troubled" place becomes imbued with multiple problematics—the gender and class identifications of the tourist and tour guide, a community's response to a tour guide—and possibly a tourist—unwelcome in a Republican cemetery, and the guide's own political sentiments and affiliations seeping into his commentary. The ethical dimensions of tourism are revealed most baldly in the visitation of a city torn by sectarian sentiments, yet these moral dimensions are inherent in any tourist encounter.

Conclusion

Tourism in Belfast is inherently problematic: how should the city's history be told? Can its history—or any history—ever be told in its entirety or is history inevitably fragmented? The questions posited and pondered in this essay regarding history, tourism, voyeurism, and silences hardly exhaust these issues, yet they do begin to outline many of the difficulties that residents and leaders in Belfast have begun to face in the last ten or fifteen years. There are many divisions among those who seek to answer the question of how to tell Belfast's history. Leaders who advocate Belfast's more banal heritage clearly differ from those who emphasize Belfast's political heritage. Yet they share one significant quality: they look to culture and history as a means for promoting Belfast as a tourist destination. The processes of remembering, forgetting, creating, and displaying history—as the Crumlin Road Courthouse and Gaol, and tours of the city's troubled past suggest—are an integral part of the ways that history and tourism have begun to unfold in this Northern Irish city.

Part III
Marketing Communism

Chapter 7

"There's No Place Like Home"
Soviet Tourism in Late Stalinism

ANNE E. GORSUCH

Between 1947 and 1953, Soviet citizens were encouraged to turn inwards, to avoid dangerous "border zones" both literal and imaginative. After the relative openness of the war period, the postwar years were ones of "containment" directed both at limiting the threat of the western other and at reinforcing Soviet patriotic identity.[1] The change could be seen in the Soviet travel and exploration magazine *Vokrug sveta* (Around the world). In 1946, a time of continuing if hesitant openness, *Vokrug sveta* included articles and images of the non-Soviet world, as well as information about prerevolutionary and Soviet-era explorers. There were stories about trips to Prague and to New Guinea, about ocean exploration at the time of Columbus, and a favorable review of Il'ia Il'f and Evgenii Petrov's 1936 book *One-Storied America*.[2] But in 1947, coinciding with Andrei Zhdanov's campaign against "servility before the west," the permissible world shrunk, and most of the articles were now about travel within the Soviet Union including pieces on Moscow, on Vladimir Lenin's exile (within Russia), on Iosif Stalin's childhood in Georgia.[3] Even in a magazine devoted to world exploration, good travel was now defined as domestic.

The late Stalin regime nourished ignorance about foreign countries in order to advance its own xenophobic interpretation of world events in which the bourgeois west was cast as the enemy.[4] Creating enemies was only part of the solution to the foreign policy and domestic challenges of the postwar period, however. The regime also demanded a heightened "Sovietness" from those still considered loyal. Domestic tourism was one response to this perceived need, intended to produce physically and ideologically healthy Soviet citizens. Moscow was a particular focus of Soviet patriotic education for the postwar tourist, but tourism also contributed to the construction of Soviet identity on the larger

collective level of the Soviet Union. It aimed to create a correct understanding of the "socialist homeland" by investing historical sites and
"exotic" spaces with Soviet significance. Last, but by no means least,
tourism was a means of reassuring a weary, war-torn, population.
Descriptions of beautiful beaches and luxurious resorts suggested to
loyal citizens that conditions would improve and their future would be
comfortable and bright. In every case, travelers were reminded that it
was only within the borders of the socialist homeland that Soviet citizens
could let down their guard and be confident of a warm welcome.

Although increasing attention has been paid to the history of tourism
in western Europe and North America and to its contributions to questions of identity formation, political mobilization, nation building, consumption, and practices of daily life, scholarly work on tourism and its
significance in the Soviet context is in its infancy.[5] This chapter is a pre-
liminary attempt to consider the contribution a history of tourism might
make to our understanding of the cultural and political particularities
of late Stalinism. That said, some aspects of tourist organization and
experience discussed here are not particular to the late Stalin period;
tourism was appropriated as a "Soviet" project in the late 1920s and
developed into a mass movement in the 1960s.[6] Indeed, this is part of a
larger project on domestic and international tourism from 1945
through the Khrushchev era. When I began, I had little expectation of
finding much on tourism in the difficult and hungry years of late Stalinism, but I found that Soviet newspapers and magazines carried multiple
articles in the postwar period about the wonderful new possibilities for
domestic tourism and healing travel now available and that archives doc-
umented significant state interest. "The tourist movement must become
a mass movement!" exhorted one enthusiastic journalist in 1951.[7]

My primary interest in this essay is on official representations of travel.
In keeping with this discursive focus, my sources include central Soviet
newspapers such as *Izvestiia* and *Pravda* and the popular press including
the illustrated magazines *Ogonek* and *Vokrug sveta*. The press is an especially good source for uncovering the particularities of late Stalinist
approaches to tourism as articles were written with changing political
demands in mind. Also useful are books about tourism, which provided
instructions on how to be a tourist, as well as guidebooks educating readers about specific localities. Many of the prominent authors writing
about tourism published throughout the 1930s, 1940s, and 1950s, however, and this fact, together with time to publication, makes them a better source on Soviet tourism in general rather than on the late Stalinist
period in particular. More essential are the archival records of the Trade
Union Tourist-Excursion Bureau, the primary agency organizing tourism in the postwar period.[8] Finally, I also use travel accounts by western

journalists and diplomats, which, although clearly influenced by the Cold War dynamic, have the great advantage of their interest in the everyday. That said, I do not explore in detail the lived experience of Soviet travelers, why they traveled, and what they experienced when they did. As Rudy Koshar reminds us in a recent book on the history of German guidebooks: "Leisure has its own history, neither wholly determined by the structures and constraints of the mode of production in which it develops, nor fully shaped by patterns of social power."[9] Soviet travel experts, travel agencies, and tour guides directed travelers toward sites of historical, political, and cultural interest and then tried to teach them how to think correctly about these spaces and about their own place within the larger Soviet sphere. The official meaning assigned to travel and the meaning(s) taken from it by those traveling could be two quite different things, however. A history of the intersection of official production and popular consumption lies ahead.

Defining *Turizm*

In its broadest possible sense, tourism can be defined as a "leisure activity" that involves a journey to "sites outside the normal places of residence or work."[10] But tourism has rarely been so simply defined, and an extensive North American and European literature explores the distinctions (and similarities) between tourism, travel, and most recently, vacationing.[11] The Russian term *turizm* has a different flavor, referring most often to walking, hiking, biking, and camping, often along excursion routes. Some excursions were nature based, such as the day hike sixty young people undertook to a picnic site on the Moscow River in 1952.[12] Others were more ideological. In the early 1950s, travelers earned the badge of "USSR Tourist" for traveling to Gori, Baku, and Tbilisi in a touristic reenactment of Stalin's childhood and early revolutionary life.[13] Often the two were combined—the student group that enjoyed the "picturesque" beauty of the Moscow River also stopped in the pouring rain to listen "with attention" to a lecture relating to nearby Borodino.[14] Tourists often stayed at tourist bases (*turbazy*) and alpine camps, using these as centers from which to take sometimes lengthy overnight walking trips of 45 kilometers in two days or 60 kilometers in three.[15] In 1949, tourism was officially recognized as a type of sport.[16] It was a form of mass action through *doing*, similar in its demand for active mass participation to "collectivizing the countryside and industrializing the periphery, doing mass calisthenics, writing poetry in workers' clubs."[17]

This understanding of turizm reflected long-held beliefs about exposure to the elements, and indeed travel itself, providing a source of physical and ideological strengthening. In Sergei Aksakov's 1852 memoir,

Years of Childhood, he attributed his recovery from debilitating illness to "movement," "air" and the "marvellous effect of travel upon health."[18] Lenin likewise "preached the virtues of clean mountain air and long hikes in the forest."[19] Although not particular to late Stalinism, the athleticism of tourism and its association with bodily strengthening was especially relevant to the postwar period when so many people were recovering from the physical challenges of war and occupation. In 1947, O. Arkhangel'skaia the author of *How to Organize a Tourist Trip,* argued that "fresh air" and movement would "strengthen the nervous system" and lead to "a healthy appetite and sleep."[20] A 1946 children's guide to the Volga similarly noted that a trip along the river would "strengthen health, pluck up vitality and energy, and provide a good rest."[21] Connections were made between the physical know-how provided through active tourism and the "practice of communist construction." In 1954, V. V. Dobkovich defined active tourism as a form of what he called "sanitary purposefulness" (*ozdorovitelnaia napravlennost*).[22] In his *Tourism in the USSR,* Dobkovich argued that vigorous tourism would "strengthen the nervous system, [and] improve the working of the cardiovascular system" thus enabling "the Soviet tourist to more successfully do his part in the active construction of a communist society."[23] Dobkovich presumably would have approved of the group of students and teachers who took a break from their hike along the Moscow River to help peasants with their mowing.[24] Indeed, many official tourist activities stretched the boundaries of what we might consider "leisure."

Turizm was not just a form of *doing,* however. Turizm was also a form of what James von Geldern has called mass action through *seeing.*[25] Excursions to cultural events, historical museums, and collective farms demanded mental concentration rather than physical agility but were also highly valued forms of touristic behavior. "There is a hush over the place," John Steinbeck observed about the Lenin Museum in 1947. "People speak in whispers, and the lecturers with their pointers talk in a curious melodic litany."[26] John Urry has drawn our attention to the fundamentally "visual nature" of the modern tourist experience in an analysis of what he calls the "tourist gaze."[27] Museums, postcards, photography, the very notion of "sightseeing," all confirm the importance of the visual for tourism. Soviet travel experts such as Arkhangel'skaia understood the way in which the photograph in particular might give "shape to travel."[28] She insisted that the subject matter of the tourist photograph was to be "figured out before hand so that after the trip the photographs reflect all sides of the trip and the life of the group."[29] Although von Geldern has argued that *doing* was seen as the ideal form of mass action during the 1920s and the Cultural Revolution, while the mid-1930s emphasized the passive spectator who visited the new "showplace for the economy, Moscow's VDNKh," or watched ritualized voting on newsreels distributed about the country,[30] after the war at least, turizm combined both *doing* and *seeing*. This only increased. By the late 1950s sailing on the cruise ship "Victory," looking at the historical monuments of Rome, and seeing the sites of Moscow and Leningrad were all enthusiastically defined as turizm.[31]

That said, all forms of turizm were distinguished from "rest" (*otdykh*) for the purposes of healing and relaxation. Rest homes (*doma otdykha*) were vacation rest houses that provided meals and lodging, but little medical care (Figure 7.1).[32] In sanatoria, health professionals were often available to design diet, exercise, and mineral water regimes specific to the needs of a particular client such as "milk days" for those with cardiovascular problems, and "apple days" for colitis and dysentery.[33] Despite the difference between turizm and otdykh, however, the boundary between the two was porous, and trips to sanatoria, and certainly to rest homes, were often closer to what we might consider a vacation than a hospital sojourn.[34] Although sanatoria were intended for those under a doctor's care, well-connected people sometimes managed to maneuver

Figure 7.1. One of the buildings of the rest home Primor'e in the Leningrad suburbs, with pensive statue of Lenin in front. From O. S. Grintsevich, *Kurortirye raion* (Leningrad, 1964).

the system to enjoy a month's holiday in the relative luxury of Black Sea and other resorts (Figure 7.2).[35]

"The Tourist Movement Must Become a Mass Movement"

In April 1945, while the Red Army was still fighting in Berlin, the Secretariat of the Central Trade Union ordered its Tourist-Excursion Bureau back to work.[36] A few of the many ambitious tasks of restoration included organizing excursions in Moscow and Leningrad; building tourist facilities in Borodino, Dombai, Kislovodsk, Sochi, and Tbilisi; providing sufficient car transport for tourists and guides; and organizing new informational materials about available tourist excursions.[37] The challenges of postwar recovery were enormous, however, and had an impact on resources available for tourism just as they did on every other facet of Soviet life after the war. Tourist bases and sanatoria struggled with poor quality facilities, with a lack of trained workers, and with a deficiency of proper "healing foods."[38] Factory clubs, which sometimes sponsored tourist activities, found it hard to support even the simplest of productions or excursions in the immediate postwar period.[39] A limited,

Figure 7.2. Sanatorium Severnaia Rive'ra, in the Leningrad suburbs. From O. S. Grintsevich, *Kurortirye raion* (Leningrad, 1964).

often damaged transportation system made it difficult to transport people from one place to another.[40] In 1948, tourist advocates complained that funding was still inadequate and that tourist work remained highly disorganized. Romashkov, a hydroelectric engineer who participated in Trade Union planning meetings about tourism both before and after the war, worried that "apart from the Crimea and Caucasus, there are no [developed] tourist locations."[41] Suggestive priority was sometimes given to tourist facilities in particularly strategic locations, however. In 1947, the Intourist hotel in Stalingrad was repaired enough to house international tourists, though its "windows looked out on acres of rubble, broken brick and concrete and pulverized plaster."[42]

In the earliest years of reconstruction and recovery, many workers had little interest in travel and little ability to pay for it.[43] According to Soviet historian V. Dvornichenko, the number of workers participating in tourist excursions increased in 1947 and 1948, but there were still fewer participants than in the prewar period. Only 70 percent of Tourist Bureau capacity was used.[44] This hardly seems surprising: after the war many Soviet citizens could scarcely think about such extravagances as tourism. "How can we continue like this?" wondered one individual in 1946, "Sacrifices and sacrifices. Understand me, if a family of three now needs 600 to 700 rubles [to buy food on ration cards], that is not all that has to be bought. The government is not giving away soap, there is no butter or lard, only substitutes, there is no kerosene. We are at the last extremity."[45] Another Soviet citizen, Mariia Nikolaevna Sadchikova, a doctor and army officer, thought little about possibilities for travel. Although she was lucky enough to move to Moscow for permanent settlement from a provincial city, she spent fifteen years living in a tiny basement room in Moscow before she could afford to move into a decent apartment. Like many Soviet holidaymakers, she visited relatives once a year (in Kuibyshev), but apart from this she could not afford any recreational travel beyond the Moscow suburbs.[46] Despite the challenges of the postwar environment, however, Soviet citizens were not immune to the appeal of a few weeks away from work. Indeed, the severe overcrowding of the postwar period in which per capita urban living space actually decreased from what it had been in 1940, surely added to the pleasure of time away from home.[47] Tourism does appear to have increased in the early 1950s, by which point the economic situation had began to improve for urban dwellers and there were also more tourist facilities. In 1952, there were seventy-six tourist bases, as compared to just twenty-two in 1947.[48]

Who traveled? According to a decree of the Presidium of the Central Council of Trade Unions from August 1950, "first priority" for Tourist-Excursion Bureau facilities was supposed to go to "working trade union members who are productive innovators, basic cadre workers, employed war invalids, and production engineers and technicians." Deserving others included nursing mothers, mothers without support, and adolescents.[49] Soviet workers were reminded that they were fortunate to have their "right to relaxation" guaranteed by the Soviet Constitution, in contrast to bourgeois countries, where tourism was said to be a means of profit operated by independent companies and available mainly to wealthy tourists.[50] But in 1947, according to *Ogonek*, it was "the best and most respected members of the nation's coal mining industry" who rested at one well-known sanatorium on the Black Sea (although the magazine insisted that in the next ten years enough spaces would be built at sanatoria to hold 18,000 people).[51] Perks for a Soviet "middle class" were part of what Vera Dunham has called the "Big Deal" in which a cohort loyal to the regime and eager for stabilization was rewarded by "material incentives" of which leisure was an important component.[52] It was professionals, for example, who could take advantage of official permission to travel for business and squeeze in extra vacation time in coveted locations. Under Stalin business trips were more closely monitored than they would be later, and the possibilities for a *tvorcheskaia komandirovka* (creative business trip) were limited,[53] but at least one Moscow lawyer managed to add a week on the Black Sea onto a brief work trip in a nearby area. She asked fellow travelers at the bus stop where to find a good hotel and good restaurants and boasted about her ability to use her lawyerly status to change compartments and travel (illegally) in the international car on the train trip from Moscow.[54] Families rarely traveled together. Despite the attention paid to strengthening the nuclear family, hard-won excursions such as a weekend pleasure cruise near Moscow, were filled almost entirely with adults, although these are just the kind of adventures that might have been full of children elsewhere.[55]

Individuals without access to desirable resorts sometimes traveled on their own in what was commonly called *dikii turizm* (wild tourism)—tourism without the usual *putevka* (pass or voucher to a tourist camp, rest home, or sanatorium). Irina Corten explains this term in her lexicon: "Because of inadequate transportation, hotel, and restaurant facilities in the Soviet Union . . . [o]ften, people ended up spending their vacation in rough conditions—hitchhiking, camping or staying in small rented rooms without basic conveniences, eating irregular meals not properly prepared, and so forth. Such circumstances validate the metaphor of living in the wild."[56] And yet, while "wild tourism" was common in the prewar period and again in the 1960s and 1970s, it appears to have been comparatively rare in the postwar period. Mary Leder, a long-term American emigrant to the Soviet Union, described her own experiences traveling "wild" to Sukhumi in July 1950, including the ease with which she purchased plane tickets and found a room to rent in a local's cabin. But Leder writes that while the practice later "became widespread," "few venturesome souls attempted to travel in this way" in 1950.[57] Leder traveled "wild" because there were no hotels or hostels "open to the public" in Sukhumi. For others, these restrictions may have proved too intimidating. Beginning in 1940, republic capitals and many *kurorty* and seaside resorts were regulated by stricter passport control laws than major industrial towns and areas.[58] Despite its challenges, however, the appeal of "wild travel" was clear. As Leder remarks: "We read no newspapers [and] talked no politics."[59] Most days were spent on the beach. The unscheduled nature of "wild tourism" contrasted with the official Soviet tourist experience, which often resembled an adult version of the Pioneer camp. The schedule for visitors to the Krasnodarsk tourist base in 1948 included an ocean swim after breakfast, an excursion to a nearby city or collective farm in the morning, a nature walk in the afternoon, and a "cultural activity" such as dancing or watching a film after dinner.[60]

Patriotic Tourism

That tourism of any kind should have been offered as an answer to postwar needs and to the anxieties of the Cold War is worth exploring given the regime's preoccupation with controlling movement and its anxiety about borderlands. Indeed, tourism was just one form of "travel" in the postwar period. Millions of people were "traveling": some returning home after the dislocations of war, others forcibly evacuated from border areas and newly acquired territories.[61] The regime was especially concerned about soldiers returning home from central Europe and Germany who often brought back personal experiences of a west different than what they had been told to expect.[62] Stalin responded to the threat generated by these "travel accounts" by arresting and imprisoning those "travelers" who seemed most dangerous, especially returning prisoners of war.[63] Posters were put up warning those at home not to believe all returning soldiers, explaining that "after all the blood and hardship that the troops had undergone, their judgments [are] lopsided, that they [are] nervous and dazed, and that some of them [will] even try to claim that the cities and villages of capitalistic countries provide everyone with a mansion filled with luxuries."[64]

Domestic tourism was a form of patriotic redress. The Komsomol Central Committee described tourism as "one of the most important forms of educational work among youth, especially patriotic education."[65] Patriotic tourism engaged the tourist in rituals of public self-admiration in which the Soviet Union's prestige was perpetually reaffirmed. In 1945, the Secretariat of the Central Trade Union emphasized tourism's role in teaching workers about "the heroic spirit of the Great Patriotic War, the socialist construction of our country, the cultural growth of our people—the peoples of the USSR—[and] the economic, geographic, [and] natural wealth of the country."[66] Some of the earliest postwar excursions were to recently erected monuments and memorials to Soviet victories. As early as 1945, a Moscow student sports group organized a twenty-three-day trip "Along the path of the Great Patriotic War."[67] Indeed, war monuments were often built before cities themselves were reconstructed. The memorial obelisk in Stalingrad stood in a fenced-in site with well-tended flowers but in the shadow of the battered shells of ruined buildings.[68] Of the many types of Soviet museum (museums of history, industry, the Russian revolution, natural history, art), "memorial" museums were one of only two types to increase in number in the postwar period (from 90 in 1941 to 163 in 1952), the other being, with a much less dramatic rise, the local lore and history museum.[69]

Moscow was a major focus of Soviet patriotic tourism. In published guides to local and regional tours in the Soviet Union, Moscow was Itinerary Number 1. In part, the emphasis on Moscow was a practical one because of the resources, both financial and personal, that could be found more easily in the capital. But Moscow, as one lengthy lecture from 1945 on the reconstruction of Moscow reminded its listeners, was also the "heart of the socialist motherland."[70] Travel articles about other parts of the Soviet Union sometimes began and ended with Moscow, just as other kinds of articles began and ended with references to Stalin. An article from *Vokrug sveta* entitled "My country," praised Moscow as the modern capital of the Soviet Union, as the place where Stalin lived, and as an example to every other city and region.[71] An opening illustration in a 1947 children's book, *Around Old and New Moscow,* was of the expanding territory of the city. Perched in the center of this growing city was the Kremlin, a reminder of how Moscow itself sat in the center of an expanding Soviet Union.[72]

Moscow's symbolic significance after the war resembled the rhetoric of the 1930s when, as James von Geldern explains, Moscow had served "as a model for the state, where power radiated out from the centre to the periphery."[73] But during the Cold War, Moscow's preeminence was also explicitly international. In Stalin's published greetings on the occasion of Moscow's eight hundredth anniversary in 1947, he emphasized the ways in which Moscow was "not only" the "center of Soviet democracy" but the capital of "all working people in the world"; "not only" the initiator of "new forms of everyday life for workers in the capital" but the world center of such efforts.[74] Some of this international superiority was military. *Around Old and New Moscow* opened with an account of Moscow's repeated victories against legions of foreign invaders.[75] Postwar Gor'kii Park offered a display of war trophies that included "German airplanes of all kinds, German tanks, German artillery, machine guns, weapon-carriers, tank-destroyers, specimens of the German equipment taken by the Soviet army."[76] Some of the superiority was cultural. A 1945 theater tour did its best to reinforce the notion of Moscow's continuing world prominence despite the destructions of war, reassuring tourists that Moscow was not only "the center of [Soviet] artistic life" but the home of "the best theater in the world."[77] (However, the instructions for the guides of this tour also reminded them to behave actively and dramatically in order to make up for the fact that the tour did not include any live performances.)[78] Moscow's architecture was said to compare favorably to Paris where Georges Haussmann's admittedly grand boulevards "had made the housing situation in the city worse [for workers]."[79] The author of *Our Moscow* argued that both Moscow and Paris were better than the "capitalist city" of New York. In Moscow, as in Paris, "one could walk along the street and think, maybe dream," whereas in New York "at every step something [unpleasant] lies in wait for you."[80]

In *Our Moscow,* the Soviet capital was represented as more civilized because of its similarities with Paris. More often, Moscow's "modern" facilities were marketed for tourists in an implicit contrast to backward-looking western countries whose monuments and churches were said to commemorate oppressive and exploitative events. In part, tours of a rebuilt, modern Moscow offered hope that other cities in the Soviet Union would also recover from the devastation of war. But the focus on the "modern" was also one way of addressing a central dilemma for Soviet tourist advocates, namely that so much of the Soviet Union's historical legacy and too many of its monumental buildings were connected to the autocracy or to Orthodoxy. As Georgii Popov, head of an organizing committee for Moscow's anniversary celebrations complained about a book on Moscow architecture: "three-quarters of the [historical monuments] shown are churches and only one-quarter [of the monuments] have been built in our Soviet period."[81] If we do not watch out, he concluded, our anniversary celebrations will look like something they might dream up to celebrate Riazan', "and not Moscow."[82] It is no surprise then that a 1947 "historical-architectural" guidebook to Moscow included pictures of prerevolutionary buildings and churches but also depicted cars speeding by new office buildings (Figure 7.3), "modern" double-decker buses, new housing that towered over older wooden buildings, and a sparkling clean Moscow metro system.[83]

Figure 7.3. Guidebook photo of 1946 office building of the Ministry of the Armed Forces of the USSR (architects M. V. Posokhin and A. A. Mndoiants) with car moving by. From Iu. Savitskii, *Moskva: Istoriko-arkhitekturnyi ocherk* (Moscow, 1947), photo 46.

A 1954 historical guidebook was similarly devoted to the seven new "high-rise" buildings now dominating the Moscow skyline.[84] In guide-books and in excursions, Moscow was presented as larger than life—a full description of Moscow was said to require tens of volumes (or tens of excursions), not just one.[85]

The Central Circulatory System

During the Khrushchev era, Moscow's privileged position was gradually reversed. Moscow might still be considered "Itinerary Number 1," but the periphery, not the center, became a place of renewal and transformation.[86] In the 1954 movie *Vernyedruz'ia* (True friends), a Moscow-based bureaucrat is rescued from inertia and returned to communist consciousness through tourism, in this case a lengthy trip on a small raft with two childhood friends. Although he returns to Moscow at the end of the film, it is his adventures in the rough, and in the periphery, that transform him.[87] In late Stalinism, however, while tourism to areas outside Moscow was encouraged, it was still with a highly centralizing and containing goal in mind. In 1951, *Pravda* published the "story" of an autoworker from Gor'kii who wanted to spend his vacation on "Mother Volga" but struggled to find a guidebook that could help him properly decipher what he would see: "He wanted to have a complete picture of the great construction projects and so naturally wanted a guide[book]. His quest was met with surprise in the book stores: 'There is no such thing as a Volga guide.' In the library he was told: 'Ah, so you are interested in books on [the] Volga? Well here is Olearius' Description of Travels in Muscovy, Tartaria and Persia, and he was given a book written in the first half of the 17th century . . . 'I would like something . . . about our times,' insisted the vacationist." The traveler finally found a guide written in 1947, but even this proved unsatisfactory to the author of the account in *Pravda*: "About Nizhny, [the book] mentions the process of food products there in the 17th century as reported by Olearius but forgets to mention what splendid automobiles are produced in the city's automobile works. [The book] never mentions a Stakhanovite by name despite the fact that at the time when the book was written the great city was famous for other things besides its monasteries. It is famous today for its innovators and scientists, but the author seems to be exclusively interested in the past." The *Pravda* article concluded with a plea for better guidebooks and travel accounts. "[Aleksandr] Pushkin, [Lev] Tolstoi, [Maksim] Gorky, [Vladimir] Mayakovsky and others have written travel books and considered this a very important literary genre because it develops love for the motherland and helps people to get to know it better."[88]

As this suggests, tourism was also a means of imaginatively and experientially integrating the Soviet body at the larger, collective level. "Travel in our country is great and purposeful; it is as beneficial as blood circulation," N. Moskvin argued in an article entitled "The Hospitality of Cities."[89] The thirtieth anniversary of the October revolution was celebrated by an almost 6,000-kilometer motorcycle and automobile race around the Soviet Union. The race began and ended in Moscow, both the literal and figurative "heart" of the collective communist body. The thirty participants raced down to the Crimea, up through the Baltic region, over to Leningrad, and back "home" to Moscow.[90] Through tourism, the more "exotic" parts of the USSR were incorporated into the central circulatory system of the Soviet Union.[91]

The happy cohesiveness of the Soviet Union was compared to the divisiveness of the United States, which was said to be torn apart by class, race, and region. In Ilya Erenburg's published travel account of his trip to the United States in 1946, he emphasized ethnic and regional differences and hierarchies. A significant portion of Erenburg's report focused on his travels in Mississippi and Alabama and the racism he observed there.[92] Soviet citizens were reassured that such was not the case in the Soviet Union. According to *Ogonek,* although thousands of kilometers separated Kaliningrad in the far west and Vladivostok in the Far East, the people of these cities lived "in a single Soviet atmosphere": "The people of Kaliningrad and those of Vladivostok greet [the anniversary of the October revolution] with the same happiness."[93] An article about the trip of artist N. M. Romanov to Lake Issyk-Kul' in the northern Tian'-Shan' mountains, similarly explained that "no matter where [Romanov] went, he was at home; everywhere was part of his Soviet homeland."[94] The "socialist homeland" even extended to the Soviet ships that provided a safe haven for those traveling to or from western Europe or the United States. Woodworker Khemaiak Kazandzhian left the United States to "return home" as part of the "Return to the Homeland" project. As he described it to the readers of *Ogonek:* "genuine democracy was evident" from the moment he received his new Soviet citizenship on board a Soviet ship while still docked in New York.[95] "Everywhere else is good, but there is no place like home," "Peoples' Artist" Nikolai Golovanov reassured the readers of *Ogonek.*[96]

Tourism helped inscribe both far-flung and new territories (the Baltic region, parts of the Far East, western Ukraine) with Soviet significance. Many accounts of non-Russian peoples minimized their exotic particularities. Thus Romanov was praised for describing everywhere he went "simply and naturally without being captivated by exoticism."[97] An article on the "sixteen capitals" of the Soviet Union admitted that they differed from each other geographically and culturally, but the photos chosen of each marked them as "Soviet," including images of monumental buildings in the Stalinist neo-classical style, trolleybuses, and in Baku, "a view of the city from the Kirov Park of Culture and Rest."[98] *Pravda* exclaimed similarly that Leninabad, "Tadzhikistan's oldest city," was no longer a "squalid feudal city" but an industrial center with streets that have been "remapped," a drama theater, a Palace of Culture, and three motion picture houses.[99] Travel accounts did sometimes describe ethnic and cultural difference, but often through photos of people in national dress.[100] This was not unlike Stalin's insistence in the 1930s that ethnic and national minorities demonstrate their uniqueness through folk dance which then became a ritualized expression of the "exotic" for popular consumption.

The tourist experience itself was also uniformly "Soviet" from the moment of arrival in a train station or airport. Although this standardization was not particular to late Stalinism, it may have helped reinforce the centralizing goal of this period. Instead of advertising regional tourist sites, local airports displayed busts of Stalin and Lenin and the same quotations from Lavrentii Beriia or Viacheslav Molotov about the importance of Soviet aviation. The only difference lay in which local heroes had their photos on the walls.[101] Most cities contained a park of culture and rest, and "the benches, the long plots of flowers, the statues of Stalin and of Lenin, the commemorations in stone of the fighting that was done in this town at the time of the Revolution" varied very little.[102] Tourist bases were similarly standardized, leading one inspector after Stalin's death to complain that a Georgian tour base had nothing in it of a Georgian nature—neither pictures, dishes in the café, curtains, or carpets.[103]

Despite all of this, the unfamiliar or "exotic" elements of the Caucasus or the Baltic region could hardly be denied. The exiled Duc de Richelieu had been appointed governor of Odessa soon after its founding, and in architecture and layout, the city still resembled a French provincial town.[104] So too with the "lush subtropical vegetation, the oleanders, the palm trees, the eucalyptus, the roses" of the Black Sea.[105] In addition, while promoting tourism to spaces of ethnic and cultural difference might have been intended as a way of "taming" these unpredictable places and minorities by Sovietizing their spaces for tourist consumption, it is not obvious that it had such an effect. In late imperial Austria, to take one comparative example, Tyrolean peasants subject to the curiosity of foreigners, "soon became aware of the distinctive elements of their particular culture."[106] Local peoples were then able to capitalize on foreigners' curiosity, promoting and emphasizing regional cultural differences in order to attract visitors. Further research on the reception and impact of tourism in non-Russian regions will tell us more about the relationship between tourism and local identity in the USSR.

The Good Life: The Promise of Tourism

The Soviet regime under Stalin did little to actually give its citizens a "good life" if by this we mean providing better living conditions and significantly more consumer goods, but officials were aware of public discontent and increased expectations following the war.[107] We associate attention to public need with the Khrushchev era.[108] What the history of tourism confirms, however, is that even in late Stalinism the state had to balance repression and terror with promises of significant material improvement. As Shelley Baranowski and Ellen Furlough argue in *Being Elsewhere: Tourism, Consumer Culture, and Identity in Modern Europe and North America*: "The competition between East and West was more than just an arms race. It amounted to a contest over which side could provide its citizens with 'the good life.'"[109] The promotion of domestic tourism was one way to remind Soviet citizens of the benefits of living in a socialist system and to discourage comparisons with the more rapid economic recovery of the west. Readers of the Soviet press could compare newspaper accounts of domestic tourism, which emphasized the healing, life-giving properties of Soviet spaces, to reports on America's "dirty and neglected" cities, which were said to be "full of rotting, messy, discarded goods, scraps of newspaper, cigarette butts and such waste."[110] Living in the west could put you "in constant danger of [your] health and life."[111] Living in the Soviet Union made you healthier and happier than ever. Thus in 1946, when most Soviet citizens were still buried under snow, and urban dwellers were provisioned only on the basis of ration cards, *Izvestiia* described the energetic efforts of the city of Sochi to prepare its resorts for the coming summer season: "Spring comes early in Sochi. In the last few days the temperature has been 20 degrees. The mimosas are magnificent."[112]

There were some contradictions inherent in this appeal to consumption in a socialist society.[113] The dominant ideology of tourism was still as presented above: tourism as purposeful and patriotic. In *Tourism in the USSR*, Dobkovich contrasted the purposefulness of Soviet turizm with the wastefulness of "bourgeois tourism," which consisted only of "entertainment" and the "pursuit of the unusual," often degenerating into "roving [*brodiazhnichestvo*] aimlessly and thoughtlessly."[114] But magazine advertisements suggested that Soviet tourists could not only travel but do so in style. A large, back cover ad from *Ogonek* in 1948 showed a luxury liner cruising in tropical waters alongside palm trees (Figure 7.4).[115] The Ministry of Light Industry promoted its leather goods with an advertisement in *Vokrug sveta* depicting six elegant leather suitcases, including a steamer trunk, stacked on the front portico of a fine resort, with car and driver pictured below.[116] Links were made between tourism, better and more comfortable forms of transportation, and the promise of a better (and more modern) future. In June 1947, an *Ogonek* correspondent described special "comfortable" express trains designed just to transport vacationers to the Black Sea health resorts. The accompanying pho-

Figure 7.4. The ship *Rossiia* at anchor off the Black Sea coast. From *Ogonek*, 1948.

tos showed happy children, an eager male worker gazing out the train window, and two men (in suits) playing chess in a spacious cabin.[117] *Ogonek* also described with evident pride the opening of the first two public car dealerships in Moscow and Leningrad in 1947. That few could buy these cars (or that few cars were available to buy) is suggested by the fact that the stores sold motorcycles and bicycles, as well as cars.[118] But the propaganda value was perhaps more important. This article was prominently located next to another on the ills of capitalist New York.

These advertisements and articles clearly suggest more than attention to material need per se. In the economically challenging conditions of postwar Russia, it is difficult to argue that elegant leather suitcases were a material necessity. What was being manipulated was public desire, and in a form inconsistent with the supposed goals of socialist advertising to teach "rational consumption," rather than to create insatiable consumer demand.[119] Why introduce the possibility of luxury cruises when so many were even unable to travel by train? Why contradict the otherwise determinedly Soviet portrayals of tourism found in earnest books and travel guides? In part, the answer was a pragmatic one: the state need for funds outweighed a commitment to ideological purity. Many of the large advertisements on the back covers of *Ogonek* and *Vokrug sveta* linked fantastical vacations with putting money aside in a state savings bank or buying a bond. This was likely meant to make the obligatory subscriptions to state bonds more palatable, though it must have been especially grating to those who had lost much of their life savings in the December 1947 currency reform in which cash had to be exchanged at a rate of ten to one, and state bonds were suddenly worth two-thirds less.[120] Tourism was a particularly useful form of state-generated fantasy because vacations are so often something dreamed about, saved for, and seen as a future reward for work well done.[121] But tourism was also useful precisely because of its indeterminate quality. After all, the state had chosen the draconian method of currency reform as a means to increase revenue when it might instead have increased the output of consumer goods. Tourism was a safer sort of "promise" than consumer goods in that its absence was not so easily noticed on local shelves.

But advertisements for luxurious tourist experiences were also examples of a postwar emphasis on "culture" (*kul'tura*). In her analysis of middle-class values in Soviet fiction, Vera Dunham emphasizes a petit bourgeois interest in freshly enameled elevators, newly waxed parquet floors, and hall lights "made in the shape of lilies," a fantasy of consumption of which tourism may surely be a part.[122] But Katerina Clark's broader understanding of postwar "culture" as "divans and bedspreads" but also as modernization ("a sewage system, paved roads") and politeness is even more apt. In her study of the socialist realist novel, Clark argues that in the postwar period, "[most of the working population] sought to rise in the hierarchy of status and enjoy a higher standard of living, and to this end they endeavored to comport themselves as was deemed fit for a person of their standing."[123] It was an "official doctrine," Clark explains, that "the experience of World War II had brought about a radical change in Soviet man, who was now more sophisticated than he had been before."[124] Travel (even if not always tourism) has long been associated with "cultured" sophistication and status. In this case, both state and society (or some elements of it) may have been in agreement that tourism was desirable for the supposedly more sophisticated postwar citizen. Just what kind of tourism was ideal, as well as possible, remained a matter of debate.

"Shortcomings and Difficulties"

The multiple articles and advertisements in newspapers and journals about tourism and health resorts were meant, in part, to reassure people that their material desires would be taken care of. They were more like fairy tales than travel accounts, however. Many of the articles about tourism and health resorts were far from accurate, as the Soviet press itself sometimes admitted. The numerous accounts of happy, health-giving tourist experiences contrasted with other reports of problems with transportation and with poor, dirty conditions. Advertisements for air travel did not mention that planes usually flew only during the day, that waits were often very long, and that in winter air travel often stopped altogether because of packed earth runways damaged by snow and mud.[125] As P. Ponomarev, deputy to the Penza Province Soviet complained in a letter to *Izvestiia:* "Recently I had to make a flight from Penza to Molotov and back. At the Penza airport they refused to sell me a through ticket by way of Moscow under the pretext that one had to put in a request for it three days before the flight. I had to get a ticket to Moscow in the hope of attracting the attention of officials at the Vnukovo airport [Moscow]. But in Vnukovo the official on duty told me that since the ticket was not a through one I had to go back to the Bykovo airport. At the Bykovo airport there were no empty seats in the plane. I had to go back to Moscow and get a train ticket."[126] G. Osipov took a train to the Crimea intending to spend his vacation at the rest home of the All-Soviet Radio Broadcast Committee. "The committee issues passes all over the Soviet Union," Osipov explained, "and persistently publicizes the merits of its rest homes." Osipov's Crimean vacation was far less than ideal, however.[127] In a letter to the editor of *Izvestiia,* I. Rudakov complained similarly about his experiences at the Lipetskii Spa: "I went there this year hoping to spend a profitable time resting and restoring my health. Alas, my hopes were not realized. . . . The rooms are destitute of comfort, containing only rusty, dirty cots. Besides, they are used as passages to reach other rooms. This is not much of a rest."[128] Not only were hotels often unattractive, they also had few free rooms, since many rooms were occupied by permanent residents who lived there full time because of a lack of other housing.[129] According to N. Makarov, who hoped that the tourist movement would become a "mass movement," by 1951 trade union societies still had not done what they should to satisfy the Soviet people.[130]

Although it is not surprising that conditions in Soviet tourist facilities and hotels were far from ideal just five years after the end of World War II, it is significant that these complaints were published in the central newspapers. This suggests that the central government wanted the directors of sanatoria and resorts, the local trade unions, and the directors of various responsible ministries to act quickly. It also suggests that the regime wanted people to think that they had popular everyday interests in mind and that these interests were foiled by local "shortcomings and difficulties," not by a lack of state attention to the "needs of man."[131] Thus, a 1952 article in *Izvestiia* gave credit to the Soviet state's ongoing efforts to organize vacations for workers, which was said to demonstrate the "constant concern of the Communist Party and Soviet government for the welfare of the people."[132] The article then went on to attribute problems in organizing summer vacations for workers to the Ministry of Public Health and the Central Council of Trade Unions, as well as the local departments of health. The author of an unfavorable article about Crimean resorts listed those at fault by name (Comrades Golenishchev, Kirsanov, Slavshchik, and Muraveva) and accused them of visiting the Crimea not to "eliminate irregularities" but for a holiday.[133] But, it was not just journalists who complained about conditions and service in health resorts and tourist bases. Letters to camp directors and comments left in opinion books show that tourists themselves were sometimes dissatisfied, most often with the food and the surly staff.[134] Archival documents show that problems with tourism were acknowledged at the upper levels. In September 1950, the Presidium of the Central Trade Union insisted that "improvements were necessary in transport, food, inventory, medicines, informational materials, and advice."[135] "We are an extraordinary people," one Russian told a visiting foreigner ten years later. "We can defeat the German armies but cannot organize the exits from a railway station."[136]

"We Know That Our Journey Must Be and Will Be the Happiest!"

In an article entitled, "The Hospitality of Cities," N. Moskvin extolled the Soviet tourist experience: "Who does not dream of seeing something remarkable and extraordinary when he arrives in a strange town? The spirit of the traveler is open to new impressions and is always bright and friendly. When he arrives at the station and alights on the platform the new arrival, as it were, holds out his hand to a strange town and awaits a joyous handshake."[137]

Moskvin's tourist sounds as if he was free, even encouraged, to seek out the unexpected and the mind-opening. But, as we have seen, postwar tourism was decidedly not about forming "new impressions" but about internalizing official ones. Although Soviet travel was at times marketed as recreational, at heart it was "serious fun."[138] Published materials on tourism assumed (or assured?) that the lessons learned from tourism were always positive. Even the "obstacles and difficulties" that were likely to occur in almost every trip served an important "moral" purpose leading to "collectivism, courage, will power, persistence, patience, endurance."[139] In the Stalinist worldview, there was no room for disappointment, frustration, or dislike of the Soviet self (just as there was no room for admiration of the capitalist other). As student tourists en route through a peasant village replied to well-wishers: "We know that our journey must be and will be the happiest!"[140]

The function assigned Soviet turizm differs from that assigned tourism in other nonauthoritarian regimes. Some scholars of mass tourism have described tourism negatively as a passive, prefabricated "pseudo-event."[141] But recently, tourism has been seen more positively as an active search for authenticity; as a potentially mind-opening experience with the possibility to reaffirm or alter "the traveler's sense of self in unpredictable ways"; and as a "cultural laboratory where people have been able to experiment with new aspects of their identities."[142] This essay does not explore the personal experience of Soviet tourists, some of whom may indeed have projected their own understandings even on such prepackaged experiences as the Soviet excursion. Further work may be able to tell us what happens to the tourist experience in an authoritarian state when the didactic elements are heightened and the alternatives minimized. Did the Soviet tourist, as Walter Benjamin described his own tourist experience, return "from vacation as a homeless person"?[143] Or was their sense of belonging to the Soviet homeland reinforced, as the state certainly hoped it would be? What I hope is clear from this more limited exploration, is that official understandings of tourism were driven by regime anxiety about loyalty. Travel can be about adventure, about self-discovery, about relaxation, about consumption, but in the late Stalin period it might best be seen as a "ritual of reassurance."[144] Tourism was a ritual of reassurance for the state: it offered a means of producing socialist-minded citizens focused internally on the advantages of the Soviet system. It may also have been a ritual of reassurance for Soviet citizens in so far as tourism offered hope that postwar life would be an improvement on what they had thus far endured.

Chapter 8

Dangerous Liaisons

Soviet-Bloc Tourists and the Temptations of the Yugoslav Good Life in the 1960s and 1970s

PATRICK HYDER PATTERSON

During the 1960s and 1970s, Yugoslavia emerged as the success story of socialist Europe, an intriguing "in-between" zone that, to many, seemed to offer a prescription for bridging the Cold War divide with a promising mix of the best of the East and West. Capitalizing on Yugoslavia's natural features, especially the stunning Adriatic coast, tourist enterprises used the country's low-cost but increasingly impressive tourist infrastructure to lure travelers from all over Europe and beyond, and tourism became a mainstay of the economy. Yugoslavia was, for many Westerners, their first or only experience of life in a communist country, and these visits by tourists and travelers helped make the Yugoslav experiment the subject of a rich, lively, and frequently quite positive literature in both popular and scholarly forums in the West. The phenomenon explored here represents a parallel development that has, until now, received almost no scholarly attention despite its critical political, economic, and cultural significance: Yugoslavia's controversial and highly influential role as a magnet for travelers from Soviet-bloc countries. Approaching the problem comparatively, this investigation asks how institutions and individuals in other countries in socialist Eastern Europe understood, represented, and managed the possibilities—and the perceived perils—of travel to welcoming yet wayward Yugoslavia.

Addressing tourism in Yugoslavia in an era when it had become both quite robust and extraordinarily meaningful, the project places special emphasis on the golden years of the Yugoslav experiment with self-management socialism, seeking to understand how travel to the country was experienced, monitored, promoted, and regulated during the period from the early 1960s through the late 1970s. By this time, Yugoslavia had already become highly suspect in orthodox communist circles. The state and party had broken away from the Soviet bloc in 1948 in a power struggle between Tito and Stalin, and the rift had been, at best, only partially repaired in subsequent years, as Yugoslavia drifted westward in both its foreign and domestic policies. Worker self-management, a system that sought to tie the performance of Yugoslav enterprises to a variety of market incentives, seemed to some Marxist critics to smack of back-door capitalism, with its reference to dubious values such as profit, return on investment, and competition. First introduced in 1950, and strengthened gradually thereafter with an especially far-reaching set of market reforms in 1965, self-management appeared to yield dramatic results: Yugoslavia, or at least its more developed northern and western regions and urban centers, became remarkably prosperous.

As in no other economy of socialist Europe, the country's productive capacities were increasingly oriented to the satisfaction of ordinary consumers' needs and wants. By the mid-1960s, a media-driven culture of consumption was flourishing, causing celebration and worry about its profound resemblances to the lively consumer societies of postwar Western Europe. Shopping in Yugoslavia was quite unlike shopping anywhere else in the socialist East. The country's attractiveness as a consumer destination for citizens of the Soviet-bloc countries was a source of considerable pride among Yugoslavs, and some Yugoslav products and brands with a reputation for "European" quality were especially sought after.[1]

It was this political, social, and economic context, and the much-discussed Yugoslav "difference," that made visits to the country by citizens of the Warsaw Pact states so potentially meaningful. After 1948, going to Yugoslavia meant going to something other than a safe, "friendly," reliably communist state. Indeed, the official regulations of the German Democratic Republic counted Yugoslavia among the "*nicht-sozialistische Länder,*" a designation that not only demonstrated the wariness shown toward the independence of "Titoist" government, but also had the practical effect of making travel to the country rather more difficult.[2] The divergence between the errant Yugoslav line and the path taken by the more orthodox, centrally planned societies became only more obvious after the boom years of the 1960s had begun in earnest.

This chapter seeks to begin the process of uncovering and interpreting the historical significance of these dangerous liaisons with the Yugoslav "difference." It looks at tourists from Hungary, Czechoslovakia, and the German Democratic Republic, states notable either for their comparatively wealthy—and hence mobile—populations, for their ease of access to Yugoslavia, or both. The unsettling implications of travel to Yugoslavia are, in turn, shown to be linked to key problems in the conceptualization of tourism and leisure travel as a historical force with global dimensions. To reach these critical issues, the research draws on a variety of primary sources, including guidebooks, promotional materials, literary representations and visitor accounts, government documents and statistics, and coverage in mass-media publications in which tourism, travel, and life in foreign lands were recurring subjects.[3]

Special periodicals devoted specifically to travel and tourism, which appeared at least sporadically in some countries, have proven especially revealing. The careful scrutiny of sources such as these, and a deeper consideration of the nature of touristic experience, help correct some of the existing imbalances in the historiography of what party leaders referred to as "really existing" socialism, a phrase that reveals both how adamant the communists were about the promise of a radiant future and how keen they were to stress their own present-day accomplishments in the face of great obstacles.

Shaped for decades by the historiographical imperatives of the Cold War, studies of socialism have long tended to privilege issues of high politics and to stress large-scale systemic functions and distinctions. This approach made socialist Yugoslavia attractive to and noteworthy within Western scholarship because of its comparative political freedom, its administrative decentralization, and its departure from centralized planning, but it has left us with only a very incomplete understanding of what life was like for ordinary people in Yugoslavia and in other socialist states. To gain a stronger sense of the elusive socialist Everyday, we need to look beyond high politics, great power struggles, and stark conflicts over human rights issues—important as these are—and move instead toward a consideration of subjects that affected more people, in more ways, more of the time. We need not trash the Cold War schemata entirely: there were indeed critical differences between the two contending systems, but when it comes to the experience of everyday life under socialism, these played out at least as much in terms of consumption practice as in the realm of political freedom. Consumption opportunities mattered far more "on the ground" than is commonly acknowledged (though many observers have noted, if typically only superficially and in passing, that the failure to satisfy consumer desires played a large part in the ultimate collapse of state socialism). And if these everyday wants, needs, hopes, and yearnings of ordinary consumer-citizens are central to the story, then so too are the practices, attitudes, and culture of tourism, a phenomenon that scholars have increasingly come to understand to be bound up tightly with consumption, and one that may perhaps best be understood as a special form or mode of consumption.

The historiographical issues that arise in connection with tourism in socialist Yugoslavia are, it turns out, extraordinarily rich and significant.[4]

Some matters, important enough in their own right, must fall outside the scope of the present investigation. The single greatest tourist "draw" in Yugoslav history was, without a doubt, the 1984 Winter Olympics in Sarajevo. Crucial as that event was for Yugoslavia's prestige and for international awareness of the country, it is best left untreated here. The hosting of an Olympic gathering is so unusual that it tends to obscure fundamental patterns: what tourists were doing when they visited the games bore little resemblance to what they regularly did when spending time in Yugoslavia. Their day-to-day activities would have been very different, the cultural and symbolic content quite out of the ordinary, and the nature of the experience dramatically altered by the huge and utterly atypical Olympic crowds. Doubts about the representative quality of the Sarajevo episode are only compounded by the fact that the games were sited in Bosnia-Herzegovina, a very infrequent and comparatively inaccessible destination for foreign travelers. Moreover, by the time of the Olympic events, Yugoslavia's economy had been in the midst of a dramatic collapse for at least five years, a period marked by unemployment, shortages, and wild hyperinflation that resulted in widespread disillusionment about the Yugoslav system both domestically and abroad and made the country somewhat less appealing to visitors from the Soviet bloc. To best capture a sense of the structural, long-term patterns that emerged from Yugoslavia's vaunted exceptionalism, this study concentrates instead on sources from the two prior decades, when the economy was booming, interest in Yugoslavia was soaring, and the country seemed to offer a genuinely socialist alternative to the "Affluent Society" of the West.

The Road Less Traveled: The Role of Tourism in Socialist Society

In many ways, the examination of Soviet-bloc tourism in Yugoslavia stands in a peculiar, (and peculiarly revealing) relationship to contemporary empirical and conceptual approaches to the historiography of tourism, travel, leisure, and the consumption dimensions of these phenomena. Indeed important commonalities exist between Soviet-bloc tourism and the classic version of tourism that has drawn so much scholarly attention of late, that is, the tourism undertaken by citizens of capitalist societies. Yet there were also number of critical ways in which socialist tourism did not neatly conform to prevailing theoretical understandings. Those distinctions warrant further consideration.

The conceptual complications caused by the specific dynamics of socialist travel arise almost immediately once we start to look at life under communism in light of the dominant theoretical and interpretative tendencies of Western scholarship. Many scholarly interpretations of the touristic experience, for example, focus on its *restorative* functions, its capacity to generate an altered state of healthy removal from the workaday world. In this view, tourism is understood as creating an "elsewhere" that is filled with meaning for the "normal" everyday life that has temporarily been left behind. As this line of analysis is often either explicitly anthropological or deeply indebted to anthropological approaches, such formulations tend to conceive of tourism as representing a form of sacred experience that gives meaning to the profane and the ordinary. Nelson Graburn, for example, frames the problem in terms of the opposition between the holiday and the everyday: "Vacations involving travel, i.e., tourism, since all 'proper' vacations involve travel, are the modern equivalent for secular societies to the annual and lifelong sequences of festivals for more traditional, God-fearing societies. Fundamental is the contrast between the ordinary/compulsory work state spent 'at home' and the nonordinary/voluntary 'away from home' sacred state. . . . Thus holidays (holy, sacred days now celebrated by traveling away from home) are what makes 'life worth living' as though ordinary life is not life or at least not the kind of life worth living." Importantly, this conception also stresses the critical purposive aspects of tourism: the journey becomes a vehicle for accomplishment, transformation, and self-improvement, while leisure *without* travel—that is, simply staying at home and doing nothing—is interpreted as idleness and hence an "improper" activity.[5]

Such restorative, extraordinary functions of leisure travel were indeed present in the tourism undertaken by citizens of communist states as well. Still, it appears that in this regard, tourism functioned rather differently in the specific context of socialism. A prime project of socialist governments was to valorize work, and in this way to praise and encourage precisely those "ordinary/compulsory" elements of life that characterized the everyday, workaday domain. Given communist commitments to the value of productive activity, any acknowledgment of the "sacred" aspects of leisure ran the risk that it might profane work itself. Yet in the end, at least in this one respect, common modes of analyzing the nature and meaning of touristic activity do assist the effort to understand socialist leisure, for even in the socialist context, where elite institutions of party and state mattered more, tourism was by no means exclusively a matter of official discourse and the top-down transmission of values and norms. Ordinary citizens were busily generating their own culture of tourism, too, and there is ample reason to conclude that for them, tourism did indeed involve the sort of quest for escape and restoration that contemporary theories have posited.[6]

Less relevant in the present context are those interpretative approaches that read tourism as first and foremost an imperialist endeavor.[7] Keyed as they are to the venues and practices of capitalism, these theories of leisure travel prove, in the end, to be of rather limited utility for an analysis of tourism within the socialist world, where a range of movement limited by travel restrictions and by the sheer lack of disposable income tended to keep tourists within the ambit of a collection of societies and cultures not all that different from their own. The prospect of visits to the Soviet Union's various Asian republics and to other exotic socialist destinations such as China, Cuba, Mozambique, and Vietnam does offer some points of contact with theoretical conceptions derived from the experiences of the capitalist West, but for all its potential symbolic potency, this sort of socialist tourism was comparatively rare. It is perhaps tempting to also look for evidence of some analogous "imperial gaze" in the record of Soviet tourism to East-bloc countries. The research for this project has not included an examination of sources from the USSR, but a review of Soviet coverage of travel to Yugoslavia could prove revealing in many ways, especially given the uneasy geopolitical relationship and ideological competition between the Soviets and the wayward Yugoslav communists. Of much greater immediate relevance to the effort to integrate the socialist experience into the theorization of tourism, however, is the recent inclination to treat leisure travel as a powerful form of, and critical venue for, practices of consumption.[8]

If tourism has only lately and partially become a subject of deep and sustained academic inquiry,[9] this is even more the case when it comes to the complex relationships between tourism and socialism, a political system that sought to offer an alternative to both capitalism and to the "consumer society" that contemporary capitalism has tended to generate. The characteristics and consequences of travel under socialism have, until now, drawn very little scholarly attention. Empirically, we are just beginning to scratch the surface, and there has been no sustained effort to determine how the particularities of the various socialist cases mesh, or fail to mesh, with the theory of tourism studies developed in—and often, *about*—the West. The parallel phenomenon of visits by citizens of capitalist states to socialist countries raises its own set of special problems, but tourism in this direction across the East-West divide has been similarly neglected as well.[10]

Recently, however, there have been some signs of an awakening to the deeper meanings of tourism for socialist societies and to the implications of the special socialist experience for the effort to conceptualize the nature and historical impact of travel and tourism more generally. Perhaps most notably, the premier interdisciplinary area-studies journal in Russian and East European affairs, *Slavic Review,* devoted a special issue to the problems that tourism presents in light of the traditionally

"backward" Russian socioeconomic structure and the aggressively modernizing Soviet response.[11] The studies assembled in that volume represent a welcome recognition of the importance of tourism as a genuinely
global historical phenomenon, yet they also underscore (and indeed
explicitly acknowledge) how little we still know about how tourism really
functioned and what it meant in communist societies. And if this shortage of empirical knowledge remains a real problem with respect to Russia and the Soviet Union, it is even more distressing when it comes to
the lands of Eastern Europe, which have traditionally elicited far less
scholarly attention.

Yet the distinctive experience of East European travelers offers a rich
source of insights into the nature and significance of everyday life under
socialism (and, I argue, socialist "high politics" as well), and it is one
that should not be ignored in favor of an overriding emphasis on the
great Cold War enemy. Without the evidence of the East European
cases, we take away only a partial and misleading picture. It is striking,
for example, that the excellent studies of Soviet tourism appearing in
the *Slavic Review* collection deal almost exclusively with *domestic* travel.
What Soviet citizens were most likely to experience thus stands in stark
contrast to the subjects of much recent scholarship on tourism, with its
focus on engagement with the foreign, the distant, and the exotic.
Because of their looser legal regimes and more developed economies,
most of the societies of the East bloc, the Soviet "satellites" in the old
Cold War parlance, undertook tourism in somewhat different (yet not
entirely dissimilar) ways. The particularities of these countries' experience thus raise a number of special empirical and conceptual issues.

It is one of the virtues of the contemporary attempt to understand
tourism in deeper conceptual terms that it alerts us to the ways in which
tourism can represent the fulfillment of various political and cultural
agendas, quite often unseen and unrecognized, and present both on the
part of the visitor and the visited. Travelers are almost never, it bears
remembering, innocents abroad. Wherever we encounter it, the discourse of tourism is usually not only richly descriptive, but in important
ways, profoundly normative as well.

In socialist society, tourism was even more a matter of expectations,
projects, and prescriptions. Perhaps surprisingly, given socialist societies' saturation with straightforward, often heavy-handed propaganda,
the touristic literature that developed in these countries was not blatantly directive. If we delve deeply into the representation of touristic
activity, however, we can find a rich set of implicit or explicit political
and cultural messages. Socialist authorities were keenly attentive to the
ideological content of tourism. Diane Koenker observes, for example,
that in the Soviet Union "travel, touring and prescribed leisure were

very much official projects," and the pairing of tight control over the press with communist ideology about "proper" leisure and tourism as a domain of the state only tended to intensify the traditional prescriptive inclinations of travel writing and travel writers, as seen in Moscow city guidebooks from the Soviet period that "told travelers what to look for and how to see."[12] A similar tendency toward this "official" conception of tourism is present in the record of other state-socialist countries as well.[13] Agents of the state explicitly construed the promotion of tourism, both foreign and domestic, as a political endeavor, and the idea that tourism must serve as a deliberate, managed part of the formation of socialist consciousness was thus a standard theme in communist discourse about tourism.

These notions emerge clearly, for example, in one comment from the editor-in-chief of *Turista Magazin*, communist Hungary's leading periodical for travel and tourism, who observed that "here at home tourism touches every level of the population; it is therefore no accident that we call it a political matter. Behind the movement there stands a powerful background. Tourism is one of the elements of education; it takes on a leading role in turning a person into someone well informed, with broad horizons. . . . Our socialist society has clarified the complex concept of tourism and established its conditions."[14] Such themes and such language—the broadening of horizons, travel-as-education, tourism as an arena for party and state intervention—are typical of the state-socialist literature of tourism. Again and again, we find both institutional and individual actors planning for, analyzing, and worrying about the complex of matters that one official of IBUSZ, Hungary's state-sponsored travel agency, called the "social, economic, and cultural-ideological influences and consequences" of foreign travel. Communists recognized that tourism *mattered*. These things were not to be left to chance.

The context of socialist governance also squarely presents us with tourism's function as a reward to ordinary citizens. This particular aspect of socialist tourism connects in important ways with the influential theoretical tendency, discussed earlier, to see tourism as restorative, as an activity that confers meaning to life by removing people from their everyday, workaday existence: implicit in that idea of a sacred, distanced, "elsewhere" state there is clearly some notion of reward as well. In capitalist societies, however, it is not at all clear just *who* is granting the rewards: Is it the vendors of transportation, lodging, meals, souvenirs, and other touristic consumables, who (for a price, of course) make available all the joys of travel and tourism? Is leisure travel instead a more reflexive process, one in which the individual tourist-consumer rewards herself? Or is the agent-benefactor something more vague and slippery, this amorphous but deeply felt "way" or "system" of "ours" that delivers the Good Life to those who work hard and play by the rules?

The complexities of capitalism cloud the subject. In socialist society, the connections between behaviors and rewards were much more explicitly conceptualized, and the source of the benefits offered was very clearly identified. As socialist states seized on the idea of leisure as a necessary counterpart to, and compensation for, the hard work that was expected of each citizen in the long struggle to "build socialism," there sprung up an impressive infrastructure of tourism, including, in some states, a vast network of government-run, heavily subsidized, low-cost tourist centers in resort areas. At little or no cost, ordinary workers could retreat to these beach communities, lakeside villages, mountain retreats, and spa towns for a few weeks each year in order to relax and escape the cares of the workaday world.

Working in tandem with this concept and practice of tourism-as-reward was the idea that tourism itself was, or should be, a form of education. Here again, the conception turns on the idea of the state as the central actor, mobilizing resources and citizens in an activity that was understood, often explicitly, as a future-oriented *project*, with the familiar communist aims of improving taste, edifying the populace, developing a specifically socialist sort of knowledge about the world and the role of socialism in it, and thereby contributing to the creation of a common socialist consciousness.[15] Here, too, the socialist experience offers some points of contact with the prevailing theories of tourism studies, especially with the notion that tourism, undertaken "properly" at least, is a mode of personal cultivation, something that is "good for you."[16] These commonalities notwithstanding, the socialist experience is probably most significant in this respect because it clearly represents something more than a simple recapitulation and reproduction of the more familiar Western practices and values. Accordingly, socialist tourism complicates and challenges the prevailing interpretations of tourism as a world-historical force.

The idea of tourism as a form of education was coupled with a belief that tourism should serve as a means of discovering the glories of one's own country, and deepening an appreciation of, and sense of loyalty to, the homeland. Socialist societies deliberately promoted tourism as both an expression of (and a means of further developing) a healthy and desirable sense of patriotism. Thus we find the East German women's magazine *Für dich*, a mass-market weekly with a huge circulation of more than 900,000, urging readers in 1963 to experience the joys of "Discovery Trips through the Republic."[17] (Note the ambiguities present here in the odd insistence on the precise legal form of the state, a symptom of the East German government's peculiar plight, especially after the closure of its borders with the West: Was this just a reference to that part of a preexisting and still-existing *Heimat*—"Deutschland"—that happened at the time to included in the GDR? Or were citizens instead being invited to take to the road to discover their "own country," a newly created "homeland"?) This emphasis on domestic tourism as a celebration of one's own state and society, and thus as an instrument of patriotic loyalty, was a constant element of *Für dich*'s coverage,[18] and it crops up frequently in numerous other Soviet-bloc sources as well.[19]

Regarding the joys and bounty of the homeland, there were sometimes deeper, more complicated messages, too. In her insightful study of the culture of tourism that developed in the Soviet Union in the waning years of Stalin's rule, Anne Gorsuch concludes that the Soviet authorities charged with the development and oversight of tourism consistently drove home the message that domestic travel was to be preferred over excursions abroad because citizens of the USSR could not be assured of a genuinely hospitable reception beyond the safe confines of the homeland. Tourism therefore functioned as what Gorsuch calls a "ritual of reassurance": for the state itself, tourism provided, or at least promised to provide, "a means of producing socialist-minded citizens focused internally on the advantages of the Soviet system," while for ordinary citizens tourism held out the prospect of a future that was continually (if only very gradually) improving, thanks to the efforts of the state.[20]

Of course, communist authorities had no monopoly on the linkage of tourism with national pride, allegiance, and well-being. Powerful actors in modern capitalist systems have frequently attempted to stimulate and manage domestic tourism with reliance on a quite similar patriotic imperative. Along these lines, for instance, Marguerite Shaffer concludes that tourism in the United States during the period from 1880 to 1940 was increasingly bound up with the production of a genuinely *national* American culture. Linked to the workings of a nascent corporate-industrial economy, tourism became, in this view, "a form of geographical consumption that centered on the sights and scenes of the American nation," developing with time into "a ritual of American citizenship" that trained citizens to be loyal, grateful, and contented, and in the end, served as one of the prime cultural forces that defined what America was and what it meant to be American.[21]

But notwithstanding the evident similarities, tourism under communism should be understood as something rather different. Viewed in comparative terms, the conceptualization of tourism that was articulated and practiced in state socialism is, in the end, at least as noteworthy for the ways in which it diverged from capitalist patterns as it is for the commonalities between the two systems. In capitalist societies, the linkages between leisure travel and national identity have been, if not haphazard, then certainly not carefully controlled, and by no means the product of tightly coordinated and consistently integrated planning. Moreover, as it has unfolded in the capitalist/corporate order, the process has been notable for its decentralization and for the almost staggering multiplicity of historical subjects involved. As Shaffer's account makes clear, the creation of a shared vision of America through "national tourism" was a project undertaken by a remarkably wide range of public and private actors, including car manufacturers and railroads, other corporations and business enterprises, civic groups and clubs, members of the good-roads movement, publishers of guidebooks and other tourist-oriented mass media, governmental entities such as the National Park Service and the Works Progress Administration, and novelists, essayists, diarists, and other private individuals.

Socialist tourism was "national tourism," if at all, in a quite different way. It would be foolish, of course, to view tourism under communism as simply a project of the state. Yet the socialist state was understood to have a special mission, and unique competencies, in developing tourism and leisure toward national ends. By exercising those powers vigorously, the party and government authorities of socialist Europe made the practice and experience of tourism something very different from what developed under capitalism. Most critically, private individuals, and non-state civil society more generally, played a greatly attenuated role in the articulation of a common national conception of tourism. Market forces, and market actors such as the business groups and corporate enterprises that so strongly shaped the American experience by pursuing national motifs to their own ends, were largely removed from the field. Of course, the complexity of the socialist state's institutions did allow for a variety of views and approaches, and individual citizens were by no means merely the passive recipients of state action. Quite to the contrary: there is every reason to believe that on the ground, in their day-to-day lives and in their personal and group experiences of travel, individual citizens did generate a potent, broadly shared, popular tourist culture.

But by and large, this bottom-up mass culture of leisure has been obscured from view; it remained popular without being popularized, although East German cinema seems to have allowed some notable exceptions. While capitalist society has hardly been a reliable conduit for transmitting genuine popular experiences of travel to the forefront of media representation, this incongruity between what was presented and what was lived proved even more acute in socialist systems, where the state and its institutions tended to occupy almost the entire field of public discourse. Much of the force of Shaffer's argument about the emergence of "national tourism" in America comes precisely from her determination that the national dimensions of tourism were not just propagated from the top by elite actors, but were also received, endorsed, cultivated, and imbued with new meaning and content by ordinary individual citizens. They, too, became the subjects of the nation. It is this popular dimension of the tourist experience, I believe, that allows us to conclude that it was truly "national."

Culture resides in the shared quality of expression. The varieties of expressive form—ideas, attitudes, values, art, practice—do not amount to a "culture" unless they are commonly embraced and broadly shared. The socialist state with its unusual powers certainly did promulgate a national vision of leisure travel, but that does not permit a straightforward determination that the popular culture of socialist tourism was indeed "national." At this early point in the development of tourism history, we do not know whether the state succeeded. As a result of party-state decisions about what sorts of expression would be encouraged, permitted, disseminated, and archived, much of the evidence of the way ordinary individuals experienced tourism—and how they worked, alongside the state, to shape and give meaning to the experience of leisure—has been lost, or was never created in the first place. These departures from capitalist paradigms, and from the intellectual paradigms of tourism scholarship developed almost exclusively with reference to capitalist practice, leave the national quality of socialist tourism open to debate and further exploration.

Innocents Abroad: The Perils of Foreign Travel

At the same time, the very urgency and transparency of the communists' efforts to make tourism "national" renders the "problem" of international travel all the more important. In the case of domestic tourism, the desiderata of socialist planning and ideology—the use of travel as a means to promote economic development, social cohesion, and civic loyalty—dovetailed nicely with hard and cold economic realities: it was perhaps a bit easier to convince citizens of the pleasures of home when few had the surplus income to sample any foreign destinations. If, in the waning years of Stalinism in the USSR, coercion thus made a virtue of necessity, we encounter a rather different pattern when the focus shifts to Eastern Europe in the 1960s and 1970s, a period marked by lasting, indeed structural, changes as the result of the "thaw" following Stalin's death. For a host of economic, cultural, political, and not least geographic reasons, ordinary citizens of socialist Eastern Europe had at their disposal many more opportunities to experience the comforts and curiosities of "elsewhere" than their Soviet counterparts, who, conversely, could point with some justification to the wide range of touristic pleasures that their territorially expansive homeland could offer. Here history matters, too: many of the "East Europeans" of the 1960s and 1970s were also once (and future) "Central Europeans": citizens of the old German and Habsburg empires or their successors who could draw on the memories and shared experiences of an increasingly cosmopolitan tourism tradition that had developed before World War II, when these peoples were the subjects—and perhaps even more frequently, the objects—of a wide variety of cross-border encounters.

Unlike their Soviet confreres, citizens of many of the East European socialist states therefore could and did travel abroad more freely, in all senses of the word, and that freedom raised a set of special concerns for those entrusted with the planning, promotion, and management of tourism. Domestic travel remained comparatively unproblematic; it implicated the joys and satisfactions of "home," a place that typically does command considerable popular loyalty and affection, however imperfect it might be.[22] Foreign travel, on the other hand, meant leaving home, seeing contrasts, looking at alternatives. If tourism was, in the lands of state socialism, habitually presented as part of a larger package of government-coordinated efforts to provide the Good Life, that approach placed the actions of government at the forefront, teaching citizens to closely associate tourism with the state. This was, of course, a two-edged sword: tourism could be used to call attention to the state's accomplishments, but it also could reveal the inadequacies and failures of government policy.

Foreign travel therefore raised a particularly thorny set of issues, highlighting the possibility that the leaders of some other society might actually be doing the job better. The widely endorsed understanding of travel-as-reward and travel-as-cultivation implicitly demanded some meaningful departure from the sites and rhythms of the socialist worker's everyday world; for leisure travel to have the value and effect desired, a journey to "somewhere else" was absolutely required. But it was safest to ensure that this "somewhere else" was ultimately still counted as "home." International travel threatened to communicate to citizens the undesirable message that, to borrow Milan Kundera's phrase, "life is elsewhere." Tourist excursions to the "fraternal" societies of the Soviet bloc appeared to present only mild and manageable problems in this regard, a matter of small distinctions that made no real difference and the finetuning of policies that remained essentially comparable and harmonious. "Home" was apparently a concept labile enough to be stretched on occasion to include other societies in a common socialist international community. But ventures to the West or, in the case of maverick Yugoslavia, to the almost West, were something else entirely: these societies represented consciously chosen alternatives to the policies of orthodox state socialism, and travel to these places threatened to teach Soviet-bloc tourists lessons about home that were distinctly unwelcome.

For these reasons, international travel per se, and with it international tourism, caused considerable worry for the governments of socialist Europe. Official conceptions of travel, especially legal doctrines, treated the question as one of *protecting* both individual travelers and the societies from which they were temporarily departing. East German law, for example, required citizens to obtain exit visas for each instance of travel outside the country; in the case of travel to nonsocialist countries, permission was conditioned on good standing in the workplace and other similar, essentially political factors, and the law left officials broad discretion in granting or denying travel permits.[23] The GDR presents one of the most restrictive cases, but similar dynamics in all the Soviet-bloc systems gave foreign travel an extraordinarily heightened political and cultural valence, making it something rare and precious to ordinary citizens and a matter of continuing concern to government authorities. In such circumstances, travel to "right-deviationist" socialist Yugoslavia was as close to the West as most ordinary tourists from Eastern Europe and the USSR were likely to ever come, and thus the chance to experience the Yugoslav "difference" took on additional meaning.

To the extent that such travel involved a significant shopping component, it was all the more suspect. As Tibor Dessewffy observes (in this case, of the Hungarian regime, but the point is one of more general application), communist authorities took a very dim view of the use of tourism to exploit consumption opportunities not available at home. "The regime," Dessewffy concludes, "supported the Enlightened, Cultural-Traveller, who was attracted by foreign landscapes and customs, and who wished to become acquainted with the cultures of other nations. On the other hand, the authorities interceded against the Speculating Tourist, portrayed as the 'insignificant minority,' who used travel for shopping, or worse, for 'earning without working.'"[24] The shopper-tourist was, from the point of view of socialist ideology, using tourism in all the wrong ways.

The consumer culture that Yugoslavia offered was not, it must be said, on a par with the more elaborate version offered in Western Europe. But what proved critical was the chance to travel from relative deprivation to relative abundance. Thus, just as tourist-shoppers from even the wealthiest parts of Yugoslavia regularly poured into Italian Trieste and Austrian Graz and Klagenfurt to sample what even their more consumer-friendly brand of socialism had failed to deliver, citizens of Romania found it attractive to compensate for the comparatively extreme scarcity of their daily lives by shopping excursions into Hungary.[25] For their part, those relatively better-situated Hungarians were, in turn, keenly interested in cross-border tourism to Yugoslavia and, when currency and travel regulations permitted, to Austria. In each case, what mattered most for the tourist-shopper was that *more* was available across a given frontier.

In this regard, the contrast between the Soviet bloc practice and the distinctive Yugoslav treatment of foreign travel proves particularly instructive. In the early 1960s, the Yugoslav state dramatically relaxed the limitations on travel to the West imposed on its citizens, restrictions that had once resembled those of other communist countries. By the 1970s, Yugoslavs could—and frequently did—boast that they held passports that were among the most valuable in the world: Yugoslavs found that they could go practically anywhere without a visa, and the state's move triggered not just the vast, much-discussed waves of *Gastarbeiter* who went temporarily to Germany and other Western industrial centers, but a less well known and less thoroughly studied flow of Yugoslav tourists abroad. This avid consumption of tourism by Yugoslav citizens was, indeed, one of the most noteworthy features of the society's enthusiastic embrace of consumerism during the fat years of the 1960s and early to mid-1970s. Moreover, this experience of eager, frequent, and far-reaching Yugoslav tourism abroad, including largely unrestricted travel to the otherwise forbidden West, provides one of the critical interpretative contexts for the evaluation of Soviet-bloc tourism undertaken here. Yugoslavs left their country—and, critically, came back—in great numbers.[26]

In the main, citizens of the Soviet-bloc countries could not entertain such prospects for freedom of movement, though by the 1980s, Hungary's comparatively liberalized policies on travel to the West had likewise become a point of considerable pride, as the similar freedom had long since been for Yugoslavs. For Hungarians it was now not exit visas but rather purchasing power, and the need for "hard" and hard-to-get Western currency, that proved the most serious restraint on travel abroad, and the literature of Hungarian tourism reflected both the shift toward a more open travel policy and the recognition that insufficient funds would typically hold in check all but the most modest international travel plans.[27]

While the Soviet-bloc states' overriding concern for protecting their populations from the contaminating influences of the West is most notable in the legal regimes surrounding travel, it shows up in subtle ways in the literature of tourism, too. In this regard, we must be sensitive to what is *not* being covered, reported, or said: with respect to both the West and, as explained later, Yugoslavia, what we encounter in the history of tourism under state socialism is the history of the lacuna, the elision, the silence. Yet there was clearly a perceived need to fill those troubling silences, and to conform to the emerging international cultural model that to be a citizen of a "modern," "developed" society was to be a tourist and traveler. If there were things that, for political reasons, could not be said, it nevertheless appeared necessary to say *something*.

In this regard, coverage of purely domestic travel options could only go so far; socialist travel writing sought to engage a public interest in the world beyond the state borders. One apparent response to this problem was to develop and disseminate an adventurist travel literature that dealt with foreign lands so exotic that few ordinary citizens could have any real expectation of going there. This provided a way of satisfying the same impulse for a little exoticism that *National Geographic* has traditionally cultivated among Americans: the chance to have the wide world and its pleasures (and beauties) available, all without leaving the easy chair.[28] Since circumstance and policy coincided to make such journeys to the far reaches of the globe out of the question for almost all socialist citizens, this sort of quasi–travel reporting acquired an even more significant role and meaning, and we see it sprinkled liberally throughout the mass-market publications of Eastern-bloc countries.[29]

In the final analysis, the treatment of foreign travel opportunities in Soviet-bloc sources tends to fall within one of four categories, depending on the actual potential for travel to the destinations in question and the nature of the representations that were offered to readers. The first of these four groupings covers the case just mentioned, that is, the welcomed exotica of places such as Africa, the Far East, Oceania, and Latin America. These (non)destinations prompted a sort of "virtual" tourism literature: actual travel to these places by socialist citizens was extraordinarily unlikely, but the coverage offered was ample and rich. With respect to the second category, the representation of travel to the capitalist West, Soviet-bloc tourism was likewise extremely infrequent. In this case, however, media representations of tourism remained quite scarce, and the discourse surrounding such tourism was severely constrained. With only very infrequent exceptions, we find nothing even remotely resembling the engaging, positive, "virtual" tourism that developed around the unthreatening exotic lands where Soviet-bloc citizens were just as unlikely to go. It may be more accurate, in fact, to characterize the rare representations that do appear from time to time as politically inspired travel reportage rather than touristic literature per se.[30]

East-bloc travelers could go, however, to other countries of the Warsaw Pact, and as the economies and tourist infrastructures of those sister states continued to develop, they did indeed flock to these destinations in ever-increasing numbers.[31] In this third category of representation, which accounted for the great bulk of Soviet-bloc international tourism, depictions of tourism in travel writing and the mass media were frequent, rich, and positive. While there was still quite obviously some "virtual" quality to this discourse as well, and a considerable effort to appeal to the armchair traveler, it was quite clearly a literature meant for real tourists who could and would go to experience the foreign pleasures they read about in the domestic press.

Homeland Insecurity: The Meanings of Travel to Yugoslavia

We come then, finally, to the last of the four categories of representation, where we find a pattern of limited, thin, and constrained coverage that in some ways resembles the cool treatment directed toward Western Europe and the United States. But whereas tourist travel to any single country in the capitalist West verged on the negligible for most of the period under consideration here, this fourth category is occupied by a lone tourist destination that drew hundreds of thousands of East-bloc travelers annually: socialist Yugoslavia. In 1977, for example, Yugoslavia was the second-most common foreign destination for Hungarian travelers, after Czechoslovakia, with an impressive 910,000 cross-border visitors for the year.[32] Travel to Yugoslavia was an extraordinarily important part of tourism in the socialist world: in any given year, the number of citizens who visited Yugoslavia was typically comparable to, or even greater than, the figure for those traveling to all the nonsocialist countries combined. In 1975, there were approximately 304,000 visits by Czechoslovak citizens to Yugoslavia, a number that exceeded the total of approximately 294,000 who traveled to all nonsocialist countries. The figures for Hungary in the same year show an even more dramatic pattern: approximately 754,000 visits by Hungarian citizens to Yugoslavia, as against a combined total of only 203,000 for Austria, West Germany, Italy, France, Great Britain, the United States, and the Scandinavian countries. It should be noted that in some instances, the number of travelers visiting Yugoslavia was not nearly as great as the number of those making much shorter trips across a single international frontier (most notably, from Hungary to Czechoslovakia or vice versa). Rather, the number of visits to Yugoslavia was often more in line with the figures for other more distant destinations in the socialist world (Romania, Bulgaria, the USSR). But when the figures are adjusted for the cumulative amount of time travelers actually spent in a given country, this difference recedes considerably, as the average length of stay in Yugoslavia was far longer than in most other socialist countries. Bulgaria, with its attractive Black Sea resorts, was a notable exception. Like Yugoslavia, it also functioned as a longer-term vacation destination, albeit without the additional lure of attractive shopping opportunities.[33] Accordingly, once the boom in foreign travel was under way, East European tourists were getting a very substantial exposure to the pleasures and temptations that Yugoslavia offered.

From meager beginnings, travel to Yugoslavia had become a hot item: as one representative of Hungary's IBUSZ noted in 1979, "every one of our colleagues who handles foreign travel knows that interest in Yugoslavia is great every year. Fulfilling the ever-increasing demand is frequently a cause of concern."[34] With the desire to travel to Yugoslavia so keen, there were ample reasons to fear the effects of a socialist citizen's sojourn there: The lumbering state-controlled economies of the Soviet bloc could easily look rigid, weak, and undesirable when viewed against the apparent successes of Yugoslavia's much-touted and highly unorthodox economic system. As Yugoslavia's truly remarkable consumer culture expanded from year to year into the 1970s, opportunities at home might seem dismayingly bleak by comparison. Furthermore, Yugoslavia allowed Western media to circulate fairly freely, stirring fears of contamination through ideological contraband. And because Yugoslavia's borders with Italy and Austria were open to its own citizens, and somewhat less carefully guarded than the Iron Curtain, there remained the discomfiting possibility that travel to Yugoslavia might be, for some, a one-way journey only.

For these reasons, the public discourse of Soviet-bloc societies treated the issue gingerly, apparently balancing fears of contamination (and worse) with the perceived need to accommodate citizens' legitimate desires for sun, sea, shopping, relaxation, and a taste of the good life. The sources reveal that when citizens of Eastern Europe were told, to use Diane Koenker's apt phrase, "what to look for and how to see" in Yugoslavia, they were consistently directed to the safe, nonthreatening aspects of Yugoslav life. Yugoslavia's abundant physical beauty was a logical and thoroughly uncontroversial subject for discussion. And so it was to nature, and especially the sea coast, that commentators in tourist publications and travel literature turned time and time again, though some observers remarked that it was a pity that the hordes of tourists, intent on reaching the Adriatic, almost always passed by some of the country's more subtle treasures. As one Czech writer lamented, "thousands of Czechs and Slovaks visit Yugoslavia every year, and only an insignificant fraction of them do not go to the sea. And thus cars, trains, and planes aim for the shortest and quickest road to the warm, blue and, for the time being, still relatively clear and clean waters of the Adriatic."[35] Complementing this heavy emphasis on the natural was a similar tendency to underscore those elements of Yugoslav history so remote as to pose no real ideological difficulties in the context of contemporary political affairs.[36]

These emphases are especially prominent in the guidebooks to Yugo-slavia produced in Soviet-bloc countries. Historians have mined guide-books for insights into the interests, motivations, biases, and agendas of foreign visitors to an ever-expanding range of destinations. So, too, guidebooks would appear to be an excellent place to start the search for the meanings of Soviet-bloc tourism. In this regard, however, we need to proceed with a due dose of scholarly caution lest we be misled by the dramatically differing circumstances of tourism in its modern bourgeois *locus classicus.* Especially recently, the American and European tendency in travel-guide publishing has been toward market segmentation and "narrowcasting"—*Fodor's* and the *Michelin* Guides for the high end, *Insight* and *Eyewitness* guides for those who like to be enticed by photo-graphs, *Frommer's* for more budget-conscious adults, and *Lonely Planet, Let's Go!,* and the *Rough Guides* for younger, cash-strapped readers and those with cultural leanings that favor a simpler style of travel. It is there-fore not hard to envision a future historiography of contemporary tour-ism that will find a multiplicity of meanings in the ways that narrow subsets of the comparatively wealthy Western tourist population have approached their exotic neighbors.

Prospects for the historiography of travel in the socialist East could hardly be more different: the limited and controlled media markets of Eastern Europe offer no such richness of sources, and no such plurality of views, tastes, and styles. Instead, we see a tendency to present a homogenized, unified, one-size-fits-all message. And ultimately, because of censorship, we have to understand that even the message of some-thing so superficially apolitical as a tourist guidebook was, in some very real sense, a constrained and managed message.

What emerges from an examination of Eastern-bloc guidebooks on Yugoslavia conforms to the larger pattern of infrequent, limited, and constrained representation that appears throughout the socialist-era lit-erature of travel more generally. The guides are noteworthy for the way in which they confined themselves to exceptionally safe rhetorical terri-tory: there were lengthy and detailed discussions of the Yugoslav federa-tion's constituent peoples and their histories (a hot topic today, but not one that especially troubled Yugoslavia's socialist neighbors at the time, with the possible exception of the Magyars), but there was precious little in the way of comments about contemporary political issues, about the recent spectacular achievements of the Yugoslav economy, or about the differences between Yugoslavia's "self-management" and the more orthodox socialist systems with which readers would be familiar. Given that tourism is now generally acknowledged as a special, and perhaps especially important, form of and venue for consumption, there was strikingly little acknowledgment that tourists might be eager to visit

Yugoslavia precisely *because* of its leaders' diversion from the path of the command economy and its (in)famous dalliances with consumerism.[37] With its dynamic economy and its audacious mixing of socialism and elements of Western liberalism, Yugoslavia had become exciting for people in both East and West, but the bloodless bureaucratese that characterized the guidebooks of the Soviet bloc obscured that fact.[38] Readers of the travel literature on Yugoslavia that appeared in various "fraternal" socialist states could thus come away with the impression that this socialist society was really not all that different from their own, except perhaps for its geography and its unusual blend of colorful "Balkan" peoples (and these, of course, were more or less matters of happenstance, for which the Yugoslavs and their unorthodox government could scarcely claim credit).

The insistence of socialist ideology that tourism serve as a means of educating the public comes through clearly in the guides to Yugoslavia, many of which reveal an extraordinary sensitivity to these didactic imperatives of socialist travel. The 1984 volume on Yugoslavia published by Olympia, the leading Czechoslovak guidebook series, thus labors on dutifully about the country's macroeconomic conditions, the social characteristics of each constituent socialist republic, the structure of the state, and Yugoslav-Czech contacts through history. It catalogues Yugoslavia's capacities for industrial production without acknowledging for readers what differences the economic experiments had created on the ground, in everyday life, for ordinary Yugoslavs (and for foreign visitors, too). Thus we find more about the machine factories of Serbia, the refineries of Croatia, the lead and zinc mines of Kosovo, and the ironworks of Zenica—with the seemingly obligatory factory photograph— than we do about any consumption opportunities, which were no doubt closer to the hearts and minds of most Czechoslovak tourists.[39] "Shopping" merits merely the most cursory treatment in this guide, only about a page in total, and much of that is dedicated to a simple listing of souvenirs and folk-art items typical of the country's regions, all comfortably unthreatening in their exotic charm: Turkish coffee sets and mills from Bosnia, filigree from the seaside, handwoven goods and embroidery from Macedonia.[40] To the extent that shopping was recognized as a possible pastime for tourists using the guide, it was, without exception, exceptionally "safe" shopping—nothing that would implicate the wisdom or shortcomings of consumer policy at home. And nowhere do we encounter an acknowledgment that Yugoslavia had become a prime shopping destination for Czechoslovaks eager to stock up on products and brands unavailable in their home markets.

Here and there, though, the guidebooks do let slip a few hints about what else, besides the craggy coastline and sparkling beaches, might have been so many luring Soviet-bloc travelers to Yugoslavia. The "shopping" sections of the guidebooks were usually limited to a few bland observations about the price of basic commodities such as bread, meat, milk, and cheese, but elsewhere in the texts there were sometimes intimations that travelers might have come with a different sort of shopping list. The leading Hungarian guidebook series, Panorama, published a 1981 guidebook to Belgrade that acknowledged shopping might be on the minds of at least some visitors to the Yugoslav capital. For those on the trail of such adventures, this book was willing to provide at least a few of the details. (East Europeans were famously savvy shoppers, however, and we might well wonder whether word-of-mouth had not already done the job for many.)

In this guide, one of Belgrade's prime shopping areas, the center-city district around Terazije Square, was repeatedly referred to as the city's "Váci utca" (Váci Street). Invoking the allure of that downtown Pest pedestrian zone sent an obvious signal to Hungarian readers: since the late 1960s, when the country's leadership pursued new consumerist strategies to encourage ordinary citizens to forgive and forget the thwarted revolution of 1956, Váci utca had become synonymous with high style, changing fashion, and rapidly multiplying shopping opportunities. Shoppers were also told they might also head for the huge Albanija store and its smaller neighbors on Prince Michael Street, sample the "old Balkan" atmosphere of the area around Balkanska and Prizrenska streets, or venture down into a glass-fronted underground commercial passageway that the guide described as "characteristic" of Belgrade: shining and bustling, with the widest variety of small shops, boutiques, cafés, and restaurants, some even open twenty-four hours a day and on weekends and holidays.

Notwithstanding the recurring comparison to Váci utca, the guide intimated that Yugoslavia was, in the end, something different. The book pointed out that the selection in the city's stores was extraordinary, and Hungarian tourists needed to know that the prices of goods varied slightly from store to store. This, the author remarked, was "a particularity of Yugoslav commerce, and a powerful tool in the competition between commercial enterprises for customers." Another remarkable product of this distinctively Yugoslav competition, readers were told, was the unusual courtesy and solicitude of the shopkeepers, who were polite and warm even when "by chance" a shopper left without making a purchase.[41] Discerning readers could see that something quite unusual was going on in Belgrade.

Yet even when they include some of these more unguarded passages, the guidebooks prove, in the final analysis, limited and limiting. The guides do not in themselves offer more than a partial and tentative indication of the contours of the Soviet-bloc experience of tourism in Yugoslavia. Thus it becomes necessary to look further afield, to a broader range of travel literature and, for evidence of the construction of tourism as a large-scale popular phenomenon, to coverage of travel issues in mass-market media sources that were not devoted to travel per se. Literary sources and quasi-literary travelogues can likewise prove extraordinarily revealing. In one such volume, for example, an artist's sketch of a bustling Yugoslav streetscape hinted at the admixture of socialism and Western consumer culture that so fascinated visitors from Eastern Europe: here readers could see Zeiss lenses, the pride of East German industry, advertised alongside prominent signs for the consummately Western Fords and Fiats that Yugoslavs, unlike their socialist neighbors, could buy with comparative ease, enjoying a wider selection without the long wait lists that so vexed consumers in the Soviet bloc.[42]

Yet the pattern that emerges from even this broader examination of the evidence is ultimately not greatly at variance with the conclusion suggested by the guidebooks: the Yugoslav "difference" went unseen or, in those rare instances when it was acknowledged, was downplayed.[43] When Yugoslavia itself could not be simply ignored, as was often the case, its political and economic system was represented in conspicuously safe terms as fundamentally similar to that of the traveler's home country. The consumerist efflorescence that had made the Yugoslav system so noticeable to Westerners served, it appears, to render it almost invisible in the discourse of Soviet-bloc tourism.

There was, however, one glaring exception to this tendency toward minimizing the distance between Yugoslavia and the Warsaw Pact states. As a Balkan country, Yugoslavia did offer another, permissible sort of difference: it offered exotica, and on this the guidebooks and travel literature could linger, savoring in particular the remnants of the Ottoman past. In this vein, Rajko Doleček, a Czechoslovak writer of Yugoslav extraction born in Yugoslavia, extolled the pleasures of sitting with friends in the well-known restaurant *Dva jelena* (Two Deer) in the "bohemian" Skadarlija quarter, awash in the ambience of the city's Balkan past.[44] Another account, this one from Hungary, describes the auto campground that had become so much a part of the East European experience of travel to Yugoslavia as nothing less than a "modern caravanserai," noteworthy both for its oriental exoticness and its mixing of cultures and peoples of enticingly varying provenance: a place where Swedes rubbed elbows with Magyars, Brits with Soviets, and Germans with Poles, where *Mitteleuropäisch* beer flowed at the same tables as the decidedly Eastern *konyak*, and where tradition was served up alongside assertive consumerist modernity in the form of "black Turkish coffee and the local version of Coca-Coca, which they call Jugo-Cocta."[45]

In this connection, the freedom given by more literary modes of expression clearly allows a little of the "impermissible" to creep in alongside the "approved" traffic in Balkan imagery: what readers find out in these revealing moments from the accounts of actual visitors to Yugoslavia is not just that this was an unusually "Eastern" East European country. They also learn that it is a country that let East *mix* with West, and Easterners with Westerners, in all sorts of unusual and pleasurable ways—a place where the rules gave way, where one could meet ordinary people from the "lands of developed capitalism" and, to some extent, bridge the Cold War division.

Elsewhere in the observations of individual travelers to Yugoslavia we see further evidence of this appealing "in-between" quality that the land offered to Soviet-bloc tourists. With its tree-lined boulevards and its "coffeehouses spilling out onto the sidewalk," Belgrade was said in one traveler's account to be, at least in certain spots, not unlike Paris, though the "dusty, provincial quality" of the little shops and the market stalls that sprawled across the center city did, the visitor admitted, weaken the comparison.[46] Two other Hungarian travel writers took up, at some length, much the same theme—Belgrade as "the Paris of the Near East"—in a collection of reminiscences about their own trip. Like the account presented in the book itself, the title of this work, *Az ismeretlen szomszéd* (The Unknown Neighbor), suggests that Yugoslavia might remain "unknown" because it was an alien, "Balkan" society, and hence in some respects ultimately *unknowable*. If this was the case for Magyars, it was likely to hold true as well for Czech, Polish, and German visitors equally confident of their "Central European" identities, distanced from most Yugoslavs by their perceived ties to a faded Germanic-Habsburg world, which communist culture had not managed to erase.

Because the phenomenon identified here is a matter of the relative *invisibility* of Yugoslavia as a tourist destination, the interpretation of sources poses some peculiar problems. The record of East European public discourse is, in some respects, not wholly satisfying, as is typically the case when one must prove a negative. The mass-media materials reviewed for this analysis do not make any obvious effort at anti-Yugoslav propaganda, but it is entirely plausible that future research may reveal evidence of a strategy of outright suppression of coverage of travel to Yugoslavia. Whether such "smoking-gun" documents will ever emerge remains, at this early stage in the historiography of East European tourism, an open question. As a result, we are left instead with a more subtle problem, and the more difficult task of divining meaning from what is evidently absent, from what is not said.

Nevertheless, the pattern of neglect and silence is so striking, and so consistent throughout so many sources, that strong reasons exist to suspect that the omissions actually amount to conscious and intentional exclusions. First of all, in sharp contrast to the infrequent and limited treatment of opportunities for travelers to Yugoslavia, Soviet-bloc travel literature devoted very heavy coverage to touristic offerings in other socialist countries; these images of the Warsaw Pact states were, not surprisingly, relentlessly positive.[47] Tellingly, even certain Western countries could elicit more attention than Yugoslavia. It was especially noticeable in the case of Finland, and Sweden also received frequent, and frequently positive, treatment in the Soviet-bloc press. These neutral Scandinavian countries, at a safe distance as they were, appeared to be reasonably untroubling targets for examination. The unsettling example of equally neutral Austria, by contrast, apparently proved too close for comfort. With a government dependent on socialist support yet beyond Soviet interference, and with its inconvenient location just over the Hungarian and Czechoslovak borders, Austria represented a much less palatable subject than faraway Finland and Sweden, and it received comparatively little coverage.

Curiously, it seems to have been easier and less threatening for the state-sanctioned publishers to talk about certain relatively "good" noncommunist countries—good because they were not thoroughly capitalist, and above all, because they were neutral—than a wayward, "bad" socialist one that took military aid from the West and had a defense policy oriented largely toward repelling a Soviet-bloc invasion. Indeed, the Soviet-bloc media even seemed more willing to report on excursions to unapologetically capitalist NATO countries—albeit as a means of criticizing capitalism—than to explore the realities of daily life in Yugoslavia.[48]

Given the importance of Yugoslavia's consumer culture to the history of postwar socialism and to the questions under consideration here, it is critical to note that the topics of consumption and consumer culture per se were by no means treated as off-limits in the Soviet-bloc media. The same mass-market periodicals that gave continuing coverage to tourism at home and abroad repeatedly engaged these issues. Though consumption took a back seat to production in both socialist doctrine and the socialist press, media outlets showed some sensitivity to their readers' abiding interest in new opportunities to shop and spend, and they demonstrated an awareness that the growth of "consumer society" had become a hot topic among cultural critics throughout the developed world. The socialist media thus proved very willing, for example, to take up the subject of consumerism in "man on the street" reportage from capitalist countries as a way of criticizing them. Moreover, representations of travel to, and everyday life in, other socialist countries of the Warsaw Pact sometimes included very prominent and positive treatment of the consumption prospects available there. In East Germany, for example, it was clearly quite acceptable for the editors of the leading women's magazine *Für dich* to depict Budapest as a center of style and fashion.[49]

Yet the same cannot be said of the approach taken toward analogous consumption opportunities in Yugoslavia. If consumption per se was quite clearly not the problem, we ought to wonder whether it was the particular Yugoslav orientation toward consumption, and Yugoslavia's achievements in this arena, that prompted the unusual silence. The cause for suspicion is only heightened by the fact that, as Wendy Bracewell has demonstrated, the Yugoslavs' own lively literature on foreign travel was overtly comparative, marvelously frank, and unabashedly responsive to the allure of foreign shopping: "What a tourist might want to acquire; how to shop—and how to pay; what you can and can't get, both abroad and at home; dealing with scarcity or abundance, choice or its absence; tipping; the attitudes of shop assistants; confronting Yugoslav customs on your return—all are subjects that are treated repeatedly, not to say obsessively."[50] In glaring contrast to the reticence that pervaded the Soviet-bloc evidence, Bracewell finds that Yugoslav travel accounts from the 1950s and 1960s, and even contemporary guidebooks for travel to the West, acknowledged candidly and at great length that Yugoslavs headed abroad would be intensely interested in shopping, consumption, and the chance to explore the difference between what the foreign markets offered and what was available at home.

Finally, there are occasional instances when tourism in Yugoslavia appears to have been deliberately omitted from East European discussions that would otherwise have naturally involved the subject. Thus we find, in one particularly telling example, that the route of one East German magazine's travel series on destinations along the Danube took an abrupt eastward turn near the Yugoslav border, leaving the watercourse only to return to it later after the river was back within the territories of the Warsaw Pact. The message here seems unambiguous and unmistakable: there was an expectation that readers would not be traveling into *nicht-sozialistisch* Yugoslavia, however logical that might have been as part of a trip down the Danube.[51] Taken on balance, the record strongly suggests that the country's relative invisibility was not a matter of mere oversights or lack of interest, but was instead the product of a practice of conscious, repeated omissions.

In Soviet-bloc representations, Yugoslavia thus seems to have fallen into a hybrid, intermediate status: a "bad" socialist country, one that was troubling to Warsaw Pact governments, attractive to East-bloc citizens, all too accessible, and in the end, best not talked about. If the appearance of comity and sheer public demand sometimes made it necessary to acknowledge Yugoslavia's popularity as a tourist destination, political considerations dictated that the country be discussed in a safe, non-threatening way, one that bled out much of the remarkable Yugoslav "difference." In the end, it seems, Soviet-bloc writers did not quite know where to place Yugoslavia. Was it Near Eastern, or nearly Western? The exotic "Eastern" and "Balkan" qualities could clearly be tolerated and celebrated; it was the evident "Western-ness" of socialist Yugoslavia that was the problem. In this respect, what made Yugoslavia beautiful made it dangerous, with the resultant need to render Yugoslav consumption altogether inconspicuous.

Appendix

TABLE 1. FOREIGN TRAVEL BY CZECHOSLOVAK CITIZENS (*PASÍVNÍ CESTOVNÍ RUCH*), 1965–1989, BY COUNTRY OF DESTINATION

Destination	*(Number of international travelers in thousands)*						
	1965	*1970*	*1975*	*1980*	*1985*	*1988*	*1989*
All countries total				10,343	8,394	7,258	8,569
Socialist countries total	1,572	3,542	7,101	9,792	7,928	6,751	6,248
Bulgaria	55	360	440	407	500	334	321
GDR	451	442	1,952	2,548	2,025	2,522	1,951
Hungary	463	1,667	2,564	4,177	3,760	1,906	2,080
Poland	375	450	1,142	1,689	274	885	1,025
Romania	18	269	250	114	119	131	124
USSR	37	166	357	344	342	414	355
Yugoslavia	*143*	*186*	*304*	*496*	*898*	*362*	*375*
Non-socialist countries total	169	212	294	551	466	687	2,322
Austria	71	52	91	137	98	136	1,562
France	9	14	18	25	25	35	42
Italy	9	23	27	44	32	46	69
Germany (FRG)	43	58	76	16	170	248	418
Great Britain	5	9	12	15	11	20	21
Sweden	3	2	3	7	5	11	15
USA	n/a	3	3	5	5	9	12

Note: Data for 1989 are partial.
Source: Statistická ročenka Československé Socialistické Republiky, 1961, 1965, 1966, 1970, 1973, 1976, 1981, 1986; *Statistická ročenka České a Slovenské Federativní Republiky,* 1990.

TABLE 2. FOREIGN TRAVEL BY HUNGARIAN CITIZENS, 1960–1985, BY COUNTRY OF DESTINATION

Destination	(Number of international travelers in thousands)					
	1960	1965	1970	1975	1980	1985
All countries total	299	884	1,007	3,477	5,164	5,333
Socialist countries						
Bulgaria	3	12	27	97	315	409
Czechoslovakia	153	382	234	1,339	2,070	1,792
GDR	23	60	133	297	591	509
Poland	10	90	103	337	542	271
Romania	44	67	110	239	435	1,055
USSR	23	37	71	145	200	158
Yugoslavia	*7*	*78*	*143*	*754*	*530*	*569*
Non-socialist countries						
Austria	16	65	52	86	168	353
France	2	9	14	16	21	24
Germany (FRG)	7	37	38	52	90	161
Great Britain	1	6	9	8	12	15
Italy	4	17	26	29	47	61
Scandinavian countries	1	5	8	8	n/a	n/a
USA	>1	3	5	4	7	9

Source: Statisztikai évkönyv, 1965, 1970, 1971, 1975, 1980, 1982, 1984, 1985, 1989, 1990.

Chapter 9

A Means of Last Resort

The European Transformation of the Cuban Hotel Industry and the
American Response, 1987–2004

Evan R. Ward

> *Don't worry; Cuba is the best place to invest on this continent, for one very*
> *simple reason: It is the only place where there is no risk of a Communist*
> *revolution.*
>
> —*Fidel Castro*

In the Spring of 1898, as Spanish hopes for retaining Cuba, its final
Latin American colony, dimmed with the entry of the United States into
the Spanish-Cuban conflict, Ramón Blanco, the leading Spanish authority on the island, desperately appealed to his Cuban adversary, Máximo
Gomez. He declared, "We Spaniards and Cubans now find ourselves
face to face with a stranger of a distinctive race and of an acquisitive
nature, whose intentions are not only to keep Spain from raising its flag
on Cuban soil, but also to exterminate the Cuban people, because of its
Spanish blood. . . . Therefore, the supreme moment has arrived in that
we forget our past differences and that united, Cubans and Spaniards,
we reject the invader for our own defense."[1] If Blanco's desperate
appeal to the Cuban independence movement appeared absurd at the
time, and even less relevant during the following years as American
hotels and retail establishments poured onto the island, the economic
difficulties of socialist Cuba in the late 1980s and 1990s made such a
reunion a patent reality. Despite the fact that American consumer culture dominated Cuba during the first sixty years of the twentieth century, its subsequent embargo of trade with the island, coupled with
Europe's willingness—and Spain's in particular—to capitalize on the

American absence in a new global era, clearly tilted the Cuban hotel industry in the direction of Europe, returning the island's elite, in a sense, to the cultural milieu that had prevailed there during the Spanish colonial period. At the same time, Fidel Castro's enthusiasm for European excellence in hotel management illustrated his willingness to reconcile capitalist tactics for the sake of a socialist revolution: in theory both required discipline and an accountability that were just as much at home in a free-market economy as in a command economy.

The Influence of American Developers (1898–1959)

Following the Spanish-American War, North American retail and hospitality institutions quickly filled the void created by the exit of Spain from the island.[2] By the 1950s, American individuals and corporations played significant roles in the Cuban hotel and tourist industry. Some of the American dominance took the form of infrastructure development, as in the case of Varadero, a twenty-two-kilometer peninsula some hundred miles east of Havana. Varadero was originally founded by the Spanish on December 5, 1887, and served primarily as a summer haven for some of Cuba's wealthiest families, who lived forty miles away in Cardenas (the hometown of Elian Gonzales). The arrival of chemical mogul Francis Irénée du Pont in 1926 set the peninsula on course to become one of the premier international beach resorts in the Caribbean. In late 1925 one of du Pont's employees, Charles Meade, approached his boss and asked if he could take a vacation. Du Pont responded by asking Meade to take a trip for "business and pleasure" to Cuba to assess the tourist possibilities of the Bay of Cardenas and Varadero. Du Pont had a hunch that the peninsula offered a "nice . . . beach where older people could buy a place for rest in the winter during their declining years." Meade quickly confirmed du Pont's hunches by telegram: "Just what you want, better come down." On May 1, 1926, du Pont and others took a United Fruit Company steamer and headed for Havana. Traveling over the pothole-filled roads between Havana and Varadero, du Pont prepared for his conquest of the peninsula. He began by purchasing nearly half of the peninsula, from Fifty-fourth Street out toward the present-day ecological reserve on the tip of the peninsula. In total du Pont purchased some 180 acres of the land on the peninsula, with several miles of virgin beach washed by transparent, multihued blue waters. He then proceeded to restore homes, make the water supply dependable, and sell real estate to Cubans and Americans interested in living on this terrestrial paradise.[3]

The crowning achievement of du Pont's domain on Varadero Peninsula was the stately Xanadu mansion, located at the most advantageous point on the island, San Bernardino Point. This rocky crag seemed to hang over the Caribbean waters below it, eternally suspended in the air. Construction on Xanadu began in June 1928 and was completed by July 1929. At a cost of $400,000, with an additional $200,000 spent on furniture, Xanadu set the mark for elite beach tourism in Cuba. Du Pont used the eleven-room mansion not only as a summer retreat, but also as a place to entertain other wealthy Americans who might desire to buy land in Varadero for a summer home. With green marble imported from Italy for the bathrooms and floors, dark-toned woods from England and nearby Santiago de Cuba for the roof and exterior accents, American fabrics for the interiors, and a nine-hole golf course to boot, Xanadu was the ultimate pleasure palace on the peninsula and encouraged lavish beach tourism, particularly during the 1950s.[4]

Du Pont's improvements to the island as a whole invited a subsequent rush of hotel investments in the 1940s and 1950s. While some of the hotels were small and reflected the old-world charm of Spanish architecture, others—the Hotel International, for example—represented the vanguard of the modern movement, with several hundred rooms arranged along the beach in the boxy architectural style reminiscent of Conrad Hilton's Caribe Hilton in San Juan, Puerto Rico. By the 1950s, then, development of Varadero caused some to boast that the peninsula was home to the finest beach in the world.

American dominance of the Cuban hotel sector was accentuated with the completion of the more urban Havana Hilton in New Havana (Vedado) in 1958. The officers of Hilton International originally agreed to build a large hotel in Havana as early as 1952. Six years later, the thirty-story concrete fortress lorded above the Havana skyline, boasting nearly six hundred rooms and the most commanding views of Havana Bay, El Morro, La Cabaña de San Carlos (the largest fortress built by the Spaniards in the New World), Habana Vieja, and the opulent eastern suburbs of Miramar and Marianao. The Havana Hilton represented the classic union of state power and corporate initiative that provided the model for hotel development in the postwar period throughout Latin America. Unbeknownst to most of the guests at the March 19, 1958, inauguration of the hotel, most of whom had been flown to Havana by Conrad Hilton on chartered airliners, the revolution in the eastern countryside was gaining power and would eventually transform the hotel into a symbol of the socialist revolution, the Havana Libre.

The Cuban Revolution and the Hotel Industry

When Fidel Castro rolled into Havana during the second week of January he selected the Havana Hilton as his temporary home and base of operations. This offered Hilton executives unusually easy access not only to Castro, but also his plans for tourism on the island. Hilton International Executive Vice President Robert J. Caverly was one of the first Americans to meet with Castro once he had settled in the Havana Hilton. He arranged to meet Castro on the first morning he arrived in Havana and ate breakfast with El Comandante on his balcony in suite 2324 as armed guards monitored the proceedings of their conversation through the glass doors of the suite. Castro expressed an interest in promoting tourism in order to earn foreign exchange, and that to facilitate such a strategy he would "consider leaving the hotel casinos open for tourists, but would discourage casino patronage by Cubans." Castro then arranged a $1-million dollar line of credit for Hilton International through the National Bank of Cuba. Caverly later met with Ernesto "Che" Guevara and Raul Castro to set up a Cuban corporation that would receive the money on behalf of the hotel.[5]

As early as February 1959, Caverly suggested that one option Hilton retained for its Cuban venture, should the new government continue to drag its feet on tourism promotion, would simply be to pull out of the hotel and let the Cuban government manage the property.[6] Caverly and other Hilton executives clearly understood that Hilton did not own the property; they merely managed it. "I believe we will have to force the issue in whatever action we decide to take," Caverly wrote to Hilton, "The Government is so disorganized that they do not have any intra-government communication or administrative procedure for reaching a major decision regarding [tourism labor issues]. It does not appear that any one Minister—and probably not Castro himself—would make such a decision on his own."[7] With only a lease agreement, Hilton International was free to leave whenever it wanted, in essence leaving the greatest financial burden on the Castro regime to run and manage the hotel. As occupation rates at the property continued to dwindle and the Cuban government failed to attract tourists in sufficient numbers to fill Havana's large luxury hotels, executive attitudes shifted toward pulling out of the venture.

Hilton International legal counsel Sid Wilner played a significant role in Hilton's exit from Havana. As lines of credit made available by the new regime early in 1959 began to dry up in the fall of the same year, Wilner approached the new Cuban government about the possibility of extending more credit for hotel operations. Che Guevara's appointment as head of the Bank of Cuba and the growing influence of communism in the labor unions portended a gloomy day for the future of mass tourism in Cuba. As a result, Wilner, according to his own recollections, wrote Fidel Castro an ultimatum, demanding that either the government provide greater support for the Havana Hilton or the government would have to take over operations of the hotel as Hilton International would pull out of the venture. "I wrote a letter to Castro, being quite bold," Wilner remembered several decades later, "telling him that we had tried cooperation with them to make this hotel a success . . . but we were now running out of working capital and I could see only two solutions. One was for the government to continue to pour in money or to, what might make more sense, was for the government to take over. *As a result of that, that was when they nationalized our company.*"[8]

In November 1959, Conrad Hilton wrote a brief letter to Arthur Elminger, who had served as the head of Latin American hotels for Hilton International. "It looks like Castro has destroyed all business," Hilton observed, "and is rapidly destroying all future business in the country. Here we are in Puerto Rico completely booked up and no one wants to go to Havana." After briefly discussing Wilner's options for Hilton in Cuba, Conrad asserted, "We are definitely not going to put another nickel down there so I am wondering what they [the government] are going to do."[9] Elminger concurred, noting that the new regime was growing increasingly more radical, looking for new channels of revenue as time went on. He also noted that the Cuban government had recently taken over operations of the Hotel Riviera. While Castro had previously been viewed as a friend (and guest) at the Hilton, such a move, in Elminger's eyes, meant that it was "not impossible for Fidel Castro to see fit to frown at [the possibility of taking over] the Havana Hilton." Elminger concurred with Conrad, noting, "Our recommendation is to continue to operate the Havana Hilton until the end of the year on a day to day basis, but we wholeheartedly concur with you that we should not put an additional nickel into the hotel."[10]

In the wake of Hilton International's expressed intent to leave Cuba if tourist-planning efforts did not improve, Fidel Castro made two separate speeches to the Hotel Workers Union and Food Workers Union on June 16, 1960. Almost identical in substance, Castro informed the tourist employees that Cuban tourism would now cater to Cuban nationals and not to foreigners. The climax of the speeches came when he announced to the workers that the Havana Hilton would shortly be renamed the Havana Libre. Castro stressed the degree to which Cubans had been exploited in the building of these hotels, laying particular stress on the financing agreement reached with the Food Workers Union for construction of the Hilton. "The Riviera was built with state financing, for the most part and then turned over to foreign interests," he remarked. "The National Hotel had been state property for many years, and then was turned over to foreign interests." "But the final straw," he emphatically noted, "was reached with one of the most immoral and shameful acts committed in our country in the case of the Hotel Hilton." Wild applause followed Castro's comments. Castro derided Conrad Hilton for owning a chain of hotels around the world and requiring Cubans to finance his hotel in Havana. With Castro having thrown down the definitive challenge to Hilton's presence in Cuba, Hilton International quickly mobilized its exit.[11]

At the beginning of the revolution exuberance hushed any concern as to how mammoth hotels with hundreds of rooms and discerning customers might be operated for the benefit of Cuba. Castro claimed a great triumph for the Cuban people when he took over management of the Havana Hilton from the American company in June 1960, changing the name to the Havana Libre,[12] built with the pension funds of the Food Industry Workers Union during the 1950s. Castro's wresting of management from Hilton seemed like a huge moral victory for the revolution, but it was a tremendous task for a country ill-equipped to manage luxury hotels. Castro's greatest concern on the night of the hotel's transfer of power seemed to be full employment more than effective hotel management. "We will make the hotels profitable," he insisted, "in the only proper way and through the only correct policy which the revolutionary government can pursue. For this reason, no worker in the food sector . . . will be dismissed."[13] Such a philosophy ran counter to the conventional wisdom of how Hilton had made his fortune: cut the number of employees to the minimum while training them to be more productive.

The deterioration of Cuba's hotel sector was almost immediately apparent. In the first years following Castro's rise to power officials decided to prohibit gambling in the casinos, especially after the number of American tourists visiting Cuba dropped. The ways in which the casinos were used illustrated the lack of sophistication that went into management of the hotel. Englishman Edwin Tetlow, who visited Cuba for an extended stay in 1959, commented, "The casino at the Havana Hilton was stripped of all its luxurious and glittering fittings and turned into a kind of exhibition hall in the service of the revolution. Drab charts and propaganda posters followed each other in dreary succession on its walls. . . . One would never have dreamed in the end that it had once echoed the click of roulette balls, the discreet and soft announcement of the croupiers, the swish of silken gowns, clink of glasses, the slowing tick-tock of the wheel of fortune and the staccato whirs and clops of the slot machines against the richly decorated walls."[14]

Tetlow also had the opportunity to visit Varadero on two occasions. In 1959, in need of relaxation after three months studying the Castro regime, he headed to the peninsula. During his first visit, Tetlow reveled in the beauty and splendor of Varadero, noting, "The flies . . . were as nothing compared with the pure joys that Varadero could still offer before it was utterly ruined as a choice resort by the revolution." Good food, gardens, and shops on First Avenue complemented the beautifully warm water. Two years later Tetlow returned to Varadero, where numerous changes were evident. A more somber mood pervaded Varadero's businesses and inhabitants in 1961. Most notably, at the Hotel Internacional, "Blocks of flats to accommodate holiday-making workers and members of the many organs of the revolution had been built."[15]

When Fodor travel writer Bruce Taylor visited Havana in 1966, he provided a very candid evaluation of hotel management in the Cuban capital. "[The] great hotels of Havana are falling apart," he observed. "Wallpaper and plaster are peeling; linen and carpets are wearing thin; room air-conditioning is unpredictable. Service, never quite up to North American standards, is worse than ever." Only two hotels, the Havana Libre and the Capri, had operating swimming pools, as plumbing problems had forced the closure of other pools. Finally, even the quality of restaurants had declined dramatically. For Taylor, "The food is best on the black market."[16]

Jamaican novelist Andrew Salkey visited Cuba one year later. He recounted his impressions of Havana's Hotel Nacional in his diary: "Slipped by the wicked French journalists and [went] out to the . . . back garden, wind-swept, cool, and with a disused cannon pointing towards Miami. The swimming pool is empty, badly in need of paint but spotlessly clean." Back inside, while waiting at the bank teller and gift shop, he remarked, "[I] glanced up at very slow-moving ancient electric fans, down at old-fashioned showcases in middle of center aisle, [filled] with humble curious and Havana mementoes. Grillework, everywhere, tarnished and painted over in parts."[17]

A decade later, in 1979, travel writer Paula Deperna noted, "The pre-1959 hotels have continued to operate ever since . . . but redecoration and restoration have never been a priority. Consequently, many hotels seem frozen in the 1950s décor." Noting the switch in emphasis from luxury to practicality (often reached by simply letting hotels deteriorate), Deperna continued: "The tourist will find adequate facilities most everywhere, but there is no hotel in Cuba at this moment comparable to the grand deluxe hotels in some other nations." Commenting on the amenities of these hotels in free fall, Deperna observed, "Most, but not all, hotels in Cuba have hot water. Cubatur [the state-directed travel agency] steers tourists to those that do, unless there is no choice." Finally, service seemed to have fallen below international standards with the decline of hotel properties: "Service is not always fast, but making requests in Spanish speeds matters considerably."[18]

When the Spanish hotel consortium Guitart began to remodel the property in 1993, three decades of deterioration and poor management of the Havana Libre were noticeable to visitors. Before the Cuban government turned management of the hotel over to the Spanish company, journalist Mauricio Vicent evaluated the condition of Havana's last great hotel built prior to the revolution: "The passage of time and the lack of resources for its maintenance punished [the hotel], converting it into a blue mastodon on the asphalt of Vedado. The slow elevators, the old pipes, the broken mirrors, the dirty *moquetas*, and the poor state of the air conditioning made it so that the Cuban authorities finally took seriously the need to remodel it."[19] Lack of efficiency exacerbated the decaying infrastructure of the building. When Guitart took over the management of the hotel on May 31, 1993, nearly one thousand employees attended the hotel's 534 rooms, a high ratio of employees to hotel rooms by European and North American standards. Furthermore, fiscal management of the hotel left something to be desired: audits revealed an average loss of two thousand dollars in cash per day from the hotel's coffers. Finally, the hotel was so filled with cockroaches that it was observed: "Upon fumigating the hotel we killed millions of cockroaches. So many that [it is still not known] why the Habana Libre was not able to walk by itself."[20]

The European Reconquest

Hotel management deficiencies were only part of a larger problem that faced the Cuban government in the late 1980s and early 1990s. By the mid-1980s Fidel Castro began looking for new forms of exchangeable currency to supplement the sagging, Soviet-subsidized economy. More important, Castro recognized the folly of trying to manage hotels and retail establishments without the proper expertise to be competitive in the global marketplace. Castro touted tourism as the economic future of Cuba, investing in the airport and road infrastructure that would be necessary to return Francis du Pont's Varadero Beach into a world-class destination. "You have a great resource in this province," he told a local crowd, "and that is the Varadero Peninsula. That peninsula has great unexploited possibilities."[21] From the two thousand rooms that existed there in 1988, Castro predicted that five thousand new rooms would be built during the next three years.

The one thing that Castro now knew he lacked was the expertise necessary to operate a world-class tourist destination. "The better the service and the more quality rooms," he asserted, "the more we will earn." Castro then proceeded to explain to the audience in Matanzas the way in which such expertise would be acquired: "Some hotels . . . will be jointly owned with [European] firms with a lot of experience in tourism, which is what we need: experience in tourism. How to run a hotel, how to treat a tourist. If there ever was anything like that here, there is none of it today." Running a hotel also demanded a capable workforce. Castro noted, "You have to train for this . . . discipline must be rigorous. Without discipline, there's no [chance] to develop those natural resources. Dealing with foreigners requires good qualifications and training."[22]

Contrary to conventional wisdom, Castro began the turn toward Western Europe and its management-rich corporations *prior* to the Soviet pullout. This would not have been possible without a reciprocated interest by the European Union. At a time when the United States was turning back the clock on U.S.-Cuban relations—President Carter had started the process of normalizing them, only to have those advances reversed by President Reagan—the European Union seized on the opportunity to invest in the Cuban economy. Spain positioned itself at the vanguard of this economic revolution. Its shared history and cultural heritage with the island made Spain the natural leader in the Europeanization of the Cuban economy. The fact that the Socialist Party ruled Spain at the time provided ideological connections that further fused the interests of the two countries.

No company better represented the European conquest of Cuba than Sol Meliá, the international hotel empire of Gabriel Escarrer Julia. Beginning in 1956, at the age of twenty-one, the ambitious Escarrer began managing hotels in the Balearic Islands, a string of islands in the Mediterranean Sea off of the southern coast of Spain, where an increasing number of Northern Europeans, particularly Britons and Scandinavians, elected to pass their vacations. Escarrer later turned to the acquisition and management of hotels in the Balearic Islands, Canary Islands, and on the Spanish peninsula. Much as the Spaniards had carved an empire out of existing empires in the fifteenth and sixteenth centuries, Escarrer bought up competing hotel groups and integrated them into his emerging Sol chain. One of the first major acquisitions involved the purchase of the HOTASA chain, which provided Escarrer with a major network of hotels throughout the Spanish peninsula. In 1987, when Escarrer outbid the likes of Hilton for the Meliá chain, he fortified his commitment to the creation of an international complex of hotels. In spite of this multitude of acquisitions, the strength of the Meliá portfolio remained its ability to manage world-class facilities, as well as provide the attendant services for hotel architecture, supply, and marketing.

In 1985, the true beginning of international expansion for Sol Meliá arose. After locating its first resort in Bali that year, Escarrer focused his attention on the market segment he knew best: vacation resorts and the two regions best known as European playgrounds for sun and sand, the Caribbean and the Mediterranean. Escarrer's decision to expand in the

Mediterranean basin was a natural fit, given the proximity of existing hotel properties. The move into the Americas was more risky, but followed historical precedents going back to the fifteenth century, when Spanish landowners used the Canary Islands as a springboard to the conquest of the Americas. The opening to establish a foothold in the Caribbean basin emerged in the form of Mexico's currency crisis in 1985. At that time the Mexican government made an appeal to various Spanish and American hoteliers to come to its planned resort communities, particularly Cancun, which had only been in commercial existence for eleven years, and take advantage of the advantageous opportunities for investing in a new market.[23]

The Spaniards lay claim to the title of "kings of Caribbean tourism" as a result of their bold entrance into the market in the mid-1980s. Sol Meliá did not enter the Caribbean alone, but went abroad with other Spanish hoteliers, including Barcelo (the dominant hotelier in the Dominican Republic) and Oasis (a competitor in Cuba as well as in Mexico). Later the Iberostar, Riu, Hotetur, Occidental, Tryp, Guitart, and Fiesta chains would join this Spanish conquest. Sol Meliá initially planted four flags in Mexico, opening the Meliá Cancun, a hotel inspired by the pyramids of ancient America; the Meliá Turquesa, also in Cancun; the Meliá Los Cabos; and the Meliá Puerta Vallarta. These four hotels gave Sol Meliá a foothold at the major FONATUR planned tourist communities and set the stage for further expansion into Mexico in succeeding decades. The foray into Mexico was followed by an invitation to build a resort community, the Meliá Bávaro, at Punta Cana in the Dominican Republic.

As Sol Meliá laid the foundation for a Latin American empire in Mexico and the Dominican Republic, even greater opportunities presented themselves in Cuba. In the mid-1980s, the Cuban government sent representatives to Spain to promote the island as a tourist destination. Curious, Gabriel Escarrer saw the potential of Cuba as a tourist destination for Canadians, Latin Americans, and Europeans, and joined forces with one of Spain's wealthiest businessmen, tobacco grower and hotel builder Enrique Martiñon. For Martiñon, the venture into Cuba was a risk, but one worth taking since he saw there much of the same tourist potential he had seen in the Canary Islands, his home base. The union between Martiñon, Sol Meliá, and other Spanish investors was known as CIHSA. After meeting with Fidel Castro and Cuban officials regarding the possibility of entering the Cuban resort industry, in 1987 CIHSA entered into an agreement with Cubanacán, the Cuban agency charged with developing tourism. The union between CIHSA and Cubanacán produced Cubacan; a mixed-enterprise in which Cubanacan would own 51 percent of any hotel built by the joint group, and CIHSA 49 percent.

In 1987, this historic consortium agreed to set its sights on building three world-class hotels at Varadero Beach, the old home of Francis du Pont's Xanadu.[24]

While there were scores of European hotel companies that entered or desired to enter the Cuban market, several important characteristics explain why Sol Meliá was able to shape the Cuban tourist sector in its own image. Gabriel Escarrer's personality and nonpolitical approach to Cuban tourism placed his group in a position of strength with the Cuban government. More important, however, was the management approach that they offered the Cuban government and the application of their global model to a particular locality. Perhaps the largest challenge for a hotel company in entering a market like Cuba involved personnel. Because of the management vacuum created by the revolution, it was very difficult to begin from the ground up and create a competent hotel staff that could cater to discriminating customers. Sol Meliá adapted to Cuba by making its then Human Resources Vice President Gabriel Canaves head of Sol Meliá's Cuban division. Working together with the Cuban government, Sol Meliá not only trained Cuban professionals for the tourist sector, but also worked to transfer knowledge and training to Cuba through interactive teaching programs originating in the Balearic Islands. This commitment to help the Cuban tourist industry grow placed Sol Meliá in a position to become the dominant leader in the Cuban hotel industry and a cornerstone of Cuban tourism since the late 1980s.

Another advantage that helped Sol Meliá dominate the Cuban hotel industry related to cultural integration into the community. After directing the construction of numerous hotels in Cuba and the Caribbean, Enrique Martiñon cast down his roots in Cuba, electing to make Havana his official residence. Furthermore, Martiñon planned his wedding to a Cuban bride to coincide with the opening of the Meliá Habana hotel in 1998. Around the first of October 1998 Gabriel Escarrer, Ian Delaney, Canadian partner in several of the CIHSA hotels and president of the Sherritt mining company, and Fidel Castro looked on as Martiñon married Janet Martinez Morán, a Cuban. Martiñon's wedding was significant not only because it coincided with the opening of CIHSA's fourth hotel on the island, but also because it followed a long-standing European pattern of social integration into the foreign society in which one chose to do business. At the end of the wedding El Comandante proclaimed, "Meliá, Sherritt, and socialism! . . . a symbol . . . of this era."[25]

CIHSA's pioneering work in Cuba also helped forge political and cultural ties between the Cuban government and the provincial governments in the Balearic and Canary Islands, the corporate homes of Sol Meliá and Enrique Martiñon, respectively. They were also in the vanguard, particularly in the case of enterprises in the Balearic Islands, of a broader Spanish conquest of Cuban tourism.[26] These connections, however, further reinforced the position of Sol Meliá and Martiñon in the Cuban tourism market. This was evident in the winter and spring of 2000 when the presidents of the governments of the Canary Islands and the Balearic Islands made official visits to Cuba, including personal visits with Fidel Castro and cabinet officials. An overriding theme in the interviews between Francisco Antich Oliver, president of the Balearic Islands, and Carlos Lage, the Cuban vice president, was the link created by tourism between the two regions. Oliver also stressed this connection in his six-hour meeting with Castro. Oliver visited the resort of Varadero, site of the highest concentration of Sol Meliá's beach resorts. Ibraham Ferradaz, ministry of tourism at the time, noted that development was "A total priority in the existing relations in the field of tourism with the businesses of the Balearic Islands." Vice President Carlos Lage further emphasized this connection: "Baleares is a region of Spain with a great deal of tourist development. Wherefore, for a country like ours where tourism is the most important activity . . . the possibility of exchanging experiences, establishing relationships, is really very significant."[27] Sol Meliá's position as the key link in the Balearic-Cuban relationship was evident at the state dinner held in honor of Oliver's visit. Gabriel Canaves, director of Sol Meliá in Cuba, was one of the guests of state. Later on that year the president of the Canary Islands made a similar state visit to Cuba, meeting with Castro for five hours, and reminding those present at the dinner of lobster, lamb, and wine that Enrique Martiñon was the pioneer who established the first tourist relations between the Spanish islands and Cuba.[28]

With these advantages, CIHSA and Sol Meliá pursued their development of Varadero Beach. The master plan called for construction of three hotels that would appeal to different tourist segments. Designed to reflect the architectural style of Sol Meliá hotels in the Canary Islands, the horizontal orientation of these properties blended into the beach landscape. The structure of the Sol Palmeras faced onto the beach and had more than six hundred rooms and villas. It was inaugurated on May 10, 1990. The second hotel, the Meliá Varadero, a four-and-a-half-star property, lay cloaked in the flora of the island's tropical brush. It opened in December 1991. Finally, the Meliá Américas, a five-star property, sat next to the Xanadu mansion and was later complemented by the refurbished and expanded golf course, which was christened the Varadero Golf Club. The Meliá Américas opened for service in July 1994. The Meliá Varadero and the Meliá Américas were connected by a convention center and a shopping plaza, Plaza Américas, located between the two properties.[29]

Fidel Castro followed the development of Varadero, as well as the Meliá hotels there, with great interest. On September 27, 1988, Castro visited the peninsula, mentally mapping out the expected thirty thousand hotel rooms he hoped to build there. Reminiscent of his yearly sugar goals, Castro insisted that Cubans could build five thousand hotel rooms by 1991. He also reiterated a point he had made earlier in the year related to hotel management: "We've lost the idea of how to treat a tourist during all those years without them. It is a culture we must acquire."[30] At the inauguration of the Sol Palmeras hotel on May 10, 1990, Castro also addressed the important lessons in hotel management that Cubans were learning from their partnership with Sol Meliá. While he stressed the high level of culture and education of Cuban hotel workers, he also bluntly conceded, "I should honestly say that we know nothing about hotel administration. Not even the most efficient of our administrators who might be around here knows a thing." Castro confessed that in the 1970s and 1980s, Cuban hotel operators had learned how to run hotels by the multitude of errors made in tending to guests. "They wanted to serve them but did not know how," he noted, "Someone said once . . . a Cuban is the most hospitable man or person in the world, the most pleasant and thoughtful, but once he puts on a waiter's uniform he is terrible."

At the opening, Castro outlined broader goals of transferring knowledge to young Cuban professionals in order that state-run ventures would also improve. "We are going to acquire an enormous amount of experience on how to manage a hotel," he asserted. "This is not an ideological matter, it is a technical matter, it is a scientific matter. . . . We have told [the Spaniards] to manage the hotel for many years until we have cadres who can do the job the way they do, with the experience they have." Recognizing the competitive struggle that Cuba found itself in with reference to the global tourism game, Castro challenged the workers to achieve the type of efficiency that would allow Cuba to rise from the bottom of Caribbean tourism to loftier heights, all on the shoulders of Sol Meliá's experience.[31]

One year later, at the inauguration of the Meliá Varadero, a short walk up the beach from the Sol Palmeras, Castro reiterated the value of the joint partnership, particularly as it enriched Cuban knowledge of planning, designing, building, and operating world-class hotels. The Comandante reflected, "Our country did not have much experience in hotel management. . . . The experience we had was very outdated and underdeveloped. We really did not have much experience in preparing hotel projects. It was a field that was truly new to us."

Castro thrust himself into the project of creating a tourist infrastructure with the same precocious zeal with which he had learned every other facet of running a country.[32] Castro boasted that the efficiency of the Sol Palmeras provided a source from which to improve the wholly Cuban-owned hotels in Varadero. After one year, Castro brimmed, "the number of workers [at the Punta Arenas and Paraiso Hotels] has been reduced." The Sol Meliá hotels became the standard and Cuban hotels would be measured against the performance of the joint-venture hotels. "I believe we would not [have] learned as much without the privilege of gaining knowledge from the international experience, from the experience of being part of this Spanish hotel chain." He further lauded the Spaniards for their ability to plan the cost of hotels on a per-room basis and then acquire the products at a better price than Castro had been able to secure. Castro also began to style himself as something of an expert on hotel design and management. He recognized that mistakes had been made in the past construction of hotels at Varadero, such as minimizing the space of guest rooms in order to build larger public areas.

Castro's observations also extended to resort planning. One of Cuba's advantages in the development of resort infrastructure was the ability to learn from what had worked in other locations and what had not worked. What is difficult to separate, in hindsight, is where Castro's emulation of Sol Meliá and his own original ideas for resort planning part ways. Castro advocated a low-density approach to resort planning in beach sectors, citing poor examples of building large hotels right next to the water in Europe. "We have been thinking a great deal about all this," he observed, "and about truly knowing what vacationers want. For example we have learned that people do not want skyscrapers for hotels, because they became a cage." Ten years later, at a conference on tourism, technology, and nature, Gabriel Escarrer elaborated on his view of resorts, architecture, and the environment. Following the pioneering work of Sol Meliá's one-time architect, and pioneer in the development of eco-resorts, Alvaro Sans, Escarrer asserted, "The vertical shoe boxes have no room in the travel industry today. . . . Hotels have to respect the environment." More than likely this parallel vision came from the innovative work of Spanish architects who worked hand in hand with Cuban architects. Some of the earliest hotel buildings built at Varadero during the revolution looked like high-rise Soviet apartment buildings, which still stick up, out of place, against the Varadero sunset.[33]

Sol Meliá was not the only Spanish firm that revolutionized the Cuban hotel industry in the 1990s. The Guitart Hotel Company, another chain primarily based on the Spanish peninsula, also took advantage of the Cuban government's invitation to transfer know-how to the island. Guitart undertook the management of several beach hotels, as well as the island's premiere business and diplomatic hotel, the Havana Libre.

Although the Guitart hotels in Cuba would eventually become part of the Meliá family of hotels, Guitart helped set the standard against which the Cuban government measured their progress in managing urban hotel properties in the early 1990s.

At the same time that Cuban architects and builders in conjunction with Spanish experts were working on the Meliá Américas, the Havana Libre had been passed to the Guitart hotel company. Castro was very intrigued to see what types of management improvements would be made as a result of foreign expertise. A November 17, 1993, meeting of the Cuban Communist Party, attended by Fidel Castro, the city historian, Eusebio Leal, and several other delegates from the Cuban Communist Party involved with tourism, revealed the profound impact that the Guitart management team had wrought in the few short months they had been in control of the Havana Libre. The main concern of those attending the meeting was the renewal of tourism to Havana, which had once been the crown jewel of Cuba's tourist offerings. Castro applauded the discipline with which the Guitart team had enacted its reforms, noting the benefits of foreign, instead of Cuban, management. "When two Cubans get together," Castro noted hypothetically, "one says: this is my cousin; he has to put up with and tolerate everything I do; he cannot demand anything from me." In contrast, Castro noted, "they listen to everything the Spaniard tells them." "The psychological make-up of the Cuban people is quite a sight," he mused, "They listen to a Spaniard; but when a Cuban speaks, they do not listen."[34]

Party delegates later answered Castro's questions about the Havana Libre. The number of employees at the hotel had dropped from 999 to 577 since June 1. The following dialogue ensued:

CASTRO:	Why were there so many workers?
FIRST DELEGATE:	Commander, in 1989 there were 1,200 workers.
CASTRO:	There were more. There were 1,200. Go ahead. Now you have fewer than half.
FIRST DELEGATE:	It was because of their inefficiency.
CASTRO:	What were all those people doing there?
FIRST DELEGATE:	I guess they wandered around, because today we do the job with 577 and we get the job done right. . . .
CASTRO:	How many people who should not haven been eating there were eating at the hotel?
FIRST DELEGATE:	Seven hundred twenty workers.
CASTRO:	How many?
FIRST DELEGATE:	Seven hundred twenty.
CASTRO:	Who were not workers at the hotel?
FIRST DELEGATE:	They were not workers of the hotel.

CASTRO:	But they ate at the hotel.
FIRST DELEGATE:	Yes, they ate at the hotel.
CASTRO:	Do you think a tourism industry can prosper that way? I ask you, comrades, tell me the truth: Do you think a hotel where approximately 700 people with nothing to do with the hotel are eating can be a hotel for tourism? In what country of the world? Until when did that go on?
FIRST DELEGATE:	This went on until June.
CASTRO:	June, this year?
FIRST DELEGATE:	Until 1 June, when the Spaniards took over.[35]

The meeting also brought to light other transformations in the Havana Libre as a result of Spanish management. Under Cuban management, the Havana Libre suffered from 10 to 11 percent absenteeism amongst employees, but the percentage had been cut to 2 percent under Guitart. Regularization of worker hours also took place in the wake of the transfer of management. The workforce also became younger, in step with the higher demands placed on tourism workers.

The Cuban experience with Spanish operations at the Havana Libre paved the way for more efficient national management of tourist properties and hotels. Even Castro was forced to recognize his indebtedness to the Spaniards:

CASTRO:	Was the experience of the Spaniards who joined the hotel not worth anything?
THIRD DELEGATE:	We have done this thanks to that, because alone, as a Cuban, I would not have been able to do any of this. This is what makes the difference.
CASTRO:	Then we had to import Galicians?
THIRD DELEGATE:	Yes, at least initially.
CASTRO:	Right, but you think that one day we can do this by ourselves?
THIRD DELEGATE:	I am fully convinced of this but I also have to be given the powers that were given to him.[36]

The delegates at the meeting also revealed that the joint-venture partners, like Guitart, had also achieved higher levels of efficiency and occupancy as a result of their ability to work around, rather than through, the politicized Cuban economic structure. Whereas the Guitart chain had the ability to order food, set its own menus, and price meals for sale in the hotel, Cuban hotel managers were required to carry certain foods requested and priced by party officials. "My hands were tied," one

Cuban hotel official complained. "In his case," referring to the joint-venture partners, "this does not happen. He estimates the cost and he sells at a profit and no one gets in his face or sets fines or takes him to court." A party delegate at the seminal November meeting asserted, "Commander, I also believe that the Habana Libre experience . . . has helped to energize the rest of the hotels." From marketing to human resources and client attention, Guitart set the mark for Cuban tourist departments to follow.[37]

The Helms-Burton Act: "The Sword of Damocles"

From the fall of the Berlin Wall in 1989 until completion of Escarrer and Martiñon's three resorts at Varadero in 1994, the United States had taken several measures to capitalize on the implosion of Soviet support for Cuba and the resultant economic uncertainty on the island. The fall of the Soviet Union sent a rush of optimism through the State Department. An internal memo dated January 24, 1990, outlined the increasing economic strains that a collapsed communist block in Eastern Europe portended for the Caribbean island. "As a result of lost markets," the memo predicted, "Cuba's balance of trade will further deteriorate, shortages of food and other consumer goods will become more acute, and hard currency reserves will be further depleted." The ouster of Noriega in Panama provided even more evidence that the end was in sight for Castro's regime. Panama had been the main offshore acquisition point of first-world consumer goods and capital for Cuba during the embargo.[38]

In 1992, Democratic Senator Robert Torricelli, in conjunction with the chairman of the Cuban American National Federation, Jorge Mas Canosa, masterminded a further tightening of the 1961 trade embargo against Cuba. Up until 1991, hundreds of subsidiaries of American countries had legally been trading with Cuba. They simply had to ask for permission from the State Department on an annual basis. In the lead-up to the 1992 election, the Torricelli bill proposed a ban on U.S. subsidiaries trading with Cuba, regardless of where they were based. Mexico, Argentina, and the European Community expressed their opposition to the law. Canada and Britain did heed the legislation once President George H. W. Bush had signed it into law. Many experts claimed that its purpose was simply to help either the Republican or Democratic Party to carry the Cuban-exile rich state of Florida, with its twenty-five electoral votes. A lawyer representing Cuba in the United States, Michael Krinsky, put it this way: "Those votes in Dade County, Florida, mean more to the George Bush right now that the whole of the [European Community] and Canada put together." Jorge Mas Canosa placed the bill's significance within the context of wresting control of Cuban consumer culture from the Europeans at the end of the Castro regime: "(When Castro falls) a market of 11 million consumers will open up overnight; a market that will need everything from toilet paper to the most sophisticated computer. And most of that will come from Florida."[39]

Anti-Castro groups also applied extra-legal pressure. Sol Meliá and Guitart hotels, as well as other European-managed hotels, became targets of vigilante terrorism aimed at scaring tourists and companies away from Cuba. According to a Cuban report submitted to the United Nations' Security Council, attacks on hotels began almost as soon as Europeans were allowed to operate in Cuba. On October 7, 1992, four Miami-based terrorists launched an armed attack on the Meliá Varadero from a boat off of the peninsula. The following January, the report alleged, the leader of the group "Commandos L" announced that more hotel attacks were imminent and that "from now on, we are at war with Cuba." Cuban diplomats further charge that in November 1993 a spokesperson for the Miami group, Alpha 66, also warned tourists to stay away from Cuba. "Those who stay in Cuban hotels," he warned, "are considered as enemies." The following March the Spanish-managed Guitart Cayo Coco Hotel was peppered with gunfire. The same hotel was attacked again on October 6, 1994. Several months later, in May 1995, another terrorist attack targeted the same property. The attacks subsided for about two years, but then gripped Havana and Varadero anew when a string of explosions rocked the Caribbean capital in the spring and summer of 1997. On April 12, 1997, a bomb exploded in the Meliá Cohiba hotel. Later that month another explosive device was found at the hotel. In July bombs exploded at the Cuban-run Capri Hotel and the Hotel Nacional in Vedado (Havana). On August 4, 1997, another bomb exploded in the Meliá Cohiba. Finally, a bomb exploded at the first of the three hotels built by CIHSA in Varadero, the Sol Palmeras, in August 1997.[40]

If terrorism and threats to American subsidiaries trading with Cuba were not enough to asphyxiate the Cuban economy, the ascension of Jesse Helms to the chairmanship of the Senate Foreign Relations Committee set the stage for the most daring attempt to thwart the European conquest of the Cuban economy. Several factors contributed to the drafting of the infamous Cuban Liberty and Solidarity Act—or Helms-Burton Act (1996). Ironically, for a bill with such far-reaching international implications, its motivations were primarily domestic. Domestically, some considered this a veiled message from Republicans to President Bill Clinton that he needed to get tougher on Cuba. Second, the Helms-Burton bill, approved by a majority Republican House and

Senate, reinforced the political importance of Florida in national politics. Internationally, the Helms-Burton Act would punish the executives of companies that trafficked in alienated property from former owners in Cuba with revocation of their visas (Title IV), as well as open up the possibility of being sued in American courts for using those properties (Title III). As a side effect, the new law would also create uncertainty for Cuba's trade partners, a condition that might ultimately benefit American corporations.[41] The bill did not, however, take into account the overwhelmingly negative international reception to a law that suggested the United States Congress could directly punish foreign businesses for activities in a third country. Furthermore, the law would be applied retroactively—that is, for business decisions made in the past—and for the benefit of many who were not American citizens at the time their property was confiscated.[42]

In theory, the Senate committee operated from a secretive, inquisitorial list that had the names of companies suspected of occupying land or using resources nationalized from American or Cuban-American exiles by the Castro regime. The Cuban American National Foundation drew up the list from the primary investors of each country in Cuba. The Senate Committee on Foreign Relations would then draw up its own list from which investigations would be made. In practice, the companies that were publicly targeted were those that had been identified by Cuban-exile families or their lawyers, many of whom advertised their services specifically for the Helms-Burton Act. Lawyers then pressed the Foreign Relations Committee to act on their behalf.[43]

On May 22, 1996, Madrid's *El País* newspaper reported that Sol Meliá would be included on a list of companies to be investigated for their operations in Cuba.[44] The Meliá case focused on the location of the Meliá Américas, which was adjacent to the Du Pont mansion. In response the Du Pont family diplomatically observed that "the global economy is dependent on reliable rules of trade and those rules would be jeopardized by the friction that would result [if the law took effect]."[45] If Sol Meliá was found to be in violation of the law, its executives, including those who worked at subsidiary offices in the United States, would be denied visas for travel to, from, and within the United States. The article also noted, "In diplomatic circles it is believed that Washington is choosing to punish those emblematic businesses from the principal investors in Cuba with the clear purpose of dissuading them from continuing investment there."[46] In response, Sol Meliá announced that it would rather pull out of its two resort hotels in Florida, one a collection of 150 villas in Orlando near Walt Disney World, and the other, a 271-room hotel on Miami Beach, than risk losing their more lucrative business ventures in Cuba. At the same time Sol Meliá pressed ahead, announcing new investments and operations in Cuba—including a new hotel in Havana (the present-day Meliá Habana), the Sol Club las Sirenas (Varadero), and a cruise ship, the Meliá Don Juan on the southern coast of Cuba.[47] A *Miami Herald* report on October 8, 1996, announced that the U.S. government would not continue to pursue a case against Sol Meliá for the time being.[48]

With strong support from the Spanish government and the European Union, Sol Meliá avoided the dreaded letter from the State Department apprising them of sanctions under the Helms-Burton Act. In 1997 the Spanish legislature reiterated its disapproval of the Helms-Burton legislation and its support for Spanish businesses in Cuba. Spain's approach to Cuban investment was reflective of European policies toward Cuba in the 1990s: while they disapproved of human rights violations and the undemocratic nature of the Castro regime, they believed that dialogue was more valuable than an embargo. Furthermore, Spain's business presence in Cuba was becoming too formidable to simply call off. Having responded to Cuba's calls for help in the late 1980s, Spanish investments in Cuba amounted to 54 million pesetas in 1996 alone. Ironically, Cuba's inability to pay back debts to lender nations made the presence of its corporations on the island even more vital. However, the Spanish legislature noted in a report, "In general, the investments are bottomed out now that the general climate generated by the said Helms-Burton Law is discouraging Spanish investments as well as investments from other countries." The report concluded by calling for a defense of Spanish interests on the island.[49]

Undeterred, Sol Meliá pressed on as the rising leader in Cuba tourism. The furor over the Helms-Burton Act seemed to be in abeyance, particularly after Madeline Albright agreed with leaders from the European Union on May 18, 1998, to work toward a suspension of Title IV with the United States Congress in exchange for a commitment by the European Union not to take the matter to the World Trade Organization.[50] The same month, Sol Meliá officially captured the title of leader in Cuban tourism, managing eight hotels on the island and committed to build and manage more resorts in connection with the Canadian mining interest, Sherritt International. By that time they had also opened the new Meliá Habana in the Miramar district across the street from the new Monte Barreto complex, a business center comparable in function to a World Trade Center. Attended by Fidel Castro, the inauguration of the Meliá Habana further cemented the strong relationship between Martiñon, Sol Meliá, and the Comandante. In 1999, the Spanish government staged the ultimate protest of the Helms-Burton law by publicizing President Aznar's stay at the Meliá Habana during the Inter-American Summit. At the summit Castro singled out Sol Meliá for their importance to the Cuban economy. The pressures of the United States Congress amounted to an "assault against the most important foreign company of tourism with which Cuba has relations."[51]

In the wake of this revelry, however, Senator Jesse Helms renewed the fight to catch Sol Meliá in violation of the Helms-Burton Law based on its operation of a new resort in Holguin, Cuba.[52] Sol Meliá was not alone. Given the fact that tourism had passed sugar production in the early 1990s as the chief generator of foreign exchange, tourism-related businesses found themselves the targets of investigation. The German hotel company LTU and French-based Club Med also received letters of inquiry from the State Department related to their operations in Cuba.[53] On July 30, 1999, the State Department served Sol Meliá with a letter of inquiry regarding its operations of the Sol Rio de Oro Hotel on Santa Lucia beach in Holguin province. The hotel sat on land once owned by the Rafael Lucas Sanchez family, where they had operated the Central Santa Lucia sugar plantation.[54] Lawyers for the family leaked rumors to the press later that fall that a sanction on the hotel chain was imminent, although nothing ever came of the matter. In an awkward move, the State Department, which was never as interested in applying the Helms-Burton Act as the Foreign Relations Committee and Jesse Helms, encouraged the two parties to agree to a settlement. Sol Meliá, citing a ban on such compensation by the European Union, rejected the proposal and continued to operate hotels in Cuba. In fact, the turmoil only strengthened Sol Meliá's resolve to expand its operations in Cuba. To add to the irony, Gabriel Escarrer was invited to New York to accept the award of Hotel Man of the Year from the International Association of Hotels and Restaurants at the Palace Hotel in November. As the subject of praise, Escarrer insightfully noted, "The American hotel operators are dying of envy because they cannot enter the Cuban market."[55] In December 1999, Escarrer, undeterred by the Helms-Burton question, emphasized the next phase of hotel management in Cuba, the keys, including joint venture projects at Cayo Coco and Cayo Guillermo.[56]

During the 1999 crisis, Sol Meliá gained its strongest support from provincial, national, and international bodies such as the European Union.[57] The strongest arguments against the Helms-Burton Law emerged during discussion in the Spanish Congress of Deputies following Sol Meliá's receipt of the State Department letter of inquiry. At a September 29, 1999, meeting, the Minister of Foreign Relations, Juan Matutes apprised the deputies of the contents of the letter of inquiry. Matutes assured the delegates that the letter was simply a request for information about the Sol Meliá hotel in Holguin, Cuba. However, he also blasted the letter for its ambiguous implications of possible punishment. In addition, he condemned the law for its extraterritorial and retroactive nature, faulting the United States for not living up to the pledge that Madame Albright had given in February 1998 to push Congress to deactivate points three and four of the Helms-Burton Act. Matutes argued that the Spanish government had a responsibility to defend Sol Meliá, given the fact that the fate of other Spanish companies in Cuba hung in the balance with that of Sol Meliá.[58]

The Helms-Burton Act had the strange effect of breaking down the often-rigid party lines in the Spanish legislature and clarifying the ironies and hypocrisies of the law. Rodriguez Sanchez objected to the fact that the letter had been sent directly from the State Department to Sol Meliá and not through corresponding channels of the Spanish government. "It is [arrogant] that a Department of State would direct itself unilaterally to a private business from another country," he noted. "In the field of international relations, I believe that this would be worthy of study. Apart from being a political intimidation, it is a sword of Damocles that is always [hanging] above us." Sanchez also welcomed news that ClubMed and LTU had received letters from the State Department. This would only strengthen support from members of the European Union against compliance with the law. Robles Fraga, from the Grupo Popular, gave perhaps the most stinging rebuke. Perhaps recalling the painful experience of Spaniards following Spanish-American War in 1898, Fraga observed: "Our businesses in Spain, assuming risks and naturally looking for the logical benefits, find themselves in the necessity of arriving at agreements with a government [the United States] that has an important original sin: For one part, that they do not respect nearly any of the international norms of protocol and, for another, that, in its own day, expropriated and confiscated determined properties from thousands of legitimate owners that had worked to acquire them, among whom, certainly, I will remind one more time, were thousands of Spaniards." Fraga concluded by urging the European Union to oppose the extraterritorial practices of the United States. Balletbo I Puig (Socialist Party) noted that the most damaging effect of the law was its tendency to create a sense of doubt amongst European investors. "What is happening," she observed, "in these moments has already had an effect that is creating instability in Spanish and European investors . . . who tend to be very prudent by definition." She also noted that the law discouraged free trade, something the Americans had actively promoted in the late twentieth century. The session ended in unanimity, with the ideas of historical irony and free trade conspiracy fresh in the air.[59]

Meanwhile, on the other side of the Atlantic, the lack of action on the part of the State Department helped explain why the Helms-Burton Act had created smoke and mirrors, but little in the way of actual sanctions.

Furious at the State Department's unwillingness to carry out his recommendations, Jesse Helms made a desperate attempt to see sanctions served to Sol Meliá. On November 16, 2000, Helms wrote a pompous letter to Thomas Pickering, Under Secretary of State, demanding that his department carry through with recommended actions against the Spanish hotelier. Helms emphasized that he had worked with the Sanchez family for three years in bringing sanctions against Sol Meliá. He underhandedly accused the State Department of dragging their feet on the mailing of the July 30, 1999, letter and admonished Pickering to carry out the mailing of sanctions to Sol Meliá. This was one of Helms' last-gasp attempts to punish the company. It brought to light the reluctance on the part of the State Department to proceed on the matter, perhaps because of conflicting interests with the European desks of the State Department. The following year, Jesse Helms retired from the Senate. The Senate Foreign Relations Committee has not assailed Sol Meliá since the State Department's letter of inquiry in the summer of 1999.[60]

Europe's success in transforming Cuba's tourist sector into the most productive segment of the economy did not go unnoticed by American corporations, the American government, or special interest groups, such as the Cuban-American community in Miami. If the purpose of the Helms-Burton legislation was to discourage foreign investment in Cuba, it did nothing to close loopholes that permitted American businesses to visit the island and plan their own post-Castro conquests. In 1995, the year prior to passage of the law, approximately 1,300 American business executives visited the islands to make their market assessments, including Colgate Palmolive, Procter and Gamble, General Motors, K-Mart, Gillette, Johnson and Johnson, Sheraton, Radisson, and Royal Caribbean Cruise Lines. Serious corporations signed memorandums of understanding with the Cuban government in anticipation of normalized relations. Others exploited a Department of Treasury loophole that allowed Americans to invest in foreign companies with Cuban operations who do not make more than 50 percent of their income on the island. By 1999 enough American brands had registered their trademarks in Cuba to fill a shopping center with stores and a supermarket with products, including the Home Depot (1993), Planet Hollywood (1991), TGIFridays (1992), Paul Mitchell (1992), Ralph Lauren (1992), Hilton (1989), Sunkist (1996), Pepsi (1992), Carolina Herrera (1994), Huggies (1994), Radisson (1995), Healthy Choice (1996), Sbarro (1997), Ace Hardware (1996), Jockey (1996), United Airlines (1996), Old Spice (1996), Heinz (1996), Visa (1996), Pizza Hut (1996), Kmart (1994), Starbucks Coffee (1997), Foot Locker (1994), Nike (1996), Rockport (1993), Sports Authority (1995), Hawaiian Tropic (1992), Tommy Hilfiger (1995), Little Caesars (1996), Goya (1992), and

McDonalds (1996).[61] While it might be argued that many of these companies were simply protecting their labels, it can also be inferred that such steps would not be taken unless the opportunity to do business in Cuba could one day be a possibility. Finally, more and more American products, by way of marketing agreements and distribution through third countries, were finding their way to Cuban store shelves. Ultimately, these developments, coupled with the tacit approval of business arrangements taking place between American companies and Cuban officials, led some Europeans to believe that the purpose of the Helms-Burton legislation actually aimed to punish the Europeans for getting to the island first before the embargo was lifted.[62]

Conclusion: Europe and the Cuban Hotel Industry

Regardless of whatever changes take place in the Cuban hotel industry after the United States decides to allow trade with its neighbor, the late 1980s through the early years of the new millennium constituted a tremendous period of Europeanization in the Cuban economy. The union between the island and the Old World so desired by Ramón Blanco in 1898 found new life as a result of the economic difficulties after the termination of Soviet assistance. Canadians, Italians, Britons, Spaniards, Germans, the French, Scandinavians, the Dutch, and others flocked to Cuba. When I traveled to Havana and Varadero in early 2004, it was clear that the fear intended by the Helms-Burton Act had largely subsided. In the Plaza San Francisco, under the imposing shadow of the Lonja de Comercio, the city's principal commercial building, the local Benetton store had shut its doors, not in preparation to leave the country, but instead for remodeling. On Obispo Street, the traditional pedestrian commercial artery of Havana Vieja since the eighteenth century, Cubans—as well as foreigners who spoke French, German, Dutch, Spanish, and distinctively British, Bahamian, and Irish strains of English—stopped to gawk at clothing stores covered with names of European clothing designers.

   In Miramar, Havana's upscale suburban area and diplomatic core, the Miramar Trade Center, Havana's equivalent of the World Trade Center, stands surrounded by European hotels: the Havana Meliá, glassy LTI Panorama (German), and the more subdued Novotel Miramar (French). Across the street from the Havana Meliá and diagonal to the Trade Center, the Galeria Comodoro, Cuba's finest shopping center, buzzed to a rock-and-roll beat and hosted upscale shoppers at its Mango (Spain), LaCoste (France), Façonable (France), and Benetton (Italy) boutiques. Workers and shoppers alike took a moment to enjoy fresh French bread at the Pain de Paris bakery.

Finally, Varadero continued to welcome the world to its beaches. Instead of traveling overland from Havana, as Francis du Pont did some eighty years ago, many Europeans, Canadians, and Latin Americans travel to the peninsula via direct flights from continental cities to the Varadero International Airport. The modest airport that has been carved out of the scrubby plain to the east of the city is a testament to the degree of Europeanization this once-isolated part of Cuba has achieved. The Cuban Ministry of Tourism lists Canadians, Italians, Germans, English, and Spaniards as the most frequent travelers to the island. An Air France office in Varadero shares building space with a Cuban snack bar on First Avenue in Varadero. Russian tourists snap photos in front of Al Capone's old home near the eastern point of the peninsula. Germans and Italians stroll the beach, darkly tanned, in their Speedoes, while Hungarians and Germans sit at a bar using English as their pidgin language to debate the merits of the best soccer players in Europe. Chinese tourists frolic in the water, snapping pictures of each other, as the sun sets to the west of the peninsula. At the upper end of the peninsula, the Dupont Mansion shares San Bernardino Crag with its Spanish neighbors: Meliá Américas, Meliá Varadero, Sol Palmeras, and the Iberostar Bella Costa. Miniature passenger trains run tourists to the Plaza Americas Shopping Center, where French and Canadian shoppers gawk at Italian and Spanish designer clothing before munching on pizza whose ingredients are flown in from Toronto by the Canadian chain, Pizza Nova. Signs in some stores offered a conversion scale for Euros, which were exchanged alongside dollars.[63] This polyglot jungle provided a stark contrast to the largely monolingual American beach haven to the west, Cancun. And so does the flat, more horizontal skyline of Varadero, whose design has largely been left in the hands of Europeans and Cubans.

The author's observations in Cuba confirmed that the policy choices made in Europe and the United States during the twentieth century, and particularly during the Castro regime, created one of the most drastic transformations of consumer culture in the history of the hemisphere. During the last half of the nineteenth century, Cuba was Spain's most "loyal" colony and the streets of Paris, London, and Madrid largely ruled its cultural preferences. The Spanish-American War in 1898 brought an abrupt transformation not only in the way Cuba was governed, but also in the precipitous domination of the consumer arena by American companies and styles. The Batista years of the 1950s brought a false sense of stability that further encouraged American investment in the retail and hotel sectors, only to be toppled by the improbable success of the Cuban Revolution.

Castro's rise to power was accompanied by the creation of a consumer culture vacuum with the de-commercialization of Cuban society and the flight of American investment and capital from the island. Perhaps Castro's greatest error was his belief that Cuba did not need management experts in order for the revolution to succeed. Castro's opening to Western Europe in the 1980s was a tacit admission that the island could not survive without some expertise in the fields of hotel and retail management. The arrival of companies like Sol Meliá returned the pendulum to its original point in the mid-nineteenth century as Cuba's economy oriented again toward Europe. Ironically, the American hotel and resort infrastructure that was supposedly erased by the Revolution, as in the cases of Varadero and the former Havana Hilton, provided the groundwork for European success on the island. After that success, the Helms-Burton Act represented an extraterritorial attempt on the part of the United States to thwart European domination on the Cuban island.

To some, these radical shifts in cultural and commercial orientation might appear chaotic. However, dramatic changes define Cuban history in general. Much like the United States' decision to conquer and control Cuba economically and politically at the end of the nineteenth century, America's decision to distance itself from the country, as well as ostracize those who attempted to pick up where they once had ruled, laid the foundations for a radical change in the island's consumer culture. The swinging pendulum also attests to the continuing colonial nature of Cuba in the global economic order. Whether that will change after the Castro regime seems doubtful. While many believe a wholesale shift in momentum in favor of U.S. corporations (including Wal-Mart, McDonalds, and Tommy Hilfiger) will take place once the embargo is lifted, these intervening years of European influence will undoubtedly affect the approach of whoever succeeds them or jostles side by side for market share.

Afterword

Janet F. Davidson

In 1915, Seymour Dunbar's lengthy tome, *A History of Travel in America*, was first published. At the time, long-distance travel and tourism were not everyday activities: most people did not have access to paid vacations, and travel was still firmly ensconced as an elite activity. Almost ninety years later, when the Center for the History of Business, Technology, and Society at the Hagley Museum and Library held a conference on tourism in fall 2004, things had radically changed. Countries around the world had seen and felt tourism's transformative economic effects as the numbers of tourists rose exponentially. By the beginning of the twenty-first century tourism was, by anyone's definitions, a mammoth global business, something to be taken seriously for its myriad economic, social, and cultural effects.

Just a few fairly random examples will highlight the range of the ways tourism has played into various nation's economies. On a winter day in 2005, an Internet search for "tourism statistics" told me that by 2005 tourism was a $1.3-trillion industry, supposedly responsible for massive job creation in the United States.[1] In 2004, "international tourist expenditure accounted to $7.4 billion or 18.5% of New Zealand's total export earnings" as well as being responsible for nearly 10 percent of the country's gross domestic product (GDP).[2] In 2003, 40,000 people flew into Tonga, and nearly 6,500 people arrived in the African nation from cruise ships.[3] In the same year, tourism provided Iceland with more than 5 percent of its GDP.[4] Although many sources hype the benefits of tourism, some countries were negatively affected by the business of tourism: United Kingdom residents' propensity to travel to overseas countries left the country with a £16.7 billion deficit in tourism spending.[5] Clearly, the business of tourism has become something to take seriously, if only because of the vast amounts of money it generated by the end of the twentieth century.

It has become a scholarly truism to point to the decades when scholars neglected the topic of tourism. As the generally told story goes, ignoring or belittling tourism was part and parcel of scholarly ideas about pleasure travelers. Making fun of tourists, and suggesting that they were somehow engaging in an inauthentic experience, has been part of the way that people understood what tourism has meant to cultures and societies. Yet, despite this narrative of those once ignored or reviled and now closely analyzed, a vast earlier literature—produced by both professional and amateur historians—touches on travel experiences and tourism. This literature is one of transportation and technology. It is not a history that is held in terribly high regard these days. But it is a literature that, ironically and durably, gave travel a respect that later historians did not.

The downsides of this literature are obvious: there isn't a great attention to the role of people and their experiences. But there are things to be learned and gleaned from reading authors such as Seymour Dunbar. Dunbar's 1905 work—published when the history profession was young, and perhaps reflecting the spirit of Frederick Jackson Turner's Frontier Thesis—is rife with ideas that have fallen out of favor: progress and white supremacy are firmly embedded it its narrative. Like many others with an interest in the transportation systems of the United States, Dunbar made the railroad into the epitome of the nation: he concluded his massive tome with the idea that "the opening of a modern travel highway across the continent marked the end of a work that began when English speaking white men landed on the shores of Virginia and Massachusetts. With its completion a destiny was realized."[6] Dunbar's turgid prose fit both into the growing history of technology and into notions about transportation's links to progress and order. Historians, as they touted the nationalizing qualities of transportation systems and travel, followed the lead of Americans who lived through the dramatic transformations of the nineteenth century. In 1869, after the telegraph announced the transcontinental railroad was complete, the Reverend Dr. Vinton, minister of New York's Trinity Church, whose bells pealed out to commemorate the event, told his congregation about the positive effects of the railroad: "It will populate our vast territory, and be the great highway of the nations; their merchants will cross it to trade with us. But there is another aspect in which we view it as a blessing, and in connection with which we esteem it of still greater import. It will preserve the union of these States."[7]

More recently, the ideas of social and cultural historians have affected the ways that people study travel and transportation. Studies with a cultural and literary bent, such as Leo Marx's *Machine in the Garden* and Wolfgang Schivelbusch's *The Railway Journey* should be required reading for historians of tourism. And in the 1990s, historians such as Amy G. Richter and Kathleen Franz have begun to examine transportation systems using ideas drawing on literary theory and using the prisms of race, gender, and class.[8] For the most part, however, although they indirectly gave us clues about leisure travelers, and they have explored travel as a window into public domesticity, tinkering, or travel as a nationalist trope, transportation buffs and scholars influenced by the history of technology have not usually focused on the tourism industry or on the experiences of tourists themselves.

That has been left to more recent studies that have focused on tourism as a topic in its own right. The revitalization of interest in the history of tourism reflects increasing professional interests in the history of mass consumption, in the intersections of public and private, in battles over the contested meanings of the past, and in the ways that tourism illuminates actual and cultural imperialism. Most accounts of tourism history in the United States mark the start of the transformation of the discipline from the publication of John Sears's seminal text, *Sacred Places*, in 1989.[9] It and other works helped create a standard narrative about the role of tourism. Basically, the newly conventional narrative runs—albeit often with some modifications and usually a dash more complexity—as managerial capitalism created wealth and an infrastructure, more wage earners had more stable jobs and ultimately gained access to the once-elite "vacation."[10] At the same time, as Cindy Sondik Aron suggests, the meanings of leisure changed; tourists as we know them didn't exist in the mid-nineteenth century. Mass production and urban capitalism thus led to the growth of tourism.

Ironically, despite the production-anchored vision embedded in this story, many scholars—influenced no doubt by cultural theory and Dean MacCannell's seminal work *The Tourist*—have been more interested in the consumption of leisure or manipulation of the symbols of tourist activity than in the actual workings of the tourism industry.[11] It is a rare scholar of tourism who does not quote a French theorist, or owe a debt to Pierre Bourdieu's *Distinction*.[12] Studying tourism in this way has provided a window into the interpenetrations of viewer and viewed, culture and identity. While much of this work is laudable, interesting, and evocative—and a number of the authors in this volume use techniques employed by cultural theorists to great advantage—*The Business of Tourism* joins a growing literature that seeks to redress the balance, taking the business of travel and tourism seriously in combination with adopting a more respectful attitude toward tourists and a more critical attitude about ideas of progress.

In the *Business of Tourism*, authors such as Brian Bixby trace the role of economics in the rise of Shaker village tourism. Transportation infrastructure is a key part of the story of tourism in Kenneth J. Perkins's Algiers, whereas even Philip Whalen's theoretically sophisticated work focuses on the "firm" called Burgundy. Gaston Gérard's life, actions, and ideas are as significant to Whalen's argument as theorist Guy Debord's ideas. In some sense the book you hold in your hands is a deeply "old-fashioned" history—empirically based, grounded in the real experiences of producers and consumers. Yet, because of its range and depth, *The Business of Tourism* offers a fresh look at the way tourism operates. These contributions from scholars interested in the histories of a variety of countries with a range of economic systems, as they explore how tourism works, move us beyond any simplistic notions of its imperialism—cultural or actual. The chapters with a religious focus are equally provocative, as they examine the business side of spiritually based tourist attractions, and take the beliefs of the adherents seriously. It would be easy for Aaron K. Ketchell to mock Silver Dollar City, but he chooses, instead, to explore its contours.

The Business of Tourism also challenges the idea that capitalist mass production leads to the growth of tourism. Evan Ward's marvelous discussion of Cuban tourism, Ann Gorsuch's work on Soviet tourism at the end of the Stalinist era, and Patrick Patterson's exploration of Yugoslavia most directly undermine the capitalist-tourism connection simply by the fact that they explore tourism in communist nations. But more important, this book suggests that we should rethink the way we examine tourism, exploring the role that stability and organization—not capitalism or communism per se—plays in tourist economies.

In the *Business of Tourism*, predictability, planning, stability, and infrastructures shape and structure tourists' experiences around the world and across time. Castro's Cuba doesn't become a tourist success because it embraces capitalism: rather, it becomes a success because the country's leaders and workers learn ways to create a quality experience for their visitors, some of whom probably flock to the nation's hotels and beaches *because* of Cuba's communism, not in spite of it. The assumption that tourism has become a massive industry because of the rise of capitalism is something that this book suggests should be questioned and challenged by all historians interested in the ways that leisure travel has helped shape and structure a wide variety of different economies across time and space. As it does so, *The Business of Tourism* makes an important contribution to the burgeoning literature on a fascinating topic.

Notes

Chapter 1. The East as an Exhibit

1. The Egyptian 24 is one in a string of themed megaplex movie theaters built by Muvico. See Ryan Chittum, "Themed Megaplexes Entice Shoppers to the Mall," *Wall Street Journal*, June 15, 2005, B1. See also http://www.muvico.com.

2. Roy Higgs, "Entertainment in Shopping Centers: Development, Design and Management Considerations," presentation to the International Council of Shopping Centers (ICSC) Asia Pacific Conference, held October 13–14, 2004, in Shanghai, China. Available from http://www.ddg-usa.com/press_room/presentations/2004Oct14-ICSC-Asia-RH.pdf.

3. Chittum, "Themed Megaplexes Entice Shoppers to the Mall."

4. In much the same way that I argue here that Egypt played a critical role in the rise of the international tourism industry, Antonia Lant suggests that "Egypt played midwife to film's birth." Antonia Lant, "The Curse of the Pharaoh, or How Cinema Contracted Egyptomania," in *Visions of the East: Orientalism in Film*, ed. Matthew Bernstein and Gaylyn Studlar (New Brunswick, N.J.: Rutgers University Press, 1997), 81.

5. Jeremy Black, *The British Abroad: The Grand Tour in the Eighteenth Century* (New York: St. Martin's Press, 1992); John Tower, "The History of the Grand Tour," *Annals of Tourism Research* 12 (1985): 301–16; James Buzard, *The Beaten Track: European Tourism, Literature, and the Ways to Culture, 1800–1918* (Oxford: Clarendon Press, 1993); Karen Kennerly, "Far Away So Close," *New Republic*, July 19–26, 1999; John Pemble, *The Mediterranean Passion: Victorians and Edwardians in the South* (Oxford: Clarendon Press, 1987); Lynne Withey, *Grand Tours and Cook's Tours: A History of Leisure Travel, 1750–1915* (New York: William Morrow, 1997).

6. Daniel J. Boorstin, *The Image: A Guide to Pseudo-Events in America* (New York: Atheneum, 1971), 85. As if anticipating the Arundel Mills shopping mall, Boorstin notes that "shopping . . . is one of the few activities remaining for the tourist" (92). Dean MacCannell, however, notes that "the commodity has become a means to an end" that holds value in terms of its meaning as a cultural experience. He also suggests that the modern "touristic consciousness is motivated by its desire for authentic experiences" and that tourists should be studied as semioticians in search of markers or signs of authenticity. Dean MacCannell, *The Tourist: A New Theory of the Leisure Class*, new ed. (Berkeley: University of California Press, 1999), 23, 101. See also Jonathan Culler, "The Semiotics of Tourism," *Framing the Sign: Criticism and Its Institutions* (Oxford: Blackwell, 1988), 153–67.

7. Edward W. Said, *Orientalism* (New York: Vintage Books, 1979).

8. Derek Gregory, *The Colonial Present: Afghanistan, Iraq, Palestine* (Malden, Mass.: Blackwell, 2004), 17.

9. Ibid.

10. Timothy Mitchell, *Colonising Egypt* (Berkeley: University of California

Press, 1991), 1–21; Zeynep Çelik, "Noble Dreams, Wicked Pleasures: Oriental-
ism in American, 1870–1930," in *Speaking Back to Orientalist Discourse at the World's
Columbian Exposition,* ed. Holly Edwards (Princeton, N.J.: Princeton University
Press, 2000).

11. Mitchell, *Colonising Egypt,* 21.

12. Ibid., xiv.

13. Ibid., 24.

14. This project is extended in Timothy Mitchell, *Rule of Experts: Egypt, Techno-
Politics, Modenity* (Berkeley: University of California Press, 2002).

15. Derek Gregory, "Colonial Nostalgia and Cultures of Travel: Spaces of
Constructed Visibility in Egypt," in *Consuming Tradition, Manufacturing Heritage,*
ed. Nezar Alsayyad (London: Routledge, 2001), 111–51; Derek Gregory,
"Emperors of the Gaze: Photographic Practices and Productions of Space in
Egypt, 1839–1914," in *Picturing Place: Photography and the Geographical Imagination,* ed. Joan M. Schwartz and James Ryan (London: I. B. Tauris, 2003), 195–
225; Derek Gregory, "Imaginative Geographies," *Progress in Human Geography* 19
(1995): 447–85; Derek Gregory, "Scripting Egypt: Orientalism and the Cultures
of Travel," in *Writes of Passage: Reading Travel Writing,* ed. James Duncan and
Derek Gregory (London: Routledge, 1999), 114–50.

16. Gregory, "Scripting Egypt," 115.

17. Ibid., 117.

18. Gregory, "Colonial Nostalgia," 115.

19. Susan S. Fainstein and Dennis R. Judd, "Global Forces, Local Strategies,
and Urban Tourism," in *The Tourist City,* ed. Dennis R. Judd and Susan S.
Fainstein (New Haven, Conn.: Yale University Press, 1999), 1.

20. Susan Buck-Morss, "Semiotic Boundaries and the Politics of Meaning:
Modernity on Tour—a Village in Transition," in *New Ways of Knowing: The Sci-
ences, Society, and Reconstructive Knowledge,* ed. Marcus G. Raskin and Herbert J.
Bernstein (Totowa, N.J.: Rowman & Littlefield, 1987), 200–236; Tim Mitchell,
"Worlds Apart: An Egyptian Village and the International Tourism Industry,"
Middle East Report no. 196 (September–October 1995): 8–11.

21. Derek Gregory makes a similar claim about visitors to the Luxor Hotel
and Casino in Las Vegas: Gregory, "Imaginative Geographies," 476.

22. Brian M. Fagan, *Rape of the Nile: Tomb Robbers, Tourists, and Archaeologists in
Egypt,* 2nd ed. (Wakefield, R.I.: Moyer Bell, 1992), 51.

23. Said, *Orientalism,* 84–85. Donald Malcolm Reid, *Whose Pharaohs? Archaeology, Museums, and Egyptian National Identity from Napoleon to World War I* (Berkeley:
University of California Press, 2002), 31–36.

24. Ali Behdad, *Belated Travelers: Orientalism in the Age of Colonial Dissolution*
(Durham, N.C.: Duke University Press, 1994), 34.

25. John Barrell, "Death on the Nile: Fantasy and the Literature of Tourism,"
Essays in Criticism 41 (April 1991): 97–127; Withey, *Grand Tours,* 230–32; Elaine
Altman Evans, *Scholars, Scoundrels, and the Sphinx* (Knoxville: Frank H. McClung
Museum, University of Tennessee, 2000), as well as the essays collected in Paul
Starkey and Janet Starkey, eds., *Travellers in Egypt* (London: I. B. Tauris, 1998).

26. Reid, *Whose Pharaohs,* 83; Withey, *Grand Tours,* 232.

27. Reid, *Whose Pharaohs,* 70–71; Withey, *Grand Tours,* 229.

28. By the 1870s, Baedeker published its first Egyptian guidebooks. At about
the same time, Cook wrote his own and later commissioned an Egyptologist
from the British Museum, A. Willis Budge, to write a new one to be published by
the firm. See Piers Brendon, *Thomas Cook: 150 Years of Popular Tourism* (London:

Secker & Warburg, 1991), 128; A. Wallis Budge, *Cook's Handbook for Egypt and the Sûdân,* 2nd ed. (London: Thomas Cook & Son, 1906); Reid, *Whose Pharaohs,* 72.

29. Behdad, *Belated Travelers,* 48.

30. See Jason Thompson, "Ossman Effendi: A Scottish Convert to Islam in Early Nineteenth-Century Egypt," in *Historians in Cairo,* ed. Jill Edwards (Cairo: American University of Cairo Press, 2002), 81–105.

31. Excerpt from *Macmillian's Magazine* published as "The Dragoman," *New York Times,* September 5, 1875, 4.

32. Budge, *Cook's Handbook for Egypt,* 27.

33. Withey, *Grand Tours,* 233.

34. As cited in Reid, *Whose Pharaohs,* 76.

35. Budge, *Cook's Handbook For Egypt,* 26–27.

36. Reid, *Whose Pharaohs,* 84, 90. See also Brendon, *Thomas Cook,* 85.

37. Withey, *Grand Tours,* 234.

38. Brendon, *Thomas Cook,* 5–8.

39. Ibid., 31–32.

40. Ibid., 16.

41. On the exhibition, see C. R. Fay, *Palace of Industry, 1851* (Cambridge: Cambridge University Press, 1951).

42. Brendon, *Thomas Cook,* 60.

43. Ibid., 15. Wolfgang Schivelbusch, *The Railway Journey: Trains and Travel in the Nineteenth Century* (New York: Urizen Books, 1979), 75.

44. Scott Lash and John Urry, *Economies of Signs and Space* (London: Sage, 1994), 262.

45. Cynthia H. Enloe, *Bananas, Beaches and Bases: Making Feminist Sense of International Politics* (London: Pandora, 1989), 28–29.

46. Brendon, *Thomas Cook,* 85.

47. Kennerly, "Far Away So Close."

48. David Weaver and Laura Lawton, *Tourism Management* (Milton, Australia: John Wiley & Sons, 2000), 66.

49. Ibid.

50. W. Fraser Rae, *The Business of Travel: A Fifty Years' Record of Progress* (London: Thomas Cook & Son, 1891), 102–3.

51. On the so-called "anti-tourists," see Brendon, *Thomas Cook,* 81–100; Buzard, *The Beaten Track;* Kennerly, "Far Away So Close"; Withey, *Grand Tours,* 162–66. For a more recent critique of Cookism, see Boorstin, *The Image.* For an anti-tourist novel about Egypt, see Pierre Loti, *Egypt (La Mort De Philae)* (London: T. Werner Laurie, 1909; reprint, ebooksLib.com).

52. For a succinct overview of actor-network theory, see Michel Callon, "Actor Network Theory," in *International Encyclopedia of the Social and Behavioral Sciences,* ed. Neil J. Smelser and Paul B. Baltes (Oxford: Elsevier Science, 2001), 62–66.

53. Gregory, "Colonial Nostalgia," 115–16.

54. Jonathan Murdoch, "The Spaces of Actor-Network Theory," *Geoforum* 29 (1998): 360.

55. John Law, "Notes on the Theory of the Actor-Network: Ordering, Strategy and Heterogeneity" (published by the Centre for Science Studies, Lancaster University, Lancaster); available from http://www.comp.lancs.ac.uk/sociology/papers/Law-Notes-on-ANT.pdf.

56. See Bruno Latour, "Technology Is Society Made Durable," in *A Sociology of Monsters: Essays on Power, Technology, and Domination,* ed. John Law (New York: Routledge, 1991), 103–31.

57. A few published studies have sought to explore tourism through actor-network theory; see V. R. van der Duim, "Tourismscapes: An Actor-Network Perspective on Sustainable Tourism Development," Ph.D. diss., Wageningen University, 2005, 91.

58. Cindy S. Aron, *Working at Play: A History of Vacations in the United States* (Oxford: Oxford University Press, 1999), 138.

59. Linda K. Richter, "The Political Dimensions of Tourism," in *Travel, Tourism, and Hospitality Research: A Handbook for Managers and Researchers,* ed. J. R. Brent Ritchie and Charles R. Goeldner (New York: John Wiley & Sons, 1987), 259.

60. Ibid.

61. Dean MacCannell likens Cook's package tours, in contrast to the travel services provided by American Express, to the building of "tourist factories, called 'resorts' and 'amusement parks,' through which people are run assembly-line fashion." See MacCannell, *The Tourist,* 163.

62. See Lash and Urry, *Economies of Signs and Space.*

63. Shelley Baranowski and Ellen Furlough, eds., *Being Elsewhere: Tourism, Consumer Culture, and Identity in Modern Europe and North America* (Ann Arbor: University of Michigan, 2001).

64. Schivelbusch, *The Railway Journey,* 41–50.

65. Richard S. Lambert, *The Fortunate Traveller: A Short History of Tourism and Travel for Pleasure* (London: Andrew Melrose, 1950), 140.

66. Brendon, *Thomas Cook,* 168–69.

67. Lambert, *The Fortunate Traveller,* 148.

68. Rae, *The Business of Travel,* 118.

69. Ibid.

70. Brendon, *Thomas Cook,* 114.

71. Withey, *Grand Tours,* 160.

72. Ibid., 149.

73. Behdad describes the transition from travelogue to guidebook in the mid-nineteenth century as one in which the discourse of tourism become marked by "the dispersion of a plurality of voices." Tourists, he notes, are encouraged "to check, to confirm or deny the validity of the information [the guidebook] provides." See Behdad, *Belated Traveler,* 41, 44.

74. Brendon, *Thomas Cook,* 163.

75. Alden Hatch, *American Express: A Century of Service* (Garden City, N.Y.: Doubleday, 1950); Ralph T. Reed, *American Express: Its Origins and Growth* (New York: Newcomen Society of North America, 1952), 18–20.

76. Laurent Tissot, "How Did the British Conquer Switzerland? Guidebooks, Railways, Travel Agencies, 1850–1914," *Journal of Transport History* 16 (March 1995), 37–38.

77. See Brendon, *Thomas Cook,* 110–14; Hugh De Santis, "The Democratization of Travel: The Travel Agent in American History," *Journal of American Culture* 1 (spring 1978): 14.

78. Tissot, "How Did the British Conquer Switzerland?" 43.

79. *Cook's Excursionist,* May 3, 1869, cited in Brendon, *Thomas Cook,* 120.

80. See Gregory, *Scripting Egypt,* 140.

81. The experience of Cook's first tour of Egypt is recorded by the unpublished diary of Miss Riggs. See Brendon, *Thomas Cook,* 122–29.

82. Florence Nightingale, *Letters from Egypt: A Journey on the Nile, 1849–50* (London: Barrie and Jenkins, 1987), 187, as cited in Withey, *Grand Tours,* 245.

83. Gregory, "Scripting Egypt," 140.

84. "The Nile," *New York Daily Times*, August 12, 1857, 2.

85. John Ward, *Pyramids and Progress* (London: Eyre and Spottiswoode, 1900), 173, as cited in Gregory, "Colonial Nostalgia," 137.

86. Michel Hani et al., letter to editor, *The Times* (London), June 9, 1874, 6.

87. Ibid.

88. Thomas Cook & Son, letter to editor, *The Times* (London), June 12, 1874, 4.

89. Ibid.

90. E. Butler, *From Sketch-Book and Diary* (London: Adam and Charles Black, 1905), 55, as cited in Gregory, "Scripting Egypt," 121.

91. Brendon, *Thomas Cook*, 120.

92. Reid, *Whose Pharaohs*, 85.

93. Dahabiyyah voyages typically sailed up the Nile as quickly as possible and only on the return voyage stopped along the way to allow visits to the ruins.

94. Reid, *Whose Pharaohs*, 84–85. Janne Ahtola, "The Lure of the Season: The Rise of Thomas Cook and Son in Egypt," *Journal of African Travel-writing* 5 (1998): 82.

95. Budge, *Cook's Handbook for Egypt*, 2.

96. Ahtola, "The Lure of the Season," 81. These so-called "popular tours" were, however, never within reach of working-class or lower middle-class travelers from Europe.

97. Budge, *Cook's Handbook for Egypt*, 29–30.

98. Brendon, *Thomas Cook*, 35.

99. F. M. Sandwith, *Egypt as a Winter Resort* (1889), 2, 107, cited in ibid., 231.

100. Ahtola, "The Lure of the Season," 80.

101. G. W. Steevens, *Egypt in 1898* (New York: Dodd, Mead, 1898), 70, 269.

102. W. Fraser Rae, *Egypt to-Day* (London: Richard Bentley and Son, 1892), 267.

103. Steevens, *Egypt in 1898*, 215.

104. Gregory, "Emperors of the Gaze," 211.

105. Budge, *Cook's Handbook for Egypt*, 30–31; Gregory, "Scripting Egypt," 121.

106. D. Sladen, *Oriental Cairo* (London: Hurst and Blackett, 1911), 332, as cited in Gregory, "Scripting Egypt," 134.

107. W. M. Thomson, *The Holy Land, Egypt, Etc. Forty-eight Photographs by Francis Bedford* (London: Day & Son and German Gallery, 1862), as cited in Deborah Bull and Donald Lorimer, *Up the Nile: A Photographic Excursion: Egypt, 1839–1898* (New York: Clarkson N. Potter, 1979), xx.

108. Bull and Lorimer, *Up the Nile*, xvi.

109. Ahtola, "The Lure of the Season," 80.

110. Cited in Withey, *Grand Tours*, 262.

111. Alain Rustenholz, "The Nearness of the East," in *Voyages Around the World*, ed. Marc Walter (New York: Friedman/Fairfax Publishing, 2001), 119.

112. *Cook's Excursionist*, May 4, 1872, as cited in Brendon, *Thomas Cook*, 129.

113. Lambert, *The Fortunate Traveller*, 148.

114. Brendon, *Thomas Cook*, 230.

115. Ruth Kark, "From Pilgrimage to Budding Tourism: The Role of Thomas Cook in the Rediscovery of the Holy Land in the Nineteenth Century," in *Travellers in the Levant: Voyagers and Visionaries*, ed. M. Wagstaff and S. Searight (London: ASTEN, 2001), 155–74.

116. Brendon, *Thomas Cook*, 3, 115.

117. See Withey, *Grand Tours*, 167–95.

118. F. Robert Hunter, "Tourism and Empire: The Thomas Cook & Son Enterprise on the Nile, 1868–1914," *Middle Eastern Studies* 40, 5 (September 2004): 32.

119. F. Robert Hunter, "Egypt Under the Successors of Muhammad 'Ali," in *The Cambridge History of Egypt: Volume 2, Modern Egypt, from 1517 to the End of the Twentieth Century*, ed. M. W. Daly (Cambridge: Cambridge University Press, 1998), 180–97.

120. Roger Owen, *The Middle East in the World Economy*, revised ed. (London: I. B. Tauris, 1993), 122–52.

121. Ahmad al-Hitta, "The Development of Transport, 1800–1870," in *The Economic History of the Middle East, 1800–1914*, ed. Charles Issawi (Chicago: University of Chicago Press, 1966), 410–14.

122. Hunter, "Tourism and Empire," 34.

123. Ibid., 35.

124. Saad, "Travel in the Good Old Days."

125. Brendon, *Thomas Cook*, 137.

126. Ibid.; Hunter, "Tourism and Empire," 38–39.

127. Brendon, *Thomas Cook*, 190–200. Hunter, "Tourism and Empire," 39–40.

128. Hunter, "Tourism and Empire," 39–41.

129. Arthur Falkner, as quoted in Brendon, *Thomas Cook*, 200.

130. Withey, *Grand Tours*, 260.

131. Rae, *The Business of Travel*, 275.

132. Edmund Swinglehurst, *Cook's Tours: The Story of Popular Tourism* (Poole: Blandford Press, 1982), 97–98.

133. "Nile Tourist Traffic May Start a Rate War," *New York Times*, August 16, 1906, 5.

134. Cook also built a hospital in Luxor.

135. Banquet transcript, 4–5, printed in Rae, *The Business of Travel* (transcript pages bound prior to volume's title page).

136. Budge, an Egyptologist and Cook's guidebook writer, notes that the Egyptians called J. M. Cook "King of Egypt." See also Brendon, *Thomas Cook*, 200, 32–33. Gregory, "Colonial Nostalgia," 128–29.

137. Swinglehurst, *Cook's Tours*, 105.

138. Brendon, *Thomas Cook*, 232.

139. Steevens, *Egypt in 1898*, 271–72.

140. Rae, *The Business of Travel*, 282.

141. Rae, *Egypt to-Day*, 266; Rae, *The Business of Travel*, 280–81.

142. Rae, *Egypt to-Day*, 266–67.

143. Fagan, *Rape of the Nile*.

144. "Relic-Hunting," *New York Times*, August 4, 1881, 4; Loti, *Egypt (La Mort De Philae)*.

145. William Charles Maughan, *The Alps of Arabia: Travels in Egypt, Sinai, Arabia and the Holy Land* (London: Henry King, 1875), 64, as cited in Gregory, "Colonial Nostalgia," 137.

146. Muhammad al-Muywaylihi, *A Period of Time* (Reading: Ithaca, 1992), 313–14, as cited in Reid, *Whose Pharaohs*, 64.

147. Donald Malcolm Reid, "Nationalizing the Pharaonic Past: Egypt 1922–1952," in *Rethinking Nationalism in the Arab Middle East*, ed. James Jankowski and Israel Gershoni (New York: Columbia University Press, 1997), 127–49.

148. Reid, *Whose Pharaohs*, 64–65. A hundred years later, even an American anthropological study of a village near a tourism site—Richard Critchfield's *Shahhat: An Egyptian* (Syracuse: Syracuse University Press, 1978)—would "ignore the village's dependence on archaeology and tourism," which "appear to be a significant source of income for the village and certainly an integral part of its life." See Mitchell, *Rule of Experts*, 143.

149. Budge, *Cook's Handbook for Egypt*, 31–32.

150. Dale F. Eickelman and James Piscatori, eds., *Muslim Travellers: Pilgrimage, Migration, and the Religious Imagination* (London: Routledge, 1990); Chris Taylor, *In the Vicinity of the Righteous: Ziyara and the Veneration of Muslim Saints in Late Medieval Egypt* (Leiden: Brill, 1999); Nile Green, "Migrant Sufis and Sacred Space in South Asian Islam," *Contemporary South Asia* 12 (December 2003): 493–509.

151. Rae, *Egypt to-Day*, 209–15.

152. Said, *Orientalism*, 84–92.

153. Reid explains that J. M. Cook organized the trip led by his best dragoman "free of charge" because he was "hopeful that [the new Khedive] Abbas II would continue to favor his company." Reid, *Whose Pharaohs*, 206.

154. As quoted in Rae, *Egypt to-Day*, 269.

155. Reid, *Whose Pharaohs*, 237, 287.

156. Loti, *Egypt*, 214.

157. Reid, *Whose Pharaohs*, 288.

158. Reid, "Nationalizing the Pharaonic Past," and Fayza Hikal, "Egypt's Past Regenerated by Its Own People," in *Consuming Ancient Egypt*, ed. Sally MacDonald and Michael Rice (London: UCL Press, 2003), 123–38.

159. Rae, *Egypt to-Day*, 268.

160. Gregory, "Colonial Nostalgia," 135. David E. Nye, *American Technological Sublime* (Cambridge, Mass.: MIT Press, 1994).

161. Michael J. Reimer, "Views of Al-Azhar in the Nineteenth Century: Gabriel Charmes and 'Ali Pasha Mubarak," in *Travellers in Egypt*, ed. Paul Starkey and Janet Starkey (London: I. B. Tauris, 1998), 276.

162. Ibid.

163. Ibid., 277.

164. Michelle L. Woodward, "Between Orientalist Clichés and Images of Modernization: Photographic Practice in the Late Ottoman Era," *History of Photography* 27 (winter 2003), 363–64.

165. "The Season in Egypt: Tourists Replaced by Soldiers," *The Times*, February 4, 1915, 11.

166. Brendon, *Thomas Cook*, 256.

167. Ibid.

168. Matthew Gray, "Economic Reform, Privatization and Tourism in Egypt," *Middle Eastern Studies* 34 (April 1998): 57–73.

169. Brendon, *Thomas Cook*, 310–11; Gregory, "Colonial Nostalgia," 113–14.

170. Mitchell, "Worlds Apart," 9.

171. Ibid.

172. Susan Slyomovics, "Cross-Cultural Dress and Tourist Performance in Egypt," *Performing Arts Journal* 33–34 (1989): 139–48.

173. Ala al-Hamarneh and Christian Steiner, "Islamic Tourism: Rethinking the Strategies of Tourism Development in the Arab World After September 11, 2001," *Comparative Studies of South Asia, Africa and the Middle East* 24 (Spring 2004): 18–26.

174. Ibid., 25.

Chapter 2. The Compagnie Générale Transatlantique and the Development of Saharan Tourism in North Africa

1. Marc Baroli, *La Vie quotidienne des français en Algérie, 1830–1914* (Paris: Hachette, 1967), 208.

2. John Pemble, *The Mediterranean Passion: Victorians and Edwardians in the South* (Oxford: Clarendon Press, 1987), 84–99; R. E. Scoresby-Jackson, *Medical Climatology or a Topographical and Meteorological Description of the Localities Resorted to in Winter and Summer by Invalids of Various Classes, Both at Home and Abroad* (London: John Churchill, 1862), was typical of the many nineteenth-century works extolling mild climates.

3. Pemble, *Mediterranean Passion*, 49; Henri Klein, *Feuillets d'El-Djezair* (Algiers: L. Chaix, 1937), 171.

4. *Cook's Excursionist and Tourist Advertiser*, February 15, 1875, 7. The estimate of wages appears in H. Phelps Brown and Sheila V. Hopkins, *A Perspective of Wages and Prices* (London: Methuen, 1981), 11. At the 1875 exchange rate, the trip cost approximately U.S. $430 (first class) or $375 (second class). In terms of comparative purchasing power, these amounts are the rough equivalent of $7,150 and $6,230 in early twenty-first-century U.S. dollars. The conversion from sterling to dollars is based on Lawrence H. Officer, "Exchange Rate Between the United States Dollar and Forty Other Countries, 1913–1999," Economic History Services, EH.Net, 2002, http://www.eh.net/hmit/exchangerates/; the adjusted dollar value is derived from John J. McCusker, "Comparing the Purchasing Power of Money in the United States (or Colonies) from 1665 to Any Other Year Including the Present," Economic History Services, EH.Net, 2004, http://www.eh.net/hmit/ppowerusd/.

5. Daniel Nordman, "Les Guides-Joanne. Ancêtres des Guides Bleus," in Pierre Nora, ed., *Les Lieux de mémoire*, Vol. II (*La Nation*), Part 1 (*Paysages*) (Paris: Gallimard, 1984), 529–67.

6. Baroli, *La Vie quotidienne*, 209.

7. Joseph Hyam, *The Illustrated Guide to Algiers: A "Practical" Handbook for Travellers* (Algiers: Anglo-French Press Association, 1899), viii.

8. Ibid., 97.

9. *L'Excursioniste*, January 1900, 7, and February 1902, 9.

10. Thomas Cook and Son, "Programme of Cook's Select Personally Conducted Tours to Algeria and Spain," Autumn 1891, 10–12.

11. *Cook's Excursionist and Tourist Advertiser*, February 1, 1886, 4; November 12, 1888, 4; and February 1, 1889, 8.

12. Arthur Griffiths, "An Algerian Winter-Resort," *Fortnightly Review*, 57 n.s. (January–June 1895): 462.

13. Alfred E. Pease, *Biskra and the Oases and Desert of the Zibans* (London: Edward Stanford, 1893), 43.

14. Malek Alloula, *Le harem colonial. Images d'un sous-érotisme* (Paris: Garance-Slatkine, 1981); Gilles Boëtsch, "La Mauresque aux seins nus: l'imaginaire érotique colonial dans la carte postale," in *Images et colonies: Nature, discours et influence de l'iconographie coloniale liée à la propagande coloniale et à la représentation des Africains et de l'Afrique en France, de 1920 aux indépendances*, ed. Nicolas Bancel, Pascal Blanchard, and Laurent Gervereau (Paris: Association Connaissance de l'Histoire de l'Afrique Contemporaine, 1993), 93–96; and Malek Chebel, "L'‘Arabe' dans l'imaginaire occidental," in *L'Autre et nous: Scènes et types*, ed. Pascal Blanchard (Paris: Association Connaissance de l'Histoire de l'Afrique

Contemporaine, 1995), 39–45. Zeynep Çelik and Leila Kinney, "Ethnography and Exhibitionism at the Expositions Universelles," *Assemblage*, no. 13 (December 1990): 34–59.

15. Allan Christelow, "Algerian Dimensions of France's Middle East Policy, 1916," in *Franco-Arab Encounters: Studies in Memory of David C. Gordon*, ed. L. Carl Brown and Matthew S. Gordon (Beirut: American University of Beirut Press, 1996), 275–76, *viz.* n14.

16. Marthe Brabance, *Histoire de la Compagnie Générale Transatlantique: Un Siècle d'Exploitation Maritime* (Paris: Arts et Métiers Graphiques, 1955), 101–14.

17. Ibid., 108. Based on figures cited by Michèle Salinas, *Voyages et voyageurs en Algérie, 1830–1930* (Toulouse: Editions Privat, 1989), 29, and on tables in Jean L'homme, "Le pouvoir d'achat de l'ouvrier français au cours d'un siècle: 1840–1940," *Mouvement Sociale*, no. 63 (April–June 1968): 46; French workers' daily wages in the early 1880s hovered around four francs a day.

18. Ellen Furlough, "*Une Leçon des choses:* Tourism, Empire, and the Nation in Interwar France," *French Historical Studies* 25 (summer 2002): 441–73.

19. Mohamed Bergaoui, *Tourisme et voyages en Tunisie: Les années régence* (Tunis: n.p., 1996), 140.

20. Arthur Clark, "Hotels with a History," *ARAMCO World Magazine* (July–August 1997): 25–26; Serge Santelli, "Les Hôtels de la Transatlantique," *Monuments historiques*, no. 130 (1984): 67–70.

21. Brabance, *Histoire de la Compagnie Générale Transatlantique*, 243. The amount is equivalent to almost $150 million in early twenty-first-century U.S. dollars.

22. A list of hotels appeared in *La Revue des Voyages* (the French language informational publication of Cook's), January 1930, 30–31; Brabance, *Histoire de la Compagnie Générale Transatlantique*, 242 (map).

23. *Traveller's Gazette*, February 1923, 8.

24. Michèle Salinas, *Voyages et voyageurs en Algérie, 1830–1930* (Toulouse: Editions Privat, 1989), 25–27. The figure for total 1927 disembarkations at all Algerian ports appears in *Les Cahiers du centenaire de l'Algérie* (Paris: Comité National Métropolitain du Centenaire de l'Algérie, 1930), Livre 8: Colonel Dhé and Jean Denizet, *Les Liaisons maritimes, aériennes et terrestres de l'Algérie*, 15.

25. Brabance, *Histoire de la Compagnie Générale Transatlantique*, 243.

26. *Traveller's Gazette*, February 1921, 11.

27. *La Revue des Voyages*, February 1926, 67.

28. Alison Murray, "Le Tourisme Citroën au Sahara (1924–1925)," *Vingtième siècle*, no. 68 (October–December 2000): 95–107.

29. At the 1925 exchange rate, these three figures equated to approximately $1,900, $240, and $715. They are the rough equivalents of $20,000, $2,500, and $7,500 in early twenty-first-century U.S. dollars. The franc to dollar conversion is based on Lawrence H. Officer, "Exchange Rate Between the United States Dollar and Forty Other Countries, 1913–1999." Economic History Services, EH.Net, 2002, http://www.eh.net/hmit/exchangerates/; the adjusted dollar value is derived from John J. McCusker, "Comparing the Purchasing Power of Money in the United States." Based on figures in L'homme, "Le pouvoir d'achat," 52, and in Institut Scientifique de Recherches Economiques et Sociales, *Tableaux de l'économie française, 1910–1934* (Paris: Librairie du Recueil Sirey, 1935), plate 34; daily wages for most French workers in 1925 ranged between 20 and 30 francs.

30. *La Revue des Voyages*, January 1925, 25.

31. Murray, "Le Tourisme Citroën," 95.

32. *Bulletin du Comite de l'Afrique Française*, 1925, 45.

33. Translations of portions of the Annual Political Report of the Lieutenant Governor of French Sudan for 1927 appear as course materials at http://courses.wcupa.edu/jones/his311/archives/anf/ap160e.htm. The original document is in the Archives Nationales de France, Section d'Outre-Mer, Affaires Politiques, Carton 160.

34. Mention of this reclassification appears in http://courses.wcupa.edu/jones/his311/archives/anf/ap150.htm. The original document is in the Archives Nationales de France, Section d'Outre-Mer. Gouverneur Générale de l'Afrique Occidentale Français, Affaires Politiques, Carton 150, Cabinet: Affaires présentées en Commission Permanente du Conseil du Gouvernement, 1931.

35. Octave Meynier and A. F. Nabal, *Guide Pratique du Tourisme au Sahara* (Paris: Société d'Editions Géographiques, Maritimes et Coloniales, 1931).

36. *La Revue des Voyages*, February 1929, 9.

37. Ibid., January 1929, 24.

38. Ibid.

39. Ibid., February 1931, 11.

40. Quoted in Furlough, "*Une Leçon des Choses*," 458.

41. Ibid., 445, quoting from the official report of the exposition. Literature on the exposition itself is voluminous; for a range, see Catherine Hodeir and Michel Pierre, *L'Exposition coloniale* (Brussels: Editions Complexe, 1991); Patricia A. Morton, *Hybrid Modernities: Architecture and Representation at the 1931 Colonial Exposition, Paris* (Cambridge, Mass.: MIT Press, 2000); Sylviane Leprun, *Le théâtre des colonies: Scénographie, acteurs et discours de l'imaginaire dans les expositions, 1855–1937* (Paris: L'Harmattan, 1986); Charles-Robert Ageron, "L'Exposition coloniale de 1931: Mythe républicain ou mythe impériale?" in *Les Lieux de mémoire*, vol. I (*La République*), ed. Pierre Nora (Paris: Gallimard, 1984), 561–91.

42. Furlough, "*Une Leçon des Choses*," 459. The goals of attracting visitors to the exhibit and inducing them to travel to the colonies occasionally collided, as in an exposition poster with the message, "Why go to Tunisia when you can visit it in Paris?" (447).

43. *La Revue des Voyages*, August–September 1937, 31; August 1938, 33. In 1933, a new edition of *Cook's North Africa (Morocco, Algeria, Tunisia and Libya)* devoted 90 pages to Morocco, more than 100 to Algeria, 60 to Tunisia, and 30 to Libya, and included, in addition to a map of the entire region, maps of Libya, the region between Tangier and Casablanca, the Aurès Mountains, and the cities of Tangier, Casablanca, Algiers, Tunis, and Tripoli.

44. *La Revue des Voyages*, Ibid., August–September 1937, 31.

45. Ibid., January 1937, no pagination.

46. Ibid., February 1937, 14. The most detailed description of festival events is in ibid., April 1938, 35.

47. Ibid., April 1936, 15–16.

48. According to statistics compiled by the local syndicat d'initiative, 600 tourists visited Bou Saada in 1938, the peak year of the prewar decade. When some tourist activity resumed in 1947, the agency put the figure at 316. Between 1948 and 1950, the annual number rose from 980 to 1308, but thereafter it declined, falling to only 90 in 1952 as political instability spread throughout the Maghrib. In that nothing distinguished Bou Saada from other centers of desert tourism at the time, a similar pattern may be assumed to have prevailed elsewhere in the Sahara. Youssef Nacib, *Cultures oasiennes: Essai d'histoire sociale de l'oasis de Bou-Saâda* (Paris: Publisud, 1986), 382.

Chapter 3. "Food Palaces Built of Sausages [and] Great Ships of Lamb Chops"

1. M. F. K. Fisher, *The Gastronomical Me* (New York: North Point Press, 1954 [1943]), 87. Also see the memoirs of her housemate, neither of which mentions the existence of the other: Gertrude Clark Powell, "Housekeeping in the Provinces" and "Summertime in Burgundy," in *The Quiet Side of Europe* (Los Angeles: GCP, 1959), 10–41 and 76–107.

2. Fisher, *The Gastronomical Me*, 52.

3. Rebecca Sprang, *The Invention of the Restaurant: Paris and Modern Gastronomic Culture* (Cambridge, Mass.: Harvard University Press, 2000).

4. Kolleen Guy, "Rituals of Pleasure in the Land of Treasures: Wine Consumption and the Making of French Identity in the Late Nineteenth Century," in *Food Nations: Selling Taste in Consumer Societies,* ed. Warren Belasco and Philip Scranton (New York: Routledge, 2002), 39.

5. Guy Debord, *The Society of the Spectacle* (New York: Zone Books, 1995 [1967]), 151.

6. T. J. Clark, *The Painting of Modern Life* (Princeton, N.J.: Princeton University Press, 1984), 11.

7. Gaston Derys, *Dictionnaire de Gastronomie Joviale* (Paris: Editions des Portiques, 1930), 34.

8. Raymond Badouin, *Revue du vin de France* 5 (March 1931): 1.

9. Press release dated October 1, 1926, in Archives Municipales de Dijon, series 2F, "Foire 1926."

10. "L'ambassadeur de la Propagande française et du vin français," in "Discours de M. Gaston Gérard" [on the occasion of the 1927 Foire Gastronomique de Dijon], *Bien Public*, November 11, 1927, 1. The sobriquet comes from J.-F. Louis Merlet, "A la Louange des Gastronomes," *Presse*, November 23, 1928.

11. Gaston Gérard, *Le Miroir du Coin et du Temps* (Dijon: Editions des Etats Généraux de la Gastronomie française, 1959), 164–65.

12. Xavier Aubert, letter from the Comité de la Foire Gastronomique dated November 4, 1926, in Archives Municipales de Dijon, series 2F, "Foire 1926."

13. Claude Chatelus, "Après les Vendanges," *La Terre de Bourgogne* 23 (1934), 372.

14. Albert David, "Dijon, Après la 5ieme Foire Gastronomique," *Progrès de la Côte-d'Or*, November 23, 1925, 2.

15. Quoted in "La Foire Gastronomique," *Bien Public*, November 11, 1927, 1.

16. A typical Gérard speech is provided in "Chronique de la Foire: Le Discours de Gaston Gérard," *Progrès de la Côte-d'Or*, November 11, 1931, 2.

17. Marion Carcano argues that the concept of "the region" was recognized as the sole guarantor of social cohesion and national unity in "Mémoire et Ethnographie Folkloriste en Bourgogne" (Mémoire de Maitrise en Histoire Contemporaine: Université de Bourgogne, 1997), 74.

18. Philippe Poirrier, "Municipalité et Culture au XXe siècle: Des Beaux-Arts à la Politique Culturelle," (thesis, Université de Bourgogne, 1995, 177–210. Also see Marion Carcano, "Regionalisme et Ethnographie Folkloriste en Bourgogne," 5–31, for an analysis and overview of the community's "réseau académique."

19. Gaston Gérard, "Les fastes et liesses de Dijon," *Bien Public*, October 31, 1935, 3.

20. Benedict Anderson, *Imagined Communities: Reflections on the Origin and Spread of Nationalism* (New York: Verso, 1991); Susan Buck-Morss, *The Dialectics of*

Seeing: Walter Benjamin and the Arcades Project (Cambridge, Mass.: MIT Press, 1989), 71.

21. Roger Thiblot, "Les Foires," *Bien Public,* November 8, 1929, 5.

22. Jean-François Bazin, *La Bourgogne* (Rennes: Editions Ouest-France, 1997), 76.

23. Quoted in ibid., 77.

24. See Henri Béraud, "Lyon, Capital du Bien Manger," in *Anthologie de la Gastronomie Française,* eds. Curnonsky and Gaston Derys (Paris: Delagrave, 1936), 340; Marcel Grancher, "Les Fêtes Gastronomiques de la France"; Raymond Baudouin, "Lyon, Capital Gastronomique de la France;" and "Les Menus de la Semaine Gastronomique Lyonnaise," *Revue du Vin de France* 76 (1933): 7–12.

25. One critic remarked that Gérard "had turned himself into the apostle of the restoration of French cuisine." J.-F.-Louis Merlet, "A la louange des Gastronomes," *Presse,* November 23, 1928, 1–2.

26. Gérard, *Le Miroir du Coin et du Temps,* 165.

27. Gérard, *Le Miroir du Coin,* 159.

28. Paul Léon, "Préface," in *Urbanisme et Tourisme,* eds. Léon Auscher and Georges Rozet (Paris: Editions Leroux, 1920), 4.

29. "La Foire Gastronomique," *Progrès de la Côte-d'Or,* November 7, 1922, 1, and "Chronique de la Foire: L'Ouverture Officielle," *Progrès de la Côte-d'Or,* November 8, 1925, 1. A 31-page section on "The Products of Burgundy" in the official guide to the sixth gastronomical fair in 1926 describes these products in terms of their significance to Burgundian culture and history.

30. "La Foire: L'animation en ville," *Progrès de la Côte-d'Or,* November 6, 1921, 2.

31. Gaston Gérard, *Dijon, Ma Bonne Ville . . . Souvenirs et Confidences* (Dijon: Etats Géréraux de la Gastronomie Française, 1928), 247.

32. Arthur Chandler, "Fanfare for the New Empire," *World's Fairs* 7.2 (1986): 11–16; "Empire of Autumn," *World's Fairs* 6.3 (1986): 2–8; "Heroism in Defeat," *World's Fairs* 6.4 (1986): 9–16; "Revolution: The Paris Exposition Universelle of 1889," *World's Fairs* 7.1 (1987): 1–9; "Culmination: The Paris Exposition Universelle of 1889," *World's Fairs* 7.3 (1987): 8–14; and "Where Art Deco was Born," *World's Fairs* 9.1 (1989): 1–7.

33. Merchants who participated in the gastronomical fair benefited from a 50-percent tariff reduction on wares shipped on the P. L. M. railroad. *Bien Public,* August 3, 1926, 3.

34. "L'Alliance des Foires," *Progrès de la Côte-d'Or,* November 14, 1925, 2.

35. "Le poste radiotéléphonique," *Progrès de la Côte-d'Or,* November 13, 1925, 2.

36. *La Terre de Bourgogne,* November 13, 1926, 762.

37. *La Terre de Bourgogne,* November 20, 1926, 781–82; and November 27, 1926, 795–96.

38. Clark Powell, *The Quiet Side of Europe,* 11.

39. Gaston Gérard, "Dijon et sa Foire Gastronomique," *L'Alsace Française,* November 7, 1925, 409.

40. J.-F.-Louis Merlet, "A la louange des Gastronomes," *Presse,* November 23, 1928, 1–2.

41. "La Foire," *Progrès de la Côte-d'Or,* November 12, 1922, 2.

42. The net gain decreased as the fair grew in size. The fair committee incurred additional expenses such as security and the rental of additional fairgrounds related to the scale of the event.

43. Gérard, *Dijon, ma Bonne Ville*, 249.

44. Christelle Guilard, "La Foire Gastronomique de Dijon" (Université de Bourgogne: Diplôme D'études Approfondies, 1999), 51.

45. Archives Municipales de Dijon, series 2F, "Foire 1926."

46. The annual records held in Dijon's Municipal Archives are incomplete and provide no statistics for numerous years.

47. Fully twenty percent of 900 merchants' stalls represented Parisian interests by 1925. See "La Foire Gastronomique," *Progrès de la Côte-d'Or*, November 9, 1926, 3.

48. Dijonnais merchantile interests alone represented 26 of 668 in 1926, 104 of 514 in 1932, 140 of 498 in 1935, and 122 of 489 in 1937. Guilard, "La Foire Gastronomique de Dijon," 51–42.

49. Gaston Gérard, "La Côte-d'Or, berceau et paradis de la Gastronomie," in *La Côte-d'Or . . .* (Paris: Alépée, 1954), 171, and "Le Discours du Maire de Beaune," *Bien Public*, November 10, 1929, 4.

50. Albert David, "Dijon, Après la 5ieme Foire Gastronomique," *Progrès de la Côte-d'Or*, November 23, 1925, 2.

51. "Communiqué de l'Hotel de Ville," July 7, 1921, Archives Municipales de Dijon, Series 2F.

52. "Le discours du Maire de Beaune," *Bien Public*, November 10, 1929, 4.

53. Gaston Gérard, "La Côte-d'Or, berceau et paradis de la Gastronomie," in *La Côte-d'Or . . .* (Paris: Alépée, 1954), 171.

54. "Chronique de la Foire: Le Discours de M. Gaston Gérard," *Progrès de la Côte-d'Or* 9, November 10, 1931, 2.

55. Stefan Zweig, *Voyages* (Paris: Belfond, 2000), 33. Henry Miller promoted Dijon's sleepy reputation in *Tropic of Cancer* (Paris: Obelisq Press, 1934). On this point, see Jean-Francois Bazin, *Le Tout Dijon* (Dijon: Editions Clea, 2003), 155.

56. A. Carreau, "5ième Foire Gastronomique," *La Terre de Bourgogne*, November 14, 1925, 729.

57. Fisher, *The Gastronomical Me*, 52, and M. F. K. Fisher, *The Art of Eating* (New York: Vintage Books, 1976), 395.

58. "Chronique de la Foire: La Décoration des Rues," *Progrès de la Côte-d'Or*, November 8, 1925, 1.

59. Henri Charrier, "Le Tourism," in *La Côte-d'Or . . .* (Paris: Alépée, 1954), 135.

60. *Art bourguignon et Bourgogne* [catalogue d'exposition] (Paris: Galerie Jean-Charpentier, 1936).

61. "La Gloire bourguignonne," *La Bourgogne d'Or* 102 (March–April 1936): 137.

62. Roupnel, "La Somptuosité de la Bourgogne," *L'Alsace Française*, November 7, 1925; "Eloge de la cuisine familiale," *Le Bien Public*, November 20, 1929; Gaston Roupnel, *La Bourgogne, types et coutumes* (Paris: Horizons de France, 1936), 128–133; Max Cappe, *Les Chants du Terroir, Poèmes Bourguignons* (Dijon: Imprimerie Lèpagnez, 1932 [dated by family members]). "L'Affair Jérémie," *XIIe Foire Gastronomique de Dijon* (Dijon: Imprimerie Lepagnez, 1932); "Bourgogne & Gastronomie," *Progrès de la Côte-d'Or*, November 9, 1925, and 'La Trêve du Cuisinier," *Dépêche de Toulouse*, December 29, 1921, 1.

63. Roupnel, "Préface," Max Cappe, *Les Chants du Terroir*, Poèmes Bourguignons, 4–5.

64. Roupnel, "La Somptuosité de la Bourgogne," *L'Alsace Française*, November 7, 1925, 415. Roupnel's article was accompanied by Henri Druout's "Le vrai

visage de la Bourgogne," Albert Thibaudet's "Le génie des écrivains bourguignons," A. Kleinclausz' "Dijon, ville d'art," and Gaston Gérard's "Dijon et sa foire gastronomique."

65. Roupnel, "La Somptuosité de la Bourgogne," *L'Alsace Française*, November 7, 1925, 415.

66. Ibid., 414.

67. Zweig, *Voyages*, 34.

68. Pierre Léon-Gauthier, *Les Clos de Bourgogne* (Beaune: Darantière, n.d.), 12.

69. One of the fathers of French gastronomy, Alexandre Grimod de la Reynière, kept the memory of the Saint Martin Fair alive in his early nineteenth-century manuals such as the *Ecrits gastronomiques* (Paris: Bibliothèque 10/18, 1997 [n.d.]).

70. "La Foire de Saint Martin," *Progrès de la Côte-d'Or*, November 11, 1925, 2.

71. Powell, *The Quiet Side of Europe*, 12.

72. "La Foire: L'animation en ville," *Progrès de la Côte-d'Or*, November 4, 1921, 1.

73. "L'Inauguration de la XIe Foire Gastronomique," *Progrès de la Côte-d'Or*, November 1, 1931, 2.

74. "Chronique de la Foire: Les enfants visitent la Foire," *Progrès de la Côte-d'Or*, November 17, 1925, 2.

75. Powell, *The Quiet Side of Europe*, 12.

76. "Chronique de la Foire: La Fête Foraine," *Progrès de la Côte-d'Or*, November 12, 1925, 2.

77. "Autour de la Foire: Illuminations et Fête Foraine," *Progrès de la Côte-d'Or*, November 12, 1931, 2.

78. "Chronique de la Foire: L'Alimentation," *Progrès de la Côte-d'Or*, November 10, 1925, 1.

79. "Chronique de la Foire: A Travers les Halls," *Progrès de la Côte-d'Or*, November 10, 1925, 1.

80. "Chronique de la Foire: Le Salon d'Honneur," *Progrès de la Côte-d'Or*, November 10, 1925, 1.

81. Marcel-E. Grancher, *Denise mène les boeufs* (Paris: Editions Rabelais, 1953), 239.

82. Gaston Roupnel, "Eloge de la cuisine familial," *Bien Public*, November 20, 1929, 5.

83. Ibid., 5.

84. Powell, *The Quiet Side of Europe*, 93.

85. "Chronique de la Foire: L'Alimentation," *Progrès de la Côte-d'Or*, November 10, 1925, 1.

86. Grancher, *Denise mène les boeufs*, 239.

87. "La Foire Gastronomique: Les Vins et Spiriteux," *Progrès de la Côte-d'Or*, November 8, 1922, 1.

88. See, for example, "Le coin du Gourmet," *L'Automobile Club de Bourgogne* (December 1937): 12.

89. Alfred Contour, *Le Cuisinier Bourguignon: Nouveau livre de cuisine pratique* (Beaune: Librairie Vinceneux-Loireau, 1921 [1891]).

90. Maurice-Edmond Saillard (Curnonsky), *Cuisine et vins de France* (Paris: Larousse, 1953), 3–4.

91. Prosper Montagné and Philéas Gilbert, "A Travers la Bourgogne Gourmande," *La Revue de Bourgogne* 12 (1922): 610–15.

92. Gaston Roupnel, "La Trêve du Cuisinier," *Dépêche de Toulouse*, December 29, 1921, 1.

93. Gaston Roupnel, "Eloge de la cuisine familial," *Bien Public*, November 20, 1929, 5.

94. Roupnel, *Bourgogne, types et coutumes*, 127–38.

95. Clément-Janin, "Toute la Bourgogne à la Foire," *La Bourgogne d'Or* 14 (1927): 33–34. Also see Jean Dagey, "Brillat-Savarin," *Progrès de la Côte-d'Or*, November 13, 1925, 1.

96. Roupnel, "Eloge de la cuisine familial," 5.

97. A reviewer provided this synopsis of Roupnel's lecture of Brillat-Savarin as godfather of popular Burgundian gastronomy: "IX Foire gastronomique de Dijon; conférence de M. Roupnel," *Le Bien Public*, November 13, 1929. On Piron's folklorizations, see "Le Patois bourguignon au XVIIe siècle," *Le Bien Public*, February 28, 1933, 3; Piron, "Aimé Piron apothicaire," *Pays de Bourgogne* 159 (1993): 21–27; and Lucien Chiselle, "Le Plaisant Piron," *La Bourgogne d'Or* 108 (1937): 121–29.

98. Patrice Higonnet, *Paris, Capital of the World* (Cambridge, Mass.: Belknap Press, 2002), 300.

99. Philippe Poirrier, "From the Fine Arts to a Cultural Policy in Dijon from 1919 to 1995," *Cultural Policy* 2 (1996): 343.

100. "Piron ou le sel bourguignon," *Progrès de la Côte-d'Or*, November 9, 1937, 6.

101. Fisher, *The Gastronomical Me*, 98–99.

102. Curnonsky, "Eloge de Brillat-Savarin," in *Anthologie de la Gastronomie française* eds. Curnonsky and Gaston Derys (Paris: Delagrave, 1936), 210.

103. Georges Rozet, *La Bourgogne tastevin en main* (Paris: Horizons de France, 1949), 148.

104. Waverly Root, *The Food of France* (New York: Vintage Books, 1992), 13. For example, see Mélanie, "Le Pot-au-feu," *Progrès de la Côte-d'Or*, November 8, 1935, 5.

105. Powell, *The Quiet Side of Europe*, 90.

106. Ibid., 84.

107. Root, *The Food of France*, 186.

108. Colette Willy, *Paysages et portraits* (Paris: Flammarion, 1958), 167–68 and 171. Also see Colette Willy, "Récriminations," *La France à Table: Bourgogne* (December 1954), 47.

109. Jean Claude Ribaut, "Le pot-au-feu de Dodin-Bouffant," *Le Monde*, June 10, 2005, 24. Also see "La Bourgogne: Les recettes de notre pays," *Cuisine de Terroir* 15 (1997): 45–62.

110. Gaston Gérard, "La Foire Gastronomique," *Progrès de la Côte-d'Or*, November 6, 1922, 2.

111. "Chronique de la Foire: Les conferences de l'Académie," *Progrès de la Côte-d'Or*, November 10, 1925, 1.

112. Gérard, *Le Miroir du Coin*, 160.

113. Ibid., 162–63.

114. Gaston Gérard, quoted in *Bien Public*, November 19, 1927, 1. Gérard's economic policies during the Great Depression, for example, are outlined in "Le discours de M. Gaston-Gérard au Congrès du Parti Radical Indépendant," *Progrès de la Côte-d'Or*, November 7, 1938, 1 and 5.

115. *Dictionnaire des Ministres de 1789 à 1989*, vol. 5 (Paris: Perrin, 1990), 1819.

116. Higonnet, *Paris,* 313.

117. See Gregory Alexis, *L'Age d'or du Voyage, 1880–1939* (Paris: Chêne, 1990); Marc Boyer, *L'invention du Tourisme* (Paris: Gallimard, 1996); Gareth Shaw, *Critical Issues in Tourism* (Cambridge, Mass.: Blackwell, 1994); and Xavier Martel, *L'iconographie Touristique Comme Propagande Géopolitique en Temps de Paix,* 2 vols. (Paris: X. Martel, 1998).

118. Patrick Young, "La Vielle France as Object of Bourgeois Desire: The Touring Club de France and the French Regions, 1890–1918," in *Histories of Leisure,* ed. Rudy Koshar (New York: Berg, 2002), 171–72.

119. Mark McGovern defines tourism as "the consumption of place and the consumption of goods and services in that place," in " 'The Cracked Pint Glass of the Servant': The Irish Pub, Irish Identity and the Tourist Eye," in *Irish Tourism,* ed. M. Cronin and B. O'Connor (New York: Channel View Books, 2003), 84.

120. Raymond Badouin, "Agriculture et Tourisme," *La Revue du Vin de France* 98 (1935): 10–11.

121. M. F. Carton quoted in "Tourisme et Gastronomie," *Touring Club de France* 421 (1929): 258.

122. Letter from The Automobile Club Féminin, dated October 5, 1931, to the Mayor of Dijon in Archives Municipales de Dijon, 1I1/ 160, "Fêtes 1931."

123. Root, *The Food of France,* 186.

124. Letter from Henri Bussiere, dated July 18, 1935, to the Mayor of Dijon in Archives Municipales de Dijon, 1I1/ 164, "Fêtes 1935."

125. L[ucien] Bonnard, *Le Touring Club de France et Son Oeuvre* (Paris: TCF, 1927), 13.

126. "Tourisme et Gastronomie," *Touring Club de France* 421 (1929): 258; "Le Mâconnais: Pays de Lamartine," *Touring Club de France* 466 (September 1933): 303–5; "Eglises du Mâconnais et fermes Bressanes," *Touring Club de France* 516 (November 1937): 327–35; and "De Montbard à Dijon à travers la Bourgogne inconnue et pittoresque," *Touring Club de France* 505 (December 1936): 389–97.

127. Français Woltner, "Les Vins de France," *Bulletin Province de L'Automobile Club de Bourgogne* (November 1929): 209–13; Georges Leconte, "Voyage à Travers les Provinces Françaises," *L'Automobile Club de Bourgogne* (October 1937): 7–8; "Tourisme et Gastronomie," *L'Automobile Club de Bourgogne* (March 1934); Gaston Gérard, "Demeure Historique de Bourgogne," *L'Automobile Club de Bourgogne* (September 1934): 2–3; and "Journée Dijon-Macon," *L'Automobile Club de Bourgogne* (June 1934): 5.

128. "Le Rail et la Route: La Foire Gastronomique," *L'Automobile Club de Bourgogne* (November 1932): 5–6, 17; and Robert Blanc, "Rallye Gastronomique de Dijon," *L'Automobile Club de Bourgogne* (December 1934): 2–9.

129. "Excursion dans le Dijonnais," *L'Automobile Club de Bourgogne* (April 1937), 9–13.

130. Robert Desnos, "Voyage en Bourgogne (1930–1931)," in *Desnos: Oeuvres* (Paris: Quarto, 1999), 632 and 615.

131. Georges Rozet, *J'ai Découvert a Dijon* (Macon: Protat Frères, n.d.), 13 and 14.

132. "Au pays bourguignon," *Touring Club de France* 373 (December 1925): 508–12.

133. Gaston Derys, "Petite Géographie Gastronomique de la France," in *Anthologie de la Gastronomie Française,* eds. Curnonsky and Gaston Derys (Paris: Delagrave, 1936), 231.

134. "L'Affair Jérémie," *XIIe Foire Gastronomique de Dijon* [catalogue officiel] (Dijon: Imprimerie Lepagnez, 1932).

135. Fisher, *The Art of Eating*, 87, 431.

136. Ibid., 431, 432.

137. Ibid., 433.

138. Gaston Derys, "Petite géographie gastronomique de la France," in *Anthologie de la Gastronomie Française* (Paris: Delagrave, 1936), 231.

139. The renewed interest in rural inns was provided a genealogy in Roger Vaultier, "Auberges du Temps Jadis," *L'Illustration*, October 2, 1937.

140. Curnonsky and Gaston Derys, *La France Gastronomique, Guide des Merveilles Culinaires et des Bonnes Auberges Françaises, La Bourgogne* (Paris: F. Rouff, 1923), 48.

141. Quoted in Gaston Gérard, "La Côte-d'Or, berceau et paradis de la Gastronomie," in *La Côte-d'Or: Aspect Géographique, Historique, Touristique, Economique et Administrative du Département* (Paris: Alépée, 1954), 170.

142. "Les Quatre Glorieuses de Bourgogne," *Le Bien Public*, November 2, 1935, 4.

143. "Menu de l'Hotel de la Côte-d'Or pour l'occasion du XIIième Congrès de l'Union Nationale des Officiers de Réserve a Dijon, 24 juillet 1932."

144. Gérard, "La Côte-d'Or, berceau et paradis de la Gastronomie," 172.

145. Ibid.

146. "A Travers les Stands: Le Pavillon du Tourisme," *Progrès de la Côte-d'Or*, November 8, 1931, 2.

147. M. Charier, quoted in "L'économie bourguignonne vue de l'Exposition," *Progrès de la Côte-d'Or*, November 13, 1937, 1.

148. Ory, *Le Discours Gastronomique Français*, 123.

149. Gaston Gérard, "La Gastronomie Bourguignonne," *La France à Table: Bourgonge* (December 1954), 8.

150. Gaston Gérard, "Les fastes et liesses de Dijon," *Bien Public*, October 31, 1935, 3.

151. Christelle Guilard, "La Foire Gastronomique de Dijon," appendix 28.

Chapter 4. Consuming Simple Gifts

My thanks to Hancock Shaker Village, Inc., David Newell, and the Vermont Historical Society for access to their collections. And thanks to Jill Mudgett, who introduced me to Daniel Pierce Thompson's life and works.

1. As of early 2005, one Shaker community remained, Sabbathday Lake, Maine, with fewer than ten members.

2. Flo Morse, *The Shakers and the World's People* (Hanover, N.H.: University Press of New England, 1987), 240.

3. Clarke Garrett, *Spirit Possession and Popular Religion: From the Camisards to the Shakers* (Baltimore: Johns Hopkins University Press, 1987).

4. Stephen A. Marini, *Radical Sects of Revolutionary New England* (Cambridge, Mass.: Harvard University Press, 1982). On the Shakers' early proselytizing, see Edward Deming Andrews, *The People Called Shakers: A Search for the Perfect Society* (New York: Dover, 1963); Stephen J. Stein, *The Shaker Experience in America: A History of the United Society of Believers* (New Haven, Conn.: Yale University Press, 1992), 10–31. Shaker village names changed over time; throughout this article I have used the names by which they are best known today.

5. Stein, *Shaker Experience*, 10–25; Morse, *Shakers and the World's People*, 30–38;

Deborah E. Burns, *Shaker Cities of Peace, Love, and Union: A History of the Hancock Bishopric* (Hanover, N.H.: University Press of New England, 1993), chs. 1–2; Edward R. Horgan, *The Shaker Holy Land: A Community Portrait* (Harvard, Mass.: Harvard Common Press, 1982), ch. 3.

6. Garrett, *Spirit Possession*, chs. 9–10; Stein, *Shaker Experience*, 41–49. On the difficulties of living as a Shaker among non-Shakers, see Elizabeth A. De Wolfe, *Shaking the Faith: Women, Family, and Mary Marshall Dyer's Anti-Shaker Campaign, 1815–1867* (New York: Palgrave-Macmillan, 2004), 29–30.

7. Stein, *Shaker Experience*, 43–50, 94–98; Morse, *Shakers and the World's People*, 120–22; Priscilla J. Brewer, *Shaker Communities, Shaker Lives* (Hanover, N.H.: University Press of New England, 1986), 53–54.

8. Economic issues generally: Stein, *Shaker Experience*, 135ff. Land purchases: Edward Deming Andrews and Faith Andrews, *Work and Worship: The Economic Order of the Shakers* (Greenwich, Conn.: New York Graphic Society, 1974), 174–84. Brewer, *Shaker Communities*, offers an extensive analysis of Shaker demographics. On controversies between Shakers and neighbors and government, see De Wolfe, *Shaking the Faith*.

9. Ellen-Rose Savulis, "Vision and Practice: Resistance and Dissent in Shaker Communities," Ph.D. diss., University of Massachusetts at Amherst, 1998, 41–43; David R. Starbuck, *Neither Plain nor Simple: New Perspectives on the Canterbury Shakers* (Hanover, N.H.: University Press of New England, 2004), 3, 17. Clay Lancaster, *Pleasant Hill—Shaker Canaan in Kentucky: An Architectural and Social Study* (Salvisa, Ky.: Warwick Publications, 2001), 20–21, 29, 35–36. Morse, *Shakers and the World's People*, 108–10; also Moritz Busch, *Travels Between the Hudson and the Mississippi, 1851–1852* (Lexington: University Press of Kentucky, 1971), 71–76.

10. June Sprigg, "Out of this World: The Shakers as a Nineteenth-Century Tourist Attraction," *American Heritage* 31, 65–73. Accounts mentioned in note 5 primarily treat eastern villages. For early visitors at a western village, see Cheryl Bauer and Rob Portman, *Wisdom's Paradise: The Forgotten Shakers of Union Village* (Wilmington, Ohio: Orange Frazer Press, 2004), chs. 1, 3, 6. Busch, *Travels*, 62–76; Capt. Marryat, C.B., *A Diary in America, with Remarks on its Institutions* (London: Longman, Orme, Brown, Green, & Longmans, 1839), 114–16, 122. For visitor numbers, see Burns, *Shaker Cities*, 133. Dona Brown, *Inventing New England: Regional Tourism in the Nineteenth Century* (Washington, D.C.: Smithsonian Institution Press, 1995), ch. 1; Richard H. Gassan, "The Birth of American Tourism: New York, The Hudson Valley, and American Culture, 1790–1835," Ph.D. diss., University of Massachusetts at Amherst, 2002. For an early visit to Mount Lebanon, see Anne Carey Morris, ed., *The Diary and Letters of Gouverneur Morris*, vol. 2 (New York, 1888), 521; see also Morse, *Shakers and the World's People*, 164–66. On Mammoth Caves, see John F. Sears, *Sacred Places: American Tourist Attractions in the Nineteenth Century* (Amherst: University of Massachusetts Press, 1998), ch. 2; and on its relation to Pleasant Hill, see W. A. H[inds], "The Pleasant Hill Shakers," *American Socialist* v. 1, no. 31 (October 26, 1876): 245.

11. The typical visit was constructed from Morse, *Shakers and the World's People*, 59–60, 141–42, 152–66; Busch, *Travels*, 72–76. The reference to a public speaker is from the microfiched Shaker collection at the Western Reserve Historical Society (hereafter referred to as WRHS), I.B.30, entry dated March 10, 1807. On change in dance styles, see Garrett, *Spirit Possession*, ch. 10; Stein, *Shaker Experience*, 48, 104. On disruptions, see Morse, *Shakers and the World's People*, 164–65; Marianne Finch, *An Englishwoman's Experience in America* (New York: Negro University Press, 1969), 120–21.

12. Jeffrey Alan Melton, *Mark Twain, Travel Books, and Tourism: The Tide of a Great Popular Movement* (Tuscaloosa: University of Alabama Press, 2002), chs. 1–2. On the circulation of Shaker and apostate writings, see De Wolfe, *Shaking the Faith.*

13. Captain Basil Hall, *Travels in North America, in the Years 1827 and 1828,* vol. 1 (Edinburgh: Cadell and Company, 1829), 111–12; Harriet Martineau, *Society in America,* vol. 2 (London: Saunders and Otley, 1837), 54–62; [James Fenimore Cooper], *Notions of the Americans: Picked up by a Traveling Bachelor,* vol. 2 (Philadelphia: Carey Lea & Carey, 1828), 247–50. Morse, *Shakers and the World's People,* 164. The tourist gaze is drawn from John Urry, *The Tourist Gaze: Leisure and Travel in Contemporary Societies* (Thousand Oaks, Calif.: Sage, 1990), 3. On visitors' perceptions of the Shakers, see Marryat, *Diary in America,* 117–22; Mrs. Basil Hall, *The Aristocratic Journey, being the Outspoken Letters of Mrs. Basil Hall Written During a Fourteen Month's Sojurn in America 1827–1828* (New York: G. P. Putnam's Sons, 1931), 40–44. On dancing, see Ann Wagner, *Adversaries of Dance: From the Puritans to the Present* (Urbana: University of Illinois Press, 1997), ch. 5; Morse, *Shakers and the World's People,* 59.

14. Morse, *Shakers and the World's People,* 68–69; Andrews and Andrews, *Work and Worship,* 198. On Millennial Laws, see WRHS I.B.37; on the seed industry, see Andrews and Andrews, *Work and Worship,* 53ff.

15. Sears, *Sacred Places,* ch. 5.

16. For the Enfield visitors' register, see WRHS III.B.1; the local area was defined as a rough circle bounded on the north by Springfield and neighboring communities, on the south by Hartford and neighboring communities. Cindy S. Aron, *Working at Play: A History of Vacations in the United States* (New York: Oxford University Press, 1999), ch. 1. On Shaker connections to camp meetings, see Bauer, *Wisdom's Paradise,* chs. 1–2. For farmer letters, see December 23 letter from Ashton Willard to the Hon. C. W. Willard, in doc. 28 (Willard Papers), and the October 12, 1857, letter from Austin E. Simmons to Achsa W. Sprague, in doc. 181, both in the Vermont Historical Society Library. De Wolfe, in *Shaking the Faith,* notes that by 1813 the Enfield Shakers were generally accepted by their neighbors (32).

17. Samuel D. Johnson, *The Shaker Lovers: A Drama in One Act* (n.p., 1849).

18. Johnson, *Shaker Lovers;* Daniel Pierce Thompson, *May Martin, and Other Tales of the Green Mountains* (Boston: Lee and Shepard, 1890), 253–306.

19. On mobs attacking the Shakers, see De Wolfe, *Shaking the Faith.*

20. Horgan, *Shaker Holy Land,* 85; Burns, *Shaker Cities,* 107; Stein, *Shaker Experience,* 288–89.

21. Morse, *Shakers and the World's People,* 159, 160, 164; Finch, *Englishwoman's Experience,* 119. On apostate dancing troupes, see Morse, 207–9. Brewer, *Shaker Communities,* chs. 1, 3, and 8 covers recruitment in the aftermath of revivals and demographic trends.

22. Spectators, see Calvin Ely diary, WRHS V.B.11. Demographics, see Brewer, *Shaker Communities,* chs. 4, 6. Sunday worship as a spiritual and social event, see Paul E. Johnson, *A Shopkeeper's Millennium: Society and Revivals in Rochester, New York, 1815–1837* (New York: Hill and Wang, 1978).

23. Andrews and Andrews, *Work and Worship;* see also Busch, *Travels,* 62. On the role of the Office, see Stein, *Shaker Experience,* 151; Savulis, "Vision and Practice," 41–42. On the antebellum Office as a retail shop, see Brewer, *Shaker Communities,* picture and caption between 114 and 115; Morse, *Shakers and the World's People,* 95; Finch, *Englishwoman's Experience,* 140.

24. Millennial Laws: WRHS I.B.37, I.B.50, I.B.52; Stein, *Shaker Experience,* 95–97; Andrews, *People Called Shakers,* 243–89. On the Shaker reputation for food, see Don Gifford, ed., *An Early View of the Shakers: Benson John Lossing and the Harper's Article of July 1857* (Hanover, N.H.: University Press of New England, 1989), 32; Charles Nordhoff, *The Communistic Societies of the United States* (New York: Schocken Books, 1965), 140. On charging for meals and giving food to the poor, see Stein, *Shaker Experience,* 269; Bauer, *Wisdom's Paradise,* 223; W[illiam] D[ean] Howells, "Shirley," in *Three Villages* (Boston: James K. Osgood and Company, 1884), 78.

25. On visitors and laborers staying overnight, see Busch, *Travels,* 60; "Journal of the Gathering Order Concerning those who visit or Stay over Night," Library of Congress Shaker collection microfiche, reel 17, container 19, item 239. For rules, see Morse, *Shakers and the World's People,* 125, but see also Mary L. Richmond, comp., *Shaker Literature: A Bibliography,* vol. 1 (Hancock, Mass.: Shaker Community, 1977), 162–63, on the problem of dating this item.

26. This theme is recurring in Brewer, *Shaker Communities,* although her treatment is more complex; see 30, 38, 64, 145. On Canterbury archaeology, see Starbuck, *Neither Plain nor Simple,* chs. 3, 5. On Marble Hall, see Bauer, *Wisdom's Paradise,* 240–41. Regarding education and periodicals, see Stein, *Shaker Experience,* 100–101, 153, 160, 203–4; Millennial Laws, WRHS I.B.50, I.B.52. For critics, see Thompson, "Shaker Lovers"; and C.B., "A Second Visit to the Shakers," in *The Lowell Offering; A Repository of Original Articles written exclusively by Females Actively Employed in the Mills,* vol. 1 (Lowell: Powers & Bagley, 1841), 337–40.

27. On closing meeting, see Bauer, *Wisdom's Paradise,* 156, 179; Savulis, "Vision and Practice," 73–74. On spectators at outdoor meetings, see "A Journal of Domestic Events & transactions In a brief & conclusive form, Commenced Jan. 1st, 1843," from Hancock Shaker Village, Shaker microfilm series, reel 2, entries dated May 14, June 4, and August 13, 1843.

28. On erosion, see examples in Brewer, *Shaker Communities,* 78, 85–86, 100–102, 162, 167, 172–73. For visitors touring the village, see Morse, *Shakers and the World's People,* 190ff, and Gifford, *Early View of the Shakers.* Information on other Shakers as visitors can be found at "A Journal of Domestic Events," entry for June 21. Registers: "Journal of the gathering Order"; WRHS III.B.4, III.B.30.

29. Brewer, *Shaker Communities,* 163.

30. For interpretations of "Mother's Work," see Andrews, *People Called Shakers,* ch. 8; Stein, *Shaker Experience,* 165–200; Brewer, *Shaker Communities,* chs. 7–8. On Millennial Laws, see note 24. For sacred writings, see "The Holy Order of the Church," dated February 18, 1844, Hancock Shaker Village, Inc. Shaker collection microfilm reel 1; see also Brewer, *Shaker Communities,* 163–64.

31. Brewer, *Shaker Communities,* 145, 160, 166, 189–92. Stein, *Shaker Experience,* 200–208, 226–28, 333–35.

32. Priscilla J. Brewer, "The Shakers of Mother Ann Lee," in *America's Communal Utopias,* ed. Donald E. Pitzer (Chapel Hill: University of North Carolina Press, 1997), 51; Ruth Alden Doan, *The Miller Heresy, Millennialism, and American Culture* (Philadelphia: Temple University Press, 1987); Clara Endicott Sears, comp., *Gleanings from Old Shaker Journals* (Boston: Houghton Mifflin, 1916), 167–68; Andrews and Andrews, *Work and Worship;* Stein, *Shaker Experience,* 272–86; Starbuck, *Neither Plain nor Simple,* 9.

33. Gifford, *Early View of the Shakers.* Andrews and Andrews, *Work and Worship,* 149–51; see also Charles B. Muller and Timothy D. Rieman, *The Shaker Chair* (Amherst: University of Massachusetts Press, 1984), 130–232.

34. Howells, "Shirley." Horgan, *Shaker Holy Land*, 90, 101. Nordhoff, *Communistic Societies*, 194, states the mill had been sold by Howell's visit. On perceptions of decline in rural New England, see Hal S. Barron, *Those Who Stayed Behind: Rural Society in Nineteenth-Century New England* (Cambridge: Cambridge University Press, 1984), ch. 3.

35. W. D. Howells, *The Undiscovered Country* (Boston: Houghton Mifflin, 1880), and *The Vacation of the Kelwyns: An Idyl of the Middle Eighteen-Seventies* (New York: Harper & Brothers, 1920).

36. Aron, *Working at Play*, chs. 1, 2, 5. On the decline of dancing and public worship, see Stein, *Shaker Experience*, 331; Brewer, *Shaker Communities*, 195; Bauer, *Wisdom's Paradise*, 228. Regarding the Shirley tavern, see Horgan, *Shaker Holy Land*, 114, 120–22, and S. Union: "Shaker Museum at South Union" travel brochure, c. 2004, page labeled "bed & breakfast." For friendships with tourists and weddings, respectively, see Frances E. Howe, *14000 Miles: A Carriage and Two Women* (Fitchburg, Mass.: Sentinel Printing Company, 1906), 4, 8, 31, 185, 210, 213–14, and Burns, *Shaker Cities*, 187.

37. Sears, *Gleanings from Old Shaker Journals*, especially the introduction and chs. 18, 24, and 30. Megan M. Kennedy, "'This Place Is not Meant for Recreation. It Is Meant for Inspiration': The Legacies of Clara Endicott Sears," M.A. thesis, University of Massachusetts at Amherst, 2005.

38. Nordhoff, *Communistic Societies*, 11–22, 115–256, 383–418.

39. James K. Reeve, "A Shaker Community," *New England Magazine*, n.s. 6 (May 1897): 349–53; Madeline S. Bridges (pseud. for Mary Ainge De Vere), "A Wonderful Little World of People," *Ladies' Home Journal*, vol. 15: 7 (June 1898): 6–7. Pseudonym identified in Gregory Clark, *Rhetorical Landscapes in America: Variations on a Theme from Kenneth Burke* (Columbia: University of South Carolina Press, 2004), 64–66.

40. "The Shakers: A Strict and Utopian Way of Life Has Almost Vanished," *Life* 26 (March 21, 1949): 142–48; Arthur F. Joy, "The Shakers, 1774–1954," *Yankee* 18 (July 1954): 86–95; "The Shakers: Serene Twilight of a Once-Sturdy Sect," *Life* 62 (March 17, 1967): 58–70.

41. Pamela Todd, *The Arts and Crafts Companion* (Boston: Bulfinch Press, 2004), 32; Eileen Boris, *Art and Labor: Ruskin, Morris and the Craftsman Ideal in America* (Philadelphia: Temple University Press, 1986); David M. Cutler, *Gustav Stickley* (New York: Phaidon, 2003). The rise of the Arts and Crafts movement was related to several broader trends. See T. J. Jackson Lears, *No Place of Grace: Antimodernism and the Transformation of American Culture, 1880–1920* (New York: Pantheon Books, 1981); Miles Orvell, *The Real Thing: Imitation and Authenticity in American Culture, 1880–1940* (Chapel Hill: University of North Carolina Press, 1989). Regarding the rise of handicrafts, see Stein, *Shaker Experience*, 269–70; Burns, *Shaker Cities*, 150, 171; Brewer, *Shaker Communities*, 164, 189; Edward Deming Andrews, *The Community Industries of the Shakers* (Philadelphia: Porcupine Press, 1972), 248–54; Marion Wire, "What the Shakers Make for Christmas," *Ladies' Home Journal* 26:1 (December 1908, Christmas issue): 77. For Victorian flourishes, see Timothy D. Rieman and Jean M. Burks, *Encyclopedia of Shaker Furniture* (Atglen, Pa.: Schiffer, 2003), 46–48. On Shaker women going out to sell goods, see Michael S. Graham, "The Sabbathday Lake Shakers and the Rickers of the Poland Spring Hotel: A Scrapbook History" (exhibit brochure, United Society of Shakers, Sabbathday Lake, Inc., 2002).

42. Graham, "Sabbathday Lake Shakers"; Howells, "Shirley," 109; Stein, *Shaker Experience*, 291, 298–99.

43. Andrews and Andrews, *Work and Worship,* 186; O[liver] P[rentiss](?), "Shaker Depletion," *The American Socialist* 4 (January 30, 1879): 35; Harriet E. O'Brien, *Lost Utopias: A Brief Description of Three Quests for Happiness, Alcott's Fruitlands, Old Shaker House, and American Indian Museum* (Boston: Perry Walton, 1929), 32–33; Julia Neal, *The Kentucky Shakers* (Lexington: University Press of Kentucky, 1982), 85, and Lancaster, *Pleasant Hill,* 104; Graham, "Sabbathday"; and David L. Richards, *Poland Spring: A Tale of the Gilded Age, 1860–1900* (Durham: University of New Hampshire Press, 2005), which appeared after this chapter was composed. On Lebanon Springs, see "Medicus" [pseud., Daniel Denison Slade], *Twelve Days in the Saddle: A Journey on Horseback in New England* (Boston: Little, Brown, 1884), 51–53.

44. Andrews and Andrews, *Work and Worship,* 53–74; James Harvey Young, *The Toadstool Millionaires; A Social History of Patent Medicines in America before Federal Regulation* (Princeton, N.J.: Princeton University Press, 1961), 199; Morse, *Shakers and the World's People,* 144–46.

45. Thorstein Veblen, *The Theory of the Leisure Class: An Economic Study of Institutions* (New York: Macmillan, 1899). See also sources at note 42.

46. Orvell, *Real Thing,* 160; Todd, *Arts and Crafts Companion,* 156.

47. Brewer, "The Shakers," 51–52; Stein, *Shaker Experience,* 241–52. Morse, *Shakers and the World's People,* 280–89, 296; Horgan, *Shaker Holy Land,* 144–45.

48. Stein, *Shaker Experience,* 371–72.

49. Ibid., 370–77; Horgan, *Shaker Holy Land,* 143, 149, 152; Kennedy, "'This Place Is Not Meant for Recreation,'" 22.

50. On drop-in visitors and tourism in this period, see Stein, *Shaker Experience,* 344; Aron, *Working at Play,* chs. 7–9; Horgan, *Shaker Holy Land,* 140. On Sears, see Kennedy, "'This Place Is Not Meant for Recreation,'" 27ff.

51. Robert and Elizabeth Shackleton, *The Quest of the Colonial* (New York: Century Company, 1913); Howells, *Vacation of the Kelwyns;* Wallace Nutting, *Furniture Treasury (Mostly of American Origin): All Periods of American Furniture with Some Foreign Examples in America, also American Hardware and Household* (Framingham, Mass.: Old America, 1928), 33.

52. Stein, *Shaker Experience,* 373–78, 396–97; Edward Deming Andrews and Faith Andrews, *Religion in Wood: A Book of Shaker Furniture* (Bloomington: Indiana University Press, 1966).

53. Andrews, *People Called Shakers,* quotation at xii; Stein, *Shaker Experience,* 380–82.

54. For Mount Lebanon, see Stein, *Shaker Experience,* 344–52, and for Hancock, see Amy Bess Miller, *Hancock Shaker Village / The City of Peace: An Effort to Restore a Vision, 1960–1985* (Hancock, Mass.: Hancock Shaker Village, 1984). See also Lancaster, *Pleasant Hill;* Morse, *Shakers and the World's People,* 119, 137–42, 181–82, 267–69.

55. Stein, *Shaker Experience,* 371–76, 378, 395–96, 421. Morse, *Shakers and the World's People,* 240, 316–17, 338–39. Discussion of current conditions for tourists is based on author's personal observations during 2004–2005.

56. Starbuck, *Neither Plain nor Simple,* ch. 2.

57. Stein, *Shaker Experience,* xiii. Rieman's *Encyclopedia of Shaker Furniture* uses Shaker history as background for analyzing the furniture.

Chapter 5. "I Would Much Rather See a Sermon than Hear One"

1. Alan Goforth, "Not Your Parent's Branson," (*Kansas City) Metro Voice* 14, no. 6 (2003): 24.

2. James A. Thompson, "Saga of the Shepherd of the Hills, Part III," *Springfield!* 15, no. 5 (1993): 56–58.

3. Don Zimmerman, "Country's Mecca in Missouri," *USA Today*, June 24, 1994, 1D; Kathy Buckstaff, "Despite Pains, Growth Moves Ahead," *Springfield News-Leader*, February 26, 1995, 8A; "First There Was Nashville . . . Then Came Branson," *Atlanta Journal-Constitution*, July 4, 1993, N4.

4. Branson/Lakes Area Chamber of Commerce & Convention & Visitors Bureau, Branson/Lakes Area 2005 Fact Sheet.

5. Stacey Hamby, "Silver Dollar City: Owners Build Empire on Christian Principles," *Word & Way*, June 10, 1999, 9; S.T. Lambert's comments were posted as a review of Silver Dollar City on the *Epinions.com* Web site, December 31, 2000, www.epinions.com/kifm-review-2307-2039366B-3A4F0229-prod4.

6. Jim Thompson, "The Herschends: Catalysts for Ozark Mountain Country's Unprecedented Growth in Tourist Trade," *Springfield!* 13, no. 4 (1992): 57–58; Lisa Gubernick, "A Curb on the Ego," *Forbes* 150, no. 6 (1992): 418–20.

7. Crystal Cody, "Silver Dollar City Hits Slump," *Arkansas Democrat Gazette*, August 8, 2003, 31.

8. Milton D. Rafferty, *The Ozarks: Land and Life* (Fayetteville: University of Arkansas Press, 2001), 8; John F. Sears, *Sacred Places: American Tourist Attractions in the Nineteenth Century* (New York: Oxford University Press, 1989), 38; *The Visionaries: The Herschends of Branson, MO*, dir. Dave Hargis and prod. Roy Speckman, Universal Midwest Media, 1992, videocassette.

9. Edith McCall, " 'Down Under' at Silver Dollar City," *Ozarks Mountaineer* 45, no. 6 (1997): 42; Ronald L. Martin, *Official Guide to Marvel Cave* (Springfield, Mo.: Ozark Mountain Publishers, 1974), 14.

10. Jerry S. Madsen, *The History: Those Who Walked with Wright* (Galena, Mo.: Ozark Trails Magazine, 1985), 30; Lynn Morrow and Linda Myers-Phinney, *Shepherd of the Hills Country: Tourism Transforms the Ozarks, 1880s-1930s* (Fayetteville: University of Arkansas Press, 1999), 38–40.

11. Capt. J. B. Emery, "Description of Marble Cave, Missouri," *Kansas City Review of Science* 8 (1885): 614–15.

12. Rafferty, *The Ozarks*, 200–204; Jane Westfall and Catherine Osterhage, *A Fame Not Easily Forgotten* (Conway, Ark.: River Road Press, 1970), 2, 7. On late nineteenth-century Eureka Springs' spa tourism, see Charles Cutter, *Cutter's Guide to Eureka Springs, Arkansas* (St. Louis: Cutter & Trump, 1884); and L. J. Kalklasch, *The Healing Fountain: Complete History of Eureka Springs* (St. Louis: Chambers' Print, 1881).

13. Morrow and Myers-Phinney, *Shepherd of the Hills Country*, 40–42; Martin, *Official Guide to Marvel Cave*, 16. In 1886, the mining town's name was changed to Marmaros (Greek for "marble"). See Madsen, *Those Who Walked with Wright*, 30.

14. "A Pioneer of Ozark Awakening," *Arcadian Magazine*, July 1931, 9; Miles H. Scott, "The Marvelous Cave," *White River Valley Historical Quarterly* 8, no. 10 (1988): 4–5; Thompson, "The Herschends," 38.

15. Crystal Payton, *The Story of Silver Dollar City: A Pictorial History of Branson's Famous Ozark Mountain Theme Park* (Springfield, Mo.: Lens & Pen Books, 1997), 24–25; Martha Hoy Bohner, "It All Started with a Hole in the Ground," *Ozarks Mountaineer* 48, no. 2 (2000): 32.

16. "Mystery of Marble Cave," *White River Leader*, December 13, 1913; Flo Montgomery Tidgwell, "A Marvel of a Cave," *Ozarks Mountaineer* 35, no. 2–3

(1987): 27; *Scientific American* 68 (1893): 65; G. Kingsley Noble, "Creatures of Perpetual Night," *Scientific American* 139 (1928): 432, 430.

17. Martin, *Official Guide to Marvel Cave,* 21; Arline Chandler, "A Tale of Two Men Leads to One City," *Branson's Review* 8, no. 3 (2000): 26.

18. Marge of Sunrise Farm, "Fresh from the Hills . . . Ozark Cave Women," ca. 1944, Shepard Room Collection, Library Center, Springfield-Greene County Public Library, Springfield, Mo.; L. C. Milstead, "Harold Bell Wright: Press Agent," *Bookman,* January 1931, 502.

19. Asa Don Dickinson, *The Best Books of Our Time, 1901–1925* (New York: H. W. Wilson, 1928), 201; Harold Bell Wright, *The Shepherd of the Hills* (Gretna, La.: Pelican, [1907] 1994), 284. According to Dickinson, Wright was the third most popular American writer between 1895 and 1926 and the first in popularity between 1909 and 1921.

20. Martin, *Official Guide to Marvel Cave,* 24; Madsen, *Those Who Walked with Wright,* 30; McCall, " 'Down Under' at Silver Dollar City," 43.

21. Payton, *The Story of Silver Dollar City,* 23; McCall, " 'Down Under' at Silver Dollar City," 43; Martin, *Official Guide to Marvel Cave,* 54.

22. Thompson, "The Herschends," 37–38; Doug Johnson, "Leap of Faith Succeeds in Branson Attraction," *Washington Times,* April 29, 2000, E2; William Childress, "A City as Popular as Pretzels," *St. Louis Post-Dispatch,* April 5, 1997, 7T.

23. Payton, *The Story of Silver Dollar City,* 39–44; "Branson Mainstays Continue to Thrive," *Springfield News-Leader,* August 26, 1996, 68.

24. Payton, *The Story of Silver Dollar City,* 40; Thompson, "The Herschends," 39; William Childress, "Silver Dollar City Gets Worldly," *St. Louis Post-Dispatch,* April 27, 1997, 8T.

25. Payton, *The Story of Silver Dollar City,* 51; "Mary Herschend Dies at 83," *Branson Beacon and Leader,* March 21, 1983, 1.

26. Silver Dollar City Chamber of Commerce, "Silver Dollar City in Marvel Cave Park" brochure, Shepard Room Collection, Library Center, Springfield-Greene County Public Library, Springfield, Mo.; Mary Hartman, "Alf Bolin's Reign of Terror," in *In the Heart of Ozark Mountain Country: A Popular History of Stone and Taney Counties, Including Branson, Missouri,* ed. Frank Reuter (Reeds Springs, Mo.: White Oak Press, 1992), 127–30; Payton, *The Story of Silver Dollar City,* 58.

27. Richard Schickel, *The Disney Version* (New York: Simon and Schuster, 1968), 267; E. L. Doctorow, *The Book of Daniel* (New York: Random House, 1971), 289.

28. On the use of religious and/or spiritual language to describe Disneyland and Disney World, see Margaret J. King, "Disneyland and Walt Disney World: Traditional Values in Futuristic Form," *Journal of Popular Culture* 15, no. 1 (1981): 116–40; and Virginia A. Salamone and Frank A. Salamone, "Images of Main Street: Disney World and the American Adventure," *Journal of American Culture* 22, no. 1 (1999): 85–92.

29. Payton, *The Story of Silver Dollar City,* 126, 58–59.

30. Peggy Soric, "A Temple of Wood, a Message of Truth," *Springfield News-Leader,* July 26, 1986, 4B.

31. Ibid.

32. Soric, "A Temple of Wood," 4B; Lucas S. Roebuck, "Coaster Thrills and Mountain Skills," *Today's Christian* July–August 2001, 48; Kathryn Buckstaff,

"They're Getting Married in a Theme Park," *Springfield-News Leader,* June 9, 1997, 3B.

33. Soric, "A Temple of Wood," 4B; Bob Deeds, pastor, Silver Dollar City Wilderness Church, interview by the author, Branson, Mo., July 20, 2003.

34. Ron Sylvester, "There's Silver in These Hills," *Springfield News-Leader,* February 13, 2000, 3B; "Mary Herschend Dies at 83," *Branson Beacon and Leader,* March 21, 1983, 1.

35. Arline Chandler, "Silver Dollar City's Future Is Its Past," *Branson Review* 8, no. 3 (2000): 23, 27–29; Rick Brunson, "Behind the Boom in Branson, Mo.," *Charisma,* July 1993, 49; Roebuck, "Coaster Thrills and Mountain Skills," 48; Thompson, "The Herschends," 69.

36. Lewis C. Daly, "A Church at Risk: The Episcopal 'Renewal Movement,'" *Institute for Democracy Studies Insights* 2, no. 2 (2001): 1–6.

37. Father Richard Kellogg, rector, Shepherd of the Hills Episcopal Church, interview by the author, Branson, Mo., September 13, 2002; Johnson, "Leap of Faith," E2.

38. R. Laurence Moore, *Selling God: American Religion in the Marketplace of Culture* (Oxford: Oxford University Press, 1994), 244–48; Brenda E. Brasher, ed., *Encyclopedia of Fundamentalism* (New York: Routledge, 2001), 402–3, 470–73; Grant Wacker, "Searching for Eden with a Satellite Dish," in *Religion and American Culture,* ed. David G. Hackett (New York: Routledge, 1995), 441.

39. Richard Corliss, "If Heaven Ain't a Lot Like Disney: Theme Parks Created in Uncle Walt's Image Offer a Sanitized Suburban Utopia," *Time,* June 16, 1986, 80; Richard N. Ostling, "Of God and Greed: Bakker and Falwell Trade Charges in Televangelism's Unholy Row," *Time,* June 8, 1987, 70; Richard N. Ostling, "TV's Unholy Row: A Sex-and-Money Scandal Tarnishes Electronic Evangelism," *Time,* April 6, 1987, 60; Johnson, "Leap of Faith," E2; "The New Jim Bakker TV Show Acquires Camelot!" *Branson Church Getaway Planner* 8, no. 1 (2005): 10.

40. Johnson, "Leap of Faith," E2; Pete Herschend, vice chairman of the board of directors, Herschend Family Entertainment Corporation, interview by the author, Branson, Mo., September 24, 2002; Hamby, "Silver Dollar City," 9.

41. Roebuck, "Coaster Thrills and Mountain Skills," 48.

42. Kathryn Buckstaff, "Ozarker Spearheads Nazareth Village," *Springfield News-Leader,* May 9, 2002, 2B.

43. Payton, *The Story of Silver Dollar City,* 126; Doug Johnson, "Branson's Silver Dollar City Theme Park Takes a Christian Slant," *Minneapolis Star Tribune,* May 21, 2000, 10G; Roebuck, "Coaster Thrills and Mountain Skills," 48; Patricia Bates, "Herschends Turn SDC into Multi-Million Dollar Empire," *Amusement Business* 103, no. 50 (1991): 3–4. The Herschend Family Entertainment Corporation's explicitly Christian mission statement has not been without controversy; see "Silver Dollar City Alters Mission Statement," *Springfield News-Leader,* December 15, 2000, 1A.

44. Orville Conrad and Alicia Bolin's comments were posted to the *Silver Dollar City Fan Club* Web site, July 12, 2005, http://groups.yahoo.com/group/SDCFans/message/866 and http://groups.yahoo.com/group/SDCFans/message/865.

45. Roebuck, "Coaster Thrills and Mountain Skills," 48.

46. Thompson, "The Herschends," 39; Sarah B. Hansen, "Silver Dollar City Turns to Gold," *Springfield News-Leader,* December 17, 1990, 2D; Gubernick, "A Curb on the Ego," 418–20; "For New Operations Chief, First Priority is to 'Glo-

rify God,'" *USA Today*, April 30, 1987, 7A; "Higher Calling," *Springfield Business Journal*, August 3–9, 1998, 2.

47. Frank Elliot, "Ozark Mountain Magic," *Fun World* (Official Magazine of the International Association of Amusement Parks & Attractions), November 2000, 58; Carolyn Olson, "Theme Park Offers Award-Winning Entertainment, Christian Values," *St. Louis Post-Dispatch*, May 14, 2000, T3; "Silver Dollar City: Missouri," *MotorHome Magazine*, July 7, 2005, www.motorhomemagazine.com/shortstops/0009silver.cfm (accessed 2 August 2005).

48. Kathryn Buckstaff, "Veggie Tales Takes Branson," *Springfield News-Leader*, June 2, 2002, 10B; "Veggie Tales Phenomenon Hits Branson," *PR Newswire*, June 3, 2002; John Wooley, "Silver Dollar City Launches Kids' Fest Celebration," *Tulsa World*, June 9, 2002, 7.

49. Johnson, "Branson's Silver Dollar City Theme Park," 10G; Brunson, 49; Hamby, "Silver Dollar City," 9; Roebuck, "Coaster Thrills and Mountain Skills," 48.

50. Silver Dollar City promotional booklet, "Sharing and Caring in the Spirit of Community," 2002.

51. Tom Uhlenbrock, "Branson Cheers President's Tune," *St. Louis Post-Dispatch*, August 22, 1992, 1A; Scott Charton, "Republican President of Education Board Praises Democrat Carnahan," *Associated Press Political Service*, January 18, 1996; David Corn and Dan Moldea, "Did Ashcroft Take the Low Road on the Highroad?" *Nation* (online edition), January 15, 2001, http://ssl.thenation.com/doc.mhtml?i = 20010129&s = corn20010115 (accessed August 7, 2005); Randy Buseman, George Klenovich, and Rusty Goode, "Honoring Achievement: The Ernst & Young Entrepreneur of the Year Awards," *Business Record (Des Moines)*, June 27, 2005, 14.

52. Kathy O. Buckstaff, "Branson Residents Oppose Gambling," *Springfield News-Leader*, September 10, 1994, 4A; Pete Herschend quoted in Robert Siegel, Noah Adams, and Dan Collison, "Boats in Moats," *All Things Considered* [radio program], October 8, 1998; Oscar Avila, "Vote for Amendment Raises Gambling Fears in Branson," *Kansas City Star*, November 12, 1998, B1; Howard Boyd, pastor, Branson Hills Assembly of God Church, interview by the author, Branson, Mo., September 29, 2002.

53. "Records Indicate Family Bankrolling Casino Opposition," *Columbia (Missouri) Daily Tribune*, July 15, 2004; Allen Palmeri, "Defeat of Branson Casino Proposal Shows 'Prayer Over Money,'" *Baptist Press News*, August 4, 2004, 30.

54. Jerry Henry, Corporate Director of Research, Herschend Family Entertainment Corporation, "Silver Dollar City Exit Summary, Summary of Positive Comments, Year to Date 2002"; Epinions.com Web site, October 15, 2002, www.epinions.com/content_78265486980; AOL CityGuide Web site, August 5, 2001, http://cityguide.aol.com/stlouis/entertainment/search.adp?cat = vt%5f%5fst%5f&page = detailReviews&id = 111907188&rskip = 20&layer = venues. Silver Dollar City conducts many exit polls to gauge customer satisfaction. In 2002, roughly 30 percent of those surveyed (92 of 307) mentioned the park's "safety," "friendliness," "cleanliness," "order," and "Christian values" as that which they most enjoyed about their experience.

55. Payton, *The Story of Silver Dollar City*, 126; TripAdvisor.com Web site, September 8, 2004, www.tripadvisor.com/ShowUserReviews-g44160-d103201-r2519146-Silver_Dollar_City-Branson_Missouri.html.

56. "Family Fun Feeds Silver Dollar City," *(Oklahoma City) Journal Record*, April 27, 2000.

57. Pierre Bourdieu, *Outline of a Theory of Practice*, trans. Richard Nice (Cambridge: Cambridge University Press, 1977), 164, 82–83.

58. TripAdvisor.com Web site, July 23, 2001, www.tripadvisor.com/ShowUser Reviews-g44160-d106415-r644301-Marvel_Cave-Branson_Missouri.html.

Chapter 6. "Troubles Tourism"

1. Geoffrey Williams, "Belfast Regains Its Charm," *Sunday Tasmanian*, July 3, 2005.

2. Catherine Morrison, "Troubles Hot Spot Warms to Tourism," *Irish News*, April 6, 2005.

3. Marie Louise McCrory, "'Vibrant, Virginal' Belfast Lauded," *Irish News*, June 11, 2005.

4. Ron DePasquale, "Destination Belfast? Tourists Flood In," *Christian Science Monitor*, September 1, 2005.

5. Padraic Flanagan, "Belfast Burns Again; Police Come Under Fire in the Third Night of Street Riots," *Express, Scottish Edition*, September 14, 2005.

6. Stuart Emmrich, "Belfast Is Ready for the Party to Begin," *New York Times*, August 21, 2005.

7. Mary Fitzgerald, "Tourism: Hard Case to Solve," *Belfast Telegraph*, August 24, 2005.

8. www.gotobelfast.com.

9. John Whyte, *Interpreting Northern Ireland* (Oxford: Clarendon Press, 1990).

10. Two examples of the debater are Susan Crane, "'(Not) Writing History: Rethinking the Intersections of Personal History and Collective Memory with Hans von Aufsess," *History and Memory* 8, no. 1 (1996): 5–29, and Alon Confino, "Collective Memory and Cultural History: Problems of Method," *American Historical Review* 102, no. 5 (1997): 1386–1403.

11. Michel-Rolph Trouillot, *Silencing the Past: Power and the Production of History* (Boston: Beacon Press, 1995), 25.

12. Joseba Zulaika, "Postindustrial Bilbao: The Reinvention of a New City," *Basque Studies Program Newsletter* 57 (University of Nevada, Reno, 1998); David B. Clarke, *The Consumer Society and the Postmodern City* (London: Routledge, 2003).

13. Robert Hewison, *The Heritage Industry: Britain in a Climate of Decline* (London: Methuen, 1987). Patrick Wright, "Heritage and Danger: the English Past in the Era of the Nation-state," in *Memory: History, Culture and the Mind*, ed. Thomas Butler (Oxford: Blackwell, 1989), 152–76; Raphael Samuel, *Theatres of Memory, Vol. I: Past and Present in Contemporary Culture* (London: Verso, 1994), 139–312.

14. "Cultural Tourism: Developing Belfast's Opportunity," Tourism Development Unit, Belfast City Council 2003.

15. Jonathan Bardon and David Burnett, *Belfast: A Pocket History* (Belfast: Blackstaff Press, 1996), 65.

16. Ibid., 68–69.

17. Albert N. Cousins and Hans Nagpaul, *Urban Life: The Sociology of Cities and Urban Societies* (New York: John Wiley & Sons, 1979), 67–68.

18. Bardon and Burnett, *Belfast*, 38, 53.

19. Ibid., 60.

20. Frederick Boal and Stephen Royle, "Belfast: Boom, Blitz, and Bureaucracy," in *Regional Cities in the UK, 1890–1980*, ed. George Gordon (London: Harper & Row), 192–93.

21. Christopher Andrae, "Cities Vie To Be Scotland's 'Culture Capital,'" *Christian Science Monitor*, September 25, 1991.

22. "Conway Mill—A Brief History" (www.conwaymill.org/building.html).

23. As noted in the brief 1989 report "EU Support for Tourism in Northern Ireland," Political Collection, Linen Hall Library, Belfast, Northern Ireland.

24. www.failteireland.ie/home/ mediapress.asp?id=9&MediaId=37.

25. www.nics.gov.uk/press/eti/010629c-eti.htm.

26. www.gotobelfast.com/index.cfm/level/page/category_key/197/Page_Key/396/ Par ent_Key/0/Content_Key/749/type/Page/PaGeName/Belfast's_Top_10_t hings _to_do!

27. When I conducted research in Belfast in 2003, the Belfast Welcome Centre employees encouraged me to take an open-top Belfast City Sightseeing Tours tour through the city—a tour that traverses both the typical historical sites as well as working-class Republican and Unionist areas of West Belfast—yet the brochures for taxi tours of these areas were relegated to small shelves on the far wall.

28. For instance, see the Northern Ireland Economic Council's report, "Rising to the Challenge: The Future of Tourism in Northern Ireland," 1997. The authors comment that the increased numbers of visitors in 1995 were "no doubt reflecting in part a 'novelty' or 'curiosity' factor" (7).

29. Ibid., 19.

30. Ibid., 15, 18.

31. Northern Ireland Tourism Board, "Growing Tourism Together," *Corporate Plan 2002–2005*, 6.

32. Trouillot, *Silencing the Past*, 27.

33. www.iol.ie/~wbelecon/tourism.html.

34. Ibid.

35. Tourism Development Unit, Belfast City Council, "Cultural Tourism, Developing Belfast's Opportunity," 2003: 16.

36. Personal interview with Professor Sophia Hillan; BBC 1 Television, "Home Truths: Belfast Black," March 15, 1994.

37. "Curious Locals and Thrifty Tourists Hop on the Bus," *Irish News*, September 1, 2005.

38. "Going to the Wall to Promote Belfast," *Irish Times*, August 23, 2005.

39. Dominic Bryan, "Belfast, Urban Space, 'Policing,' and Sectarian Polarization," in *Wounded Cities*, ed. Jane Schneider and Ida Susser (New York: Berg, 2003), 266.

40. Ann Laura Stoler, "Developing Historical Negatives: Race and the (Modernist) Vision of a Colonial State," in *From the Margins: Historical Anthropology and Its Futures*, ed. Brian Keith Axel (Durham, N.C.: Duke University Press, 2002), 156–85.

41. "The Crum—Belfast's History and Our Future," Report of a Community-led Conference on the Future of the Crumlin Road Prison (April 2002).

42. Ibid., 4.

43. Ibid., 4–5.

44. Ibid., 10.

45. Ibid., 11.

46. Ibid., 15.

47. Alan Erwin, "Notorious Belfast Court Could Become a Major Tourist Attraction," *Irish Examiner*, September 16, 2003, http://archives.tcm.ie/irishexaminer/2003/09/16/story358191156.asp.

48. Des Crowley, "Hostilities at Dunloe Drive Away Buyers," *Sunday Business Post On-line,* September 1, 2002, http://archives.tcm.ie/businesspost/2002/09/01/story 326989.asp.

49. Ibid.

50. www.northbelfastcommunityactionunit.org/gaol/htm.

51. www.heritageopendays.org.

52. http://nics.gov.uk/press/sd/050912a-sd.htm.

53. www.inyourpocket.com.

54. http://nics.gov.uk/press/sd/050912a-sd.htm.

55. Carolyn Strangea and Michael Kempab, "Shades of Dark Tourism: Alcatraz and Robben Island," *Annals of Tourism Research* 30, no. 2 (April 2003): 386–405.

56. Adriana Brasiliero and Eleena de Lisser, "Tourists Take a Walk on the Wild Side," *Wall Street Journal,* November 5, 2003.

57. Schneider and Susser, *Wounded Cities,* 2.

58. James Bone, "Why We're Drawn to the Roots of Terror," *Times of London Online,* September 6, 2003.

59. Ibid.

60. Edward Tabor Linenthal, *The Unfinished Bombing: Oklahoma City in American Memory* (Oxford: Oxford University Press, 2001); Lisa Yoneyama, *Hiroshima Traces: Time, Space, and the Dialectics of Memory* (Berkeley: University of California Press, 1999); Jack Kugelmass, "The Rites of the Tribe: American Jewish Tourism in Poland," in *Museums and Communities: The Politics of Public Culture,* ed. Ivan Karp, Christine Mullen Kreamer, and Steven D. Lavine (Washington, D.C.: Smithsonian Institution Press, 1992), 382–427; Molly Hurley and James Trimarco, "Morality and Merchandise: Vendors, Visitors, and Police at New York City's Ground Zero," *Critique of Anthropology* 24, no. 1 (2004): 51–78; Molly Hurley-Dépret and James Trimarco, "Wounded Nation, Broken Time," in *The Selling of 9/11,* ed. Diana Heller (New York: Palgrave Macmillan, 2005), 27–53.

61. www.nycvp.com/ground_zero1.html; www.hi.hkg.ac.jp/peace/eng/peace.html; www.remember.org/4/auschwitz-tour.html.

62. Frederick Boal, "Encapsulation: Urban Dimensions of National Conflict," in *Managing Divided Cities,* ed. S. Dunn (Keele: Ryburn, 1994). Cited in Bryan, "Belfast, Urban Space, 'Policing,'" 252.

63. Florence E. Babb, "Recycled Sandalistas: From Revolution to Resorts in the New Nicaragua," *American Anthropologist* 106, no. 3 (2004): 541–56.

64. www.spearofthenation.co.za/Print.asp?TourID=39.

65. Nick Hawton, BBC News, June 11, 2004, http://newsvote.bbc.co.uk/mpapps/pagetools.

66. Explore! Worldwide, www.explore.co.uk/worldwide/Articlepage.jsp?ArticleID=1151.

67. "Developing Belfast's Opportunity," 13.

68. Ibid., 10. It is not clear who visits murals or takes political tours, though in 2003 I did participate in the International Summer School at Queen's University's Institute for Irish Studies. Among this group of thirty people—whose ages ranged from late teens to postretirement—almost everyone took some type of political tour independently. This was not a typical group, however.

69. Strangea and Kempab, "Shades of Dark Tourism," 403.

70. Neil Jarman, "Painting Landscapes: The Place of Murals in the Symbolic Construction of Urban Space," in *Symbols in Northern Ireland,* ed. Anthony Buckley

(Belfast: Institute for Irish Studies, Queen's University Belfast, 1998). Accessed as electronic document, http://cain.ulst.ac.uk/bibdbs/murals/jarman.htm.

71. Dominic Casciani, All Aboard Belfast's Terror Tour, *BBC On-line*, December 1, 1999, http://news.bbc.co.uk/1/low/northern_ireland/544851.stm.

72. This particular form of political tourism was pointed out to me by a Basque scholar when I presented a version of this paper at the European Association for Social Anthropology (EASA) in September 2004 in Vienna, Austria.

73. Jarman, "'Painting Landscapes."

74. Dr. Ida Susser, personal correspondence, 2004.

75. Betsy Wearing and Stephen Wearing, "Refocussing the Tourist Experience: The Flaneur and the Choraster," *Leisure Studies* 15 (1996): 229–43.

Chapter 7. "There's No Place Like Home"

Reprinted by permission of *Slavic Review,* Winter 2003.

I would like to thank Diane Koenker and Susan Reid for their constructive criticism and encouragement. An early version of this article was presented at the workshop "Observing and Making Meaning: Understanding the Soviet Union and Central Europe Through Travel" at the University of Toronto, and I am grateful to the organizer, Susan Solomon, and to the participants for their suggestions. I would also like to thank the participants and audiences at seminars and lectures where I presented various versions while on sabbatical in England, including St. Antony's College, Oxford; the Oxford Russian Graduate Seminar; the School for Slavonic and East European Studies; the London School of Economics; the University of Birmingham Centre for Slavic and East European Studies; and the Department of Russian and Slavonic Studies at the University of Sheffield.

1. This, of course, evokes George Kennan's famous arguments in 1946 and 1947 about "containment." George Kennan, *Memoirs, 1925–1950* (Boston: Little, Brown, 1967), 559.

2. *Vokrug sveta,* no. 1 (January 1946): 63; *Vokrug sveta,* nos. 3–4 (March–April 1946): 16, 20, inside back cover; *Vokrug sveta,* no. 7 (July 1946): 48–51.

3. *Vokrug sveta,* no. 1 (January 1947): 2–4; *Vokrug sveta,* no. 9 (September 1947): 2–3, 8–11. On Zhdanov, see Robert D. English, *Russia and the Idea of the West: Gorbachev, Intellectuals, and the End of the Cold War* (New York: Columbia University Press, 2000), 46–47.

4. Jeffrey Brooks, "The Press and Its Messages: Images of America in the 1920s and 1930s," in *Russia in the Era of NEP: Explorations in Soviet Society and Culture,* ed. Sheila Fitzpatrick, Alexander Rabinowitch, and Richard Stites (Bloomington: Indiana University Press, 1991), 231–52; Brooks, "Official Xenophobia and Popular Cosmopolitanism in Early Soviet Russia," *American Historical Review* 97 (December 1992): 1431–48; Denise Youngblood, "Americanitis: The Amerikanshchina in Soviet Cinema," *Journal of Popular Film and Television* 19 (Winter 1992); English, *Russia and the Idea of the West,* 148–56.

5. See the special issue of *Slavic Review* (Winter 2003) dedicated to "Tourism and Travel in Russia and the Soviet Union." Also see Anne E. Gorsuch and Diane P. Koenker, eds., *Turizm: The Russian and East European Tourist Under Capitalism and Socialism* (forthcoming, Cornell University Press).

6. See Diane P. Koenker, "Good Travel and Bad: Creating the Proletarian Tourist," paper presented at the workshop "Observing and Making Meaning: Understanding the Soviet Union and Central Europe Through Travel," Univer-

sity of Toronto, October 18–20, 2002; I. I. Sandomirskaia, "Novaia zhizn na marshe: Stalinskii turizm kak 'praktika puti,' " 9, no. 4 (1994); B. B. Kotelnikov, ed., *Sputnik turista*, 2nd ed. (Moscow-Leningrad, 1941), 6–7.

7. N. Makarov, "For Mass Touring," *Trud*, May 27, 1951, 4, in *Current Digest of the Soviet Press* (hereafter *CDSP*) 3, no. 21 (July 7, 1951): 28.

8. This material is from archival collections: Gosudarstvennyi arkhiv Rossiiskoi federatsii (GARF), f. 9520, op. 1 (Central Soviet for Tourism and Excursions). Also useful were GARF, f. 9228, op. 1, 2 (Central Administration for Spas and Sanatoria) and Rossiiskii gosudarstvennyi arkhiv sotsialno-politicheskoi istorii (RGASPI), f. 1, op. 47 (Komsomol records on the development of youth tourism). Also see the collection of archival documents published in A. A. Kiselev et al., *Moskva poslevoennaia, 1945–1947: Arkhivnye dokumenty i materialy* (Moscow: Mosgorarkhiv, 2000).

9. Rudy Koshar, *German Travel Cultures* (Oxford: Berg, 2000), 5.

10. John Urry, *The Tourist Gaze*, 2nd ed. (London: Sage, 2002), 2–3.

11. James Buzard, *The Beaten Track: European Tourism, Literature, and the Ways to Culture, 1800–1918* (Oxford: Oxford University Press, 1993). Jean-Didier Urbain introduced the question of tourism's relationship to the "vacation." See Jean-Didier Urbain, *Sur la plage: Moeurs et coutumes balnéaires XIXe–XXe siècles* (Paris: Payot, 1994).

12. GARF, f. 9520, op. 1, d. 252, ll. 2–4 (tourist journals, 1952).

13. *Trud*, February 29, 1952, 4, in *CDSP* 4, no. 9 (April 12, 1952).

14. GARF, f. 9520, op. 1, d. 252, ll. 2–3.

15. Ibid., ll. 2–9, 13–16.

16. Iu. Efremov, "Kvoprosy o kulture turizma," in *Turistskie tropy* (Moscow: Gosudarstevnnoe izdatel'stvo "Fizkul'tura i sport," 1958), 12.

17. James von Geldern, "The Centre and the Periphery: Cultural and Social Geography in the Mass Culture of the 1930s," in *New Directions in Soviet History*, ed. Stephen White (Cambridge: Cambridge University Press, 1992), 71.

18. Serge Aksakoff, *Years of Childhood*, trans. J. D. Duff (London, 1916), 7–8.

19. John McCannon, *Red Arctic: Polar Exploration and the Myth of the North in the Soviet Union, 1932–1939* (New York: Oxford University Press, 1998), 83.

20. O. Arkhangel'skaia, *Kak organizovat turistskoe puteshestvie* (Moscow: Izdatel'stvo VTsSPS "Profizdat," 1947), 4, 6.

21. I. I. Fedenko, *Volga—velikaia russkaia reka* (Moscow-Leningrad: Gosudarstevnnoe izdatel'stvo detskoi literatury, 1946), 35.

22. V. V. Dobkovich, *Turizm v SSSR* (Leningrad: Vsesoiuznoe obshestvo po razprostraneniiu politicheskikh i nauchnykh znaii, 1954), 10.

23. Ibid., 11.

24. GARF, f. 9520, op. 1, d. 252, l. 2.

25. Von Geldern, "The Centre and the Periphery," 71.

26. John Steinbeck, *A Russian Journal* (New York: New York Herald Tribune, 1949), 37.

27. Urry, *Tourist Gaze*.

28. Ibid., 128.

29. Arkhangel'skaia, *Kak organizovat turistskoe puteshestvie*, 32.

30. Von Geldern, "The Centre and the Periphery," 71.

31. G. A. Zelenko, "Chto takoe turizm," in *Turistskie tropy* (Moscow: Gosudarstevnnoe izdatel'stvo "Fizkul'tura i sport," 1958), 8.

32. At least one observer condemned rest homes as places of slothful indulgence: A "young, healthy man whose organism craves physical activity . . . falls

into the hothouse environment of a dom otdykha where he spends idiotic . . . numbing hours of fattening and obesity, putting on weight." GARF, f. 9520, op. 1, d. 69, l. 7 (transcript of a 1948 Tourist-Excursion Bureau meeting about the development of mass tourism).

33. GARF, f. 9228, op. 1, d. 302, ll. 64–76, 106–8, 143–45 (medical reports on how to heal various conditions). In 1937 there were more than 60,000 All-Union and republic health resorts of various kinds. GARF, f. 9228, op. 1, d. 3, l. 1 (report on desired expansion of kurorty).

34. Louise McReynolds, *Russia at Play: Leisure Activities at the End of the Tsarist Era* (Ithaca, N.Y.: Cornell University Press, 2003), 171; Sheila Fitzpatrick, *Everyday Stalinism: Ordinary Life in Extraordinary Times: Soviet Russia in the 1930s* (New York: Oxford University Press, 1999), 246, n50.

35. See, for example, Ronald Hingley, *Under Soviet Skins: An Untourist's Report* (London: Hamish Hamilton, 1961), 45.

36. GARF, f. 9520, op. 1, d. 24, l. 85 (1945 report on the status and expansion of tourist facilities).

37. Ibid., ll. 87–89.

38. GARF, f. 9228, op. 1, d. 302, l. 56 (medical inspection of a kurort), and op. 2, d. 3, ll. 6–7 (report on sanatoria).

39. "Informatsiia orginstruktorskogo otdela MGK VKP(b) G.M. Popovu—o rabote fabrichno-zavodskikh klubov," in Kiselev et al., *Moskva poslevoennaia,* 646–47.

40. The railroad authorities were unprepared, for example, for the enormous number of people using the trains simply to return home in 1946 and 1947. Holland Hunter, "Successful Spatial Management," in *The Impact of World War II on the Soviet Union,* ed. Susan Linz (Totowa, N.J.: Rowman and Allenheld, 1985), 55–56.

41. GARF, f. 9520, op. 1, d. 69, l. 8.

42. Steinbeck, *A Russian Journal,* 120.

43. Dvornichenko, *Razvitie turizma v SSSR,* 44. Soviet experts admitted that not every worker could afford to pay for a trip, especially to places other than the discounted rest homes. GARF, f. 9520, op. 1, d. 69, l. 29.

44. Dvornichenko, *Razvitie turizma v SSSR,* 44.

45. As cited in Elena Zubkova, *Russia After the War: Hopes, Illusions, and Disappointments, 1945–1957,* trans. Hugh Ragsdale (Armonk, N.Y.: M. E. Sharpe, 1998), 42.

46. Interview by research assistant Victor Zatsepine of his great-aunt, June 2001.

47. Sheila Fitzpatrick, "Postwar Soviet Society: The 'Return to Normalcy,' 1945–1953," in *The Impact of World War II on the Soviet Union,* ed. Susan Linz (Totowa, N.J.: Rowman and Allenheld, 1985), 137.

48. Nonetheless, the number of individuals who could be accommodated was still less than 10,000. RGASPI, f. 1, op. 47, d. 412, l. 11 (1957 Tourist-Excursion Bureau report for TsK KPSS).

49. *Trud,* December 13, 1951, 4, in CDSP 2, no. 50 (January 27, 1951): 30.

50. Dobkovich, *Turizm v SSSR,* 3–4.

51. Aleksandr Shinskii, "Zdravnitsa ugolshchikov," *Ogonek* 38 (September 1947): 23–24. The Komsomol also earmarked places for its members. "Vosem tysiach putevok dlia studentov," *Izvestiia,* May 23, 1946, 1.

52. Vera S. Dunham, *In Stalin's Time: Middle-Class Values in Soviet Fiction* (Cambridge: Cambridge University Press, 1976), 5, 17.

53. Irina H. Corten, *Vocabulary of Soviet Society and Culture: A Selected Guide to Russian Words, Idioms, and Expressions of the Post-Stalinist Era, 1953–1991* (Durham, N.C.: Duke University Press, 1992), 148.

54. Michel Gordy, *Visa to Moscow,* trans. Katherine Woods (London: Victor Gollancz, 1953), 381. Official travelers on state business, including the Army Colonel and the Komsomol teacher, often stayed in local hotels [*gostinnitsa*] with their simple rooms, hard beds, and communal sinks in the corridor. Marie Noële Kelly, *Mirror to Russia* (London: Country Life, 1952), 51.

55. Kelly, *Mirror to Russia,* 195.

56. Corten, *Vocabulary,* 41.

57. Leder, *My Life in Stalinist Russia,* 307.

58. Gijs Kessler, "The Passport System and State Control over Population Flows in the Soviet Union, 1932–1940," *Cahiers du monde russe* 42 (April–December 2001): 495; Paul M. Hegenloh, "'Socially Harmful Elements' and the Great Terror," in *Stalinism: New Directions,* ed. Sheila Fitzpatrick (London: Routledge, 2000), 286–308.

59. Leder, *My Life in Stalinist Russia,* 310.

60. GARF, f. 9520, op. 1, d. 79, l. 108 (1948 report on the Krasnodarsk tourist base).

61. Fitzpatrick, "Postwar Soviet Society," 130–37.

62. English, *Russia and the Idea of the West,* 44. See also Zubkova, *Russia After the War,* 18, 33.

63. Zubkova, *Russia After the War,* 105–6.

64. Walter Bedell Smith, *Moscow Mission 1946–1949* (London: Heinemann, 1950), 280.

65. As summarized by Dvornichenko, *Razvitie turizma v SSSR,* 46.

66. GARF, f. 9520, op. 1, d. 24, l. 85.

67. Dvornichenko, *Razvitie turizma v SSSR,* 41–42; L. M. Loginov and Iu. V. Rukhlov, *Istoriia razvitiia turistsko-ekskursionnogo dela* (Moscow: Tsentral'noe reklamno-informatsionnoe biuro "turist," 1989), 38.

68. Steinbeck, *A Russian Journal,* 125.

69. *Kulturnoe stroitelstvo: Statisticheskii sbornik* (Moscow: Gosudastevnnoe statisticheskoe izdatel'stvo, 1956), 286–88.

70. GARF, f. 9520, op. 1, d. 23, ll. 1, 5, 27–34, 35 (information on Moscow tours and a lecture for excursion guides).

71. N. N. Mikhailov, "Moia strana," *Vokrug sveta,* 1 (January 1946): 10.

72. P. V. Sytin, *Po staroi i novoi Moskve: Istoricheskie raiony, glavnye ulitsy i ploshchady velikogo goroda* (Moscow-Leningrad: Detskoi literatury, 1947), 7–8.

73. Von Geldern, "The Centre and the Periphery," 64.

74. "Privetstvie I. V. Stalina k 800-letiiu Moskvy," in Kiselev et al., *Moskva poslevoennaia,* 249–50.

75. Sytin, *Po staroi i novoi Moskve,* 5–6.

76. Steinbeck, *A Russian Journal,* 114.

77. GARF, f. 9520, op. 1, d. 23, l. 66 (instructions for Moscow theater excursion leader).

78. Ibid.

79. Anatolii Loginov, *Nasha Moskva* (Moscow: Moskovskii rabochii, 1947), 111.

80. Ibid., 112.

81. "Iz stenogrammy soveshchaniia sekretarei RK VKP(b) i predsedatelei ispolkomov raionnykh sovetov g. Moskvy—o podgotovke k prazdnovaniiu 800-letiia Moskvy," in Kiselev et al., *Moskva poslevoennaia,* 226.

82. Ibid., 225.

83. Iu. Savitskii, *Moskva: Istoriko-arkhitekturnyi ocherk* (Moscow: Moskovskii rabochii, 1947).

84. N. Kuleshov and A. Pozdnev, *Vysotnye zdaniia Moskvy* (Moscow: Moskovskii rabochii, 1954).

85. Sytin, *Po staroi i novoi Moskve*, 8.

86. See, for example, O. A. Arkhangel'skaia, *Turistskie marshruty po SSSR* (Moscow: Izdatel'stvo VTsSPS "Profizdat," 1956), 280.

87. *Vernye druzia*, director M. Kalatozov (1954). I am grateful to Susan Reid for bringing this film to my attention. Katerina Clark traces the "reversal of the symbolic meaning of Moscow" in post-Stalin fiction in *The Soviet Novel: History as Ritual*, 3rd ed. (Bloomington Indiana University Press, 2000), 227–29.

88. A. Yerokhin, "Guide Through Antiquity," *Pravda*, September 23, 1951, 3, in CDSP 3, no. 38 (November 3, 1951): 33–34.

89. N. Moskvin, "The Hospitality of Cities," *Literaturnaia gazeta*, July 5, 1951, 28, in CDSP 3, no. 28 (August 25, 1951): 28.

90. G. Shirshov, "Pervyi vsesoiuznyi motoprobeg," *Izvestiia*, October 15, 1947, 2.

91. On the expansion of tourism and the Russian state into non-Slavic areas in the late imperial period, see McReynolds, *Russia at Play*, ch. 5.

92. Ilya Ehrenburg, "Ilya Ehrenberg's America," *Harper's Magazine* (December 1946): 568. The portions of Erenburg's travel account devoted to race relations were reprinted (with some of the more optimistic parts deleted) and accompanied by photos from Ebony, in Ilya Erenburg, "Belye i chernye," *Vokrug sveta*, 1 (1947): 22–27.

93. S. Gerasimov, "Na beregu Tikhogo okeana," *Ogonek* 1:43 (October 1947): 24.

94. "Rodnaia sovetskaia zemlia," *Ogonek* 1:43 (October 1947): 28.

95. Khemaiak Kazandzhian, "Amerikanskaia deistvitelnost," *Ogonek* 2:2 (January 1948): 3.

96. L. Rusanovoi, "Pervyi transatlanticheskii reis zakonchen," *Ogonek* 1:28 (July 1947): 11.

97. "Rodnaia sovetskaia zemlia," 28.

98. V. V. Pokhishishevskii, "Shestnadtsat stolits," *Vokrug sveta*, no. 11 (November 1947): 2–11.

99. "Tadzhikistan's Oldest City," *Pravda*, June 10, 1949, 3, in CDSP 1, no. 24 (July 12, 1949): 62.

100. "V novoi Mongolii," *Ogonek* 1:51 (December 1947): 16; Aleksandr Gutorovich, "Na plotakh cherez vodopady karpat," *Ogonek* 1:45 (November 1947): 23; Vladimir Dmitrevskii, "Na turetskoi granitse," *Ogonek* 1:29 (July 1947): 7.

101. Kelly, *Mirror to Russia*, 211.

102. Steinbeck, *A Russian Journal*, 172.

103. GARF, f. 9520, op. 1, d. 361, l. 10 (report from a tourist base in Georgia, June 1958).

104. Kelly, Mirror to Russia, 192.

105. Leder, *My Life in Stalinist Russia*, 307.

106. Jill Steward, "Tourism in Late Imperial Austria: The Development of Tourist Cultures and Their Associated Images of Place," in *Being Elsewhere*, ed. Baranowski and Furlough, 116.

107. Jeffrey Brooks, *Thank You, Comrade Stalin! Soviet Public Culture from Revolu-*

tion to Cold War (Princeton, N.J.: Princeton University Press, 1999), 196; Zubkova, *Russia After the War*, 97, 148.

108. See, for example, Susan E. Reid, "Cold War in the Kitchen: Gender and the De-Stalinization of Consumer Taste in the Soviet Union under Khrushchev," *Slavic Review* 61 (summer 2002): 211–52.

109. Baranowski and Furlough, eds., "Introduction," *Being Elsewhere*, 20.

110. G. Rassadin and I. Filippov, "Gorod neboskrebov i trushchob: Pismo iz Niu-Iorka," *Pravda*, April 7, 1950, 4.

111. E. Litoshko, "V trushchobakh Niu-Iorka," *Pravda*, September 23, 1952, 3.

112. "V gorode-kurorte," *Izvestiia*, March 26, 1946.

113. On the conflict between communist morality and consumerism in the Khrushchev era, see Catriona Kelly, *Refining Russia: Advice Literature, Polite Culture, and Gender from Catherine to Yeltsin* (Oxford: Oxford University Press, 2001), ch. 5, esp. 312–21.

114. Dobkovich, *Turizm v SSSR*, 4.

115. *Ogonek* 2:18 (April 1948): back cover.

116. *Vokrug sveta* 9 (September 1952): back cover.

117. L. Mikhailov and A. Shin, "Passazhiry 'Chernomorskogo ekspressa,'" *Ogonek* 1:23 (June 1947): 10–11.

118. "Prodazha avtomobelei, mototsiklov I velosipedov," *Ogonek* 1:41 (October 1947): 12.

119. Philip Hanson, *Advertising and Socialism* (London: International Arts and Sciences Press, 1974), 29–30; Catriona Kelly and Vadim Volkov, "Directed Desires," in *Constructing Russian Culture in the Age of Revolution, 1881–1940*, ed. Catriona Kelly and David Shepherd (Oxford: Oxford University Press, 1998), 293.

120. John Keep, *A History of the Soviet Union, 1945–1991* (Oxford: Oxford University Press, 1995, 2002), 23–24.

121. On vacationing as "an arena in which fantasy has become an important social practice," see Löfgren, *On Holiday*, 7.

122. Dunham, *In Stalin's Time*, 46. On lamp shades and other consumer items, also see Julie Hessler, "Cultured Trade: The Stalinist Turn Towards Consumerism," in *Stalinism: New Directions*, ed. Fitzpatrick, 182–209.

123. Clark, *The Soviet Novel*, 197.

124. Ibid., 198.

125. Gordey, *Visa to Moscow*, 354.

126. P. Ponomarev, "Letter to the Editor," *Izvestiia*, June 28, 1951, 3, in CDSP 3, no. 26 (August 11, 1951): 28–29.

127. G. Osipov, "Sanitary Shower," *Izvestiia*, August 5, 1951, in CDSP 3, no. 31 (September 15, 1951): 31.

128. I. Rudakov, "Neglected Resort," *Izvestiia*, August 22, 1950, 2, in CDSP 2, no. 34 (October 7, 1950): 53.

129. Moskvin, "The Hospitality of Cities," 17.

130. Makarov, "For Mass Touring," 28.

131. "Soviet Workers' Vacations," *Literaturnaia gazeta*, May 27, 1952, in CDSP 4, no. 23 (July 19, 1952): 33.

132. S. Makarov, "Behind a 'Favorable' Figure," *Trud*, June 24, 1952, in CDSP 4, no. 26 (August 9, 1952): 32.

133. Makarov, "Behind a 'Favorable' Figure."

134. See, for example, GARF, f. 9520, op. 1, d. 54, l. 121 and d. 35, ll. 49, 51, 61, 83, 89.

135. Dvornichenko, *Razvitie turizma v SSSR*, 45–46.
136. Wright Miller, *Russians as People* (London: Phoenix House, 1960), 93.
137. Moskvin, "The Hospitality of Cities," 2.
138. I have borrowed this very useful notion from Robert Edelman, *Serious Fun: A History of Spectator Sports in the USSR* (New York: Oxford University Press, 1993).
139. Dobkovich, *Turizm v SSSR*, 3–4.
140. GARF, f. 9520, op. 1, d. 252, l. 13. "Get to know [your country] and fall in love with everything about it," concluded N. N. Mikhailov in *Nasha strana* (Moscow: Molodaia gvardiia, 1945), 100.
141. Daniel J. Boorstin, *The Image: A Guide to Pseudo-Events in America* (New York: Atheneum, 1962).
142. Dean MacCannell, *The Tourist: A New Theory of the Leisure Class* (New York: Schocken, 1976); Koshar, *German Travel Cultures*, 8; Löfgren, *On Holiday*, 7.
143. As cited in Koshar, *German Travel Cultures*, 8.
144. I have adopted the notion of travel as a "ritual of reassurance" from Linda Ellerbee, "No Shit! There I Was . . . ," in *A Woman's Path: Women's Best Spiritual Travel Writing*, ed. Lucy McCauley, Amy G. Carlson, and Jennifer Leo (San Francisco: Travelers Tales, 2000), 63.

Chapter 8. Dangerous Liaisons

1. Household appliances made by the Slovenian company Gorenje, for example, were especially popular. Ferenc Hammer, "The Saga of the Gorenje Refrigerator," *Civic Arts Review* (Winter 1995): 19. On the workings of consumerism in Yugoslavia, see Patrick Hyder Patterson, "The New Class: Consumer Culture Under Socialism and the Unmaking of the Yugoslav Dream, 1945–1991" (Ph.D. diss., University of Michigan, 2001); Patrick Hyder Patterson, "Truth Half Told: Finding the Perfect Pitch for Advertising and Marketing in Socialist Yugoslavia, 1950–1991," *Enterprise & Society* 4, no. 2 (June 2003): 179–225.
2. Margita Grossman et al., *Reiseabsichten der DDR-Bürger 1990* (Berlin: Verlag für universitäre Kommunikation, 1990), 7.
3. This study samples the coverage of two important weekly women's magazines: East Germany's *Für dich* and Hungary's *Nők lapja*. While travel and tourism represented only a fraction of the wide-ranging coverage of these publications, these themes were nevertheless repeated and consistent, and they remained so throughout the Yugoslav consumerist heyday of the 1960s and 1970s.
4. A comprehensive bibliography is published at: http://www-gewi.kfunigraz .ac.at/suedost/tourism/#Bibliography (accessed October 16, 2005).
5. Nelson H. H. Graburn, "Tourism: The Sacred Journey," in *Hosts and Guests: The Anthropology of Tourism*, ed. Valene L. Smith (Philadelphia: University of Pennsylvania Press, 1977), 17–31, at 21–22; see generally 18–23.
6. See, e.g., Igor Duda, *U potrazi za odmorom i blagostanjem: O povijesti dokolice i potrošačkog društva u Hrvatskoj 1950-ih i 1960-ih* (Zagreb: Srednja Europa, 2005).
7. Dennison Nash, "Tourism as a Form of Imperialism," in *Hosts and Guests: The Anthropology of Tourism*, ed. Valene L. Smith (Philadelphia: University of Pennsylvania Press, 1977), 33–47; Valene L. Smith and Maryann Brent, eds., *Hosts and Guests Revisited: Tourism Issues of the 21st Century* (New York: Cognizant Communication, 2001).
8. Shelley Baranowski and Ellen Furlough, eds., *Being Elsewhere: Tourism, Con-

sumer Culture, and Identity in Modern Europe and America (Ann Arbor: University of Michigan Press, 2001).

9. Among the most influential studies are Dean MacCannell, *The Tourist: A New Theory of the Leisure Class* (Berkeley: University of California Press, 1999) [1976]; Valene L. Smith, ed., *Hosts and Guests: The Anthropology of Tourism* (Philadelphia: University of Pennsylvania Press, 1977); Chris Rojek and John Urry, eds., *Touring Cultures: Transformations of Travel and Theory* (New York: Routledge, 1997); and John Urry, *Consuming Places* (New York : Routledge, 1995).

10. But see, e.g., Igor Duda, "Dokono mnoštvo otkriva Hrvatsku: Engleski turistički vodiči kao izvor zapovijest putovanja na istočnu jadransku obalu od 1958. do 1969," *Časopis za suvremenu povijest* 35, no. 3 (2003): 803–22 (on English tourist guides to Yugoslavia's Adriatic coast).

11. Special issue on Tourism and Travel in Russia and the Soviet Union, *Slavic Review* 62, no. 4 (Winter 2003). See also Wendy Bracewell, "East Looks West: East European Travel Writing on Europe," in *Călători români in Occident*, eds. Nicolae Bocşan and Ioan Bolovan (Cluj-Napoca: Institutul Cultural Român, 2004), 11–23; Igor Duda, "I vlakom na vikend: Prilog socijalnoj i kulturnoj povijesti slobodnoga vremena u Hrvatskoj krajem 1960-ih," *Časopis za suvremenu povijest*, 34, no. 3 (2002): 659–78 (on domestic tourism in Croatia in the 1960s).

12. Diane P. Koenker, "Travel to Work, Travel to Play: On Russian Tourism, Travel, and Leisure," *Slavic Review* 62, no. 4 (Winter 2003): 657–65, at 659.

13. See, e.g., László Taál, "A vállalat szociálpolitikai tevékenysége" [The Sociopolitical Activity of the Company], *IBUSZ tájékoztató* [IBUSZ Bulletin] 1, nos. 2–3 (March 1978): 6. On the "social, economic, and cultural-ideological influences and consequences" of foreign travel, see "Nyílt idegenforgalmi politika" [Open Foreign-Tourism Policy], *IBUSZ tájékoztató* 2, no. 9 (n.d.) [1979]: 11; T. Házi Zsuzsa, "Pártszerű, reális, objektív tájékoztatás" [Party-spirited, Realistic, Objective Information], *IBUSZ tájékoztató* 3, no. 2 (n.d.) [1980]: 1–2; "Természetjárás a forradalmi munkásmozgalom szolgálatában" [Nature Walks in the Service of the Revolutionary Workers' Movement], *Turista magazin* 6, nos. 11–12 (November–December 1960): 3–4.

14. "90 éves a Turista Magazin" [*Tourist Magazine* Celebrates 90 Years], *IBUSZ tájékoztató* 2, no. 12 (n.d.) [1979]: 8 (emphasis in the original). *Turista* editor Lajos Endrődi stressed in this interview that his magazine's aim was to describe destinations accessible to all parts of the Hungarian population. Implicitly and explicitly, this necessitated a heavy emphasis on travel in Hungary and in other socialist countries. Ibid.

15. See, e.g., György Szomory, "A jó turisztika egyenlő a műveltséggel" [Good Tourism Is Equivalent to Cultivation], *Turista magazin* no. 6 (June 1980): 18. In this regard, the tourism policies of the Eastern European states and the USSR share some characteristics with efforts by a variety of western European Marxists to organize a socialist alternative to capitalist travel and leisure. More uncomfortably, there are also certain parallels to the attempt by the Nazi party-state to build a "healthy," solidary society in the *Kraft durch Freude* ("Strength Through Joy") movement. See Shelley Baranowski, *Strength Through Joy: Consumerism and Mass Tourism in the Third Reich* (Cambridge: Cambridge University Press, 2004). I am grateful to James Brophy for calling attention to these correspondences between state-socialist practice and other collectivist conceptualizations of tourism and leisure.

16. See Graburn, "Tourism: The Sacred Journey," 18.

17. "Entdeckungsreise durch die Republik," *Für dich* no. 18 (April 1963).

18. See also the travel and tourism monthly *Unterwegs: Magazin für Wandern, Bergsteigen, Zelten, Reisen,* published from 1957 to 1962 by the East German government's Komitee für Touristik und Wandern der DDR.

19. On the connections between tourism and patriotism in the USSR, see Anne E. Gorsuch, "'There's No Place Like Home': Soviet Tourism in Late Stalinism," *Slavic Review* 62, no. 4 (winter 2003): 760–85, esp.771–75. Reprinted in Chapter 7 of the present volume.

20. Gorsuch, "'There's No Place Like Home,'" 785. See also Gorsuch, "Time Travellers: Soviet Tourism to Eastern Europe in the Khrushchev Era," in *Turizm: The Russian and East European Tourist under Capitalism and Socialism,* ed. Anne E. Gorsuch and Diane P. Koenker (Cornell University Press, forthcoming).

21. Marguerite S. Shaffer, *See America First: Tourism and National Identity, 1880–1940* (Washington, D.C.: Smithsonian Institution, 2001), 3–4.

22. On domestic tourism in the GDR, see Wolfgang Albrecht and Gertrud Albrecht, "Stadttourismus in der Ehemaligen DDR," in *Stadt, Kultur, Freizeit; Freizeit und Tourismus in der ehemaligen DDR,* 8. Sitzung des Arbeitskreises "Freizeit- und Fremdenverkehrsgeographie" in *Frankfurt am Main 1990* (Berlin: W. Moser/Verlag für Universitäre Kommunikation, 1992).

23. See Heidrun Budde, *Reisen in die Bundesrepublik und der "gläserne" DDR-Bürger: Eine Dokumentation* (Baden-Baden: Nomos, 1997); William Sólyom-Fekete, *Legal Restrictions on Foreign Travel by the German Democratic Republic* (Washington, D.C.: Library of Congress, 1978).

24. Tibor Dessewffy, "Speculators and Travellers: The Political Construction of the Tourist in the Kádár Regime," *Cultural Studies* 16, no. 1 (January 2002): 44–62.

25. See Alenka Švab, "Consuming Western Image of Well-Being—Shopping Tourism in Socialist Slovenia," *Cultural Studies* 16, no. 1 (January 2002): 63–71; Liviu Chelcea, "The Culture of Shortage during State-Socialism: Consumption Practices in a Romanian Village in the 1980s," *Cultural Studies* 16, no. 1 (January 2002): 16–43.

26. See Patterson, "The New Class," 10–11.

27. Budget issues, for example, pervade the pull-out "mini-dictionary" entitled "Mit kell tudniuk a külföldre utazóknak?" [What Do We Need to Know for Travels Abroad?], *Turista* 6 (June 1980): 19–26. On the growth and significance of cross-border travel between Hungary and Austria, see also József Böröcz, *Leisure Migration: A Sociological Study on Tourism* (Oxford: Pergamon, 1996).

28. See Catherine A. Lutz and Jane A. Collins, *Reading National Geographic* (Chicago: University of Chicago Press, 1993).

29. See, e.g., Dénes Balázs, "A nagy kaland" [The Great Adventure], *Természetjárás* 5, no. 2 (February 1959): s.n.; Balázs, "A nagy kaland," *Természetjárás* 5, no. 7 (July 1959): 4–5 (portions of a multipart series describing travels in China); György Lewald, "Indiában a gazdagok sportja a turistaság" [In India the Sport of the Rich Is Tourism], *Turista* 6, no. 8 (August 1960): 14.

30. See, e.g., Albert Donle, "Barkarole 1957," *Unterwegs* 2, no. 2 (1958): 24–28, on the grandeur and the misery of Venice: gouging restaurateurs, extortionist gondoliers, and above all, grinding poverty. Cf. György Csapó, *Utak, terek, emberek* [Roads, Squares, People] (Budapest: Gondolat, 1976), 274, where the author depicted Italy as mired in an economic and social crisis typical of the contemporary West and asked, "where is the *dolce vita?*"

31. See the statistical tables included in Appendices 1 and 2.

32. N.L., "IBUSZ—Belgrád," *IBUSZ tájékoztató* 1, no. 11 (November 1978): 6.

33. See Appendixes 1 and 2. Statistics on foreigners traveling to Yugoslavia can be found in *Statistički bilten* (Belgrade: Savezni zavod za statistiku); issues reviewed include nos. 63, 585, 613, 673, 737, 797, 851, 915, 974, 1046, 1093, 1143, 1251, 1364, 1416, 1632, 1677, and 1752. See also *Jugoslavija 1918–1988: Statistički godišnjak* (Belgrade: Savezni zavod za statistiku, 1989). For Czechoslovak travel abroad, see *Statistická ročenka Československé Socialistické Republiky*; see especially the reports for 1961, 1965, 1966, 1970, 1973, 1976, 1981, and 1986; data covering the end of the communist period can be found in *Statistická ročenka České a Slovenské federativní republiky 1990*. For Hungary, see *Statisztikai évkönyv* (Budapest: Központi Statisztikai Hivatal); see especially the reports for 1965, 1970, 1971, 1975, 1980, 1982, 1984, 1985, 1989, and 1990. For the GDR, see Staatlichen Zentralverwaltung für Statistik, *Statistisches Jahrbuch der Deutschen Demokratischen Republik* (Berlin: VEB Deutscher Zentralverlag, 1956–1990); see especially the reports for 1963–1989. Condensed data can be found in English in some issues of the *Statistical Pocket Book of the German Democratic Republic* (Berlin: Staatsverlag der Deutschen Demokratischen Republik, various dates).

34. T. Házi Zsuzsa, "Öt évre szóló szerződés a Generaltourist-tal" [A Five-Year Contract with Generaltourist], *IBUSZ tájékoztató* 2, no. 8 (n.d.) [1979]: 2.

35. Rajko Doleček, *Na cestách: příběhy z jednoho světa* (Ostrava: Profil, 1989), 113.

36. See, e.g., Lajos Endrödi, "Az Adria úszó kőbárkái" [The Floating Stone Boats of the Adriatic], *Turista* 10 (October 1980): 8–10; Endrödi, "Bosznia és Hercegovina hegyei között" [Among the Mountains of Bosnia-Hercegovina], *Turista magazin* no. 11 (November 1980): 10–12.

37. See, e.g., Gyula Bács, *Jugoszlávia* (Budapest: Panoráma, 1968); Bács, *Jugoszlávia*, 5th ed. (Budapest: Panoráma, 1983); Bács, *A Jugoszláv tengerpart* [The Yugoslav Seaside] (Budapest: Panoráma, 1987).

38. Along these lines, see also Gyula Várady and István Roman, *Mit kell tudni Jugoszláviáról?* [What Do We Need to Know about Yugoslavia?] (Budapest: Kossuth Könyvkiadó, 1978). Though the volume represents a different type of source material—a handbook rather than a tourist guidebook—the similarities in content and tone between the language used here and the corresponding sections of many guidebooks are striking and revealing.

39. Nina Heřmanová and authors' collective, *Jugoslávie* (Prague: Olympia, 1984), 19–33, 43–47. A particularly revealing mixture of photographs in a well-illustrated Polish guidebook appears in Maria Krukowska, *Jugosławia* (Warsaw: Wiedza Powszechna, 1965); see, e.g., 161 (electrical generators), 256 (Bosnian metalworks).

40. Nina Heřmanová and authors' collective, *Jugoslávie*, 126–27.

41. References here and in the preceeding paragraph are to Gyula Bács, *Belgrád*, 2nd ed. (Budapest: Panorama, 1981), 48, 33; see also 13, 48. The traditional socialist reflexes apparently died hard, however: the book also describes in fairly numbing detail the heavy industries of the city and its environs. See also Henryk Zdanowski, *Belgradzkie ABC* [Belgrade ABC] (Warsaw: Iskry, 1966).

42. Gyöngyvér Udvary and Lajos Vincze, *Az ismeretlen szomszéd* [The Unknown Neighbor] (Budapest: Gondolat, 1968), 97.

43. See, e.g., Éva Nyárádi and Róbert Nyárádi, *Hat év Jugoszláviában* [Six Years in Yugoslavia] (Budapest: Kossuth Könyvkiadó, 1980). The account largely steers clear of Yugoslavia's consumerist success. But there was a brief nod to the commercial culture found in Maribor, ibid., 114.

44. Rajko Doleček, *Na cestách: příběhy z jednoho světa* (Ostrava: Profil, 1989), 132.

45. István Lázár, *Adriai nyár: Jugoszláviai útinapló* [Adriatic Summer: A Yugoslav Travel Diary] ([Budapest]: Koszmosz, 1968), 21.

46. Ibid., 20.

47. Examples are legion. See, e.g., "Abends an der Moskva," *Für dich* no. 4 (January 1963): 30–33; "Reisejournal Debrecen," *Für dich* no. 8 (1980): 23–26; and the series of articles on Bulgaria appearing in *Für dich* nos. 28, 29, 33, and 35 (1980).

48. See, e.g., Anna Földes, "Rajnaparti jegyzetek" [Notes from the Banks of the Rhine], *Nők lapja* 24, no. 3 (January 15, 1972): [s.n.]; Földes, "Rajnaparti jegyzetek," *Nők lapja* 24, no. 4 (January 22, 1972): 6–8; see also, e.g., Irén Németi, "Párizsi történetek" [Paris Stories], *Nők lapja* 24, no. 43 (October 21, 1972): 6–7; B.K., "25 éves a Disneyland" [Disneyland Celebrates 25 Years], *Turista* no. 8 (August 1980): 31.

49. See, e.g., "Budapester Modellalltag," *Für dich* no. 33 (August 1972): 18–21, 40; "Modisches aus Budapest," *Für dich* no. 46 (1980): 33–37.

50. Wendy Bracewell, "Adventures in the Marketplace: Yugoslav Travel Writing and Tourism in the 1950s–1960s," in *Turizm*, ed. Gorsuch and Koenker (forthcoming).

51. See "Von der Kettenbrücke bis zu den Pelikanen," *Für dich* no. 36 (September 1972): 12–15. In contrast, see the quite favorable treatment given to Yugoslavia in another, much earlier down-the-Danube travelogue from the GDR: Helmut Hauptmann, *Donaufahrt zu dritt: Streiflichter von einer kleinen Grossfahrt durch Deutschland, Österreich, die Slowakei, Ungarn und Jugoslawien* (Berlin: Neues Leben, 1957). The peculiar characteristics of Hauptmann's account bear noting: it appeared before the dramatic tightening of travel restrictions that accompanied the erection of the Berlin Wall, and well in advance of Yugoslavia's emergence as a socialist version of consumers' paradise. Moreover, the unusual mode of travel—a tiny boat taken down the river—distances the work from the mass-tourism experiences of later years. As such, the substantial and positive coverage found here does little to counteract the prevailing invisibility of Yugoslavia in East German sources.

Chapter 9. A Means of Last Resort

The author would like to thank the University of North Alabama for research support in writing this chapter, including a College of Arts and Sciences Research Grant. Ms. Cathleen Baird, Director and Archivist at the Hospitality Industry Archives and Library provided crucial assistance and intellectual inspiration for this project. All newspapers and periodicals have been accessed electronically, unless they are part of an archival collection. If page numbers are not available, please consult electronic format of specified journal or newspaper. All speeches by Fidel Castro have been accessed through the University of Texas's electronic LANIC Castro database at http://lanic.utexas.edu/la/cb/cuba/castro.html.

Note to epigraph: As quoted in "El encanto de las playas de Varadero," *El País* (August 12, 1994).

1. Letter from Ramón Blanco, Capitán General de Cuba, to Máximo Gomez, April 1898, on exhibit in the Palacio de los Capitanes Generales, Havana, Cuba.

2. See Louis Perez, Jr., *On Becoming Cuban: Identity, Nationality, and Culture*

(Chapel Hill: University of North Carolina Press, 1999) and *The United States and Cuba: Ties of Singular Intimacy* (Athens: University of Georgia, 1990).

3. Author's notes and interview with Graciela Perez Sanchez, Museum Official, February 10 and 11, 2004, Varadero Municipal Museum, Varadero, Cuba.

4. "Muestra del Mes: Mansión Xanadu, Características Constructivas," August 1998, Varadero Museo Municipal, Varadero Cuba, pamphlet in author's collection.

5. Robert Caverly to Conrad N. Hilton (CNH), February 11, 1959, Hospitality Industry Archives and Library, University of Houston (HIAL), CNH Collection, Hilton Hotel Corporation Record Group (RG HHC), Box 10, Folder 12.

6. Ibid.

7. Ibid.

8. Sid Wilner, oral history interview by Cathleen Baird, HIAL, August 1, 1995, 15.

9. CNH to Arthur Elminger, November 21, 1959, HIAL, CNH Collection, RG HHC, Box 10, Folder 2.

10. Elminger to CNH November 23, 1959, HIAL, CNH Collection, RG HHC, Box 10, Folder 2.

11. See Fidel Ruz Castro (FRC), "Castro Speech to the Food Industry Workers," *Obra Revolucionaria*, no. 9 (June 16, 1960), 5–20; Also see FRC, "Castro Speaks to Hotel Workers Union," Radio Progreso transcript, June 16, 1960.

12. Michael M. Lefever and Cathleen D. Baird, "The Expropriation of the Habana Hilton: A Timely Reminder," *International Journal of Hospitality Management*, 9, no. 1 (1990), 14–20.

13. FRC, "Castro Speaks to Hotel Workers Union."

14. Edwin Tetlow, *Eye on Cuba* (New York: Harcourt, Brace and World, 1966), 55.

15. Ibid., 132–33.

16. Bruce Taylor, "Cuba: Revolution vs. Tourism," in *Fodor's Guide to the Caribbean, Bahamas, and Bermuda, 1967*, ed. Eugene Fodor (New York: David McKay Company, 1967), 200, 204.

17. Thomas Salkey, *Havana Journal* (New York: Penguin Books, 1971), 23.

18. Paula DiPerna, *The Complete Travel Guide to Cuba* (1979), 26.

19. Mauricio Vicent, "El capitalismo llega al Habana Libre," *El País*, March 22, 1993.

20. Mauricio Vicent, "La Coca-Cola revoluciona Cuba," *El País*, September 2, 1993.

21. FRC, "Mass Rally at Giron Victory Square," *Havana Domestic Service*, June 30, 1988.

22. Ibid.

23. Much of the information on Sol Meliá's expansion came directly from the Director of Communications office at Sol Meliá. Ms. Cristina Molina in the Sol Meliá office graciously researched and drafted a document in response to my questions. The director of Sol Meliá in Cuba, Gabriel Canaves, also contributed critical information to this account of Sol Meliá's entry and growth in Cuba.

24. "El Grupo Martiñon incia a final de año las obreas de tres nuevos hoteles en Cuba," La provincia section, *Diario de las Palmas*, February 17, 2000.

25. Mauricio Vicent, "La bendición de Fidel Castro," *El País*, October 2, 1998.

26. The seminal article, "Baleares. El Prestigio empresarial de una región; Las companías mas activas," *Expansión* (Madrid), November 19, 2003, provides

the most thorough overview of the tremendous impact that the islands' hotel operators have had in Spain and the Caribbean.

27. *EFE Spanish Newswire Services (EFE)*, "Cuba-España: Presidente Autonomia Balear Visita Varadero," February 5, 2000.

28. *EFE*, "Cuba-España: Presidente Autonomia Balear Se Reunion Seis Horas con Castro," February 6, 2000; *EFE*, "Cuba-España: President Communidad Canaria se entrevisto con Fidel Castro," May 14, 2000.

29. Author's communication with Gabriel Canaves, March 4, 2004.

30. Candido Dominguez, "Castro, Others Analyze Varadero Development," *Gramna*, September 27, 1988, LANIC Castro Database; FRC, "Mass Rally at Giron Victory Square," Havana Domestic Service, June 30, 1988; FRC, "Castro Discusses Tourism Plans, Medical Issues," *Tele-Rebelde* Network transcript, September 26, 1988.

31. FRC, "Castro Speaks at Partnership Hotel Inauguration," *Havana Cuba Vision* Network transcript, May 10, 1990.

32. FRC, "Fidel Castro Speaks at Hotel Opening 14 December," Meliá Varadero, December 14, 1991, *Tele Rebelde* Network transcript.

33. Ibid.; www.dr1.com, "Nature in Harmony with Tourism Development," June 26, 2001.

34. "Castro, Delegates Comment at Havana PCC Meeting," *Tele Rebelde* Network transcript, November 17, 1993.

35. Ibid.

36. Ibid.

37. Ibid.

38. Robert B. Morley to Mr. Aronson, "Cuba's Declining Trade Prospects," www.foia.state.gov/documents, January 24, 1990.

39. Elizabeth Pisani, "Cuban Trade Caught in Battle for Florida Vote: A New Law Aimed at Winning Support from an Exile Community," *Financial Times*, October 27, 1992, 6.

40. Bruno Rodriguez Parrilla, "Measure to Eliminated International Terrorism," "Measures to Eliminate International Terrorism," General Assembly, Fifty-Sixth Session, Agenda Item 166, Security Council, October 29, 2001.

41. The Cuban American National Foundation (CANF) published a study in 1993 suggesting that the Cuban economy and polity would collapse by July 1993.

42. See Joaquin Roy, "The Helms-Burton Law: Development, Consequences, and Legacy for Inter-American and European-U.S. Relations," *Journal of Inter-American Studies and World Affairs*, 39, no. 3 (fall 1997), 77; For a more rigorous treatment, see Roy, *Cuba, the United States, and the Helms-Burton Doctrine: International Reactions* (Gainesville: University of Florida Press, 2000).

43. Mauricio Vicent, "La Helms-Burton amenaza otra vez a Sol Meliá las reclamaciones de antiguos propietarios ponen en jaque a la practica totalidad del sector turístico en Cuba," *El País*, November 7, 1999.

44. *New York Times*, "Spanish Companies in Crossfire of U.S.-Cuba Battle," July 20, 1996, section 1, 39. David Ing, "Spanish Chain Nixes Cuba Deal," *Hotel and Motel Management*, 211, no. 13 (July 22, 1996): 10.

45. "Spanish Companies in Crossfire of U.S.-Cuba Battle," *New York Times*, July 20, 1996, section 1, page 39. Vicent, "Sol Meliá y la herencia de los Duponts," *El País*, July 17, 1996.

46. "La lista negra de ee uu incluirá al grupo sol por sus hotels en cuba," *El País*, May 22, 1996.

47. Mauricio Vicent, "Sol Meliá ampliará inversiones en Cuba pese a la ley Helms-Burton," *El País*, May 24, 1996.

48. "U.S. Won't Punish Spanish Group 'For Now,' " *Miami Herald*, October 8, 1996, A7.

49. Administración del Senado, "Informe sobre las relaciones con Cuba," Boletín Oficial de las Cortes generales, Senado, VI legislatura, serie I: *Boletín General*, March 17, 1997.

50. The United States also established a Registry of Claims at the same time in order to facilitate the due process of reclamations by Cuban exiles.

51. Sixto Martinez, "El presidente Cubano acusa al país norteamericano de una 'permanente conspiración,' " *La Estrella Digital*, March 11, 1999, www.fut.es/~mpgp/amigos266.htm.

52. G. Gonzales and G. Manzano, "Presiones y intereses," *Cinco Días*, August 13, 1999, 16. The authors noted, "The renewal of the investigations concerning Sol Meliá took place immediately after the pressure exerted this past July by Senator Jesse Helms over the government of Bill Clinton."

53. "EEUU aplica la ley Helms Burton a Club Med y a la alemana LTE," *El País*, September 10, 1999.

54. Vicent, "La Helms-Burton."

55. Olata Arrieta, "Los hoteleros de EE UU premian a Sol Meliá y el Gobierno investiga sus inversiones en Cuba," *Ideal*, November 10, 1999, www.cubanet.com.

56. Radio Havana Cuba on *BBC Summary of World Broadcasts*, December 4, 1999.

57. The governor of the Balearic Islands, Francesc Antich, vowed to "do what is necessary to not leave these businesses without support that operate 'outside of Spain.' " *EFE* Spanish Newswire Services, "Sol Meliá 'Desconoce' Ultimatum y Recuerda apoyos España y EU," October 30, 1999.

58. Cortes Generales, Diario de Sesiones del congreso de los diputados, comisiones, 1999, VI legislatura, numero 754, Asuntos Exteriores, Sesion 58, Sr. D. Francisco Javier Rupérez Rubio (president), www.senado.es/boletines/CO0754.html.

59. Ibid.

60. See Jesse Helms to Honorable Thomas Pickering, November 16, 2000, www.cubatraderpublications.com/Helmsletter/index.htm; also see "Helms Demands Helms-Burton Sanctions Against Spanish Hotel Chain," November 21, 2000, www.cubatraderpublications.com/story5/.

61. U.S.-Cuba Trade and Economic Council, "Trademark and Patent Registration Procedures."

62. Antonio Cano, "Negocios, si; en Cuba, tambien," *El País*, February 8, 1996.

63. Mauricio Vicent, "Array," *El País*, June 3, 2002.

Afterword

1. Tourism Institute of America, "Did You Know? Tourism Facts," http://www.tia.org/index.html, accessed November 16, 2005.

2. New Zealand Ministry of Tourism, "Keytourism Statistics, accessed online at http://www.trcnz.govt.nz/NR/rdonlyres/6A3DA5F7-2CAD-4618-B610-EFC 861876A8F/17074/KeyTourismStatistics1.pdf.

3. "Tonga Statistics Department—Tourism," http://www.spc.int/prism/Country/TO/stats/Tourism/Tourism/htm.

4. "Statistics Iceland—Tourism Industry," http:///www.statice.is/?pageid = 1512&src = /tempt_en/feedamal/ferdaidnadur. asp.

5. Office of National Statistics, *Travel Trends, 2003: A Report on the International Passenger Survey* (London: Her Majesty's Stationery Office, 2004), 9, accessed online at http://www.statistics.gov.uk/downloads/theme_transport/tt2003web .pdf.

6. Seymour Dunbar, *A History of Travel in America: Being an Outline of the Development in Modes of Travel from Archaic Vehicles of Colonial Times to the Completion of the First Transcontinental Railroad: The Influence of the Indians on the Free Movement and Territorial Unity of the White Race: The Part Played by Travel Methods in the Economic Conquest of the Continent: and Those Related Human Experiences, Changing Social Conditions and Governmental Attitudes Which Accompanied the Growth of a National Travel System* (New York: Tudor Publishing Company, 1937, [1915]), 1357.

7. *Harper's Weekly*, "The Pacific Railroad," May 29, 1869.

8. Leo Marx, *The Machine in the Garden: Technology and the Pastoral Ideal in America* (New York: Oxford University Press, 1964), Wolfgang Schivelbusch, *The Railway Journey: The Industrialization of Time and Space in the Nineteenth Century* (Berkeley: University of California Press, 1986); Kathleen Franz, *Tinkering: Consumers Reinvent the Early Automobile* (Philadelphia: University of Pennsylvania Press, 2005); Amy G. Richter, *Home on the Rails: Women, the Railroad, and the Rise of Public Domesticity* (Chapel Hill: University of North Carolina Press, 2005).

9. John Sears, *Sacred Places: American Tourist Attractions in the Nineteenth Century* (Oxford: Oxford University Press, 1989).

10. Warren James Belasco, *Americans on the Road: From Autocamp to Motel, 1910–1945* (Cambridge, Mass.: MIT Press, 1979); Marguerite S. Shaffer, *See America First: Tourism and National Identity, 1880–1940* (Washington, D.C.: Smithsonian Institution Press, 2001); and Cindy Sondik Aron, *Working at Play: A History of Vacations in the United States* (New York: Oxford University Press, 1999).

11. Dean MacCannell, *The Tourist: A New Theory of the Leisure Class* (New York: Schocken Books, 1976).

12. Pierre Bourdieu, *Distinction: A Social Critique of the Judgement of Taste* (Cambridge, Mass.: Harvard University Press, 1984).

Contributors

Brian Bixby is interested in how the history of interactions between tourists and hosts affects them both. He is completing his doctoral dissertation on visitors to Shaker communities at the University of Massachusetts at Amherst.

Janet F. Davidson has spent the past decade studying transportation and travel in the United States. As project historian for the Smithsonian Institution's "America on the Move" exhibition, she co-authored *On the Move: Transportation and the American Story*. She is currently historian at the Cape Fear Museum in North Carolina.

Anne E. Gorsuch is associate professor of history at the University of British Columbia. She is the editor (with Diane P. Koenker) of *Turizm: The Russian and East European Tourist under Capitalism and Socialism* (2006) and author of *Youth in Revolutionary Russia: Enthusiasts, Bohemians, Delinquents* (2000).

Waleed Hazbun teaches international political economy and Middle East politics at the Johns Hopkins University. He is currently writing a book about the politics of tourism and globalization in the Middle East.

Molly Hurley Dépret is a doctoral candidate in cultural anthropology at the Graduate Center of the City University of New York. Her dissertation focuses on space, place, history, and violence in Belfast, Northern Ireland, through interviews and participant-observation with police, taxi drivers, their dispatchers, and residents.

Aaron K. Ketchell received his Ph.D. in American studies from the University of Kansas. He is a lecturer at the University of Kansas and the author of the forthcoming book *Holy Hills: Religion and Recreation in Branson, Missouri* (Johns Hopkins University Press).

Patrick Hyder Patterson is a historian and lecturer in Eleanor Roosevelt College at the University of California, San Diego. He is currently com-

pleting a book manuscript on consumption and market culture in socialist Hungary, Yugoslavia, and the German Democratic Republic. His
articles have appeared in *Slavic Review, Enterprise and Society*, and *East
European Politics and Societies*.

Kenneth J. Perkins is a professor of Middle Eastern and North African
History at the University of South Carolina who specializes in the study
of indigenous responses to colonialism. He is currently researching the
development and impact of tourism in the Maghrib from the 1870s until
World War II.

Philip Scranton is University Board of Governors Professor of History at
Rutgers University, Camden, and serves as director of the Center for the
History of Business, Technology and Society at the Hagley Museum and
Library. He is currently researching the development of jet propulsion
by the United States, Britain, and France during the Cold War.

Evan R. Ward is assistant professor of history at the University of North
Alabama. He is currently working on a book-length comparative study of
national tourism development in Puerto Rico, the Dominican Republic,
Mexico, and Cuba.

Philip Whalen is assistant professor of history at Coastal Carolina University. He is currently working on a book manuscript entitled "The Making
and Marketing of Modern Burgundy 1919–1939: Wine, Gastronomy,
and Tourism."

www.ingramcontent.com/pod-product-compliance
Ingram Content Group UK Ltd.
Pitfield, Milton Keynes, MK11 3LW, UK
UKHW041023190225
455302UK00001B/65